JANE ADDAMS AND THE MEN OF THE CHICAGO SCHOOL, 1892-1918

JANE ADDAMS AND THE MEN OF THE CHICAGO SCHOOL, 1892-1918

Mary Jo Deegan

91-152

Transaction Books
New Brunswick (U.S.A.) and Oxford (U.K.)

First paperback edition 1990
Copyright (1988) by Transaction Publishers
New Brunswick, New Jersey 08903.

Library of Congress Catalog Number: 86-6964
ISBN 0-88738-077-8 (cloth); 0-88738-830-2 (paper)
Printed in the United States of America

Library of Congress Cataloging-in-Publication Data

Deegan, Mary Jo, 1948-
  Jane Addams and the men of the Chicago school, 1892-1918.

  Bibliography: p.
  Includes index.
  1. Addams, Jane, 1860-1935–Contributions in sociology. 2. Chicago school of sociology. I. Title.
HM22.U6D4   1986
ISBN 0-88738-077-8
301'.092'4

                                        86-6964
                                        CIP

To My Mother,
Ida May Scott Deegan

Contents

List of Tables and Figures

List of Illustrations

Following page 142

Preface

This book started from a very modest wish. Over a decade ago, I wanted to write a popular paper, only eight or ten pages long, on an early woman sociologist. I believed there must have been at least one woman who worked in my discipline, and I wanted to remember and celebrate that work. To my utter amazement, when I examined the early sociology journals, I found not one but dozens of early women sociologists. The story of their lives and work has fascinated me over the ensuing years. I haunted archives, read musty organizational records, and pored over correspondence. These were unfamiliar tasks for a sociologist of our era and I fear that many friends and colleagues thought I was on a wild goose chase. This book is a partial answer to their many questions concerning the nature of my work and that of the early women sociologists.

Reading the work of Jane Addams has been a pleasure and an education. I began this study thinking she was a popular and sentimental sociologist, and her importance today was as a historical figure in sociology. I did not think much of her intellectual stature and was primarily interested in recording how the profession had changed since she worked in its founding years. I have radically altered my perception of her and of the male Chicago School today. Although I differ with Addams on many points, I share many of her fundamental concerns and assumptions. In particular, I found her analysis of a cooperative model to be innovative and her study of women's lives to be integral to my own feminist studies today. Her work rounded out my training in sociology and provided a new way of thinking about symbolic interaction, applied knowledge, and the role of women in shaping a profession.

Archival work was a new adventure for me. I sincerely thank the generous and kind archivists who endured my many questions, my requests to read and copy large numbers of files, and my foraging around in areas where I was unsure of what I was seeking. There were many people who helped me in these tasks at the following centers: the Hull-House Archives, the University of Illinois Chicago Memorial Collection, the University of Chicago Special Collections, the Swarthmore College Peace Collection, the Wisconsin Historical Society, Wellesley College Archives, The Library of Congress, the Children's and Women's Bureau Archives, The Chicago Historical Society, the Sophia Smith Collection, and the Schlesinger Library. I particularly thank Dan Meyer of the University of Chicago, Mary Lynn McCree formerly of Hull-House, Bernice Nichols formerly of the Swarthmore Peace Collection, Debby Boone of Sophia Smith, and Archie Motley of the Chicago Historical Society. These archivists have been advisors over a period of years and have pointed out many areas that I would have overlooked without their assistance.

Financial support for this research was very difficult to obtain. Because Jane Addams has been defined as "not a sociologist" and because I was using historian's techniques instead of "mainstream" sociological methodology, peers who read my funding application did not feel that my project was justifiable as a sociological inquiry. I applied for numerous grants and these requests were turned down with one notable exception. The University of Nebraska Research Council has been the sole source of funds, and they have given generously on a number of occasions. They provided three summer fellowships and one semester's leave over the course of a decade. Their willingness to continue their aid enabled me to finish this work at a much faster rate than I could have done alone. I am extremely grateful to that body. Similarly, Dean Gerry Meisels of the College of Arts and Sciences at the University of Nebraska-Lincoln financed secretarial help that was crucial to completing this work.

A number of people read all or parts of the manuscript or listened to presentations of it at various professional meetings. They asked penetrating questions, suggested further lines of study, and supported the project with great enthusiasm. My thanks go to Alan P. Bates, Andrew Barlow, Jessie Bernard, John S. Burger, James T. Carey, Ruth Shonle Cavan, Emily Dunn Dale, Virginia Kemp Fish, Joan Huber, Glenn Jacobs, Heather Kurtz, Valerie Malhotra, Helen Moore, Jane Ollenburger, Jack Nussan Porter, the late Gregory P. Stone, Sherry Tillson, and Mary Roth Walsh. In addition, Ceceilia Dawkins and Chet Veal opened their homes and hearts to this project. Mary Kay Schleiter gave me the key to her Chicago apartment and an open invitation to stay during my many archival visits. Allen F. Davis suggested major cuts and revisions which I undertook; Morris Janowitz told me to cut my very large project on all early women sociologists down to one initial volume on Addams; Irving Louis Horowitz pointed out the need to clarify my position on the relation between Addams as a sociologist and a social worker; and Alan Booth helped me to edit so many drafts that his patience and sound advice go beyond any debt I can repay. Pat Palmieri extended an invitation on behalf of the Smith College Women's Studies Program to participate in the Professional Women's Conference in June 1983. I was fortunate to meet many scholars in this area of study. Their dedication and skill helped inspire me the next year during my seemingly endless revisions.

Many early sociologists and relatives of the Chicago men have shared their time and knowledge and I gratefully acknowledge their help: Nels Anderson, Jessie Bernard, Ruth Thomas Billingsley, Herbert Blumer, Ruth Shonle Cavan, the late Everett C. Hughes, the late Irene Tufts Mead, and several others who requested that their names not be used. Ruth Shonle Cavan, Ellsworth Faris, Arthur Hillman, and the late Winifred Rauschenbush also provided helpful correspondence.

The typists who have worked on this manuscript have been tried beyond human eyesight. They have included Joleen Deats, Cheryl Drummond, Laurie Eells, Michael R. Hill, Carol Kokes, Margaret Kullinane, Sharon Selvage, Baja Stack, and Inge Worth. All of them have good-naturedly shared in the work of preparing the manuscript and often gave helpful advice on how to edit awkward passages. I would also like to acknowledge the help and support of the people at Transaction Publishers, especially that of Irving Louis Horowitz, president; Scott B. Bramson, publisher, Dalia Buzin, editor, and Janice Handler, editor.

Michael R. Hill has been a strong and steady force behind my sometimes wavering commitment. He has put up with complaints, multiple readings of sections, travels to faraway cities, the expenses involved, and my single-minded devotion to finishing this book. He even typed the second draft when I was unwilling to do it and could not find any institutional support. He has given me the kind of help that women have needed for centuries but only rarely found. In addition, my mother Ida May Scott Deegan has helped me through years of advanced training and listened to long and detailed monologues about my ideas and writings. This book is dedicated to her as a small token of my love and respect.

The city of Chicago is also due a note of thanks. I was born "back of the yards" where the University of Chicago Settlement was located. I attended the University of Chicago, and have lived many years in that city. Although I spent most of my childhood and early adult years in Michigan, Chicago has been part of my life and vision of the world. The early immigrants to that city with whom Addams shared her life could very well have been my relatives and their neighbors. Thus, my ties to the city are part of this endeavor and exploration of social life.

1

Introduction

In 1892 an exciting experiment in education began on a desolate prairie: The University of Chicago opened its doors and an academic era was born. William Rainey Harper, its first president, was an aggressive upstart who used persuasion, money, and promises of institutional power to lure prominent, but often young, scholars to the "wild" West. Although the university was located on an urban frontier, it wanted to rival the intellectually preeminent East. Largely eschewing the areas of established excellence, the early administrators sought out new disciplines and ambitious faculty. Both groups wanted to build a national and international reputation for the institution, and they did it with a pioneer spirit compatible with the surging city growing rapidly and haphazardly around them.

It was this intellectual whirlwind that brought academic sociology to Chicago. At that time, sociology was an amorphous area of study. It had found a tenuous niche in many universities, as an adjunct to more established and legitimized disciplines. A little bit of history, a dash of political economy, and a pinch of social amelioration comprised the general hodgepodge of the "field." Sociology even gained a reputation for being associated with "radical" ideas about changing society: socialism, feminism, and secularism were all trends that sociologists dared to study and even advocate. Although the Eastern sociologists were just as likely to be conservative as radical, the intellectuals on the "Left" of mainstream America were attracted to this new science of society and the possibility of systematically critiquing established rules and institutions.

The University of Chicago was seeking exactly this type of new discipline. As a new academy, it was in a position to offer legitimacy to a specialization without a home. As a coeducational institution, women faculty and ideas that supported women's "new" demands were also welcome. Women, moreover, were seen as ideally suited to studying social change, improving society, and questioning the old restrictions of the more established order. Each of these factors combined to make the University of Chicago a center for sociological research and development, and a haven in

1

the heartless academic world previously closed to women's higher education.

Over time, the University of Chicago and its Department of Sociology
fulfilled, and perhaps even surpassed, Harper's grand ambitions. Chicago
Sociology began to dominate the new discipline.[1] As it did so, its more
lusty youth passed and a more conservative and powerful structure
emerged. The early years of sociology's development became embedded in
myths. As sociologists became members of a new establishment, their early
association with radical ideas, especially feminism, became less desirable
memories of their past. Sociologists who specialized in criticizing the economic structure of society and women's limitations within it were particularly subject to neglect or damning interpretations. Although these
early Chicago sociologists were prominent, if not notorious, citizens, their
effect on urban America and its political life was seen as less important to
their successors in sociology than the historical development of an academic discipline. The early passion, political forays, and verve were abstracted from accounts of "scientific" sociology. Thus early male Chicago
sociologists were frequently not interpreted as important figures in sociological thought because their more important ideas and contributions
were evaluated as "nonprofessional" activities and interests.

In such a repressive context, it is not surprising to learn that early female
sociologists fared even worse than their male counterparts. Although
women flocked to the University of Chicago and to its Department of
Sociology, they were unable to gain a foothold in academic sociology. At
first, this did not seem to be problematic because there was employment for
women sociologists outside of the academy. A dual system of sex-segregated labor was thereby established. Male sociologists were expected to be
abstract thinkers, capable of teaching both sexes. Academic positions were
to be held by men who were institutionally encouraged to become professors. Female sociologists were expected to work in "women's" sociological institutions. These employing organizations included social
settlements, where sociologists lived in an impoverished community as
friends, neighbors, and community organizers; the new Young Women's
Christian Association; and women's colleges. Female sociologists were expected to be "practical" thinkers, capable of reaching out to strangers in a
hostile world and in this way mimicing the female roles of wife, mother,
and daughter in the home. In general, both sexes accepted this sex-segregated network. Many "academic" male sociologists forged a bridge between the two groups through their work with female students and their
ideological support of women's equality. In addition, a few outstanding
female sociologists were recognized as leaders by the men, and the most
important woman in this position was Jane Addams.[2]

Her preeminence as a sociologist is easy to understand. She had a seminal mind, political acumen, administrative brilliance, and moral leadership. she was one of the greatest American leaders of her day, and she is one of the most influential and famous women in our history.

Considerable scholarship on her life and influence is now available, yet none of it discusses or documents her central role as a sociologist. The only profession today that acknowledges her preeminent role in its founding is social work. Despite the lack of recognition in sociology, Addams' social thought as well as her institutional and professional ties were originally grounded in this discipline. She left a legacy that formed a basis for sociology as a way of thinking, an area of study, and a methodological approach to data collecting. Despite her vision and contributions to sociology, her authorship of this work has been obliterated from the annals of the discipline and many of her ideas were only selectively used and thereby distorted. Documentation of Addams as a sociologist and leader of the newly founded discipline is the goal of this book. There is no attempt to elaborate on her vital relationship to social work or other professions, such as political science or philosophy, or to examine her public leadership. The focus here is on sociology and her relationships with the men of the Chicago School. These men and the institution in which they worked were central to the development of sociology, and Addams worked closely with them for decades. Her sociological concepts were incorporated into the profession through their work.

Before proceeding with my task, a little sidetrip is necessary. Addams' leadership in sociology was based on considerably more than her relationship to the now recognized male Chicago School of Sociology. She coordinated and led a massive network of women sociologists who either worked at the "daring" new university or who studied there as graduate students. This book, therefore, is only the first in a series of three volumes. The second book analyzes the role of other female sociologists who worked as marginal faculty members in the Department of Sociology at the University of Chicago. The third book analyzes the work and careers of the female graduates of the department. These three volumes will describe the "female" Chicago School of Sociology and document the existence of a flourishing and influential school of thought that was systematically discriminated against in the profession. The existence of a dual, sex-stratified network in sociology has rarely been documented.[3] This first volume, then, is only a step toward establishing Addams as a central figure in sociology. Since the University of Chicago and the men who worked there as sociologists are already recognized as the earliest and most powerful institution and figures in Chicago, her work in Chicago and with these men are strong starting points for legitimating her work as a sociologist. Moreover, because the women's network and practice of sociology was ultimately less powerful and visible than the male's, Addams' most lasting influence over the discipline was channeled through these early male colleagues.

In this introductory chapter, Addams' biography and role as a historical figure are briefly presented. Formal criteria for considering her a sociologist are also given. This is followed by a short biographical introduction to each of the eight male sociologists who were the core faculty of the early Chicago School of sociology. The last section of this chapter is an overview of the organization of the book and the central arguments used to establish Addams as a founder of American sociology.

Jane Addams

More books and articles have been written about Jane Addams than any other American woman.[4] She captured the dreams, ideals, and imagination of a generation. In the process, her intellectual significance was obscured in light of her popular image as a "saint" or "villain," a woman who was larger than life and often portrayed as a simple follower of her convictions.[5]

Born in 1860, she was a contemporary of the early Chicago men. Addams was raised in a small Midwestern town where she was profoundly influenced by her father, a Quaker, state senator, and mill owner. Her family background was based on several generations of Americans. In 1879 she entered Rockford Female Seminary, in Rockford, Illinois, which was one of the pioneering colleges for women. Unresponsive to the religious message of the school, Addams sought to get "back to a great Primal cause—not nature, exactly, but a fostering Mother, a necessity, brooding, and watching over all things, above every human passion."[6] After she graduated in 1881, she entered an extended period of unhappiness, nervous strain and depression. Like many of her colleagues, notably George Herbert Mead and William James, Addams sought a meaning for her life but rejected traditional religion as an answer to her questions.[7]

This year, 1881, was crucial in her search for a place in the world. In August, her father died and his absence left her confused and despairing. But she also entered the Women's Medical College in Philadelphia. Before the year was out, she dropped out of medical training and returned home to Cedarville, Illinois. There, she was caught between the demands of her stepmother, a pressing suitor, and her ambition to have a career. Ill and surrounded by family problems, Addams drifted for a year. Finally taking some action, in 1883 she traveled to Europe. Although she was interested in the problems of the poor at this time, she was not too troubled by their plight. "Socially, too, she was still very much the product of her background and education. She was the Victorian young lady, the epitome of American feminine innocence that Henry James was so fond of depicting."[8]

Her family attempted to "enter her" into society, but she rejected their social plans. She remained frustrated and sick for the next two years and stayed primarily in Baltimore. Then, once again she traveled to Europe. On this journey, accompanied by her college friend Ellen Gates Starr, she finally found a direction for her life.

When she visited Toynbee Hall in London's East End, she became impressed with their work for the poor. This social settlement was associated with Oxford University and was designed to provide leadership to a district populated by the exploited working classes. Emphasizing urban disorganization as a barrier to needed education and "culture," Toynbee Hall provided a model for Addams' resolution of her personal and occupational crisis.

Years later, she theorized that one of the most difficult tasks for women was managing the conflicting demands between their "family" and "social" claims. For Addams, this resolution occurred through social settlements where she could remain a "lady" while making a social and political impact. Simultaneously, she was independent of traditional female roles and responsibilities in the family and home. Because of these self-benefits for those who helped others, she always emphasized both the "subjective" and "objective" needs for social settlements. This stress on the dual function of settlements prevented her from becoming the sentimental or insensitive "matrician" she is often portrayed as being. With her internal battle in abeyance, she quickly succeeded in assuming leadership of the American social settlement movement and subsequently altered the course of American thought and politics.

This dramatic public role began soon after she returned to the United States in January 1889. Addams and Starr moved to Chicago and rented an apartment there. Within a few months they moved onto one floor of a house owned by the Culver and Hull family. "Hull-House," as it was called, quickly abandoned the British Toynbee Hall model and became more egalitarian, more female-dominated, and less religious. These changes were important intellectual innovations, often implemented by Addams but frequently instigated by the women with whom she surrounded herself. Moreover, in 1892 the University of Chicago opened its doors bringing many faculty members, predominantly men, as visitors and lecturers to Hull-House. But it was Addams and Hull-House who were the leader and leading institution in Chicago in the 1890s, not the University of Chicago. Not only was she the charismatic head of a rapidly expanding social movement, but she was also considered one of the leading sociologists of her day.

The 1890s were lively and controversial years at Hull-House. Anarchists, Marxists, socialists, unionists, and leading social theorists congregated there.[9] John Dewey and George Herbert Mead, among others, were frequent visitors, lecturers, and close friends of Addams.[10] Chicago pragmatism was born through their collegial contacts and intellectual exchanges. They wanted to combine scientific and objective observation with ethical and moral values to generate a just and liberated society. A groundbreaking sociological text, *Hull-House Maps and Papers*, was published by Hull-House residents in 1893, predating and establishing the interests of the early Chicago male sociologists. During this time, Hull-House and Addams gained a national and international reputation as a radical, innovative, and successful institution. Oriented toward social change, they articulated an American dream, particularly adapted to bright, educated, Anglo women who wanted a new role in life and society.[11]

Addams surrounded herself with brilliant and dedicated people, particularly women. These women formed a core group who lived at the settlement, wrote together, gathered statistics, investigated factories and industries, conducted health examinations, examined sanitary conditions, lobbied for legislative and political reform, and organized for social betterment in their congested, immigrant, working-class district. Out of this welter of activity, Addams was the charismatic leader who translated the "facts" into everyday language, articulating the problems and needs of the community, and forming American ideals and social thought.[12]

Author of eleven books and hundreds of articles, Addams continued her teaching and educating efforts through lectures across the country and at Hull-House. She became the spokesperson of her era and, in particular, for women and the working-class immigrant. She led social reform organizations, campaigned for the Progressive Party, and helped to found numerous government agencies—notably the Childrens, Women's, and Immigration Bureaus. She practiced and advocated free speech for all and "radical democracy—she believed that equality must extend beyond citizenship rights and pervade all aspects of economic and social life. A "critical pragmatist" (defined and discussed in detail in chapters 10 and 11), she sought not only answers to problems, but those answers that were in the best interests of all, including the poor and disenfranchised.

· Addams was a cultural feminist and her views on women were little understood then or now. Having a popular image as a "saintly" woman who worked for the poor, Addams in fact believed that female values were superior to male ones and that a society built on feminine values would be more productive, peaceful, and just. Despite the lack of complete understanding of her intellectual thought, her innovative and critical ideas were accepted by the public for over two decades, when she was the "Saint Jane" of the popular press. Simultaneously, she was an intellectual leader in sociology as well as in related disciplines.

Only her pacifist ideas were truly understood in terms of their radical import. As a pacifist prior to World War I, Addams was lauded as a "good woman." However, with the building of patriotic feeling from 1913 until

America's entry into the war in 1917, she became the increasing target of animosity and personal attack. By 1917 she was socially and publicly ostracized. She went from being a saint to a villain. Booed off speaking platforms, abandoned by her friends, colleagues, and, most notably here, other sociologists, Addams was a social pariah.

This was an agonizing time for her. Committed to her values based on "feminine" ideals, she maintained her pacifist position. The culmination of her politically untouchable status occurred in 1919, when she was targeted by the U.S. government as the most dangerous woman in America. It is at this point that this book ends, for after 1919 Addams' role as a sociologist rapidly declined and she was ostracized by succeeding generations of sociologists until the present.[13] To summarize the remainder of her life, however, is important for understanding her total impact on American thought.

In 1920, women were granted the franchise, and to Addams and many other suffragists this was a major victory. Contrary to their expectations of a powerful women's vote, the decade of the 1920s led to an eclipse of the former power of women activists, including Addams. In addition, Progressive leadership was squelched following World War I and the liberal vision of a changing, optimistic, and scientifically rational society was doomed. Addams gradually resumed leadership in American thought during this decade, but it was primarily the impact of the Depression which once again restored her to the forefront of American leadership.[14] Winner of the Nobel Peace Prize in 1931, Addams became the spokesperson for many of the values and policies adopted during the New Deal. She and her female colleagues were instrumental in establishing social security and many other government programs which altered the nature of American capitalism. Dying in 1935 she was mourned worldwide as a great leader and interpreter of American thought.

Surrounded by the imagery of a "good and noble woman," she was able to articulate radical changes in American life and politics, altering the possibilities for human growth and action for the working class, immigrants, youth, the aged, and women. On the one hand, her significant contributions to public life are well known and lauded. On the other hand, her intellectual stature is barely appreciated, and her contributions to sociology totally obscured.[15] This intellectual biography begins a serious reevaluation and assessment of her social thought and its impact on this profession and discipline. The first and most superficial step is to establish her credentials as a sociologist.

Jane Addams, Sociologist

The lack of documentation of Addams as a sociologist is due to a number of factors. Looking first at her own ideas, she was opposed to academic sociology, elitism, partriarchy, and intellectualism. Each of these belief systems is intrinsic to the assumptions of sociology as it was practiced after World War I. Although she considered herself a sociologist, she wanted the profession to develop in a radically different direction than it did.

Addams was the greatest woman sociologist of her day. The fact that she was female is vital, for sociology had a sex-segregated system. After World War I, these two tracks within the profession split into social work as female-dominated and sociology as male-dominated. Almost all the women trained in Chicago Sociology prior to 1918 were ultimately channeled into social work positions. Discrimination against hiring women in academic sociology departments was rampant. The major professional association, the American Sociological Society (ASS), limited women's participation in most of its offices and programs; and the social thought developed after 1918, especially at the University of Chicago, was dramatically patriarchal and opposed to Addams' vision.[16] An applied, professional component of sociology died when Addams' severance from sociology occurred, and it has never become a respected alternative to sociologists in the academy.[17] Other social sciences, like geography, economics, and history have developed more than one professional career line, but sociology failed to do this to any considerable extent.

Finally, despite the extensive scholarly and popular study of Addams' life, it is extremely difficult to trace her influence on sociological thought. Because many sociologists claim that she is not a sociologist while many social workers claim that she is a social worker, it has appeared that Addams' "professional home" has been found. It is as if people assume she must be one or the other! This assumption has led to a profound misunderstanding of Addams' intellectual contributions and impact on sociology. There is absolutely no attempt here to minimize her impact on social work. Social workers correctly acknowledge Addams as a major thinker and professional model. The problem lies not with social workers but with sociologists. Addams was a preeminent sociologist, and an understanding of her role in sociology is integral to an understanding of this profession. To undertake any analysis of the role of women sociologists or the sociological study of women during the era of interest in this book, Addams' sociological career and concepts must be considered. When Addams is limited to membership in only one field, social work, the impact she had on sociology is entirely overlooked. Concomitantly, there is an unstated assumption that her ideas and model for action were adopted by social workers and rejected by sociologists. Instead of this dichotomy between two different specialties, a complex pattern of incorporating and modifying her ideas in each profession has occurred. It is beyond the scope or intent of this book to trace Addams' influence on social work; the task of discovering her role in sociology is difficult enough.

Addams' influence on sociology must often be inferred because most early sociologists rarely cited the work of their closest colleagues. This has been a problem in documenting the interaction among all the early Chicago men. People who coauthored writings or trained students together, such as Park and Burgess, are easily seen as important colleagues. But people who spoke to each other with great frequency, visited each other's homes, and engaged in organizational work together have few records of their shared interests that are easily accessible to scholars who study only published writings. Academic sociologists tend to rely heavily on academic publications, organizations, and institutions while overlooking applied sociology that is directed to nonacademic audiences, organizations, and institutions. For applied sociologists such as Addams, indications of mutual influence must often be sought in nonacademic records. Original archival data containing correspondence, newspaper reports, and organizational records relevant to applied sociology can help to fill the gaps in our academic documentation. Such alternative resources are particularly vital in a situation like Addams' where her influence has been buried over the course of several decades.

Because of the lack of scholarship on Addams as a sociologist, some formal criteria are needed to begin this investigation. Käsler, studying early German sociologists, has determined that if one of five criteria is met, then the individual was a member of the profession. He wrote:

> As *sociologist* I define those who fulfill at least one of the following five criteria:
>
> - occupy a chair of sociology and/or teach sociology
> - membership in the German Sociological Society (changed here to membership in the American Sociological Society)
> - coauthorship of sociological articles or textbooks
> - self-definition as a "sociologist"
> - definition by others as a sociologist[18]

Addams meets not one but all of the above criteria, in addition to other more complex associations with the profession. Each of these points is briefly examined here.

Teaching

Addams lectured through the country, at numerous colleges and social settlements. For example,

> In February 1899, she went on a typical lecture tour—leaving Chicago on February 13, she spoke at Wells College in Aurora, New York on the 14th; at

Auburn Seminary the next day; at Wells again on the 16th; then to New York for a quick stopover; then to Boston where she made two appearances at woman's (sic) clubs on the 18th; two more appearances on Sunday; on to the University of Vermont on Monday; back to Boston for two more appearance (sic) on Tuesday; two more on Wednesday, and two on Thursday; then she was off to Meadville, Pennsylvania; to Harrisburg, Richmond, Virginia, and Columbia, South Carolina, before returning home.[19]

Although many of these speeches were not academic, others were, and Addams' division between academic and everyday thought was dramatically different from that of her male academic colleagues. In addition, she offered college courses through the Extension Division of the University of Chicago.[20] The university offered her at least two chances to become directly affiliated with its staff, both of which she refused.[21] Albion Small, chair of the Department of Sociology there, even offered her a half-time graduate faculty position.[22] She declined these offers because she wanted to be outside of the academy, although she was deeply dedicated to teaching. She wanted to teach adults who could not otherwise enter the academy, because of their poverty or lack of credentials. Furthermore, she was concerned about the limits of speech and political activism associated with university settings.

Membership in the American Sociological Society

Addams was a charter member of the ASS, founded in 1905. She remained an active member from then until at least 1930.[23] She addressed the group, one of the few women to do so, in 1912, 1915, and 1919. These major presentations resulted from invitations extended by the presidents of the association. In 1928 she again addressed the group and was a discussant of a paper in 1908.[24] So not only was she a member, she was the most active and illustrious woman member during this period.

Coauthorship of Sociological Articles or Textbooks

The most prestigious and central journal to the new discipline, the *American Journal of Sociology* (*AJS*), was established at the University of Chicago in 1895. Although Addams published in a number of popular and scholarly journals, using only the *AJS* as one indicator of her sociological publications, she published five articles there plus a discussion of another paper.[25] In addition, five of her books were reviewed in the journal's pages, often by leading sociologists.[26] Clearly her work was read and recognized by sociologists of her day.

Most telling of all, however, is her publication and editing of the most central text to Chicago sociology, *Hull-House Maps and Papers*. This groundbreaking book outlined the major issues of the Chicago School of

Sociology and used a methodological technique employed by Chicago sociologists during the next forty years after its publication. Chapter 3 here is an analysis of its role in sociological thought.

Addams believed that her books were to be read and used by sociologists. Concern with ethics was central to the work of sociologists at this time; especially to Albion Small, Charles Henderson, and Charles Zeublin, all Chicago Sociologists. Thus her book *Democracy and Social Ethics* was a major sociological and theoretical statement on the construction of social order and its meaning.[27] Again, while writing on women's self-reflection, she felt that her daily observation of this phenomenon while living "in a Settlement with sociological tendencies" almost impelled her to write of this event.[28] The reviews of these two latter books and others in *AJS* indicate that both Addams and sociologists believed them to be sociological treatises.

Self-Definition as "Sociologist"

Addams was opposed to formal titles and ties. For example, she felt forced to assume the title of "Head" of the settlement for its board of trustees. In her own speech, however, she referred to herself only as "Jane Addams of Hull-House."[29] Opposed to hierarchical and elitist structures, she resisted all formal categorizing of her work and profession. Nonetheless, she did consider herself a sociologist during the period studied here. For example, Farrell noted:

> Miss Addams later identified herself professionally with these sociologists. In 1908 she wrote of her attendance at the American Sociological Association: "I simply have to take care of my professional interests once in a while and this little trip was full of inspiration."[30]

Similarly, in her writings she referred to her sociological work[31] and clearly taught sociology, wrote it, and participated in sociological events.

Addams worked within a sociological network, as well. For example, when a representative from the MacMillan Company requested names of college professors who might be interested in her book *Newer Ideals of Peace*, Addams responded that she only wanted those professors who knew her personally to receive a copy. The male sociologists (the largest single category of professors) included on her list were: Charles Henderson, George H. Mead, George Vincent, William I. Thomas, John Dewey, Graham Taylor, Charles Zeublin, Charles H. Cooley, and Sidney Webb.[32]

Definition by Others as "Sociologist"

All of the above information indicates the high esteem of her colleagues. In this book, her extensive collegial contacts with the men of the Chicago

School are documented. She was thereby a resource for both the most influential sociological school of thought of her day and for the succeeding generation of sociologists who expanded and modified this early work.

Addams was also considered a major sociologist by men outside of the Chicago school. E.A. Ross, one of the leading early figures in sociology, was a frequent visitor to and lecturer at Hull-House. Whenever he came to Chicago he lived at the settlement, and extended her two invitations to speak at the ASS when he was an officer.[33] Furthermore, Addams shared the platform with sociologist Franklin Giddings in 1892 when they taught at the Summer School of Applied Philanthropy and Ethics. At this meeting, crucial to women sociologists, it was Addams and not Giddings who made the most impressive statements, thereby drawing a group of women around her and organizing their interests through her leadership.[34] A year later she again assumed a leadership position when she presided over a two-day conference at the Chicago World's Fair. Sponsored by the International Parliament of Sociology, Addams chaired the sessions as a worldwide leader in applied sociology.[35]

Addams' writings were rarely cited by her male colleagues as significant influences. There were, however, notable exceptions. Charles Cooley, an early president of the American Sociological Society, for example, cited Addams seven times in his seminal text *Social Organization*.[36] E.A. Ross (another early president of the American Sociological Society) also used Addams as a sociological reference and authority. For example, Ross recommended her book *The Spirit of Youth* to a student who wanted "the best sociological books" to read. Ross also assigned her writings in his coursework. His syllabus for a "Seminary on the American Family" used Addams' *Spirit of Youth*, *Twenty Years at Hull-House*, and *Democracy and Social Ethics* for major reading material, and her *A New Conscience and an Ancient Evil* was an additional reference work.[37] E.S. Bogardus, yet another leading early sociologist, provides further documentation of her works being used in sociology seminars.[38] Since her books were reviewed in *AJS*, as noted above, these specific references are only documenting a small portion of her use in sociological coursework and acknowledgement as a colleague.

In addition to recognition by her sociological contemporaries, Addams was often referred to as a sociologist by the popular press. In 1912, one Philadelphia newspaper reported her holding this title.[39] She was also called a sociologist when she presented a paper on crime and the ineffective action of the criminal justice system. Both the publication of the proceedings of the conference and its newspaper reporting endowed her with this title.[40]

Thus, by all formal criteria, Addams more than meets the definition of a sociologist. But these qualifications only reveal a small portion of her influence. For she was the leader of a large number of women sociologists whose work and influence on sociology have also been neglected. The criteria listed above were primarily evidence of male sociologists' recognition. To women, Addams provided a new legitimate career as a female sociologist. She epitomized the woman who lived outside of the traditional female role and who was esteemed and honored as a result. Addams was not only the image of a society's "good woman" but she also served as a role model for women professionals. She articulated a vision of sociology adopted by many women, all of whom have been deleted from the annals of sociological history.

Male American sociologists otherwise ignored or ostracized from the profession a number of sociologists who were also associated with Addams. For example, she was a close friend and colleague of W.E.B. DuBois, the great Black sociologist. Together they formed a sociological network marginal to academic thought, but central to American political and social thought.[41] Similarly, Addams was directly associated with British sociology, exemplified in the work of Beatrice and Sidney Webb. This British influence, however, never flourished in mainstream American male sociological thought, which was dominated by Germanic and French influences.

Finally, Hull-House itself was a central institution to sociology. The home to several women sociologists, it was a meeting place for intellectual discussion and debate. Sociologists, both male and female, visited the settlement frequently, thereby influencing American sociological thought. Addams, as the leading figure in the settlement, played a key role in the institutional power of Hull-House, an additional criterion for her inclusion as a sociologist. These wider influences are beyond the scope of this book. Here one central aspect of her sociological influence is studied: her work with the Chicago men, each of whom is introduced later in this chapter.

The Significance of Addams as a Sociologist

Because Addams is now recognized as one of the greatest women leaders of the United States, it is necessary to address the issue of the importance of documenting her role in one, predominantly academic, discipline. There are several vital reasons why this is a task affecting more than an esoteric minority.

First, Addams is a major intellectual who interpreted American life, its heritage, and values. She is a social theorist of major proportions, but because her most radical ideas are unpopular and she has been stigmatized by being reduced to an image of womanhood, her intellectual leadership has been obscured. Lasch's book on her social thought is an excellent exception to this treatment, and there are a few other texts on her life that counter this trend toward adulation rather than analysis.[42] This book, then, is part of a larger body of work documenting Addams as a force shaping American thought.

Second, this neglect of a major American theorist is partially due to patriarchal ideology. When an intellectual of such magnitude can be neglected and distorted, it is clear that the fate of less eminent, but nonetheless significant, women analysts is similar. This book documents the process of selectively using Addams' social thought in sociology while denying her significant contributions to it. Simultaneously, knowledge of other segments of her thought has been repressed and her sociological leadership denied.

Third, the social thought itself is underanalyzed and has potential impact on the future of ideas in the United States, if not internationally. Addams was an articulate theorist of women's roles and values as well as a critical thinker of social institutions and social change. This thought is worthy of re-examination in its own right.

Fourth, Addams profoundly affected the course of American sociology. The discipline, then, needs to examine its roots in her work in order to understand its own history and epistemology. Concomitantly, the sexism of sociology is revealed in the study of Addams' thought and professional affiliations.

And fifth, Addams was the leader of an extensive network of women sociologists. This entire group of women, ranging in number between fifty and 100, formed a complex network of professional ties, institutions, social activism, and intellectual contributions that has never been seriously analyzed. This vast world of American women professionals has been submerged in a patriarchal society and its academic disciplines. Documentation of this wide and influential group and the study of its erasure from history would require a series of books.[43] This volume is an introduction to this other world, where Addams was the spokesperson for women who were later to be disenfranchised.

Any of the above reasons would be sufficient to justify an examination of Addams as a sociologist. As a set of reasons, they are impelling. Addams' career as a sociologist was a significant one, although it does not encompass her entire contributions to American society, social thought, or academic development. Her greatness exceeds her influence on this one profession. Nonetheless, an analysis of Addams the sociologist reveals a role, her intellectual leadership, and the broad practice of sociological patriarchy that cannot be shown in any other way. She is the key to understanding an era and a discipline.

The Men of the Chicago School

The Chicago School of Sociology is unique in the annals of the discipline. Many books and articles have been written on this early sociological institution and the men who staffed it.[44] There is a continual theme underlying most of these efforts: that the University of Chicago was significant from 1892 to 1918 because of its role in establishing and legitimating the discipline. Historical precedence, administration, teaching, and a vision of what *could be* achieved are the major strengths assigned to the period examined here.[45] Only W.I. Thomas is widely recognized as an early intellectual force. In fact, there is a kind of embarrassment over the early scholarship of the male faculty at Chicago (and the women faculty are not even evaluated as an influence or figures in the drama). This book, then, is a study of these early men as well as Addams. Both the men and Addams were erased in many ways from accounts of the intellectual growth and development of sociology due to the bias of their successors, frequently ungrateful students, who were faculty at the University of Chicago during the 1920s. Furthermore, the men of the Chicago School after 1918 often claimed that their ideas originated within themselves, disassociating themselves from their reform roots and intellectual forebears.

The men of the Chicago School were a strongly in-bred group. As Figure 1.1 shows, the early men were largely trained within the university itself after the original staff was recruited by President William Rainey Harper. During 1892-1918, only Park was "imported" from "outside" the university. (The next "outsider" to be recruited was W.F. Ogburn, who came from Columbia University in 1928.)[46]

George Herbert Mead, the Chicago philosopher, is included as a Chicago Sociologist because of his nearly universal recognition as a major figure there.[47] He is now recognized as the founding figure of "symbolic interactionism" along with his Chicago colleagues W.I. Thomas, Robert E. Park, and Ellsworth Faris.[48]

The major criteria for including the men, with the exception of Mead noted above, were employment at the university as a sociologist and service there for over fifteen years (the shortest tenure was Zeublin's seventeen years). It is clear from Figure 1.1 that all of the men except Zeublin enjoyed close collegial ties, lengthy years of service, and mutual influences.

There were three additional men who were important influences or served on the faculty for an extended period who were excluded: Graham

FIGURE 1.1

The Men of the Chicago School, Their Ties and Tenure

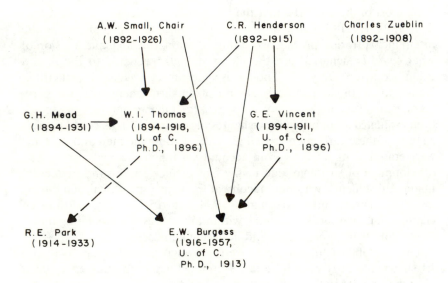

A.W. Small, Chair
(1892-1926)

C.R. Henderson
(1892-1915)

Charles Zueblin
(1892-1908)

G.H. Mead
(1894-1931)

W.I. Thomas
(1894-1918,
U. of C.
Ph.D., 1896)

G.E. Vincent
(1894-1911,
U. of C.
Ph.D., 1896)

R.E. Park
(1914-1933)

E.W. Burgess
(1916-1957,
U. of C.
Ph.D., 1913)

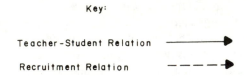

Key:

Teacher-Student Relation

Recruitment Relation

Taylor, Ira Woods Howerth, and Edward Bemis. The two former men are briefly mentioned here. Graham Taylor was a "theological sociologist" at the Chicago Theological Seminary.[49] Although affiliated with the University of Chicago, the seminary was never an administrative unit. Taylor held an appointment in the Department of Sociology at the University of Chicago formally for over two years. Since he was a close colleague of Addams, if his work were included here, her influence on the Chicago School would be documented as even more pervasive. Ira Woods Howerth worked in the Extension Division, as did Zeublin, but no references to his work with the other men or Addams came to light during the course of my investigations.[50] Although he worked for eighteen years at the University of Chicago, the lack of information on his career made references to him superfluous. Perhaps more data would reveal additional ties or confirm his isolated position, but this is a moot point here.

The third man, Edward Bemis, had a very short tenure at the University of Chicago. Teaching at the University Extension Division as a political economist and sociologist, he was summarily dismissed because of his support of the railroad workers in the 1894 Pullman Strike. His major influence on the Chicago School was his battle for free speech, discussed in more depth in chapter 7. Each of the eight men who formed the early Chicago School are briefly introduced below.

Albion W. Small

Small was nearly universally accepted and liked by his colleagues, friends, students, and administrators. Becker finds this characteristic a key to understanding Small's sociological vision,[51] for Small wanted to serve humanity and strove for fairness and justice in his relationships and social thought.

Born in 1854 in Buckfield, Maine, he was largely responsible for the development of sociology at the University of Chicago and ultimately throughout the nation. In 1879, he studied history in Germany which established the basis for his lifelong interest in Germanic social thought, government, and economics. He was trained in both the ministry and history, and he served as president of and history professor at Colby College from 1889-1892. Committed to social change and wedded to many Victorian and religious ideals, Small reflected the strains between a desire for ethical reform, the then-modern world, and objective science.[52]

After his appointment by Harper to open the first Graduate Department of Sociology in 1892, Small became a major figure in defining a special area of expertise for sociology. He hired all of the Chicago faculty studied here and established a strong position for them in the newly founded university. In addition, he was administratively adept at organizing the profession into powerful alliances. For example, in 1905 he was a charter member of the American Sociological Society and served as its president for two terms, in 1912 and 1913. Similarly, he founded the *American Journal of Sociology* (*AJS*) in 1895, quickly establishing it as the foremost journal in the discipline. Its major editorial staff and contributors were Chicago faculty, students, and associates. Small was its editor from 1895 to 1935, so he directly intervened in accepting articles that reflected his vision and control of the emerging discipline.[53]

Small set several scholarly precedents as well. With his former student and later colleague, George E. Vincent, Small co-authored one of the most influential introductory textbooks in sociology.[54] His two primary interests, ethical reform and economic organization, were later ignored by his successors at Chicago, and as a result he has been traditionally defined as a weak and relatively unimportant scholar.[55]

Profoundly disillusioned by World War I, aging and in ill health, his last years at the University of Chicago were spent in a withdrawal from many of the department's and discipline's politics and leadership. Small, nonetheless, was a formative figure in establishing sociology as an academic specialty and in building a powerful institutional basis for it. After a period of academic neglect, his scholarly work is being reconsidered and reevaluated, providing a new basis for broader understandings of his leadership and influence.

Charles R. Henderson

Henderson is almost entirely forgotten in the annals of Chicago Sociology, but he was one of the most far-thinking and influential men on the faculty. Closely sharing Addams' ideas on sociology, he was, nonetheless, more religious and less brilliant than she. Born in 1848, he, like Small, his contemporary, was a Baptist minister. Henderson graduated from the old University of Chicago in 1870, and for nineteen years he was a pastor, first in Terre Haute, Indiana, and then in Detroit, Michigan. Hired by Harper in 1892, he became a central figure at the University of Chicago. In 1895 he took a year's leave of absence and obtained a doctorate in Leipzig, Germany, and reaffirmed the Germanic base of the early male Chicago School. He established a Department of Practical Sociology in the School of Divinity as well as holding a full professorship in the Department of Sociology. As university chaplain, he held dual roles as minister and sociologist throughout his life.[56]

In addition to being the author of seven books and numerous articles, Henderson was a local, national, and international reform leader. He combined his interest in social amelioration with a continuing commitment to statistical research. His areas of specialization were criminology and prison reform, juvenile delinquency, health insurance, and the integration of modern man in a religious and secular context. Graham Taylor, his close colleague and friend, wrote in Henderson's obituary that the latter's untiring efforts to relieve the plight of the unemployed in Chicago led to a premature death from exhaustion.[57]

Charles Zeublin

Zeublin is not mentioned in any of the major books on Chicago Sociology,[58] although he taught sociology in the Extension Division of The University of Chicago from 1892 until 1908, and was a controversial figure in the city and at the university. Born in Pendleton, Indiana, in 1886, Zeublin did his undergraduate work at the University of Pennsylvania and Northwestern University, followed by graduate work in the ministry at Yale. While there he was influenced by the young biblical scholar William Rainey Harper, who would later become the first president of the University of Chicago.[59] Zeublin furthered his studies of the Old Testament in Leipzig, but wrote Harper in January of 1891 that he was abandoning this scholarly work for "political and social science."[60] Shortly thereafter, Zeublin moved into Hull-House and became one of its earliest residents. This contact with Addams ultimately led to his making social settlement work one of his major interests, and he founded Northwestern University Settlement in 1892.[61] Simultaneously, he was hired by Harper as secretary of one of the University of Chicago's extension divisions and an instructor in sociology, "rising in ten years to full professorship and continuing as such through 1908."[62]

An extremely popular lecturer, he augmented his low salary in the Extension Division by lecturing throughout the city, often on controversial subjects. In one eulogy he was remembered as having "a searching courage."[63] He made his audiences see social institutions, their communities, and their economic life with fresh eyes.[64] Unfortunately for his academic career, his powerful and critical analysis of society, especially the work of businessmen, led to his ultimate removal from the University of Chicago.[65]

The author of four books and numerous articles, Zeublin edited the popular *Twentieth Century Magazine* for three years. He devoted most of his remaining years, from 1908 until his death in 1924, to being a public lecturer or "publicist," as he called himself.[66]

George E. Vincent

Vincent was the son of Bishop John H. Vincent, the founder and first president of Chautauqua, a system of popular education and home study for adults. William Rainey Harper was also intimately involved with Chautauqua, so there was a bond between Vincent and Harper prior to their association at the university. While a student at the University of Chicago, Vincent studied with Small and Henderson, as well as John Dewey, the noted philosopher and educator.[67]

Born in Rockford, Illinois, near the birthplace of Jane Addams, on March 21, 1864, he lived until February 1, 1941. In the intervening years his major interests were Chautauqua, sociology, and educational administration. During his early work at the University of Chicago, from 1894 until 1900, he was at the forefront of sociological thought. Gradually, however, he became increasingly interested in administration, holding various positions as a dean there. In 1911 he left to accept the presidency of the University of Minnesota, and in 1917 he left this position (which he had successfully filled) to accept the presidency of the Rockefeller Foundation. This latter group was founded by John D. Rockefeller, who had also been the major initial benefactor of the University of Chicago. Vincent served as head of the foundation until his retirement in 1929. Throughout this period he kept actively involved with sociology, but more as an avocation than as his major occupation.

An example of his continuing interest in sociology can be seen in his association with *AJS*. A founding member in 1895, Vincent served as an associate editor from 1895 to 1915 and advisory editor from 1915 to 1933.[68] His professional association with sociology was a continuing thread in his career, enabling him to exert his views during several decades crucial to the development of the discipline. His long-term association with Chicago Sociology is rarely acknowledged in accounts of the profession.

William I. Thomas

A flamboyant, vital, and charismatic man, Thomas established himself as a leading sociologist in terms of his writings and dedicated students. He was born on a farm in Virginia in 1863, and in 1884 graduated from the University of Tennessee with majors in classical and modern languages. He became an instructor at that university, and then he traveled to Germany in 1888-89, where he studied languages and developed an interest in folk psychology and ethnology. Upon his return, he taught at Oberlin until 1894 when he entered the Department of Sociology at the University of Chicago as a student. Here he studied not only with Small and Henderson, but also enrolled in more "marginal courses" such as biology, physiology, and brain anatomy.[69]

From 1895 until 1918, Thomas was a leading figure in the department. His scholarly apogee was reached with the publication of a five volume work between 1917 and 1918, coauthored with Florian Znaniecki, *The Polish Peasant in Europe and America*. This book was the leading scholarly text in the discipline for almost twenty years.[70] It focused on the need for careful methodology and analyzed the effect of rapid social change on the immigrant who moved from a stable rural society to the brutal and fast paced urban life found in the United States.

Tragically, in 1918 Thomas was dismissed from the University of Chicago on an unproven charge concerning a violation of the Mann Act, i.e., crossing state lines to commit an illegal deed. This abridgement of his rights to fair trial plagued his later year, spanning almost three decades. Although he never held a full-time academic position again, he was restored to professional respectability with his election to the presidency of the American Sociological Society in 1928.[71]

George H. Mead

Mead's position in sociology has been increasingly the subject of debate. Clearly an influence on many sociology students, his relationships to the early faculty, particularly to Small, Henderson, and Zeublin, have been generally interpreted as more tenuous.[72] In this book, the social reform work of these men will be seen as close and frequently interactive, thereby documenting a number of clear ties between them.

A philosopher, Mead was born in South Hadley, Massachusetts, in 1863, the same year as Thomas' birth. In 1883 he graduated from Oberlin, where his father was a professor of homiletics and where the young Mead formed an abiding friendship with another student, Henry Castle. From his undergraduate days through his studies in Berlin, Germany, from 1888 to 1891, Mead was plagued with a depression and a lack of direction in his life. Paralleling the feelings of William James and Jane Addams during the same period, Mead felt that religion was not an answer to modern questions and that it failed to provide the deepest meaning, motivation or method to resolve modern ills.[73] Although he did not complete his doctorate in Germany, he joined the faculty at the University of Michigan in 1891 where he met John Dewey. His doubts and anguish subsided and he found his place in life. He was invited by Dewey to come to the University of Chicago in 1894, and Mead worked there until his death in 1931.[74]

A shy man with strong opinions, he impressed his students with the profundity of his thought. Many of his most important books were written posthumously by his students who appeared to have taken extensive, precise notes in his classes.[75] Although his brilliant exposition of the genesis of the self, society, and the mind are notable contributions to American social thought, his pragmatism and work in social reform were to Mead the core of his life's work and writings. This deep concern with the restructuring of society has been consistently overlooked by sociologists, partially explaining the interpretation of his influence as due to an "oral" tradition of learning at the University of Chicago (an institution otherwise lauded for its written research tradition).[76] Mead taught many sociology students, becoming a founder of Chicago symbolic interactionism. This perspective is said to be a common intellectual tie between Thomas, Park, Burgess, and their later colleague, Ellsworth Faris.[77] In this approach to the study of society, humans are the central figures in ordering and maintaining social structures built on language and the capacity to understand and respond to others.

Ernest W. Burgess

Burgess has been characterized by his student Donald J. Bogue as "young, naive, and possessed of a brilliant mind and an affection-starved soul—ripe to be proselyted to a great cause" when he arrived at the University of Chicago in 1908.[78] Born in 1886 in Tillbury, Ontario, he received his undergraduate education at Kingfisher College in Canada. Immediately continuing his education at the University of Chicago, he was one of the first men on the faculty to be trained primarily in the new discipline by its early male founders.[79]

Although he taught at three universities in Ohio and Kansas from 1912 until 1916, the majority of his career was spent at Chicago. Another quiet and retiring man with humanitarian interests, he was basically conservative and worked with meticulous detail and diligence. There were many parallels between his views and Small's during the former's early years. Gradually, Burgess became increasingly influenced by the charismatic and opinionated Park, with whom he shared an office and the coauthorship of important texts on sociology and urban life.[80]

In 1934, Burgess was elected to the presidency of the American Sociological Society. He was also an associate editor of the *AJS* during his long career at Chicago, from 1916 until 1952.[81] Although generally robust and good-natured, Burgess spent his later years in a nursing home where he declined physically and mentally. His friends and associates were distressed by the dramatic change in him and in 1966, he died there.[82]

Although Burgess was a leader in professional associations, his independent scholarly work is not held in high esteem, while the books he wrote with Park are seen as the foundation of the Chicago influence during the 1920s and 1930s. Many of their students became powerful sociologists who published numerous texts in what became known as the Chicago School series of ethnographic studies.

Robert E. Park

Park was a gruff man, dramatically different in self presentation from any of his colleagues. According to his loyal and professionally successful students, this brusqueness and offensiveness hid a "truly affectionate man."[83] Park was a strong influence on his students, directing their work and shaping their ideas. He attained a major role in the development of Chicago Sociology from 1920 until World War II. Extremely egotistical, his one autobiographical statement reads as if he founded sociology alone with few collegial influences on his social thought or development.[84] Like Vincent, he was born in 1864 (a year after Thomas and Mead). Throughout his childhood, he lived in various cities and towns in the Midwest. From a poorer background than his colleagues, Park had a checkered career as an adult. While studying at the University of Michigan, he enrolled in several of Dewey's courses.[85] After graduating from there in 1887, he worked as a muckraking newspaper reporter for over a decade.[86] Loving urban life and its vitality, Park roamed the streets looking for human-interest stories and excitement. From 1899 until 1905, like his sociological colleagues, Park traveled to Germany to study where he "read deeply into the work of the founders of sociology."[87] (Park was particularly fascinated with the work of Simmel who was later introduced into American sociology by Small.[88]

After Park worked as an assistant in philosophy at Harvard from 1903 until 1905,[89] he left to become the secretary and companion of Booker T. Washington. In this capacity, he met W.I. Thomas who recruited him to a marginal position at the University of Chicago in 1913. Park was hired to teach one course in one academic quarter, a position that he filled from 1913 until Thomas' dismissal in 1918. It was only in 1919 that Park was given a full-time appointment "instead of his temporary summer quarter tenure which had been renewed from year to year."[90] In 1923, Park was finally appointed a full professor.

This long period of apprenticeship must have been a bitter pill for Park to swallow. One indication of his estrangement from Small, Henderson, and Zeublin is his total disregard for their works in his writings and acknowledgements. Park formally recognized only Thomas as a "Chicago" influence on his sociological thought.

With a virulent ideology against social reform and "do-gooders," Park was paradoxically deeply involved with reform movements throughout his life. With Burgess he coauthored *Introduction to the Science of Society* in 1921, thereby supplanting the 1894 introductory text written by Small and Vincent. The Park and Burgess text became a famous and influential book, defining the field of sociology for beginning students over the next two decades. Similarly, their work on urban ecology became known as the basis for Chicago Sociology and its related social policy studies.[91]

Park developed a number of strong relationships with his students whose books were published in a thirty-volume series of studies covering numerous urban districts, ethnic groups, and occupations.[92] Dismissed until recently as an effective teacher but relatively insignificant scholar, his role in

Chicago Sociology is now being reexamined by several scholars.[93] In this book, he is seen as a major factor in obscuring the early history and influence of Chicago sociologists.

The Outline of the Book

Each chapter supports the major thesis that Addams was a central figure in applied sociology, especially in the Chicago School of Sociology. Hull-House, which she headed and was the major women's sociological institution, is discussed first (chapter 2). Some of the brilliant women sociologists who lived and worked there are introduced, and the relation of social settlements to male sociology is analyzed. The influence of a core group of residents at Hull-House upon Chicago Sociology is dramatically revealed in the next chapter (chapter 3), which discusses the cooperatively produced and critical text *Hull-House Maps and Papers*. This book, drawing upon detailed maps of social life on the South Side of Chicago, analyzed the effects of social disorganization, immigration, and the economy on the everyday life of an urban neighborhood. In other words, this book established the major substantive interests and methodological technique of Chicago Sociology that would define the School for the next forty years. Because of its central role in defining the Chicago School of Sociology, an entire chapter is devoted to a discussion of the problems of getting it in print, its contents, and use by male Chicago sociologists. The erasure of its central role in shaping Chicago Sociology is also documented.

The next three chapters also examine an interrelated set of ideas. Each of these chapters examines the men's relation to social reform as it changed over time. The earliest men, Small, Henderson, Zeublin, and Vincent, all worked on topics directly related to the concerns of Addams. Their work differed from her work, however, due to their greater religious emphasis and more conservative politics. Despite these differences, Addams and these "religious" men shared a significant common core of interests centered on urban life and the particular problems besetting Chicago (chapter 4).

Addams' relationship with the Chicago men reached its fullest development through her work with Mead and Thomas (chapter 5). With these three as colleagues, a flowering of sociological theory and practice occurred. Uniting an interpretation of the world as social in origin with a commitment to social change, they set the foundation for a separate school of thought—symbolic interactionism. Although all of them were originally intimately tied to pragmatism and to Addams' particular practice of sociology, the linkages between symbolic interactionism and social reform have been consistently overlooked in historical accounts of the development of the theoretical perspective.

This distortion of their work and the role of applied sociology in its development is largely attributable to Burgess and Park. These two men, therefore, comprise another distinct position toward social reform and sociology that is found within the male Chicago School (chapter 6). With Park's active hostility to the "label" of social reformer (although he frequently engaged in social reform activities) and Burgess' wavering commitment to it, the applied, political component of sociology languished and finally died within the Chicago School. Although Park and Burgess denied the significance of the work of Addams and many of the male founders of the Chicago School, these successors in the Chicago School were still affected by the early ideas, substantive concerns, and methodological techniques of their predecessors.

But Park and Burgess were not the only cause of the decline of Addams' type of sociological practice at the University of Chicago. Part of the reason for the transition in emphasis from social reform to "scientific," apolitical sociology, is due to the limits placed on faculty activism at the University of Chicago. Chapter 7 documents the form and type of political control exercised by the academy concerning the conduct of sociology, and the direct impact such censorship had on the careers of Chicago sociologists.

Addams' relationship to sociology was also directly tied to the status of women as a topic of inquiry and as colleagues in the sociological enterprise. Both of these aspects are discussed in chapter 8 in reference to the eight Chicago men. A direct link between the men's generalized attitudes toward women and their specific attitudes towards Addams as a colleague and intellectual is thereby established.

The final major topic is the sociology of Addams as an intellectual legacy. Her work in this area is analyzed as a function of two major streams of thought: cultural feminism and critical pragmatism. Chapter 9 is a discussion of "cultural feminism," a theory of society that assumes that traditionally defined feminine values are superior to traditionally defined male values. Chapters 10 and 11 are both discussions of "critical pragmatism," a term coined here, which is a theory of science that emphasizes the need to apply knowledge to everyday problems based on radical interpretations of liberal and progressive values. Chapter 10 is an intellectual history of Addams' sociological influences that range beyond the men of the Chicago School. Chapter 11 is an analysis of her explication of critical pragmatism. After both components of her thought have been analyzed, the incompatibility between cultural feminism and critical pragmatism is briefly considered. This internal inconsistency of her work is also partially responsible for the decline in her sociological leadership. Clearly, her choice of emphasizing cultural feminism with its preference of feminine values over masculine ones was the major reason for her "fall from grace." Her national censure as a pacifist coincided with her "failure" as a sociologist, and for many years she remained a social outcast. A brief summary of her life and sociological career after 1920 is presented in the concluding chapter. Here, too, a review of the changing times and profession is included and an overview of her legacy provided. Some areas for future research are then considered. Her profound influence on the course and development of sociology can only be suggested in one volume. This book is a beginning analysis of a little-examined, alternative heritage and tradition of American sociology.

Notes

1. Lester R. Kurtz documents the extensive literature on the Chicago School of Sociology in *Evaluating Chicago Sociology: A Guide to the Literature, with an Annotated Bibliography* (Chicago: University of Chicago Press, 1984). More than 1000 references to the school's first sixty years of influence are annotated there. Out of this vast literature, major statements on the school can be found in Steven Diner, "Department and Discipline," *Minerva* 8 (Winter 1975):514-53; Robert E.L. Faris, *Chicago Sociology, 1920-1932* (Chicago: University of Chicago Press, 1967); Ernest W. Burgess and Donald J. Bogue, *Contributions to Urban Sociology* (Chicago: University of Chicago Press, 1964); James F. Short, Jr., *The Social Fabric of the Metropolis* (Chicago: University of Chicago Press, 1971); and Edward Shils, "Tradition, Ecology and Institution in the History of Sociology," *Daedulus* 94 (Fall 1970):760-825. More general references to the school can also be found in texts on the history of the discipline. A good critical article of the Chicago role in sociology is found in Patricia Lengermann, "The Founding of the *American Sociological Review*," *American Sociological Review* 44 (April 1979):185-98. A more uneven analysis of the school and men is found in Herman and Julia Schwendinger, *The Sociologists of the Chair* (New York: Basic Books, 1974). Books and articles written on the men of the Chicago School are referenced in the short introductory statements of each (see notes 52-87 below and in notes throughout the book).
2. One of the best bibliographies on Addams and her era can be found in John C. Farrell, *Beloved Lady* (Baltimore: Johns Hopkins University Press, 1967), pp. 217-61. This book provides an excellent interpretation of her social reform ideas. The most critical and insightful analysis of the myth of Addams is Allen F. Davis, *American Heroine* (New York: Oxford University Press, 1973). Another fine study of her life is Daniel Levine, *Jane Addams and the Liberal Tradition* (Madison: State Historical Society of Wisconsin, 1971). A good, more informal biography was written by her nephew, James Weber Linn, *Jane Addams* (New York: Appleton-Century Crofts, 1935). Although not extensively documented, Linn provides inside views and information not found in other biographies. Addams documents her life and era best. See her *Twenty Years at Hull-House* and *The Second Twenty Years at Hull-House* (New York: Macmillan, 1910 and 1930, respectively).

3. See Mary Jo Deegan, "Early Women Sociologists and the American Sociological Society," *The American Sociologist* 16 (February 1981):14-24, "Women in Sociology: 1890-1930," *Journal of the History of Sociology* 1 (Fall 1978):11-34. An excellent discussion of women's work in the sciences is found in Margaret Rossiter, *Women Scientists in America* (Johns Hopkins University Press, 1982).

4. See Davis, *American Heroine*, p. vii.

5. Ibid.

6. Jane Addams to Ellen Gates Starr, 11 August 1879, Starr Papers, Sophia Smith Collection, Smith College.

7. Addams' life is documented in many sources. Those used primarily here were Farrell, *Beloved Lady*, Davis, *American Heroine*; and Linn, *Jane Addams*. Their information is based on archival evidence or personal knowledge of Addams and is mutually reinforcing.

8. Davis, *American Heroine*, p. 35.

9. The best account of these early years is presented by Jane Addams, *Twenty Years at Hull-House*, hereafter referred to as *Twenty Years*.

10. Mead is discussed in-depth throughout this book. See esp. chs. 2, 4, 9. Dewey's friendship with Addams is documented by Jane Dewey, "Biography of John Dewey," in *The Philosophy of John Dewey*, ed. Paul A. Schilpp (New York: Tudor, 1951, c. 1939), pp. 1-45. See also Jane Addams, *Twenty Years*, pp. 236-37, 435; John Dewey, "Introduction," in Jane Addams, *Peace and Bread in Time of War* (Boston: Hall, 1960, c. 1918, 1922). Jane Addams wrote the eulogy for Dewey's son Gordon, reprinted in *The Excellent Becomes Permanent* (New York: Macmillan, 1932). Dewey even named his daughter after Jane Addams. He is central to Chicago Sociology, but documenting this is beyond the scope of this book. See C. Wright Mills for an introductory analysis of the topic in *Sociology and Pragmatism*, ed. and intro. by Irving Louis Horowitz (New York: Paine-Whitman, 1964).

11. See ch. 2 in this volume.

12. The best documentations of her influence can be found in the books mentioned in note 3 above. See also a general overview of the contributions of Hull-House in *Eighty Years at Hull-House*, ed. Allen F. Davis and Mary Lynn McCree (Chicago: Quadrangle, 1969); Jane Addams, *Twenty Years*; and *The Second Twenty Years at Hull-House*, with the latter book hereafter referred to as *Forty Years*. One of the few serious, although limited, treatments of Addams' intellectual thought is the work by Christopher Lasch. See his introduction to the collected writings of Addams, *The Social Thought of Jane Addams* (Indianapolis, Ind.: Bobbs-Merrill, 1965), pp. vii-xxvii; and *The New Radicalism in America, 1889-1963* (New York: Knopf, 1965).

13. Davis' excellent documentation of the red-baiting of Addams and other women sociologists is discussed in *American Heroine*, ch. 14, "The Most Dangerous Woman in American," pp. 251-81.

14. Ibid., p. 282.

15. In addition to the books noted above, two articles also examine her intellectual contributions: Merle Curti, "Jane Addams on Human Nature," *Journal of the History of Ideas* 22 (April-June 1961):240-53; and Staughton Lynd, "Jane Addams and the Radical Impulse," *Commentary* 32 (July 1961):54-59.

16. See Mary Jo Deegan, "Early Women Sociologists and the American Sociological Society."

17. The role of nonacademic sociologists has been problematic for decades. Professional debates about their unequal status in the profession abound and efforts to develop "applied sociology" are continually being made. See discussions, in *Footnotes* (January 1983):2-3; and newsletters of the Clinical Sociology Association and the Humanist Sociologists.

18. Dirk Käsler, "Methodological Problems of a Sociological History of Early German Sociology," paper presented at the Department of Education, University of Chicago, 5 November 1981.

19. Davis, *American Heroine*, p. 125.

20. Addams is listed as lecturer in the Extension Division of the University of Chicago for several years (e.g., 1902, 1909, 1912). For a copy of the syllabus of one of her courses, see "Survivals and Intimations in Social Ethics," Ely Papers, Wisconsin State Historical Society, 1900. Farrell noted the syllabus of another course in his footnotes, see *Beloved Lady*, p. 83. This was titled "A Syllabus of a Course of Twelve Lectures, Democracy and Social Ethics."

21. Addams declined Harper's offers to annex Hull-House with the university on at least two occasions. She refers to this in a letter to William R. Harper, then president of the University of Chicago, on 19 December, 1895, Presidents' Papers, box 1, folder 9, University of Chicago Special Collections, hereafter referred to as UCSC. This attempt to affiliate Hull-House with the university is discussed in depth in chapter 7 in this volume.

22. Small to Addams, 1913, Addams Papers, DG1, box 4, Swarthmore College Peace Collection, hereafter referred to as SCPC.

23. The *Publications of the Sociological Society* included a list of members in each of their annual publications from 1906 to 1930. This practice was discontinued after the latter date.

24. Discussant of John Commons, "Class Conflict in America," *Publications of the American Sociological Society*, vol. 2 (1907), pp. 152-55; "Recreation as a Public Function in Urban Communities," *Publications of the American Sociological Society*, vol. 6 (1911), pp. 35-39; "Americanization," *Publications of the American Sociological Society*, vol. 14 (1919), pp. 206-14.

25. Jane Addams' *American Journal of Sociology* articles: "A Belated Industry," 1 (March 1896):536-50; "Trade Unions and Public Duty," 4 (January 1899):488-62; "Problems of Municipal Administration," 10 (January 1905):425-44; "Recreation as a Public Function in Urban Communities," 17 (March 1912):615-19; "A Modern Devil Baby," 20 (July 1914):117-18. Addams also wrote a comment on an article by John R. Commons, "Class Conflict in America," 13 (May 1908):772-3.

26. Book reviews in *American Journal of Sociology* on Addams books: Charles R. Henderson, "*Review of Democracy and Social Ethics*," 8 (July 1902):136-38; George H. Mead, "Review of *The Newer Ideals of Peace*," 13 (July 1907):121-28; Harriet Thomas and William James, "Review of *The Spirit of Youth City Streets*," 15 (January 1910):550-53; Florence Kelley, "Review of *A New Conscience and an Ancient Evil*," 18 (September 1912):271-72; Jessie S. Ravitch, "Review of *The Child, the Clinic and the Court*," 31 (July 1925):834-35.

27. *Democracy and Social Ethics* (New York: Macmillan, 1902).

28. *The Long Road of Women's Memory* (New York: Macmillan, 1916), p. xi.

29. Lionel Lane, "Jane Addams and the Development of Professional Social Work," p. 2. Unpublished paper, Addams Papers, DG1, Box 10, Series 4, SCPC.

30. Farrell, *Beloved Lady*, p. 68.

31. *Hull-House Maps and Papers, by Residents of Hull-House, A Social Settlement, A Presentation of Nationalities and Wages in a Congested District of Chicago, Together With Comments and Essays on Problems Growing Out of the Social Conditions* (New York: Crowell, 1895), p. iv; and *The Long Road of Woman's Memory*, p. xi.

32. Addams to A. Huelson, n.d. (attached to letter from Huelson to Addams, 11 January, 1907), Addams Papers, DG1, SCPC. The pragmatists Janes Tufts, Ella Flagg Young, and William James were also on the list.

33. Ross to Addams, 12 January, 1912, Ross Papers, box 5, Ross to Addams, 12 September, 1915, Ross Papers, box 7, Wisconsin State Historical Society, hereafter referred to as "Ross Papers".

34. Addams' paper on "The Subjective Necessity of Social Settlements" became a classic statement on the need for settlement workers to be in that setting and relying on their neighbors and friends. See *Philanthropy and Social Progress: Seven Essays by Miss Jane Addams, Robert A. Woods, Father J. O. S. Huntington, Professor Franklin H. Giddings and Bernard Rosanquet*, intro. Henry C. Adams (New York: Crowell, 1893), pp. 1-26.

35. E.W. Krackowizer, "The Settlement Idea," *Boston Evening Transcript* (8 June 1895), in Hull-House Scrapbooks, B-27, p. 40, SCPC.

36. See C.H. Cooley, *Social Organization* (New York: Scribner's, 1909), pp. 431-32.

37. E.A. Ross to Dean F.B. Taylor, 25 February, 1914; Ross Papers, box 6; E.A. Ross, Seminary On the American Family, Economics 262 (discipline boundaries, as this book continually notes, were very blurred during these years), "List of Books on Reserve" and "List of Additional Books and Bulletins Not on Reserve." These lists were submitted in 1926 but the course itself is undated. Dummer Papers, box 409, Schlesinger Library.

38. E.S. Bogardus. "Leading Sociology Books Published in 1916," *Journal of Applied Sociology* 4 (May 1917):14.

39. "More Campaign Contributions," *North American*, Philadelphia (2 October 1912):647-45; (p.148; J.A. Scrapbooks, #5, SCPC).

40. "Problem of Crime Unresolved, Let Us Start at It Anew," by Jane Addams; "Famous Sociological Authority of Hull House, Chicago," *The Proceedings and Cure of Crime*, 1929; and "Jane Addams Discusses Problem of Crime," *Baltimore American* (3 July 1927):2-E +. Series 3, box 7, Addams Papers, DG1, SCPC.

41. Addams was one of the founders of the National Association for the Advancement of Colored People, which DuBois led. The close relationship between DuBois and Addams is noted in several places and deserves an analysis beyond the scope of this topic. For example, see references to their joint activities in *Twenty Years*, p. 255; Levine, *Jane Addams and the Liberal Tradition*, pp. 134, 185. See also W.E.B. DuBois to Addams, 11 January, 1932, Addams Papers, DG 1, SCPC.

42. Jane Addams, *The Social Thought of Jane Addams*, ed. Lasch; Davis, *American Heroine*. Another book which partially demystified Addams' leadership is Farrell's *Beloved Lady*. As its title suggests, however, there is still an overlay of mythmaking as "lady" and an emotional image in this work. Two excellent articles are Lynd, "Jane Addams and the Radical Impulse," and Curti, "Jane Addams on Human Nature." Although there are some other good resources, especially for documentation of her life and career, there are literally hundreds

of articles on Addams that refer to her saintliness (or villainy) and mythologize her public image. As a group of writings, they symbolize Addams as an unreflective but often holy woman.

43. A large segment of this women's network was located at or through the University of Chicago and Hull-House. See Mary Jo Deegan, "Women in Sociology: 1890-1930," *Journal of the History of Sociology* 1 (Fall 1978):11-34; and "Early Women Sociologists and the American Sociological Society." Other women sociologists are also briefly examined in a number of other articles. See Barbara Keating, "Elsie Clews Parsons," *Journal of the History of Sociology* 1 (Fall 1978):1-11. The writings of a series of women sociologists are summarized in the articles written by Deegan for the *American Women Writers* series (New York: Ungar Publishing, 1978-81). These include entries on Sophonisba Breckinridge, Edith Abbott, Emily Green Balch, Marion Talbot, and Helen Merrell Lynd. See also Mary Jo Deegan, "Sociology at Wellesley College, 1900-1919," *Journal of the History of Sociology* 6 (December 1983): 91-115.

44. Faris, *Chicago Sociology*; Burgess and Bogue, *Contributions to Urban Sociology*; Short, *The Social Fabric of the Metropolis*; Shils, "Tradition, Ecology and Institution in the History of Sociology"; Lengermann, "The Founding of the *American Sociological Review*; Schwendinger and Schwendinger, *The Sociologists of the Chair*.

45. This is clear in Faris, *Chicago Sociology*, pp. 3-36; Short, *The Social Fabric of the Metropolis*, pp. xiii-xx; Burgess and Bogue, *Contributions to Urban Sociology*, pp. 1-14.

46. Faris, *Chicago Sociology*, pp. 113-16, 159.

47. There is now some debate over the significance of Mead's role. See J. David Lewis and Richard L. Smith, *American Sociology and Pragmatism* (Chicago: University of Chicago Press, 1980); Bernice Fisher and Anselm Strauss, "George Herbert Mead and the Chicago Tradition of Sociology (Part One)," *Symbolic Interaction* 2 (Spring 1979):9-26 and "(Part Two)" 2 (Fall 1979):9-20. These authors aver that Mead's role was marginal in sociological thought. This "debate" however is of recent origin and evidence supporting Mead's significance is very strong. See Herbert Blumer, *Symbolic Interactionism* (Englewood Cliffs: Prentice-Hall, 1969); Faris, *Chicago Sociology*, pp. 88-99; *Symbolic Interaction*, 3rd Ed., ed. Jerome Manis and Bernard Meltzer (Boston: Allyn and Bacon, 1979).

48. See Faris, *Chicago Sociology*; Manis and Meltzer, *Symbolic Interaction*.

49. Jane Addams, "Pioneers in Sociology: Graham Taylor," *Neighborhood* 1 (July 1928):6-11.

50. References to Howerth in Faris, *Chicago Sociology*, were limited to only the titles of his master's and doctoral theses. Diner mentions him in two of his publications, largely in reference to his work for the Illinois Education Commission, "Department and Discipline," *Minerva* 8 (Winter 1975):514-43, p. 529; and *A City and Its Universities* (Chapel Hill: University of North Carolina Press, 1980), p. 86. No archival deposit of his work and writings is known to the author nor was his name mentioned in the hundreds of letters and reports read in the course of this investigation.

51. Ernest Becker, *The Lost Science of Man* (New York: Braziller, 1971), pp. 3-4.

52. Faris, *Chicago Sociology*, p. 153; Becker, *The Lost Science of Man*, pp. 3-21.

53. Harper decided between Small and Richard Ely, a close colleague to Addams. The decision for Small led sociology in a less political direction than the choice of Ely would have. See Diner, "Department and Discipline," pp. 515-21; Faris, *Chicago Sociology*, pp. 12, 120.

54. Albion W. Small and George E. Vincent, *An Introduction to the Study of Society* (New York: American Book, 1894).

55. Faris, *Chicago Sociology*, p. 153. A review of these statements is found in chapter 4, nn. 16-20 below.

56. See Steven J. Diner, "Department and Discipline," pp. 523-25; Graham Taylor, "1848—Charles Richmond Henderson—1915," *Survey* 34 (10 April 1915):55-56.

57. Taylor, "1848—Charles Richmond Henderson—1915," p. 56.

58. See Faris, *Chicago Sociology*, 1967; Short, *The Social Fabric of the Metropolis*; Burgess and Bogue, *Contributions to Urban Sociology*. The only references to Zeublin found in sociology texts was a condescending and inaccurate one in the Schwendingers. They state that he was not a radical, left the University in 1901, and never published in the *American Journal of Society*. These are all inaccurate statements, p. 510. He was an American Fabian, albeit not a Marxist, left the university in 1908, and published four articles in *AJS*.

59. Steven J. Diner, "Department and Discipline," p. 519.

60. Zeublin to Harper, 31 January, 1891, Presidents' Papers, Box 71, Folder 13, USSC.

61. Northwestern University—College of Liberal Arts—Alumni Record, #489. Northwestern University Archives.

62. "Social Work Shoptalk," *The Survey* 53 (15 October 1924):108.

63. Ibid.

64. Ibid.

65. This is discussed in more depth in ch. 4 below.

66. Diner, citing *Who's Who in America* (Chicago, 1911). A.N. Marquis, vol. 6, p. 1257.

67. Diner, "Department and Discipline," p. 526. Note that this also was a possible source of linkage to Mead's ideas, which were closely tied to those of Dewey.

68. E.W. Burgess, "George Edgar Vincent," *American Journal of Sociology* 46 (May 1941):887.

69. See Edmund Volkart, ed., "Biographical Note" in *Social Behavior and Personality* (New York: Social Science Research Council, 1951), pp. 323-24; Paul J. Baker, "The Life Histories of W.I. Thomas and Robert Park," *American Journal of Sociology* 79 (September 1973):243-60.

70. Herbert Blumer, *An Appraisal of Thomas and Znaniecki's The Polish Peasant* (New York: Social Science Research Council, 1939), pp. 5-6.

71. Mary Jo Deegan, "Early Women Sociologists and the American Sociological Association," p. 17.

72. See J. David Lewis and Richard L. Smith, *American Sociology and Pragmatism*.

73. Neil Coughlan, *Young John Dewey* (Chicago: University of Chicago Press, 1975), pp. 113-49.

74. Faris, *Chicago Sociology*, p. 155.

75. See George H. Mead, *Mind, Self and Society*; *The Philosophy of the Act*; *The Philosophy of the Present* (Chicago: University of Chicago Press, 1934, 1938, 1932, respectively). Each book was edited by a former student with *Mind, Self and Society* based on 1928 class notes and edited by Charles W. Morris.

76. Gregory P. Stone and Harvey Farberman, eds., *Social Psychology through Symbolic Interaction* (Waltham, Mass.: Xerox College Publishing, 1970); Jerome Manis and Bernard Meltzer, eds., *Symbolic Interaction*.

77. Faris, *Chicago Sociology*, pp. 88-99; Stone and Farberman, *Social Psychology through Symbolic Interaction*; Manis and Meltzer, *Symbolic Interaction*.

78. Donald J. Bogue, *The Basic Writings of Ernest W. Burgess* (Chicago: Community and Family Study Center, 1974), p. ix.
79. Faris, *Chicago Sociology*, p. 157.
80. Ibid, pp. 37-133.
81. Ibid, p. 157.
82. Bogue, *The Basic Writings of Ernest W. Burgess*, p. xxii; interview with Nels Anderson, 28 August 1979.
83. Faris, *Chicago Sociology*, p. 30.
84. Robert E. Park, "An Autobiographical Note," in *Race and Culture* (New York: Free Press), pp. v-xiv.
85. Fred Matthews, *Quest for an American Sociology* (Montreal: McGill-Queen's University Press, 1977), p. 5. Dewey's influence on Park was quite extensive, see esp. pp. 20-30.
86. Ibid, pp. 8-30.
87. Ibid, p. 68.
88. See Small's translations of Simmel, "The Sociology of Secrecy and Secret Societies," *American Journal of Sociology* 11 (January 1906):441-98.
89. Matthews, *Quest for an American Sociology* p. 85.
90. Ibid, p. 86.
91. Faris, *Chicago Sociology*, pp. 37-133.
92. For a list of the books see Winifred Rauschenbush, *Robert E. Park* (Durham, N.C.: Duke University Press, 1979), pp. 196-97.
93. Rauschenbush and Matthews are outstanding examples of this renewed interest. See also Ralph H. Turner's anthology of Park's writing, *Robert E. Park: On Social Control and Collective Behavior* (Chicago: University of Chicago Press, 1967).

2

Hull-House and Sociology

Hull-House was for women sociologists what the University of Chicago was for men sociologists: the institutional center for research and social thought. Although each sex worked in an institution dominated by one sex, both groups engaged in a considerable exchange of ideas and interests. Institutionally, however, each sex had a distinct power base and professional network. Women controlled Hull-House and men controlled the University of Chicago. In the founding days of sociology the work of female sociologists at Hull-House developed a firm foundation for the intellectual thought of the male sociologists at the University of Chicago. In addition, while the University of Chicago developed a professional, academic basis for the profession, Hull-House developed a professional, nonacademic basis for it.

Each sex, moreover, had a different perception of his or her role and work. Although both sexes assumed that the application of knowledge was intrinsic to the sociological enterprise, the men believed that they were intellectually superior and that the best institutional home was the university. They expected women to be "out in the world" applying abstract ideas and testing them in the process. Women were the "data collectors," the doers of the "mundane," according to the view of the early Chicago men. The women, however, believed that their work was superior to the men's. They thought that the men were more concerned with "safe" abstract ideas than with the real problems of everyday life. The men were in an "ivory tower" while the women were at the forefront of change and challenge. Each sex believed that his or her work was superior to that of the opposite sex. The women, on the one hand, wanted to be disassociated from established institutions and vested interests like the Rockefeller-funded University of Chicago. They also wanted to be part of a multidisciplinary approach to the world emphasizing the totality of social problems. The men, on the other hand, wanted academic respectability and an area of specialized expertise. The academic community needed to legitimate a "new field."

33

In this chapter Hull-House is introduced as the institutional home of Addams and the center of a "women's sociologists" network. Before presenting its cast of characters, a brief analysis of the male academics' view of this institution is needed. As a group, the male sociologists tended to interpret the social settlement as a "sociological laboratory." This conception of the settlements' work was resisted by Addams ideologically when she denied the validity of the "sociological laboratory" analogy, and administratively, when she rejected an offer to have Hull-House join the University of Chicago.

Locating the Sociological Laboratory: The Social Settlement or the City?

One of the "catchwords" of the Chicago Sociologists was "the city as a sociological laboratory." For example, Park wrote in 1919: "As a matter of fact civilization and social progress have assumed in our modern cities something of the character of a controlled experiment."[1] The study of urban life was a defining characteristic of Chicago Sociology, and viewing "the city as a laboratory" was part of the perspective.[2] But this theoretical interpretation of the significance of the setting for observing human behavior was first assigned to social settlements and not to "the city." This view of the sociological function of social settlements was vehemently rejected by the women sociologists. This is particularly true for Addams and the Hull-House residents. In order to understand this debate, it is necessary to analyze its origins in the settlements.

The University Settlement as a Sociological Laboratory

During the founding years of sociology, social settlements were viewed by male sociologists as "windows" on the world. Small clearly held this view as one of the founders of the University of Chicago Settlement.[3] Started by

> An organization known as the "Christian Union," composed of a number of the first faculty members of the University of Chicago, it wished to express its religious and educational principles in the creation of a laboratory of social service in the city. It was to serve as a "window" for the sociological department of the University, the first such department in the country, and at the same time to serve the needs of a Chicago neighborhood in the same way that Hull-House ministered. After a close survey made by sociology students at the new university, it was agreed that the district just back of the Union Stock Yards, a district which had been the scene of rioting and bloodshed in the strike of 1894 (the Pullman Strike), was most in need of such a social center.[4]

This concept of the settlement as a social science laboratory can be traced directly to Robert Woods, a male leader in the social settlement movement. First addressing the audience at the Summer School of Ethics in 1892, where Franklin H. Giddings and Addams were also speakers, Woods established his broad outlines of University Settlements.[5] The following year, he gave another major address titled "University Settlements as Laboratories in Social Science." At this time, he noted that this was the "transcendent function of the university settlement."[6] In this setting, the workers became "experts": "And as a poor and crowded neighborhood is a microcosm of all social problems, the resident by his study and experiment in the microcosm becomes equipped for study and work in the broader sphere."[7] This "colonization" of social settlements was a popular idea among male sociologists and social settlement leaders. It was unacceptable, however, to the women sociologists. The latter's resistance to analyzing populations as "specimens" was a fundamental divergence between the male and female sociologists.

In 1894, Daniel Fulcomer, a short-lived University of Chicago instructor, asked Julia Lathrop to speak on the subject of Hull-House as a sociological laboratory. Following an address by Fulcomer where he defined the academic nature and interests of sociology, Lathrop did not know how to proceed. This was not her concept of sociology or Hull-House. This definition was so foreign that she side-stepped the issue: "I say nothing except to state what I can about Hull-House in the time allotted to me, and then to leave it to you to determine if it may be called a laboratory of sociological investigation."[8] Although not openly antagonistic to the perspective, Lathrop avoided the use of the viewpoint throughout her speech. She did emphasize that *Hull-House Maps and Papers* (hereafter referred to as *HH Maps and Papers*) was a sociological investigation, but this was her major concession to sociological experimentation.[9]

Addams clearly stated in the preface to *HH Maps and Papers* that the residents did not usually engage in sociological investigation.[10] This was not due to her lack of concern with sociology or sociological investigations. Rather, it was the view of settlements as "laboratories" which she rejected, believing that the needs of the people took precedence over the needs of researchers.[11] Her sensitive approach to the issue is eloquently revealed in her book on the first twenty years at Hull-House. There she noted her rejection of this concept of the settlement, but her acceptance of sociological research.

> I have always objected to the phrase "sociological laboratory" applied to us, because Settlements should be something much more human and spontaneous than such a phrase connotes, and yet it is inevitable that the residents should know their own neighborhoods more thoroughly than any other, and that their experience there should affect their convictions.[12]

Similarly, McDowell resisted the University of Chicago's pressure to become a "sociological laboratory." One author wrote that when the academy's original goal was thwarted, the sociologists turned from the University of Chicago Settlement to the Research Department of the School of Civics and Philanthropy. This latter department was headed by two Hull-House residents and sociologists, Edith Abbott and Sophonisba Breckinridge.[13] Thus, the influence of the Hull-House residents was still felt, but through academic channels and not through a continuous research "window" on settlement communities.

Another male Chicago sociologist who advanced the notion of the social settlement as a laboratory was Zeublin. In an 1899 article, published in *AJS* and following one on Hull-House, Zeublin called Edinburgh's University HAll "the first sociological laboratory."[14] Describing its work and direction under Patrick Geddes, Zeublin analyzed the mix of social settlement and university studies as a "natural" part of the city and social progress. In this way, he united the themes of the city, the university, and the social settlement. Since Zeublin was also a director of a social settlement, in his work as a sociologist he incorporated this vision of the settlement as a "laboratory" into his own work. This sex-linked difference between male and female "practical" sociology reveals one of the reasons why the networks remained distinct.

Thus, the women closed their sociological "windows," placing the needs of the community first. The view of people as "objects" and not participants in social studies was rejected by them, although they continued to support extensive data collection that responded to the demands of the community.

The Laboratory's Transition from the Settlement to the City

Lundberg, Bain, and Anderson condescendingly documented both the early significance of social settlements for research and the end of this role. Writing in 1919, they credited the early social settlement

> as a point of observation and contact center for budding scholars and social philosophers of the past generation. . . . It was a forum and discussion circle, until social science passed from its empirical stage to a more mature stature and began to range abroad for more substantial data than the inspiration of the round table.[15]

Although footnoting that (HH) *Maps and Papers* "represents the zenith reached by social science under the tutelage of the settlement,"[16] their major point was that "Social science left the dialectic laboratory of the settlement with the rise of research foundations. The point of departure might be put at 1909, which was the date of the publication of the first volume of the Pittsburgh Survey."[17]

Thus, ignoring the continuity of Addams and Hull-House personnel in both studies, these male sociologists marked the transition of the "sociological laboratory" from the social settlement to the city as occurring after 1909. (It is notable that this 1919 text appeared after Addams vilification due to her pacifism during wartime.)

But it had actually begun earlier than that. Small was calling the social settlements "laboratories" in 1894, but in 1896 he was already beginning to call "the city a laboratory" as well. In a seminal statement uniting the ideas of social action and study, Small wrote: "The most impressive lesson which I have learned in the vast sociological laboratory which the city of Chicago constitutes is that action, not speculation, is the supreme teacher."[18]

In this passage, Small articulates a view of the city as a sociological laboratory that receives its fullest statement in 1929 by Robert E. Park. At this later date, however, Park denigrated the significance of the early studies conducted by social settlements and claimed the concept of "the city as a sociological laboratory" as originating with the work of the 1920s Chicago sociologists. In the process, the idea of the city as a sociological laboratory becomes even more objectified and subject to abstraction than Small's original intent. The study of the city became divorced from social action and practice, while Small's role in generating the concept is not acknowledged.[19]

In the transitional years from 1909 until 1929, Burgess also noted that the city was a "laboratory."[20] Similarly denigrating "earlier studies" as less generalizable and unscientific, Burgess laid the groundwork for denying the value of his early work (as well as the women's) while elevating his later work with Park written in the 1920s.[21]

Between 1892 and 1929, the transition of the sociological laboratory from the social settlement to the city was complete. The early debates over the concept, its association with objectification and exploitation, and its rejection by female sociologists are all issues never discussed in the literature on Chicago Sociology.[22] By devaluing the early settlement studies and inflating the value of academic research, the Chicago sociologists of the 1920s disassociated their study of urban behavior from politics and social change. In the process, the commitments of the early male sociologists were slighted while the females were almost entirely dismissed.[23]

Hull-House and the University of Chicago

When social settlements were seen as "sociological laboratories," the University of Chicago was strongly motivated to establish a tie with Hull-

House. However, the university represented a different organization and philosophy from the settlement's. Addams resisted inclusion in the university because she foresaw a power struggle that Hull-House might well lose.

This negotiation between the university and the settlement became a public issue on one occasion. In 1895, Helen Culver donated a million dollars to the University of Chicago, primarily in the form of real estate. Since she also owned the land on which Hull-House was built, the press assumed that she had also deeded this property to the university. On 15 December, the *Chicago Tribune* published a front page account of the gift with a subheading that Hull-House had been included in the transaction. Although Small stated in one part of the article that the donation probably did not include Hull-House, he was also quoted as saying: "Hull-House is a part of the property Miss Culver gives the university and our former interest in that institution will be greatly increased. This gift will give the greatest facilities possible for work in which all sociologists will be interested."[24]

Immediately, Addams and Hull-House were inundated by calls and visits. The local press noted that the independence of Hull-House would be diminished by the Rockefeller-dominated university. Addams, denying the transfer the following day, also feared this takeover.[25]

It is clear that Harper wanted such a transaction to occur. For on 19 December, 1895, Addams specifically declined such a liaison. In a dramatic and strongly worded letter, Addams explained her position:

> Of course, we must feel that any absorption of the identity of Hull-House by a larger and stronger body could not be other than an irreparable misfortune, even although it gave it a certain very valuable assurance of permanency. Its individuality is the result of the work of a group of people, who have had all the perplexities and uncertainties of pioneers. This group is living in the 19th Ward, not as students, but as citizens, and their methods of work must differ from that of an institution established elsewhere, and following well defined lines. An absorption would be most unfair to them, as well as to their friends and supporters, who believe that the usefulness of the effort is measured by its own interior power of interpretation and adjustment.[26]

Noting that such a transfer of land would not necessitate the emergence of an "authoritative influence over Hull-House," all the comments of the press, friends, and residents indicated that such an event was feared. "Such an impression would work most disastrously to our institution, and require constant explanation which would be embarrassing for the sociological department of the University as well as for ourselves."[27]

Thus, there were strong arguments in favor of annexing Hull-House to the University of Chicago from the academy's point of view. To Addams, however, the university represented a structure threatening to overpower the settlement. To understand her resistance to incorporation, the settlement's goals, sociological practice, and personnel need to be explained and this is my next task.

Hull-House and Sociology

In 1889, Jane Addams and Ellen Gates Starr returned from a European tour filled with enthusiastic new ideas about society and their roles in it. Long despondent over her "snare of preparation"—her long training without a goal—Addams found the answer to her problem in England. She would live with the poor and disenfranchised, communicating with them across class, sex, religious, and ethnic divisions. From the very beginning, she realized that the social settlements provided a necessary outlet for educated women who wanted to learn, use their training, and retain their "feminine" worldviews and values.[28]

Although originally borrowing freely from the goals of Toynbee Hall, a community for university men with similar goals, Addams soon altered her ideas.[29] She rejected the ideal of an elite leadership and adopted a more democratic model where a settlement resident needed to be in the district as much as people in the district.[30] First emphasizing religious motivation, a kind of Christian humanism, Addams quickly deemphasized this and began increasingly to stress the need for a "radical democracy." By this latter term, coined here, Addams intended democratic principles to be carried to their extreme for total social, economic, and political equality. All people were to have a voice in decisions affecting their daily lives and society. This extreme application of democracy was the foundation of the settlement and Addams' philosophy. Also, because of the idealization of women as nurturant and humanitarian, she rapidly became the spokesperson for this approach to social life and settlements, and she embodied the symbol of what a settlement leader could be.

As graphic as this symbol was, it remained nonetheless only an "image" of Addams and the social settlement. For she and many of her followers wanted dramatic, structural alterations in American society. They believed these changes could be accomplished by providing a mechanism for people of all classes, races, and sexes to "speak together." Anticipating the extreme conflict that could result, they argued that "facts" and "scientific" evidence could persuade all fair-minded people, the members of the community, to formulate the "right way" for action. Therefore, Addams and Hull-House became a center for empirical analysis, study, and debate.

"Education" was to be the key to radicalizing America. The settlement was to provide a setting for such exchanges of knowledge. But this was a particular type of learning, one based on community involvement and challenges, especially by workers and the poor. As early as 1892, Addams articulated this special role of the settlement. Education, for her, was a form of liberation and "deliverance." It enabled people to articulate their desires, to understand complex issues, and to back up opinion with facts.[31] Although personally supporting the goals of economic equality espoused by socialists, she wanted this form of economic distribution to be selected by the people and not imposed upon them by "leaders."[32]

In order to create the type of institution she wanted, she needed independence, freedom from exploitation or manipulation of herself or her community, evidence to document the problems of the community, and methods to alleviate or eliminate these social ailments. In the next sections, Hull-House is briefly examined in terms of its goals and personnel, and as the site of numerous significant, sociological studies. This empirical work underlies the Chicago School of Sociology, forming an intrinsic, major intellectual heritage for the discipline. The network of studies and personnel at the social settlement other than Addams are emphasized in the remainder of this chapter.

Hull-House: The Settlement and Personnel

In 1889, Addams and Starr did not suspect that they would soon be the leaders of a national social movement. By 1891, "there were six settlements, by 1897 there were 74, and in 1900 there were well over 100."[33] Part of the reason for Addams' ascendancy to leadership was her stellar role in 1892 at a summer conference where she delivered two lectures on the subjective necessity of settlements and the work of Hull-House. At this meeting, Addams met a number of other women sociologists and the "women's network" was initiated.

Meanwhile, the physical facilities of Hull-House rapidly expanded. For example, during the first few months, Addams and Starr occupied only the second floor of the building that was leased to them a year later. They then named it Hull-House after its original owner, Charles Hull. In 1891 they built the Butler Art Gallery on adjacent property. This two-story structure housed a branch of the public library, had an art gallery, and space for clubs and classes. In 1893, they erected another building with a coffee house below and a gymnasium above. The original Hull-House was enlarged by a third story a year later, providing space for a kindergarten, nursery, and music school. In 1896 another story was added to the Butler Art Gallery for a men's residence, and in 1898 an entire building was added for the "Jane Club," a women's cooperative apartment. Another coffee house was built with a theater above it in 1899. This set of buildings was designed by Allen and Irving Pond who were part of the settlement movement in Chicago from its very early days.[34] During this period, the first public playground in Chicago was started at Hull-House, in 1893.[35]

From 1900 to 1914, the physical plant continued to grow apace. A succinct description of this large institution is given by Davis and McCree:

> In 1902 the Hull-House apartment building was completed with a Men's Club on the first floor. Bowen Hall, the Women's Club building, was erected in 1904, and by the next year the resident's dining hall had been constructed. In 1906 the Boy's Club building was finished, and in 1907 the Mary Crane Nursery completed the complex of buildings which covered a large block and made up Hull-House as it would remain until 1963.[36]

Divided by two alleys, there were one large and two small groups. All of them were interconnected with a courtyard that generated a park atmosphere. All of the buildings except the main house were demolished when the University of Illinois built its Chicago Circle campus. (Significant destruction of the ethnic neighborhoods in this locale also occurred at this time.)[37]

With Addams as Head Resident, others quickly moved into the social settlement to join her. These other "residents" were predominantly women. They lived together for various periods of time, from at least three months to decades, taking their meals in common and working together on numerous projects.

This group approach to living encompassed a holistic view of women's professional and personal lives. For they wrote together, formed organizations together, and campaigned as a united force. In these projects they would suspect that a certain problem existed, gather data documenting that such a problem did exist, form a policy for social action based on this factual evidence, and then lobby political and community forces to alleviate or eliminate the problem.

This team approach to problem solving and social research was Mead's idea of a "working hypothesis"[38] and is integral to Addams' sociology. Although she rarely used statistical data in her popular articles and books, she depended upon the more scholarly and detailed data collected by other residents at Hull-House to formulate her ideas and support her plans before more scholarly and political audiences. Thus Addams assumed the crucial role of translating more abstract information into its everyday meanings. She was able to transform esoteric knowledge into pragmatic programs of action. The early men of the Chicago School had this same ideal, to bring sociological knowledge to everyday life to enable people to make intelligent decisions, but they were never as successful as Addams and her cohort of predominantly female sociologists.

Because literally hundreds of women were residents at Hull-House, only the most outstanding women sociologists can be briefly mentioned in this book. These are Florence Kelley, Edith Abbott, and Sophonisba Breckinridge.

Kelley was one of the few Hull-House women to have married and borne children. Born in 1853, she was feisty and outspoken. As a female barred from graduate training in the United States, she traveled to Zurich and received a doctorate in political economy there in 1886. The early translator of Engels' writings (see chapter 3), Kelley brought to Hull-House a scholarly and radical platform for social action. For example, by 1887 she had written a pamphlet for the Association of Collegiate Alumnae (ACA, later the American Association of University Women) entitled "The Need of Theoretical Preparation for Philanthropic Work." Discussing the difference between "bourgeois" and "working class philanthropy" she noted that the latter is reciprocal and mutual. Calling for an understanding of the class background of educated women she urged their union with the workers in order to understand the laws of social and industrial development:

> to spread this enlightenment among the men and women destined to contribute to the change to a higher social order, to hasten the day when all the good things of society shall be the goods of all the children of men, and our petty philanthropy of today superfluous.[39]

Divorced and the mother of three, she was bitterly disappointed by the socialists, particularly Engels, who had treated her as a marginal and second-class comrade. Turning from Marxist thought, she nonetheless remained a radial theorist and practitioner. All her writings were based on extensive, large scale survey data concerning working conditions and constraints on the working class. Author of at least thirty-seven articles, two books, five book-length reports on factory inspections, and translator of three Marxist books and pamphlets, Kelley was a militant and brilliant theoretician. She articulated the need for a successful, American program of social change eliminating class differences and inequalities.[40]

Coming to Hull-House in the winter of 1891, she graphically described her arrival:

> Reaching Hull-House that winter day was no small undertaking. The streets between car-track and curb were piled mountain high with coal-black frozen snow. The street cars, drawn by horses, were frequently blocked by a fallen horse harnessed to a heavily laden wagon. Whenever that happened, the long procession of vehicles stopped short until the horse was restored to its feet, or as sometimes occurred, was shot and lifted to the top of the snow, there to remain until the next thaw facilitated its removal.[41]

Kelley stayed, despite this grueling introduction to the slums on the prairies. In 1899 she left to become the Secretary of the National Consumers League, an organization that lobbied for consumers and union workers' rights. Throughout her life, Kelley retained her strong ties to Hull-House and was a frequent visitor.

Edith Abbott and Sophonisba Breckinridge were such closely associated figures that their students used to refer to them as "A and B."[42] Chicago sociologists, they held numerous marginal positions in the Department of Sociology. (Breckinridge and Abbott identified themselves as primarily "social workers" after 1920. At that time, the former was 54 years of age and the latter 44.) Although it was their joint efforts that made them so remarkable, they will be introduced separately.

Sophonisba Breckinridge was recruited to the University of Chicago because she, like Addams before her, was despondent after leaving college. Born in 1866, she trained to practice law in Kentucky, the first woman to pass the bar there in 1894. However, because of sex discrimination, she was unable to find any clients who would use her skills. She wrote of her discouragement to a former college friend living in Chicago. The latter contacted Marin Talbot, Breckinridge's former instructor at Wellesley College and then employed in sociology and as the Dean of Women at the University of Chicago. Talbot quickly created a job as Assistant Dean and invited Breckinridge to come to work at the University of Chicago. Breckinridge accepted with alacrity. While employed there, Breckinridge earned two doctorates as well: one in political economy and another in law. Again, she was a "first woman" in law, being the first woman to graduate from the Law School at the University of Chicago. Nonetheless, during these early years, Breckinridge remained aimless and dissatisfied. She felt she had little control over many of her major life decisions. For example, she described her entry into the doctoral program in political economy as follows:

> I don't know how it was managed but I moved over to a room on the fourth floor of Kelly Hall (a dormitory) and became a student in Political Science at the University. I was very poor, I had almost no clothes, and money that first year, I found no way of earning.[43]

The victim of sex discrimination again, she was unable to articulate this as a source of her malaise. Reflectively, she wrote:

> I had a well known name and an academic experience with Miss Talbot, and I had enough in the way of manner. But it seemed to me that the university presidents were at that time more concerned with the outsides of their women students' heads than with their "gray matter" and so long as I could

be in contact with Mr. Freund 1), Mr. Laughlin 2), and Miss Talbot 3), I was only too glad to scrape along, getting room and board by assisting at Green Hall.[44]

It was only when she became actively associated with Addams and Hull-House that she found her niche in life. Thus it was at the age of forty-one that Breckinridge "took off" and became a prolific author, lobbyist, teacher, and leader. In 1908 she moved into Hull-House and lived there intermittently until 1920.

In 1899, Talbot arranged for a separate Department of Household Administration to be organized under the auspices of the Department of Sociology. Breckinridge was hired as a lecturer to teach five courses, beginning a "sex-segregated" women's structure within the Department of Sociology.[45] Always a distinct entity, with less status than the men's, it was nevertheless a major training and teaching area for the students, especially the female ones. It was here that Breckinridge trained Abbott, whose course work ultimately resulted in her classic statement on women's role in the marketplace, *Women in Industry*.[46] In 1908, both Abbott and Breckinridge moved into Hull-House, beginning an intimate and collegial career pattern unparalleled by any other male sociologists. To better understand it, more background on Abbott can now be introduced.

Born in 1876, Abbott was the youngest Hull-House woman to influence Chicago Sociology. Trained as an undergraduate at the University of Nebraska by the sociologist E.A. Ross and as a graduate student of Breckinridge at Chicago, Abbott was the most academically oriented sociologist of the Hull-House women. Receiving her Ph.D. in Political Economy from the University of Chicago in 1905, she continued her studies at the London School of Economics with Beatrice and Sydney Webb. Accepting a position in sociology at Wellesley College in 1907, she returned to Chicago the following year to work with Breckinridge and the Hull-House women. She filled a number of marginal faculty positions in the Sociology Department at the University of Chicago from 1908 to 1920. In the latter year, a separate school of social work was established within the university.[47]

From Abbott's arrival in Chicago until 1920, however, she and Breckinridge engaged in a series of empirical studies on education, housing, urban childhood, labor, and working women. They established the major topic areas of what was later considered "social policy" studies of the Chicago School.[48] With Breckinridge's training in law, they combined their statistical interests with massive legal case studies and briefs, achieving a highpoint in the sociology of law that has never been recognized in the profession.[49]

To adequately assess their work is considerably beyond the scope of this background chapter to Hull-House. Suffice it to be noted that they were intellectually integral members (albeit with marginal status) of the Department of Sociology and the sociological enterprise at the University of Chicago as well as residents of Hull-House.[50] Breckinridge and Abbott, moreover, worked intensively with Henderson and Mead, forging a strong link between themselves as a subgroup.[51]

Other forceful and intellectual women were residents at Hull-House, such as the first industrial physician in the United States, Alice Hamilton, and the first head of the Children's Bureau, Julia Lathrop, and her successor, Grace Abbott, sister to Edith. It was this network of women, all laboring with massive "scientific" data at hand that formed the empirical and intellectual foundation of Hull-House. Addams was clearly their leader, but they all depended on each other and their division of labor within the women's settlement. Originally conceiving of themselves as sociologists, they became increasingly dissatisfied with the direction and orientation of their male colleagues. Ultimately, most of them associated themselves with social work and disassociated themselves from sociology. Before this occurred, however, they left a significant heritage to the profession of sociology.

Some more sociological ties at Hull-House are investigated below, before returning to the major focus of this book—Addams as a sociologist.

Hull-House and Empirical Investigation

The men of the Chicago School are often interpreted as being "antiquantitative." The Chicago School of sociology, therefore, came to epitomize a "qualitative" approach to studying the world. Emphasis on "life document" studies, "participant observation," "sympathetic introspection," or even "armchair philosophy" were seen as their dominant styles of using data to interpret social life and its order. The "mapping" of demographic factors in urban regions was the only "quantitative" technique adopted by the Chicago School of urban ecology. In fact, there was, supposedly, a major "overthrow" of this Chicago antistatistical tradition with the advent of W.F. Ogburn's entry into the Department of Sociology in 1928.[52] For example, Short wrote that Ogburn "is the intellectual godfather of modern statistical methods as applied to demography, human ecology, and the study of social change."[53] If Ogburn is the godfather, then Addams, Kelley, Abbott, Breckinridge, and other Hull-House women were all his godmothers.

Recent scholarship by Bulmer has gone to extreme lengths to show that there was some "early" statistical influence on the Chicago men by examining departments at the University of Chicago other than sociology. Thus men working with quantitative methods in political science or psychology are seen as influencing male sociologists while female sociologists are not only overlooked, but even denigrated![54]

All this patriarchal scholarship consistently ignores the concern with statistics central to the work of female sociologists at Chicago. This statistical work, moreover, was frequently organized at Hull-House or through other social settlements. Collecting quantitative data was considered "women's work" by the University of Chicago's male sociologists prior to Ogburn's introduction to the staff in 1928. Because this work has been defined by patriarchal scholars as nonsociological, *voilà*! there was no statistical Chicago sociology before 1928. Men with similar interests to the women, including Henderson and Mead, also had this aspect of their work "forgotten."

To fully document the wide range of statistical work completed at Hull-House would require a separate volume. Therefore, only a sample of major figures and research works is given here. For example, my next chapter is devoted to a discussion of *HH Maps and Papers*, because of its singular influence on Chicago Sociology. But this influential book was only part of a generalized empirical approach that consistently set high standards of research excellence, later adopted by male sociologists at Chicago. This surfeit of empirical evidence is illustrated by the residents' approach to "mapping," and the publication of their empirical work in *AJS*, the most respected sociological journal of its era.

Maps

The mapping of social and demographic characteristics of a population in a geographic area was the core methodology of Chicago Sociologists of the 1920s, their only "recognized" quantitative technique. For example, Palmer's book *Field Studies in Sociology*, the major methodological text for Chicago students in the late 1920s and early 1930s,[55] devoted a complete chapter to an examination of mapping as a research tool.

Acknowledgement of this methodological technique as associated with Hull-House residents is singularly lacking. Such a systematic exclusion of the women's work can only be explained as academic dishonesty. Not only was this methodological technique first used in Chicago with *HH Maps and Papers*, but Hull-House residents openly continued this tradition and practice. *Any* visitor to Hull-House, let alone a scholarly one, was immediately exposed to their enchantment with mapping.[56] As the settlement's neighborhood became an area of ever-increasing study, "Nationality, distribution, occupation and income level, size of families, kind and character of housing, were reduced to *charts and maps, some of which were put on the walls of Hull-House so that the neighbors could also have the benefit of this research* [emphasis added]."[57] The settlement was permeated with maps.

The use of these maps by female Chicago sociologists was radically different from their subsequent "scholarly" use by male Chicago sociologists. On the one hand, the maps of the "scholars" were intended to reveal to experts and decisionmakers the lives of the people of the neighborhood. On the other hand, the maps of Hull-House were intended to reveal to the people of the neighborhood that their lifestyles had patterns and implications that they could use to make more informed decisions. These maps were part of the community, and integral to the settlement's goals of democracy and education.

Repeatedly, these Chicago women sociologists brought their information to the community and initiated major social changes. Such radical alterations in governmental structures and everyday life are certainly meritorious, but since this book is oriented to an examination of the academic influences of Addams my analysis of empirical work is limited primarily to this latter arena. One indicator of this scholarly input can be found by analyzing the residents' contributions to the major sociological journal— *The American Journal of Sociology (AJS)*.

Hull-House and the AJS

Founded in 1895 by Albion Small, *AJS* immediately became the foremost journal in the discipline and a major influence in defining sociology's subject matter, methodology, and professional issues. Although *AJS* was not limited to publications by the Chicago faculty, it did supply a market for their writings and lent support to many issues that Small favored.[58] Therefore, with Small's interest in social reform and his many ties with Addams and Hull-House, it is not surprising that many residents of the settlement published in the journal.

Using the *AJS Index* for volumes 1-40 (1995-1935), over fifty articles were written by Hull-House residents and published in the *AJS*.[59] A much larger number of articles referred to topics of interest to the residents, e.g., on social settlements, legislation, immigrants, or juvenile delinquency. The number of fifty articles is a conservative estimate of the Hull-House influence on the journal. For there were people, such as Annie Maron McLean, who worked closely with the residents and who also published in the journal. McLean alone accounts for an additional ten articles.[60] Hull-House residents were also prolific authors of books, so that over twenty-seven of their books were reviewed in *AJS*. Clearly, sociologists were reading and discussing their work.[61]

This group influence on the character of the journal is amplified even more because Addams and other Hull-House residents were affecting the work of the Chicago men who were also publishing in *AJS*. They were simultaneously writing for other scholarly publications such as the *Annals of the American Academy of Political and Social Science*, the *Journal of Political Economy*, and the *Proceedings of the National Conference on Social Work*.

But rather than be led astray into these additional indicators of scholarly production, it is sufficient to note that the Hull-House residents wrote a large number of articles in the most respected sociology journal. For the first quarter of the twentieth century, their work was recognized as sociologically significant, and it was only subsequent accounts of sociological thought which have denied this impact.

Hull-House: The Professional Woman's Commune

Hull-House is rarely interpreted as a commune, although it clearly was such an enterprise.[62] All the women who lived there had a communal domestic arrangement, freeing their time and energy for other tasks. As predominantly unmarried professionals, they developed complex and intimate friendships, difficult to document because of their unrecorded daily interactions. There are few intimate letters between the residents that remain, with Addams a notable exception in this regard.[63] One of the remaining personal recollections of this close-knit living arrangement written by Abbott gives a "feel" for their daily atmosphere:

> There was a residents' dining-room where we had dinner together and a residents' breakfast table in the public coffee-shop—where we argued in relays, over the morning newspapers. Although we were a large group of residents, we were a kind of family group together—a very argumentative family group, for we often disagreed. Our political opinions varied widely, and our arguments not infrequently began at the breakfast table; and during the day the various participants in the current controversy seemed to have sharpened their weapons and prepared for the new arguments that were sure to be heard at the dinner table—with Miss Addams often serving as mediator and laughing as verbal shots were fired. And in the late evening hours the arguments were still going on with those who sat around together when the House was officially closed and the neighbors had all gone home and the residents could use the reception room and the library for themselves.[64]

Thus, women sociologists had a radically different career pattern from that of men. Centered around communal life, these women rarely developed nuclear family structures and were liberated from the usual restrictions on women's lifestyles. They could survive on their lower salaries because they shared housing costs, domestic duties, and were indifferent to clothing fads. Interestingly, because these women were seen as fulfilling women's "nurturant and humanitarian" needs, they were not viewed as living radical lives. Their total rejection of women's everyday lives with men and in families was camouflaged by this legitimated role.

An amazing professional style emerged. These women wrote together, lived and ate together, taught together, exchanged books and ideas, vacationed together, became officers in each other's organizations, developed a pool of expertise on a wide range of topics, and generated numerous changes in the social structure of government.[65] There is no corollary among men, and male sociologists followed a much more traditional life than did their female counterparts.

Social settlements became an alternate lifestyle for women. Anna Garlin Spencer, an early woman sociologist, articulated this role as a new one for the "spinster." Heads of settlements, in particular, had a "recognized place in the social control, reform and uplift of a vast city" providing a uniquely female service. Although a bit maudlin and now sounding dated, Spencer continued: "She might be painted as the new Portia pleading at the bar of justice, her cap and gown not assumed for the occasion, but worn by right as certificate of her assured place in the world of letters and thought, not used as disguise, but as token of her official standing."[66] It is easy to see why women were so drawn to sociology. With few job possibilities if they married, or few places for social approval if they chose to work or live outside of a traditional home, the social settlement provided the answer to this dilemma. Their lives, moreover, were to be models for overall social change.

Hull-House generated an alternative lifestyle for all working women, not only for its professional residents. The settlement sponsored a group of apartments cooperatively owned and operated, called the Jane Club. Managed by the residents, it "was unique in its relative cheapness, independence from philanthropic assistance, and freedom from fussy rules. . . . In 1898 the new building opened, and the Jane Club existed as a self-supporting project for several decades."[67] This club had largely working-class women as its boarders, with private rooms and individual privacy. Its success "spurred wide discussion of cooperative housekeeping arrangements among small and large groups of single working women."[68]

Hull-House provided a function for women of all classes. But for women sociologists it provided a professional role model and ideal based on the philosophical assumptions of Addams. It was a pragmatically enacted and successfully designed arrangement for everyday life. It freed professional women from the restraints imposed upon them by society and, in particular, by male sociologists. Combining theory and practice in this way, the women built a strong professional network, undivided by patriarchal ideas of public versus private, professional versus everyday, or work versus home.[69] By combining their economic resources and knowledge, the women were formidable opponents of sexual discrimination. As a group, they defined their own world views and feminine values as superior to men's and built a sub-world within a society that otherwise restricted their place to the traditional family and home. For a few decades, they flourished.

Conclusion

Hull-House was the central institution for women sociologists from 1892 until 1920. During this period, Hull-House residents worked closely with the men of the University of Chicago. Together, they formed a basis for American sociology. Because of sexism within the profession and the ultimately marginal status of the applied sociologist's career, this entire institutional network and foundation for Chicago sociology has been significantly devalued.

In this chapter, Hull-House was described as an institution with unique characteristics. It was developed by women sociologists who engaged in massive statistical studies that were subsequently translated into everyday language and application. Hull-House was a sociological "home" radically different from academic, male-dominated sociology.

Addams resisted every effort to include her and her social settlement within the University of Chicago's definition of the sociological task. She refused an offer to be a faculty member in the department and to affiliate Hull-House directly within the university's administration. She rejected the definition of her institution as a "sociological laboratory" or outpost for the men. Instead, she built an institution with a different philosophy of education and knowledge. For Addams, education was a life-long project available to all and integral to democratic citizenship. Education was intended to empower the "student" and heal the divisions of class, ethnicity, religion, and poverty. Statistical data were needed to document the oppression of the disenfranchised and information was needed on the whole problem, not the specialized component defined by academics in various departments. Nonetheless, sociology was the "home" for Addams and many of the women at Hull-House, notably Kelley, Abbott, Breckinridge, and McDowell.

This sociological enterprise was one they shared with the early men of the Chicago School. Thus, the men came to Hull-House as lecturers, visitors, and colleagues. They participated in its programs and its social thought.

Addams was the major link between the male and female sociological worlds. As she interpreted her female colleagues' work to the public, she interpreted the female sociological task to the male sociologists. Nowhere is this intellectual heritage and leadership role in Chicago Sociology more evident than in the innovative, empirical book *Hull-House Maps and Papers*, analyzed in depth in the next chapter.

Notes

1. Robert E. Park, "The City as a Social Laboratory," in T.V. Smith and L. White, eds., *Chicago: An Experiment in Social Science Research* (Chicago: University of Chicago Press, 1921), pp. 1-19. Since Abbott also participated in this volume, and in the Chicago Social Science Research Council from which this book was a product, her presence in the project may have helped "jog" Park's memory.
2. James F. Short, *The Social Fabric of the Metropolis* (Chicago: University of Chicago Press, 1971), p. xi.
3. Small also considered Hull-House in this way. He called the supposed acquisition of Hull-House an opportunity to gain one of the greatest "facilities" for sociologists. See "Miss Culver's Rich Gift," *Chicago Tribune* (16 December 1895):8, col. 4.
4. Howard Eugene Wilson, "Mary E. McDowell and Her Work as Head Resident of the University of Chicago Settlement, 1894-1906." Unpublished Master's Thesis, Department of History, University of Chicago, 1927, p. 26.
5. See *Philanthropy and Social Progress: Seven essays by Miss Jane Addams, Robert A. Woods, Father J. O. S. Huntington, Professor Franklin H Giddings and Bernard Rosanquet*, intro. Henry C. Adams. (New York: Crowell, 1893).
6. Robert A. Woods, in *The Neighborhood in Nation-Building* (Boston: Houghton Mifflin, Riverside Press of Cambridge, 1923), pp. 30-46. See p. 42.
7. Ibid., p. 43.
8. Daniel Fulcomer, "Instruction in Sociology in Institutions of Higher Learning," *Proceedings of the Twenty-First National Conference of Charities* 21 (1984):67-85; Julia Lathrop, "Hull-House as a Laboratory of Sociological Investigation," *Proceedings of the Twenty-First National Conference of Charities* 21 (1984):313-20. See p. 313.
9. Ibid., pp. 317-18.
10. *Hull-House Maps and Papers, by Residents of Hull-House, A Social Settlement, A Presentation of Nationalities and Wages in a Congested District of Chicago, Together with Comments and Essays on Problems Growing Out of the Social Conditions* (New York: Crowell, 1895), pp. vii-viii.
11. Ibid.
12. *Twenty Years at Hull-House* (New York: Macmillan, 1910), p. 308.
13. Lea Taylor, "The Social Settlement and Civic Responsibility," *Social Service Review* 28 (March 1954):33.
14. Charles Zeublin, "The World's First Sociological Laboratory," *American Journal of Sociology* 4 (March 1899):577-92.
15. George A. Lundberg, Read Bain, and Nels Anderson, eds. *Trends in American Sociology* (New York: Harper and Brothers, 1929), p. 269.
16. Ibid., p. 270.
17. Ibid.
18. Albion W. Small, "Scholarship and Social Agitation," *American Journal of Sociology* 1 (March 1896):581-92.
19. Robert E. Park, "The City as a Social Laboratory."

20. Ernest W. Burgess, "Can Neighborhood Work Have a Scientific Basis?" *Proceedings of the National Conference of Social Work* 51, (1924):406-11. Reprinted in Ernest W. Burgess on *Community, Family and Delinquency*, ed. by Donald Bogue (Chicago: University of Chicago Press, 1967), citation from pp. 143-44. In this same article he supports the idea of returning to the settlements as sociological laboratories, noting that it is against the tide of ideas.

21. Ibid. Also Pauline Young, *Scientific Social Surveys and Research* (New York: Prentice-Hall, 1942); or even Burgess's later interpretation, "A Short History of Urban Research at the University of Chicago before 1946," in *Contributions to Urban Sociology*, ed. Ernest W. Burgess and Donald J. Bogue (Chicago: University of Chicago Press, 1970).

22. Of course the treatment of the disenfranchised by social researchers has been a subject of considerable debate in the discipline. This particular debate, however, has never been noted before.

23. See especially Martin Bulmer, "Quantification and Chicago Social Science in the 1920s: A Neglected Tradition," *Journal of the History of the Behavioral Sciences* 17 (July):312-31, 318.

24. "Gives It a Million," *Chicago Tribune* (15 December 1895):1, 4. Small cited on p. 4.

25. "Miss Culver's Rich Gift," p. 8, col. 4.

26. Addams to Harper, 19 December 1895, Presidents' Papers, box 1, Folder 9, p. 1. UCSC.

27. Ibid, pp. 1-2.

28. Jane Addams, "The Subjective Necessity of Social Settlements," in *Philanthropy and Social Progress* (New York: Crowell, 1893), pp. 1-26. See also Jane Addams, *Twenty Years at Hull-House*, pp. 65-88.

29. Allen F. Davis, *American Heroine* (New York: Oxford University Press, 1973), pp. 49-50; John C. Farrell, *Beloved Lady* (Baltimore: Johns Hopkins Press, 1967), p. 52.

30. See Farrell, *Beloved Lady*, p. 52; Addams, "The Subjective Necessity of Social Settlements."

31. Addams, ibid., pp. 33-35.

32. Addams, *Twenty Years*, p. 187. Pp. 177-97 is a general discussion of the problems of economic determinism versus free speech and choice.

33. Davis, *American Heroine*, p. 92.

34. Allen F. Davis and Mary Lynne McCree, *Eighty Years at Hull-House* (Chicago: Quadrangle, 1969), p. 22.

35. Ibid., p. 55. The Chicago sociologist Charles Zeublin specialized in the study of "playgrounds."

36. Ibid., p. 67.

37. For a discussion of the Hull-House neighborhood until the early 1960s see Gerald Suttles, *The Social Order of the Slum* (Chicago: University of Chicago Press, 1968). The original Culver mansion is now a historical landmark and museum on the campus of the University of Illinois-Chicago.

38. G. H. Mead, "The Working Hypothesis in Social Reform," *American Journal of Sociology* 5 (March 1899):369-71.

39. Florence Kelley, "The Need of Theoretical Preparation for Philanthropic Work," ACA pamphlet, 1887, quoted in Dorothy Rose Blumberg, *Florence Kelley* (New York: Augustus M. Kelley, 1966), p. 79.

40. See bibliography in Blumberg, *Florence Kelley*, pp. 181-85.

41. Florence Kelley, "I Go to Work," *Survey* 60 (1 June 1927): 271-74. Reprinted in Davis and McCree, *Eighty Years at Hull-House*, p. 37.
42. Elizabeth Wisner, "Edith Abbott's Contributions to Social Work Education," *Social Service Review* 32 (March 1958):2.
43. Sophonisba Breckinridge, "Coming to the University," Breckinridge Autobiography, UCSC, p. 2.
44. Breckinridge Autobiography, The Russell Sage Foundation, 12, p. 1, UCSC.
45. Ibid., p. 2.
46. Edith Abbott, *Women in Industry* (New York: Macmillan, 1910). An indication of Abbott's ties to Addams rather than the university is the publication of this book by Addams's publisher rather than the University of Chicago Press.
47. See Mary Jo Deegan, "Women in Sociology," *Journal of the History of Sociology* 1 (Fall 1978):11-34.
48. See James Carey, *Sociology and Public Affairs*, Sage Library of Social Research, No. 16. (Beverly Hills: Sage, 1975).
49. This is particularly noticeable in their "document" series of books. Five were published between 1924 and 1940 and authored by either Abbott or Breckinridge singly or together. See a discussion of them in Mary Jo Deegan, "Edith Abbott" and "Sophonisba Breckinridge" in *American Women Writers*, vol. 1 (New York: Ungar, 1979). Pp. 3-5 and 219-23 respectively.
50. See Mary Jo Deegan, "Women in Sociology."
51. Mary Jo Deegan, "George Herbert Mead and the Sociology of Women" and "The University of Chicago Settlement and the Department of Sociology," unpublished papers, 1981.
52. Faris, *Chicago Sociology* (Chicago: University of Chicago Press, 1967), pp. 34, 113.
53. Short, *Social Fabric of the Metropolis*, n. 20, pp. xvi-xviii.
54. Martin Bulmer, "Quantification and Chicago Social Science in the 1920's," *Journal of the History of the Behavioral Sciences* 17 (July 1981):12-31.
55. Vivian M. Palmer, *Field Studies in Sociology* (Chicago: University of Chicago Press, 1928).
56. Alex Elson, "First Principles of Jane Addams," *Social Service Review* 28 (March 1954), pp. 6-7.
57. Ibid., p. 6.
58. Faris, *Chicago Sociology*, p. 121.
59. The residents' and authors' names are given here with the number of articles they published listed in parentheses following their names: Edith Abbott (6); Grace Abbott (4); Jane Addams (5 plus 1 discussion); Emily Balch (1); Eveline Beldon (1); Sophonisba Breckinridge (5); John R. Commons (10); Paul H. Douglas (1); Florence Kelley (6); Julia Lathrop (1); Dorthea Moore (1); Mabel Carter Rhoades (1); Victor Yarros (16); Charles Zeublin (4). Titles of articles are listed in the *American Journal of Sociology Index*, 1895-1935.
60. See *American Journal of Sociology Index*, 1895-1935, p. 35. MacLean's relationship with Hull-House is documented by Mary Jo Deegan, "Annie Marion MacLean: The Chicago Sociologist Who Taught by Correspondence," unpublished paper, 1982.
61. See *American Journal of Sociology Index*, 1895-1935.
62. See Addams, *Twenty Years at Hull-House*; Gerda Lerner, "Placing Women in History," *Feminist Studies* 3 (Fall 1975):5-15. See also Jane Addams, "The Settlement as a Way of Life," *Neighborhood* 2 (1929):139-46. This article continues under the same title by Mary McDowell, pp. 146-58.

63. Davis has an excellent analysis of Addams' numerous close relationships, especially with Julia Lathrop and Mary Rozet Smith. See *American Heroine*.

64. Edith Abbott, "Grace Abbott and Hull-House," *Social Service Review* 26 (September 1950):3, 377.

65. The best indicator of this complex network can be found by reading the numerous biographies of women in settlements. For example, Jane Addams wrote, with Grace Abbott's help, *My Friend, Julia Lathrop* (New York: Macmillan, 1932).

66. Anna Garlin Spencer, *Woman's Share in Social Culture* (New York: Mitchell Kennerly, 1913), p. 112.

67. Dolores Hayden, *The Grand Domestic Revolution* (Cambridge, Mass.: MIT Press, 1981), p. 168.

68. Ibid., p. 169.

69. See Mary Jo Deegan, "Feminist Sociology," paper presented at the Midwest Sociological Society Meetings, April 1979.

3

Hull-House Maps and Papers: The Birth of Chicago Sociology

In 1895 the residents of Hull-House coauthored a sociological master-piece. Their book, *Hull-House Maps and Papers*, had a monumental influence on Chicago sociology and, in turn, American sociology.[1] Despite its preeminence, this scholarly classic has been erased from the annals of sociology. Fortunately, its influence, insight, and historical precedence cannot be expunged.

This brilliant sociological document is significant here for the following reasons. First, it established the Chicago tradition of studying the city and its inhabitants. Second, its central chapters on immigrants, poverty, and occupational structures became the major substantive interests of Chicago sociologists. Third, it used the methodology of mapping demographic information on urban populations according to their geographic distribution. This "mapping" technique is now recognized as one of the major contributions of Chicago Sociology in the 1920s and 1930s. Fourth, it undisputedly shows the intellectual influence of Addams on the men of the Chicago School. Fifth, it reveals the development of her social thought and intellectual antecedents. Sixth, it sharply illuminates the hostility of male sociologists who failed to acknowledge her groundbreaking work in founding the profession. *Hull-House Maps and Papers* (hereafter referred to as *HH Maps and Papers*) may be the most important sociology text published during the era studied here.

Albeit a cooperative venture, there were two outstanding contributors: Jane Addams and Florence Kelley. Addams was central in her role as Head Resident of Hull-House and editor of the volume. Furthermore, she wrote two chapters and the preface. Kelley was more crucial from a scholarly and professional standpoint. She was a powerful and well-trained scholar who had access to publishing resources and statistical data. She also contributed to two chapters.

Drawing on British and Germanic scholarship, *HH Maps and Papers* was nonetheless an American product. For it was the American city in the throes of industrial expansion and explosive population growth that was the heart of the book. The problems generated by these new social conditions were embodied in the lives of the people in the Hull-House neighborhood.

The development of the book, its substantive concerns, and influence on the men of the Chicago School are all documented below. The repression of this sociological heritage is also revealed by citing historical accounts of the development of Chicago Sociology.

The Start of the Project

In 1889, Addams visited London's East End. While there, she was inspired by the social settlement Toynbee Hall and began a life-long professional interest in sociology.[2] Charles Booth studied this same urban area in his exhaustive seventeen-volume *Life and Labour of the People in London*. (In 1891, an early two-volume edition was published. This was later revised and included in the series published between 1892 and 1897.)[3] Thus when Addams edited *HH Maps and Papers* in 1895, Booth's work was available to her. Furthermore, as she acknowledged in her preface, her volume was modeled after his work.[4] Booth's influence, however, was greatly modified by the Marxist tradition that Kelley brought to the project.[5]

Trained in Zurich, Kelley became a leading advocate of socialism there. An early English translator of Frederick Engels and a New York activist, she was a recognized intellectual radical prior to her arrival at Hull-House.[6] It was this same leadership that brought her to the attention of Richard T. Ely, Albion Small's mentor. United by joint interests in socialism, Kelley and Ely began an extensive correspondence. When Ely accepted a position at the University of Wisconsin, Kelley introduced him to Addams. This was crucial for *HH Maps and Papers* since it was published as part of the series of books that Ely edited, "The Library on Economics and Politics."

It was again Kelley's scholarship and training that led to her employment as the director of a census of the Hull-House district in 1893. The statistical data collected at this time became the information used to compile the maps in *HH Maps and Papers*. During the course of this massive investigation, Kelley was corresponding with Engels, and she actively interpreted her work in light of their shared theoretical approach. For example in the spring of 1894 she wryly noted that she was herself a proletarian working at a "piece rate" for the government which paid her fifty cents for every completed schedule. Despite her reflective criticism, she had compiled impressive evidence of the poverty and oppressive conditions found in "sweat shops." In the letter noted above, she continued:

The greater part of the investigation is now completed and there remain 10,000 schedules to be filled in by "sweaters' victims" in the clothing trades. . . . The work consists in shop visitation, followed by house to house visitation and I find my polyglot acquisitions invaluable. The fact of living directly among the wage earners is also an immense help. The municipal arrangements are so wretched that the filth and overcrowding are worse than I have seen outside of Naples and the East Side of New York. . . . This aggravates the economic conditions greatly, making possible child labor in most cruel forms and rendering the tenement house manufacture of clothing a deadly danger to the whole community.[7]

Kelley's combination of qualitative and quantitative methodology provided a dense interpretation of the workers' lives. Furthermore, her application of Marxist thought to the historical context of Chicago in the 1890s was a major advance in critical analysis. In this way, Kelley was a significant influence not only on *HH Maps and Papers*, but on Addams as well.

Organizing the Project

With Ely's sponsorship, Kelley's statistics, and the residents' cooperation, the project officially began. Unfortunately, but predictably, there were a series of administrative problems. One of the biggest barriers was coordinating the work of twelve contributors. Few of these authors, moreover, were trained scholars. As Addams noted in her preface, the energies of the residents were usually directed toward "constructive work" rather than "sociological" investigation.

While Addams became frustrated with the editorial process, she was concomitantly being pressured by sociologists and other social scientists who wanted to use her findings. Writing to Ely, she complained:

We have letters every week asking about it. Professor Small told me the other day that he could not "get on" any longer without it, and we feel that the matter will be so old and out of date if we wait much longer. Mrs. Kelley's office is already making great changes in the conditions of the sweater [sic] shops in the neighborhood, and the Jewish population is rapidly moving Northward, and all the conditions are of course more or less, unlike what they were July 1st, 1893, when the data for the maps was finished.[8]

Ultimately, these administrative problems were minor compared to the publisher's decision to delete the maps. Graphically complex, color-coded, and to be inserted in pockets in the book, the maps were considered too expensive to publish.

By this time, Kelley like Addams, was highly frustrated with the project. Unlike Addams, she was hot-tempered. Firing off a letter to Ely, she wrote:

But the disappointment over the delay is trivial in comparison with the dismay which I felt when you suggested cutting the maps. This I positively decline to permit. The charts are mine to the extent that I not only furnished the data for them but hold the sole permission from the U.S. Department of Labor to publish them. I have never contemplated, and do not now contemplate, any form of publication except as two linen-backed maps or charts folding in pockets in the cover of the book, similar to Mr. Booth's charts. If Crowell and Co. do not contemplate this, it will be well to stop work at once, as I can consent to no use of my charts in any other form.[9]

Ely exploded in anger. He did not have to "take" the ultimatum about the maps nor Kelley's style of delivering it. Addams moved into the breach and wrote him conciliatory notes. She explained that Kelley was under extreme pressure and that the residents appreciated Ely's labor on their behalf.[10] Presumably, she soothed Kelley, too. Thus, it was Addams' role as arbitrator that finalized the production.[11] The problem of the costs of publishing the maps was also eliminated through her negotiations. As she wrote Ely, all the book's royalties would be waived "as we have little thought about the financial gain."[12]

Upon its publication, the reviews were highly favorable. The book was rarely considered in-depth by scholarly publications although it received notices in the more popular presses.[13] Less than 1000 copies were printed, and within two years the first edition was exhausted. As Addams ruefully noted, "The Boston publisher did not consider the book worthy of a second."[14] Despite the fact that it was quickly out of print, the volume made a considerable imprint on Chicago Sociology, examined in more depth below.

The Substance of *HH Maps and Papers*

The Maps

Two multicolored maps were printed that depicted the demographic characteristics of residents within a third of a square mile near Hull-House. These were large, pull-out inserts contained in two pockets at the front and back of the volume. Their significance was noted in the title of the book, and they were its central organizing concept. One map provided information on the distribution of eighteen national groups within the district. The other map concerned their wages, occupations, and housing conditions. These maps became the prototype for Chicago Sociology. They introduced the major substantive concerns of urban sociologists in Chicago plus the method for displaying this information graphically and simply.

Chapter 1: Methodology

The methods used to collect the data, its categorization, and the maps themselves are discussed in the first chapter. Descriptions of the geographic boundaries, means of data collection, and decisions on categories are discussed by Agnes Sinclair Holbrook. Although simplistic by today's standards, the information was comprehensive and based on the participation of thousands of people. This mapping technique was used repeatedly by Hull-House residents over the next decades,[15] as noted in chapter 2.

Chapters 2 and 3: Worker Exploitation

These chapters were written by Kelley, with one coauthored by Alzina Stevens. Both articles documented the low wages, unhealthy working conditions, and injustice of capitalism. The targeted industry was the "sweating system" and the most exploited population, wage-earning children.

The criticisms and style of argument were modeled after Marx. Similarities between worker exploitation in England and the United States, the former found in *Das Kapital* and the latter in *HH Maps and Papers*, are clear.[16] These powerful chapters authored by Kelley condemned the scandalous working conditions of garment workers. Laboring in tenements for pennies per "piece" of article produced, the workers exchanged their health for less money than they needed to survive.

No comparable analysis to Kelley's can be found in the men's writings. Although *HH Maps and Papers* profoundly influenced the male Chicago School, men needed to fit into the restrictive political climate of the academy.[17]

Chapter 4: The Ghetto

Immigrants' lives were a central concern of this book, establishing a tradition that would become of major importance to later male Chicago Sociologists. Zeublin's chapter on the Jewish community in Chicago was definitely a model for Wirth's book *The Ghetto* published in 1928. In fact, Zeublin was quoted in Wirth's book, and the latter acknowledged that the original observations were still accurate.[18]

Contrary to many other writers of his day, Zeublin stressed the strengths and not the weaknesses of the community. Home-centered and guided by the synagogue, the Jewish community was an active and strong element in everyday life. The extreme poverty of the workers, however, undermined this cohesion.

Zeublin also discussed geographic and social displacement as a function of urban changes. Here, too, he predated many other male Chicago sociologists, namely Park and Burgess. As a member of the Sociology Department, Zeublin clearly affected the social thought developed there. His participation at Hull-House was central to his work in urban sociology.[19]

Chapters 5 and 6: Bohemian and Italian Immigrants

The Bohemian peasants were analyzed as a conservative and patient group. Like Zeublin's chapter, both the strengths and weaknesses of the community were noted, although the wider society saw this world as a chaotic slum. Thus poverty areas had their own "social order."[20]

The political machine actively structured the daily lives of the Bohemians, who were captured as a group when a Bohemian alderman was elected. Chicago politics have been an underlying theme in many Chicago School studies, with the latest book in this long tradition written by Thomas Gutterbock.[21]

The Italian immigrants differed from other peasants in their intense drive to return to the Old World. This resulted in their extreme tolerance of bad working and living conditions. They identified themselves as temporary immigrants. Advocating the immigration of Italians to rural rather than urban areas, the author noted that Italians were skilled peasants and farmers and unskilled laborers. When they became demoralized with their lack of knowledge they passively accepted their fate in industry.[22]

Chapter 8: Social Agencies

Social agencies, primarily Cook county institutions, were critiqued by Lathrop as dirty, crowded, degrading, and despised. Nonetheless, the commitment of the workers often made these dismal conditions more tolerable. Despite their drawbacks, increased government support and intervention were desperately needed.

In 1928, the Thomases published a book on social agencies serving children, carrying on Lathrop's interests. Since the whole Hull-House community was involved in juvenile services, this later volume was operating out of a well-established tradition based at Hull-House and articulated by Lathrop in this particular chapter.[23]

Chapter 9: Art and Labor

HH Maps and Papers again differed form the male Chicago sociologists in the sociology of art. The men neglected it while the women explored it. In a brilliant piece, Starr wrote that art emerged from a people and was an expression of their common life. When their labor was oppressive and their living conditions degrading, people often lost not only their verve for life, but also its artistic expression. Contrary to the "Bohemian" philosophy of art, Starr linked creativity with adequate housing, health, and group respect.

She also criticized American ethnocentrism and capitalism. Instead of trying to assimilate the immigrants into American life, she tried to have the "natives" understand the grace and beauty in the cultural inheritance of the peasants. More specifically, capitalism was a barrier to art when workers were alienated from themselves. Even in their homes, the poor were oppressed. For example, renters were often forced to leave their dwellings because of the landlord's control over private property. Evicted and despairing, the poor could not find the energy to express creativity, hope, and beauty.

There is no other tradition of the sociology of art within the male Chicago School. The neglect of this specialty has been linked by Tuchman to a general sexual division of labor within the profession, where art is not considered a male area of interest.[24]

Chapter 10 and the Preface: Labor and Hull-House

Addams' chapter on labor laid the groundwork for her future writings on conflict. Her analysis of labor unions was never matched by the male Chicago School of the 1920s and 1930s. The topic was, in fact, avoided. For example, Park and Burgess in their landmark textbook on sociology have an entire section devoted to social movements, but labor movements were not discussed in depth nor was Addams' work cited.[25] Addams thought it imperative to side with the laborers. Their efforts to improve their bargaining power was a way to break the cycle of poverty.

Women were often excluded from these negotiations. One simple but effective barrier was for unions to hold meetings in saloons, where no "lady" could enter. Women, moreover, often had a particularly low awareness of the need to organize. Often working from necessity, they thought only of their immediate needs and family demands. Their first priority was their children, because they were trained to think in terms of the family and not workers. In order to change their worldview, women needed to become full citizens. This required not only political equality, but also social equality. This required, in turn, equality in wages.

Despite her advocacy of unions, Addams decried the unions' support and use of military actions. She called this "negative power." Although it worked in the short-term, it could not meet the community's long-term goals. "Positive power" was built on the community's perception of its group goals and joint fate. This latter power could be harnessed under the following conditions: (1) organizing labor, (2) with a consciousness of historical development of the community, and (3) an emphasis on ethical goals based on cooperation rather than conflict.

Addams shared Marx's goal of community equality and freedom from economic restrictions emerging from a particular historical context. However, she supported unions, while he did not. She also opposed the "negative power" of war between the classes advocated by Marx. Thus this early essay reveals Addams' critique of Marxism, capitalism, and patriarchy that is without any parallel in the male Chicago School.[26]

The appendix, also authored by Addams, was a brief discussion of Hull-House. Its institutional approach to education, community organizing, and political activism were briefly introduced (see chapter 2 here). Again, there is no analogue to this work in the male Chicago School.[27]

Summarizing the Book

HH Maps and Papers established the following precedents: the use of mapping as a statistical technique to reveal patterns of social groups; emphasis on the city as a factor structuring daily lives; the analysis of immigrant groups and their disorganization in the city, primarily as a function of debilitating economic conditions; and a direct link between the work of Hull-House residents and sociologists at Chicago.

The authors of *HH Maps and Papers* also differed from the male Chicago School in that (1) they stressed economic conditions as a major cause of social problems that needed to be altered; (2) they studied art as a function of everyday life; (3) they often focused on the study of women; (4) they advocated direct social changes such as government intervention for the needy or labor organizing, and (5) they decried conflict as a method of social interaction and did not believe it was the basis of society or social order.

Clearly, these differences arise from the work of the later, male Chicago sociologists writing in the 1920s and 1930s. The early male Chicago sociologists shared the concerns and fate of the women who were dismissed from later accounts of the development of Chicago Sociology. It is the men's work that is analyzed further below.

Chicago Sociology and *HH Maps and Papers*

Small, as noted above, was directly involved with the use of this volume. Zeublin as a resident and coauthor clearly supported the work. Henderson was a strong advocate of statistics, attempting to establish a statistical laboratory at the University.[28] He even cited the volume in his writings (see chapter 4); Mead was in favor of "mapping", citing the "charities" and women's use of it in his activities.[29] Thomas was influenced in his study of immigrants and juveniles through his contacts with Hull-House and the work done there.[30] Succinctly, the city as a focus of study was a strong theme in the writing of Addams and the men of the early Chicago School. *HH Maps and Papers* established the precedent for connecting and organizing their study of the city.

The problems in seeing the connections occur only after Park and Burgess. Burgess was considerably influenced by the book, although he subsequently downplayed it. Park was influenced too, but his antisocial reform ideology made his acknowledgement of it even more tenuous.

Burgess and the Chicago School Origins

In 1916, Burgess wrote:

> Social studies of permanent importance were made, not by departments of
> sociology, but by individuals, or by groups of social workers. Examples of
> these are Booth's *Life and Labour of the People of London*, Rowntree's *Pov-*
> *erty, A Study :f Town Life*, and Jane Addams', *Hull-House Maps and Pa-*
> *pers*."[31]

Citing the "brilliant Pittsburgh study" (largely conducted by women
sociologists and involving both Addams and Kelley in the process), Burgess
continued that at the University of Chicago "practical sociology has always
been correlated with the investigation of city, state, and national problems."[32] Burgess himself emulated these studies in a social survey he conducted at the University of Kansas.

In yet another article, written in 1924, Burgess noted that *HH Maps and*
Papers was an illustration "of careful study and keen observation of these
very early efforts to determine and take account of the many and different
conditions affecting neighborhood work."[33]

This clear intellectual heritage, becomes cloudier after his success as a
Chicago sociologist. By 1946 as a leader in urban studies he was writing: "If
you go back as far as 1895 in the Hull-House papers, you will find urban
studies in Chicago began with these Hull-House studies."[34] He modified
this acknowledgement by adding that "there were other isolated studies of
Chicago during the early decades of the twentieth century."[35] Contrary to
being few in number and separate, there were numerous, connected, and
exhaustive studies often conducted at or through Hull-House.

Burgess continued to downplay the significance of *HH Maps and Papers*
when he wrote that the later social scientists at Chicago were "scientific and
objective" while the early so-called social workers were not:

> Much of the earliest "social research" was little more than the discovery and
> reporting to the public that the feelings and sentiments of those living in the
> ethnic slums were, in reality, quite different from those imputed to them by
> the public. By the early 1920's this "social work" orientation had given way, in
> the Department of Sociology to an ambition to understand and interpret the
> social and economic forces at work in the slums and their effect in influenc-
> ing the social and personal organization of those who lived there. Although
> the objective was scientific, behind it lay a faith or hope that this scientific
> analysis would help dispel prejudice and injustice and ultimately lead to an
> improvement in the lot of slum dwellers.[36]

This passage, a significant one in interpreting the role of Addams and the
influence of *HH Maps and Papers*, is completely inaccurate. *HH Maps and*

Papers was based on the collection of economic, social, and demographic data according to a fixed schedule. Thousands of people were so interviewed. The alleged social work orientation never existed, and the goals of social improvement were, in theory, the same. However, *HH Maps and Papers* was more politically radical and applied than the writings of Park and Burgess and these differences are clear.

In this same article, Burgess takes credit for making the first juvenile delinquency maps when this was frequently undertaken by Hull-House and by the Juvenile Protective Association.[37] Stretching the male Chicago sociologists' claims even further, Burgess has the gall to name this and similar mappings, "Discovering the Physical Pattern of the City." He recalls this "discovery" with self-satisfaction:

> We were very impressed with the great differences between the various neighborhoods in the city, and one of our earliest goals was to try to find a pattern to this patchwork of differences, and to "make sense of it."
>
> Mapping was the method which seemed most appropriate for such a problem.[38]

Mapping was the stated purpose of *HH Maps and Papers*. Burgess noted its significance and role in 1916 and 1924, clearly revealing his knowledge of the work and its influence on his thought. Yet thirty years later, this was forgotten and the work of Park and himself gained in prominence.

Finally, Burgess' description of Chicago urban research is exactly that of Addams and her colleagues. Burgess wrote:

> The city had a characteristic organization and way of life differentiated from rural communities. Like rural communities, however, it was composed of natural areas, each having a particular function in the whole economy and life in the city, each area having its distinctive institutions, groups, and personalities. Often there were wide differences between communities which were very sharply demarcated.[39]

In *HH Maps and Papers*, the characteristic organization of the district by ethnic communities, housing, and income was clearly demarcated. Separate functions, such as that of the brothel area, were also located. Variations in the communities—Jewish, Italian, and Bohemian—were clearly explicated and analyzed. The description of Chicago urban research by Burgess is a description of *HH Maps and Papers*.

The practice of shortening the title of the book to *Maps and Papers* and omitting the reference to Hull-House obscured the institutional significance of the social settlement. Although this may or may not have been intended, the political consequences were significant in masking the origin of Chicago's interest in mapping and urban ecology.

Park and the Chicago School Origins

Because Park was so vehemently antireform in his speech, it is often forgotten that he, too, was influenced by *HH Maps and Papers*. His ambivalence toward this work is clear, however. Within the same article, Park first labeled the study as laying the groundwork for the more systematic and detailed studies that followed.[40] Although generally slighting the book, he gave extensive credit to the Pittsburgh Study, for which Addams was an advisor. However, Park also distorted the context of *HH Maps and Papers* when he wrote:

> The first of these local studies were, as might be expected, *practical rather than theoretic.* They were the studies of health and housing; studies of poverty and crime. They became the basis for a whole series of reforms: model tenements, playgrounds, vital statistics. They created a new and romantic interest in the slum. [Emphasis added.][41]

Such a distortion of *HH Maps and Papers* is poor scholarship. Both theoretical and political, *HH Maps and Papers* helped define major areas of study in Chicago Sociology as well as establish the mapping methodology and use of statistics. Brilliantly analyzing the social factors structuring the lives of people in the district, the authors did not portray a romantic image at all. Park was mistaken.

Nonetheless, it must be noted that Park did recognize *HH Maps and Papers* as an early part of the tradition of studying the city. Jessie Bernard, who studied with him in the late 1920s, also recalled references to the book in class. There he stressed the volume's significance in his own social thought.[42] Despite these references, however, his formal writing rarely acknowledged the work of Addams and other Hull-House residents. For example, the book is mentioned only *in passim* in Park and Burgess' introductory text on sociology.[43]

Other Interpretations of the Origins of Chicago Sociology

In his volume on Chicago Sociology, Faris did not recognize Addams at all nor the influence of *HH Maps and Papers*. Instead, he emphasized the role of the men, particularly Park and Burgess (although he did note the significant role of Booth's writings).[44]

Short briefly acknowledged the intellectual heritage of the volume when he noted: "The Hull-House Papers [sic] provided an early model for systematic urban studies."[45] Again, however, Short derogates this type of work as:

> characterized by highly partisan purposes of immediate social reform. Those which were disinterested, as was the case with Booth's work, were unguided by explicit theoretical premises and hence not productive of generalized, objective statements about urban structure and social life. Urban sociologists soon moved away from the comprehensive social survey—with its "shotgun" approach to data gathering—and, with Chicago taking the lead, undertook more detailed and conceptually guided studies of specific social phenomena.[46]

Thus, Short has the peculiar interpretation that "social reform" work was atheoretical and shotgun in its approach plus highly biased. Clearly, not scientific work. However, atheoretical work like Booth's was "not productive." Only subsequent Chicago urban sociology had the answer.

Thus, a pattern of denying the methodology and intellectual impact of *HH Maps and Papers* in Chicago Sociology became institutionalized in sociology. Starting with the writings of Burgess, the accounts have gathered momentum that *HH Maps and Papers* was a byway to instead of the grounding for Chicago Sociology. Fortunately, *HH Maps and Papers* can speak for itself.

Conclusion

HH Maps and Papers marks the intellectual birth of Chicago sociology. Urban concerns of the community, immigrants' lifestyles, and the economic conditions structuring the neighborhood were all major concerns for the residents. Moreover, the mapping of social indicators characterizing the population was clearly established in the volume. This is indisputable.

The ideas of Addams and Kelley were central to the volume and were based on the work of Booth in London and of Marx and Engels in London and Germany. The women wrote from a more radical political tradition than Park and Burgess and their subsequent interpreters.

The failure to recognize the role of *HH Maps and Papers* in shaping Chicago Sociology can be traced to the series of factors examined further in succeeding chapters: (1) the increasing shift in the male Chicago School from an "applied" to "academic" emphasis, (2) the mounting political restrictions in the academy, (3) the sexism of male sociologists, particularly the type exhibited by Park and Burgess, and (4) the different collegial networks of the early and later male Chicago sociologists in reference to Addams and Hull-House. In this chapter we have studied the factor of Park's and Burgess' personal, vested interests in the study of the city. These men claimed their work was primarily a product of their own independent scholarship. As shown in chapter 1, however, Park and Burgess were a product of the early male Chicago School. This founding group was, in turn, directly linked with Hull-House and Jane Addams. It is clear that Park and Burgess were neither as creative nor as original in their writings as they claimed.

Therefore, the significance of *HH Maps and Papers* has been obscured in the annals of sociology. Despite this intellectual burial, the foundation of the Chicago School is clear. The origins of work on maps and selected urban problems can be directly gleaned from the text. *HH Maps and Papers* also provides a basis for understanding Addams' social thought and its growing divergence from that of the men in the academy. The seeds of this difference were planted in 1895 and came to full flowering with the advent of World War I.

Notes

1. *Hull-House Maps and Papers, by Residents of Hull-House, A Social Settlement, A Presentation of Nationalities and Wages in a Congested District of Chicago, Together With Comments and Essays on Problems Growing Out of the Social Conditions*, hereafter referred to as *HH Maps and Papers* (New York Crowell, 1895).
2. Jane Addams, *Twenty Years at Hull-House*, hereafter referred to as *Twenty Years* (New York: Macmillan, 1910), pp. 68-88.
3. Charles Booth, *Life and Labour of the People in London*, 9 vols. (London and New York: Macmillan, 1892-97). Eight additional volumes (London: Macmillan, 1902). (The first volumes were originally published under the title *Labour and Life of the People: London*, 2 volumes. (London and Edinborough: Williams and Norgate, 1891).
4. *HH Maps and Papers*, p. viii.
5. Allen F. Davis, *American Heroine* (New York: Oxford University Press, 1973), p. 98.
6. For an outstanding discussion of her relationship to Engels see Dorothy Rose Blumberg, *Florence Kelley* (New York: Agustus M. Kelley, 1966), pp. 43-97. Kelley's bibliography is also included there.
7. Ibid., p. 128.
8. Addams to Ely, 31 October 1894, p. 2, and 27 November 1894, Ely Papers, Wisconsin State Historical Society (hereafter referred to as Ely Papers).
9. Kelley to Ely, 14 November 1894, Ely Papers.
10. Addams to Ely, 31 October 1894, p. 2, and 27 November 1894, Ely Papers.
11. Davis, *American Heroine* p. 101.
12. Addams to Ely, 31 October 1894, p. 1, Ely Papers.
13. Addams to Ely, 4 December 1894, 22 August 1895; "Settlers in the City Wilderness," *Atlantic Monthly* 77 (January 1896): 119-23. Samuel McCune Lindsay, Review, *Annals of the American Academy* 8 (September 1896):177-81. *The American Journal of Sociology* was not founded until March 1895, partially explaining a lack of review there.

14. *Twenty Years*, p. 153.
15. See the extensive and detailed maps in Sophonisba Breckinridge and Edith Abbott, *The Delinquent Child and the Home*, intro. Julia Lathrop (New York: Charities Publication Committee, 1912). They used maps throughout their extensive writings. They also used statistical tables as well as case histories in their 1912 book, again predating other Chicago sociologists who began using these techniques after them (W.I. Thomas with the life history method and W.F. Ogburn in statistics).
16. Karl Marx, *Capital*, ed. Frederick Engels, Tr. Samuel Moore and Edward Aveling (New York: Modern Library, c. 1906). (First published as *Das Kapital* in Germany in 1859.) See esp. pp. 258, 284-89, 502-14.
17. The relationship between the Chicago men and Marxism is a complex one yet to be seriously evaluated. Nonetheless, the women as a group, particularly Kelley and Addams, were markedly more radical in their study of the economy and society than the men.
18. Louis Wirth, *The Ghetto* (Chicago: University of Chicago Press, 1928), p. 200.
19. See discussion of him in ch. 2 in this volume.
20. Gerald Suttle, *The Social Order of the Slum* (Chicago: University of Chicago Press, 1968).
21. Thomas Gutterbock, *Machine Politics in Transition* (Chicago: University of Chicago Press, 1980). An earlier study in a similar tradition is that of Harold F. Gosnell, *Machine Politics*, foreword W.F. Ogburn (Chicago: University of Chicago Press, 1937).
22. Alessandro Mastro-Valerio, *HH Maps and Papers*, pp. 131-42.
23. Julia C. Lathrop, "The Cook County Charities," *HH Maps and Papers*, pp. 142-164; William I. Thomas and Dorothy Swaine Thomas, *The Child in America* (New York: Knopf, 1928).
24. See Gaye Tuchman, "Women and the Creation of Culture," in Marcia Millman and Rosabeth Moss Kanter, eds. *Another Voice* (Garden City, N.Y.: Anchor, 1976), pp. 171-202.
25. Robert E. Park and Ernest W. Burgess, *Introduction to Sociology* (Chicago: University of Chicago Press, 1921), pp. 895-924.
26. Jane Addams, "The Settlement as a Factor in the Labor Movement," *HH Maps and Papers*, pp. 183-206.
27. Jane Addams and Ellen Gates Starr, "Hull-House," *HH Maps and Papers*, pp. 207-30.
28. See "Statistical Laboratory," box 62, folder #1, Presidents' Papers, 1889-1925, UCSC.
29. "Statistics," box 9, folder 23, Mead Papers, UCSC.
30. See Mary Jo Deegan and John S. Burger, "W.I. Thomas and Social Reform," *Journal of the History of the Behavioral Sciences* 17 (January 1981):114-25.
31. Ernest W. Burgess, "The Social Survey," *American Journal of Sociology* 21 (January 1916):492-500. See p. 493.
32. Ibid.
33. Ernest W. Burgess, "Can Neighborhood Work Have a Scientific Basis in the City?" (c. 1924), in *Ernest W. Burgess on Community, Family and Delinquency*, ed. Donald Bogue (Chicago: University of Chicago Press, 1973). p. 143.
34. Ernest W. Burgess, "Research in Urban Society: A Long View," in Ernest W. Burgess and Donald J. Bogue, eds., *Contributions to Urban Sociology* (Chicago: University of Chicago Press, 1964), pp. 1-14. See p. 4.

35. Ibid.
36. Ibid., p. 5.
37. See nn. 16, 27 above.
38. Burgess, "Research in Urban Society: A Long View," p. 6.
39. Ibid., p. 7.
40. Robert E. Park, "The City as a Social Laboratory," in *Human Communities: The City and Human Ecology* (New York: Arno, 1974), pp. 73-87. See p. 75.
41. Ibid.
42. Jessie Bernard to author, interview, 21 June 1978.
43. Robert E. Park and Ernest W. Burgess, *Introduction to the Science of Sociology* (Chicago: University of Chicago Press,1921), p. 355.
44. Robert E.L. Faris, *Chicago Sociology* (Chicago: University of Chicago Press, 1967), p. 52.
45. James F. Short, Jr., ed., *The Social Fabric of the Metropolis* (Chicago: University of Chicago Press, 1971), p. xvi.
46. Ibid.

4

Jane Addams, Social Reform, and the Religious Men

Social amelioration was the central core and thrust of the early Chicago School. It was the *raison d'être* of its existence and work. This devotion to society and its liberation has been generally interpreted as an embarrassing mistake by its successors, particularly the Chicago sociologists who followed in the 1920s. The founders were fervent advocates of a sound community based on social justice and they were generally replaced by "disinterested" statisticians, bureaucrats, and people who "studied" but did not "make" policy.

Because social reform had a central role in defining the discipline, Addams' applied sociology was integral to the profession. Many of the male sociologists considered themselves "abstract," "theoretical," or "scientific" versus the complementary branch of "applied." In general, the males were associated with the first branch and the females with the second. Both sexes, however, were united in their goal of social reform, and both crossed over into theoretical and applied areas. In this and the next chapter, I examine the ideas and their application of the male Chicago sociologists concerning this topic of social reform. These provide a direct link with their relations with Addams as a friend and colleague.

In this chapter and the next, the applied sociology of the early male Chicago School is presented as the flawed and sometimes timid dream of men who cared. The products of their age and time, they wanted to heal a society fractured by rapid change, extremes of wealth and poverty, and alienated labor. For these early sociologists, including Addams,

> The social problem was uppermost in everyone's mind—at least in the minds of those who thought about man in society and wanted to do something to ease man's lot, or further his well-being. It was the problem of social reconstruction posed by the Industrial Revolution: the problem of building a society fit for man, for the optimum development of the human spirit.[1]

Die Soziale Frage plagued the lives of these sociologists who were torn from their religious moorings. The abandonment of religious answers for secular ones is a common theme in the applied sociology of the men and Addams. But the earliest men, Small, Henderson, and Zeublin, were of an earlier generation than Addams, Vincent, Thomas, Mead, Park, and Burgess. The men of the first generation were all trained in the ministry. They were more openly religious and their Christian beliefs and convictions were recurring themes in their advocacy of social change.

Although Vincent was less openly religious, he served as a transitional figure between the early religious men and their successors. During his tenure at the University of Chicago, Vincent channeled his educational energies into the Chautauqua religious system, thereby justifying his inclusion in this chapter. But he was also beginning to write in a more secular tradition than his earliest colleagues did, and after he left the University of Chicago his major work was in administration. Clearly, he did not follow the sociological paths of either the "religious" men studied here or the more secular men studied in the next chapter. He served as a connecting link between religious and secular applied sociology, especially between Small's work and that of the later men.

In the next chapter, a continuation of this one, Thomas and Mead are portrayed as close colleagues to each other and to Addams. They represent an abstract and applied peak for Addams' sociology although Addams' sociological ties with all the men, except for Park and Burgess, were notable and enduring.

Park and Burgess are a strong contrast to these men, especially to Mead and Thomas. Park and Burgess ushered in an era of sociological thought that was rhetorically opposed to applied sociology and tolled the death knell for the women sociologists' network. Hostile to the ideas of Addams, feminism, and the language of social reform, they epitomized the depth of Addams' relations to the early Chicago men. Thus, the succeeding chapter reveals the heights and depths of the relations of the Chicago men and Addams. It maps the rapid transitions of Addams' sociological career between 1894 and 1918, the years encompassing the careers of Thomas and Mead at the University of Chicago.

Before discussing the two groups, their common ties in social reform are briefly summarized. Except for Park and Burgess they were all involved in the University of Chicago Settlement. Again, except for Park and Burgess, they were all Addams' colleagues, and they frequently visited and lectured at Hull-House. The only remaining institutional and network ties not discussed elsewhere were the men's participation in the labor issues surrounding the Chicago garment industry, in the Chicago City Club, and in the Chicago School of Civics and Philanthropy. These latter reform topics are examined briefly below.

The Chicago Garment Industry, 1893-1915

In 1893, Chicago was emerging as a great industrial city with garment manufacturing as a leading industry. Sweat shops abounded, and the working conditions for the laborer were unbearable and inhumane. Crowded into small rooms without bath facilities, air ventilation in summer or heat in winter, and working long hours, the laborers were exploited and miserable. These conditions were documented by Florence Kelley in *HH Maps and Papers* and a major concern to the Hull-House women. Similarly, the workers themselves were highly agitated and fought against these conditions for years. So, too, did the Chicago men.

Beginning in 1893, Small, Vincent, Bemis, Addams, and Kelley joined other community leaders to generate legislation banning the sweat shops and, in particular, the employment of children. A series of meetings were held, petitions written, and hearings addressed. Finally in 1895 massive social legislation ameliorating these conditions was passed.[2]

This became the first victory in a long war waged by the workers and citizens against the manufacturers. Soon Chicago became a leading center for organizing the garment unions. Ultimately, the Women's Trade Union League (organized in Chicago at Hull-House), the Amalgamated Garments Workers, and the National Garment Workers Union were formed here.[3]

This social movement reached another crisis in 1910, when a massive wildcat strike was started by two young socialist women. Immediately, thousands of workers followed them to the streets and a long, bitter strike ensued. Henderson, Mead, Addams, and the whole Hull-House community became directly involved with supporting the workers who had no food, heat, or money during the long, harsh Chicago winter.[4] Defeated, most of the workers returned to the same conditions in January of 1911. A major victory was obtained, however, through the establishment of arbitration at one of the garment industry houses.

In 1915, the workers once again went on strike. This time, they were better organized, more successful in the resolution of their strike, and fewer male sociologists were involved. Only Mead stands out as a participant and even his support is muted compared to 1910.[5]

Therefore, over a period extending from 1893 to 1915, various Chicago men were active figures in the garment industry battles in Chicago while the Chicago women led by Addams remained major figures in the contests. This concerted work by Chicago sociologists has never been noted in the annals of this volatile history of labor unions and organizing but was a strong tie between the male and female sociologists and the community.

The Chicago City Club

Chicago was a hotbed of reform from 1892 until World War I. To a considerable degree this was due to the people studied here. They agitated for social legislation, collected information on social problems, had bureaucratic skills, were lecturers and orators, and combined their talents systematically through numerous organizations. Similar activities went on elsewhere at the same time, but Chicago provided much of the initiative and leadership for what historians have dubbed "urban progressivism."[6] Diner, in his outstanding analysis of these Chicago reformers, noted that of the 169 leading men, 113 were members of the City Club.[7] Founded in 1903, this male-only group discussed and debated civic issues. Through an extensive committee structure, virtually every area of urban problems was covered. It was these committees that formed the basis for concerted action on any given issue. Oriented to the collection of facts on a given problem, each committee led a municipal drive to achieve its goals. They were frequently powerful and successful advocates. Addams was often a guest lecturer,[8] but it was the men who controlled and organized the group.

G.H. Mead was a member of the City Club from its founding until the 1920s. He served on the education committee for years, developing several statistical studies that are crucial to understanding his scholarship, reform commitments, and ties to sociology. He was president of the organization from 1919 until 1920, and frequently served on the board of directors. Henderson served on the employment committee, Zeublin was on its municipal parks committee, and W.I. Thomas was a member for two years.[9]

Thus this group formed a subunit of collegial contacts, organizing the men around specific municipal interests and united in one organization for urban planning and reform. Rather than only discussing each man's participation, it is important to note that this was a group bond that united their reform interests, most strikingly forming a basis for collegial work between Henderson and Mead.

The Chicago School of Civics and Philanthropy

The female sociologists knew that their "special" interests in women, the home, the family, and housing were not well-represented in the male faculty's course offerings. Moreover, although "applied" sociology was integral to the discipline, it increasingly suffered a second-class status compared to "theoretical" sociology. This was true even for abstract discussions of social reform compared to the concrete examination of specific issues. Therefore the "practical" sociologists, dominated by females and including males later ostracized from the sociological tradition, joined in 1904 to form a separate institution: the Chicago School of Civics and Philanthropy (CSCP). Although there was a long history of different names and founders, this particular institution later merged in 1920 with other campus divisions to become the School of Social Service Administration (SSA), the professional school of social work at the University of Chicago.[10]

A detailed analysis of its history and relationship to the male Chicago School sociologists is beyond the scope of this book. Nonetheless, even a brief look at this organization reveals a consistent area of mutual influence and exchange between Addams and the men. For example, in 1904 Henderson gave six lectures in "Personal, Institutional and Public Report for Dependents", while Julia Lathrop gave an additional four. Lathrop was a resident of Hull-House at the time and a close friend of Addams.[11] In yet a second course, "Preoccupying and Preventive Policy, Agencies, and Methods," Zeublin, McDowell, and Addams each presented a lecture.[12] Mead was very active in delivering lectures at the CSCP, while later Chicago sociologists such as Park, Burgess, and Faris, also participated.[13]

Examining the years from 1907 to 1914, the only years for which complete catalogs for the CSCP are available,[14] the network of these ties is easily discerned. Table 4.1 charts the job "title" of the Chicago men and Addams, and their participation on the board. This reveals Addams' role as an instructor in the academy, her frequent interaction with CSCP and the men's work, too. Henderson and Addams even cotaught one course, showing their collegial contact and mutual influence. Addams and Vincent also attended the same board meetings and were therefore in a face-to-face relationship there.

As a group, then, Addams, Henderson, Zeublin, Mead, and a number of Hull-House residents frequently taught at CSCP, weaving their social thought and activism into a nexus of praxis. This common institutional tie can only be briefly considered here, but its overall effect was extensive.

Albion Small and Social Reform

For Small, sociology was a tool for "improving" society. Believing in the intrinsic soundness of American life, he adopted a rational model of man based on liberal assumptions and the progressive thought of his day. Because he had such extreme faith in this country and its people, he believed there was a community consensus and goodwill underlying its major institutions. Clearly dedicated, moral, kindly, and a "gentleman" by the standards of his day, he was unable to see the conflict between his views and those of dissenters. He assumed that rational people would be able to agree with one another and therefore share his vision.

TABLE 4.1
**Jane Addams and the Chicago Men at the Chicago School
of Civics and Philanthropy, 1907-1914***

Names	Lecturer	Staff of Instruction	Board Member
Jane Addams	1907-08	(course listed-1907-08)	
	1909-10	(course listed-1909-08)	
		(4 courses listed-1910)	
		winter	1910
		(1910-11)	1910-11
	1911-12	(1 course listed-1911-12)	1911-12
		(1 course listed-1912-13)	1912-13
	1913-14	(1913-14)	1913-14
C.R. Henderson	1907-08	(2 courses listed-1907-08)	
	1909-10	(3 courses listed-1909-10)	
	1911-12	(2 courses listed-1911-12)	
	1912-13	(2 courses listed)	
George E. Vincent			1910
			1910-11
			1911-12
			1912-13
			1913-14
G.H. Mead	1909-10	(1 course listed-1909-10)	
	1910-11	(1910-11)	
	1911-12		
	1912-13		
W.I. Thomas	1910-11	(1910-11)	
	1911-12		

*These are the only years that have existing catalogs.

This clear picture of the man and his vision has been misunderstood by numerous interpreters of his work. Until recently, Small has been dismissed primarily as a poor scholar. For example, Faris wrote that of all the leading sociological figures of his day, Small "was perhaps also the least important in making enduring substantive contributions to the field of sociology."[15] Similarly, Barnes evaluated Small as a good economist but a poor sociologist.[16] Radicals have viewed him as an ineffective liberal,[17] or a corporate capitalist, doing the bidding of the business interests of the community.[18]

Dibble's recent analysis of Small interprets him as a clear predecessor to contemporary sociologists, particularly the Chicago Sociologists who followed him. Dibble found that Becker's analysis of Small as a tragic figure, torn by a tension between his values and commitment to social change and his drive for an "objective" science, was unfounded. Unable to see the congruence between Small's vested interests in the middle class and "value free" sociology, Dibble found Small to be consistent, logical, and "objective."[19]

Becker's work is considered here as more accurate and sympathetic than Dibble's. Small was a victim of his assumption that his position was logical and consistent when it was not. He was an agent of the comunity's power group, but because he accepted their values he could not see his vested interests. Thus he set the early precedent of believing that "objectivity" could abide with the values of the status quo.

Small was a moral man in the sense that he believed in doing what he saw as the right thing regardless of the cost, but he paid a high price for his blindness to his own ambitions. Since he was profoundly committed to an activist role for sociology, he often took strong stands against prevailing interests. But these positions were generally compatible with the demands of the liberal community and the politically conservative academy. This paradox of high moral standards and inability to see his biases is the root of his sexism, his oppression of free speech at Chicago, and his openness to many stances considered radical in his day which were a result of considerable soul-searching and innovative ideas.

Prime among his sociological strengths was his vision of sociology as a method to help solve life's problems and help understand "the possibilities of good inherent in man."[20] Despite his failure to practice what he preached, he believed that "No sociological perspective is correct unless it turns out at least to have a place for the angle of vision which belongs to people at different posts in the social process."[21] Although he himself rarely collected the information he considered central to sociology, he considered such work of primary importance. In 1924, he noted his own role as follows:

> If I may trust my own impressions—in the absence of precise statistics—the largest number of genuine research sociologists today are at work upon problems of the *survey* type. Next in number come the *social psychologists*. Then, among the also-ran, are the few, among whom I belong, the methodologists or general sociologists.[22]

Thus Small was caught in the dilemma of all liberals (which Addams resolved by becoming a radical pacifist). This "democratic" dilemma occurs when the "group consensus" leads to doing something unjust.

Repeatedly, Small supported narrow-minded and repressive acts: the dismissal of Bemis, the termination of coeducation for the first two years of training at Chicago, and his lack of support for other *causes célèbres* within the profession.[23] Simultaneously, however, he supported the hiring of women in "special" roles within the department, treated Addams as a colleague and friend, even when others turned against her, protested Thomas' dismissal from the department, and agitated for social change in Chicago. In general, however, when the decisions became crucial to his career or that of the department's, Small made expedient decisions.

Despite his timidity in politics, he laid out many programs for study that, had they been pursued, would have made sociology a more politically challenging profession today. It is these aspects of his thought that are examined next.

Small and the Economy

According to Small the economy was the most crucial institution for understanding society. A follower of Adam Smith, he claimed that both Smith and Marx were sociologists because of their wholistic approach to society and the economy. Contrary to other interpretations of Smith, Small thought that Smith was a socialist who had important ties with Marxism.[24] Such a claim only makes sense when the community is seen as adjusting to market demands according to an idealized, participatory democracy.

After publication of his 1907 book on Adam Smith, Small continued his economic analyses with a book on the German Cameralists. He labeled this group "pioneers in social policy" because they initiated state planning, albeit for an aristocracy rather than a democratic community. Although Small always advocated democratic principles, he believed that the German social policy of government intervention in the management of business and daily life was a good step.[25]

In his third volume on economics, Small unsuccessfully wrote a book that he thought would appeal to the "common" person and not just the scholar. Trying to capture the voices of various interests, the author let all sides speak for themselves in the form of idealized stereotypes. Education of the general community was a major goal in Small's vision of sociology,[26] but he lacked the brilliance, literary skill, and clarity that Addams used in such endeavors.

Small's final economic treatise was *The Origins of Sociology*. Again striking the theme that the economy was central to the study of society and, ergo, sociology, he based his thought on Germanic policy adapted to a democratic and American context.[27]

Barnes appraised these texts as major contributions to institutionl economics.[28] They were an important, substantive exposition of the relation of the economy to society and the government's responsiveness to the community. Nonetheless, the study of the economy by American sociologists has been a marginal field when compared to studies of organizations, bureaucracies, business, or liberal politics. Socialism and Marxism have rarely been given significant attention by American sociologists, while the institutions supporting capitalism have been examined repeatedly in isolated, specialized areas of study. Park and Burgess, moreover, greatly aided in this transition from a holistic approach to the study of the economy to one fractured in its analysis by their emphasis on competition and piecemeal change. Competition is more like a game to them than a war between the classes. Small's continual emphasis on a holistic science of society, one that understood the central roles and relations between the state and the economy based on an educated and free-speaking democratic public, was a vision of sociology that was lost by Park and Burgess. Although Small was not as critical a thinker as Addams, he had many ideas and assumptions that were compatible with hers, particularly during the early years of his work at Chicago. After World War I, however, he became increasingly withdrawn, frightened, and aloof. His vision of sociology was dying before his eyes. In 1924, two years before his retirement, he addressed the sociology students as follows:

> I confess that for several years past I have had my seasons of depression over the prospect that your generation will not go my way, but will go its own way. I have felt keen sorrow over indications that your generation will not build directly upon the work of my generation, any more than my generation built directly upon the work of Lester F. Ward. . . . In the long economy of the ages, it turns out that, on the whole, each generation knows its own business better than any previous generation could have defined it.[29]

Perhaps Small's cycle of esteem is returning and his optimism justified. Whatever the evaluation of his work, his continual withdrawal to more conservative positions is noteworthy. As a younger man, he was more optimistic about reform and progress than in his later years.

Small and Reform Activities

Small is repeatedly mentioned in biographies of Addams as a frequent visitor to Hull-House.[30] Nonetheless, there are few occasions where Small's name appears in the paper as a supporter of a particular *cause célèbre*, while those of Henderson, Zeublin, Mead, and Thomas were frequently at the forefront of politics.

The only reform group that Small openly supported was the Civic Federation of Chicago. A visible and active member during the 1890s, in the first volume of *AJS* he wrote an article on it. Formed by a prominent group of Chicago men, it was particularly active from 1893 to 1900. Small felt that their success was based on the use of experts: "The work of the Federation was conducted as a business man would manage his commercial enterprises, vis, by securing specialists for special work, and by depending upon them to know their business."[31] Thus Small emphasized the masculine role of reformers like himself, modeled after the business world and its ethic. It is also important to note that when Small was active in the Civic Federation, President Harper headed the educational committee which led in social agitations for reform of public schools, teacher training, and increasing the university's control over education in the city.[32]

A 1915 *Chicago Tribune* article about Small's ideas concerning the Germans and war in Europe embroiled him in a brief local controversy. This was at least part of the reason why he developed such an extreme desire to be out of the limelight and away from public censure.[33] Clearly, Small was an active social reformer who was relatively obscure and unflamboyant.

Albion W. Small and Jane Addams

Small was deeply dedicated to Addams and her work. More than any other Chicago sociologist, he believed in the "ideal woman" that she symbolized. As early as 1893 Addams was referred to as "Saint Jane," an appellation adequately summarizing the veneration she aroused in many people.[34] "She was the epitome of the nineteenth-century heroine who had 'never a selfish thought,' who was 'wonderfully gentle' and sexually pure and innocent, and thus in a sense superior to men."[35] Although this public image did not reveal the intellectual, administrative, and radical views of Addams, it was useful for her public role as spokesperson for the immigrant poor in her neighborhood. This image was also one that Small believed appropriate for women (see chapter 8). For Small, Addams was the role model for women sociologists. Throughout his active career, especially prior to World War I, Small firmly supported Addams in a number of ways.

References to their joint interest and activities have appeared in several places and are worth recalling here. Addams and Small worked together to combat child labor and poor working conditions in the garment industry, and Small used *HH Maps and Papers* in his teaching and urged its publication. He actively fought for the incorporation of Hull-House within the University of Chicago. When this failed, he worked with her to help establish the University of Chicago Settlement. This nexus of events and specific interests are augmented even further, however, when his relationship to Addams as a sociologist and to Hull-House as a significant sociological institution are examined. Moreover, in 1907, he strongly advocated her being awarded an honorary doctorate from the University of Chicago, which was denied at that time.

This collegial relationship was also apparent when he eagerly sought her writings for publication in *AJS*, including an article by her in the first volume.[36] Writing in 1899, Small urged Addams to submit a paper she had just presented:

> Let me repeat what I tried to say as we were leaving the train, that if there is any portion of the results which you would be willing to publish in advance of its use in book form, we should be glad to use it in the AJS . . . but I need not say that whatever you write has an importance to our constituency whether it would be in demand by a larger audience or not.[37]

In addition to this article, Addams published another four plus a comment in *AJS* prior to World War I.[38] Although she spoke at the American Sociological Society (ASS) in 1919, this article was not published in the *Journal*, as was customary, but in the *Survey* instead.[39] Thus, Addams participated frequently in the *AJS* and was the most frequent woman speaker at the ASS.[40] Although only partial documentation is available, it is probable that Small actively solicited each article. For example, in 1904, Small wrote Addams asking that her paper presented at the annual ASS meetings be reprinted in *AJS* since the Congress was "trying to publish all of the Sociological papers. Those of Henderson and Müensterberg will appear in the November number, and I wish that yours and Dr. Shaws' together with those of Ross and Thomas, could appear in the January number."[41] This request resulted in her publication of "Problems of Municipal Administration" in *AJS* in January 1905.

The most dramatic evidence of Small's belief in the outstanding sociology of Addams was his offer to hire her for a half-time position in the Department of Sociology. This was in 1913 when the department was well established; the offer for only a half-time position was due to Addams' limited time. This request is worthy of citation:

> I am writing entirely on my own responsibility, and without assurances that any specific recommendation which I might make would be adopted by our Trustees. I am wondering however whether you could consider a professorship which would call for one half the work at the University which a professor would ordinarily give, i.e., four class room hours per week for seven months in the year (October-June).
>
> This work would be with graduate students limited to classes of thirty (30). It would mean not merely lecturing, but training, and supervision of the individual work to the extent of keeping tab whether real work was being done by each individual. A graduate student—(Fellow)—could probably be assigned as your assistant in reading papers.
>
> Of course this would be more tiring work than mere lecturing, but it would be incomparably more valuable in the end than admitting a miscellaneous company of students merely to hear lectures.[42]

Since Addams lectured frequently around the city and country, as well as at the University of Chicago Extension and the Chicago School of Civics and Philanthropy,[43] Small was probably alluding to these lectures which were not systematically limited to only sociology graduate students. His recommendation and Henderson's, he said, would be forwarded to the trustees if Addams would consider the position. Although her precise answer to Small is unknown, she did not teach in the graduate Department of Sociology in any recognized status. Moreover, a faculty position in the department had little to commend itself to Addams, who worked independently and primarily with women through her established contacts at Hull-House and the University of Chicago.

Small and Addams were in agreement on a variety of reform issues, but their joint activities are largely undocumented at this time. However, one issue they both supported was an event occurring in March of 1908. This was probably the reform outcry against "the Averbuch affair." This incident had involved the unprovoked killing of a young Russian immigrant, Averbuch, by the Chicago Chief of Police. The city at the time was in a state of considerable agitation over Russian anarchists, which precipitated the Chief of Police's brutal act. Averbuch, a delivery messenger, was standing silently in the hallway of the Chief's home, delivering a package. The Chief of Police saw Averbuch, suspected him of being a Russian anarchist with a bomb, panicked, and shot him.[44]

Small wrote Addams at this time that he had written a letter to the *Chicago Tribune*. Although his position was against the stance of the paper and the general public, he optimistically wrote: "I don't believe the sober second thought of Chicago will permanently endorse the preposterous attitude of confounding things."[45]

Small is mentioned as participating at Hull-House activities on a frequent basis, but usually as a "known" fact. One of the few remaining indicators of this tie is Small's lectures at Hull-House. On 20 November 1892, only a few weeks after Small's arrival in Chicago, he spoke at the settlement on "The Social Philosophy of Jesus." In January of the following year he repeated this lecture.[46] The selection of his topic reveals his association of social settlements with religious issues. Whether he continued to offer this lecture for an extended period of time is unknown.

Small and Addams also worked together in the Civic Federation of Chicago. This was in response to the problems initiated by the economic "panic" of 1893 when Addams was appointed secretary of the Civic Federation Committee on Industrial Arbitration.[47]

Information about their relationship after 1915 is sorely lacking. It is clear, however, that Small increasingly restricted his political activities through time. In a pathetic and revealing passage on the limits of academic freedom of speech, he told his student Barnhardt that he felt he had to protect himself, even in his classroom, from political attacks. Teaching from a boring, lengthy, prepared syllabus, Small read every word directly from the text. When asked why he did this, Small replied:

> To protect myself, to prove what I said in class, I have prepared this material and I stick with it and read it and this is the proof of what I am telling my classes. The only thing I have to be real careful of is when you ask me questions and I have to answer there and then. What do I actually say in the answer? I can't take care of that problem.[48]

This attitude affected his relationship with Addams, but to what degree is unknown. By the 1920s, Small was physically ailing and aging, leaving the leadership of the department to younger men. Clearly, however, he sought out Addams throughout his active career at Chicago. He recognized her leadership as a sociologist and activist, urging greater contacts with the department, discipline, and university whenever feasible. Theirs was a strong and active tie, although never reaching the status of citing her work frequently in his own or changing his ideas about women to include an understanding of total equality.

Charles R. Henderson and Social Reform

Henderson embodied the spirit of the men of the early Chicago School. Bright, dedicated, religious, and socially active, Henderson became one of the most influential political and social leaders in the department. Nonetheless, almost all his contributions are dismissed by contemporary sociologists.

Although the historian Diner also discounts many of Henderson's ideas, he does credit him with being a central figure in the development of the discipline. Acknowledging that Henderson was not the first to support first-hand observation and intimate experience with the lives of a people to be studied, Diner concluded that the institutional support at the University of Chicago did put Henderson at the forefront of legitimating and expanding a new profession.[49]

Here, Henderson is interpreted as an important sociological figure because of this crucial institutional access and his role as an applied sociologist. Thus, his research, teaching, and public leadership were all factors in making him a significant founder of sociology.

His Writings

Role of the Scholar. The sociologist's duty, according to Henderson, was vastly different from that proposed by his Chicago successors, especially Park. Henderson captured the earliest Chicago ideals when he wrote: "The scholar's duty is to aid in forming a judicial public opinion, as distinguished from the public opinion of a class and its special pleaders."[50]"Social technology" would develop information on issues and interests affecting everyday life. He described it as follows:

> Social technology can render its best service by dealing with a body of knowledge and a system of principles. The statement, location, and analysis of a situation are made comprehensive, and the facts which are essential for a judgment are arrayed in an intelligible form for the use of administrators, voters, and reformers.[51]

Thus, like Addams, Henderson thought information should be systematically collected and then dispersed throughout the community to be used to obtain the groups' goals.

His method of analysis was consistent and straightforward (it was also adopted by G.H. Mead in his statistical work). He examined a problem of social policy by looking at its causes and treatment in other parts of the United States, past and present. From all these data, he extrapolated commonsense guidelines for present policy.[52]

Henderson was motivated by and committed to Christianity, and this underlying theme was increasingly derogated by his students.[53] His major areas of scholarship are examined below, revealing his strong interest in social problems and their resolution.[54]

Social Settlements. In a small book published in 1898, Henderson set down his basic pragmatic program combined with its implementation in social settlements. Like Zeublin and Addams, he stressed the role of the British university and settlement in helping shape the American system.[55]

Addams is the most frequently cited authority in the book. Her ideas on settlements as part of the community, the labor movement, and an expression of democracy are all noted by Henderson and are elements in her critical pragmatism. Hull-House is the most central American institution mentioned. Chicago Commons, in which Henderson was active, was only mentioned twice. Comparing the two institutions, Henderson noted that they sometimes held conferences together and were very similar except "the Commons adds the word 'religious'" to its purposes.[56]

Henderson revealed a clear understanding of the conflicts between the academic sociologist and the settlement workers when he noted:

> Workers very naturally resent the notion that a Settlement is a "laboratory" where inquisitive investigators may pursue methods of vivisection and torture, in order to illustrate or test sociological theories. They cry out against the outrage of cold analysis and theory in the presence of hunger, pain and

sensitiveness. The protest is just. And yet science is merciful. Exact, comprehensive and digested knowledge is a boon to the race.

The Hull House Papers and Maps [sic] are very striking illustrations of the kind of social investigation which may be carried on in connection with the most gentle, sympathetic and devoted labor on behalf of the population studied. Indeed, only he who loves can see. Sympathy opens not only heart, but intellect.[57]

Henderson operated on a social science model akin to that of Addams. His different vision of sociological practice is now neglected and forgotten. Nonetheless, despite sentimental overtones and religious exhortations, he reveals a depth of understanding often lacking in his successors.

Democracy and Labor. Again, like Addams, Henderson was concerned with not only political democracy, but economic democracy as well. This theme and linkage of ideas consistently appeared in all his major books, especially *The Social Spirit in America* (1907), *Industrial Insurance in the United States* (1909), and *Citizens in Industry* (1915).[58]

In *The Social Spirit in America* Henderson started from a belief in the "giveness" of Christianity and social progress. Although these are seen now as questionable assumptions, Henderson elaborated his ideas about American life from a much more flexible perspective than such a beginning would suggest.

Criticizing an overemphasis on "self-interest" as an explanatory variable, Henderson stressed the self as "a social product, and our interests are in our children, our friends, our neighborhood, our country, our church. It is just as well to call these larger and more generous impulses by higher titles."[59]

Asserting that "'competition' expresses a very real and terrible fact," Henderson combined this later Chicago School concept of Park and Burgess with other influences. As Henderson noted: "Competition itself is softened and sweetened by the sympathies which began in the family, extended to the family stock, and finally expanded into the feeling of humanity, universal philanthropy."[60]

Supporting voluntary associations as community extensions of the "social spirit," Henderson revealed a knowledge of many groups associated with Addams and Hull-House, such as the Jane Club and the National Consumers League.[61] Although supportive of labor unions and organizations to advance the goals and rights of minorities, Henderson firmly believed that all Americans shared a "spirit of cooperation." Naively affirming the openness and generosity of Americans, Henderson's critiques revealed a harmony in American life that needed to be discovered and uncovered. In this way, he was less critical than Addams in his thought.

Crime and Delinquency. Henderson's early work with deviance led to the subsequent characterization of sociology as work with the "three Ds": drunks, delinquents, and deviants. Mired in Christian philosophy and ethics, his work was often imbued with a moral tone and judgment. Simultaneously, he spoke out against parochial restrictions and inequities. This latter component of his thought, however, has been consistently overlooked, and the former stressed.

His prison reform work was international in scope and influence. His documentation of inadequate facilities, the systematic patterns of this neglect, and the lack of rehabilitation in prisons were all accurate. Often his writings appeared to be split. The statistical data were dry while his interpretations of them were impassioned. The combination appealed to the people of his era, speaking to their vision of science and progress as well as their ethical understanding of good behavior and justice.

Henderson and Social Reform Activities

Leadership in Reform Organizations. Henderson's list of leadership positions in reform organizations is impressive. He was president of the Chicago Society for Social Hygiene, a sociological forerunner of psychiatric social work. He, along with Thomas, was a member of the 1911 Chicago Vice Commission. He was a member of the board of Chicago's United Charities and president of the American Association of Prison Reform and of the International Prison Reform Association, both in 1910. Immediately prior to his death, he was on the Mayor's Commission on Unemployment. He was also active in the University of Chicago Settlement from 1894 until 1915, a member of the Chicago Civic Federation, president of the National Conference of Charities and Correction, (a forerunner to the National Association of Social Workers), and in 1911 president of the National Child Welfare Association. He was secretary of the Illinois State Commission on Occupational Diseases, along with Alice Hamilton, in 1911.[62]

Like Addams and Zeublin his reform efforts were similar to the Fabians'. His articles on social insurance and workmen's compensation paralleled many of the English programs, as well as some German ones.

The Use of Statistics. During the 1920s, the Chicago School had a reputation for being "antistatistical."[63] Thus the important work of the female Chicago sociologists, as well as that of Zeublin and Henderson, were "forgotten." One evidence of Henderson's commitment to this methodological technique was his attempt to establish a "statistical laboratory" at the University of Chicago. This venture reveals the department's interest in the subject and its response to women.

On 29 November 1908, Henderson contacted John Koren at the Department of Commerce and Labor in the Bureau of the Census. With the support of Small and Vincent, Henderson wrote that they wanted to study the multitude of problems affecting people throughout the state in reference to social reform. A statistical laboratory would be established and funded by the Russell Sage Foundation. Interestingly enough it was Koren who wrote: "I have not the pleasure of a personal acquaintance with Miss Abbott. Judging from my correspondence with her, I should think her quite capable of filling the position you mention."[64]

President Judson replied that although they could only offer $500.00 instead of the $3,000.00 requested by Koren, they were offering him the title of "Professorial Lecturer on Statistics."[65] The work would cover only part of the year and a series of lectures. Not surprisingly, Koren did not accept the position, but Abbott did. However, she was made the associate director of the Department of Social Investigation and not "officially" recognized as part of the Sociology Department. In 1914 she was finally recognized as a "Lecturer in Methods of Social Investigation" in the Sociology Department, providing the sociological training there in statistics.[66]

Thus, Henderson and the male sociology faculty wanted a "statistical laboratory," but they did not want one headed by a woman. Koren acknowledged his limited academic training while Abbott had obtained her doctorate from the University of Chicago. She worked closely with Henderson, but not as an equal.

Social Settlements. Henderson also worked closely with Mary McDowell, a former Hull-House resident, through the University of Chicago Settlement. On the board of trustees from its founding in 1894 until his death in 1915, Henderson was a strong advocate for freedom of speech and scientific observations at the settlement. His death led to a decline in the strength of the ties between sociology and the settlement, for no one else was as strong an advocate of this bond as he. His efforts at promoting his ideas and those of his women colleagues were more successful at CSCP than at the University of Chicago Settlement.[67] As a cofounder of the former institution, Henderson worked closely with Edith Abbott and Sophonisba Breckinridge along with Graham Taylor, Jane Addams, and Julia Lathrop.[68]

Worker Compensation. Henderson strongly supported worker compensation and government programs for their health services. A frequent visitor to Germany and advocate of their insurance system, Henderson struggled to have a similar program adopted in Illinois. As Dr. Alice Hamilton recalled his efforts:

> The first step . . . [was] an inquiry into the extent of our industrial sickness, and he determined to have such an inquiry made in Illinois. Governor Deeneed was then in office and Henderson persuaded him to appoint an Occupational Disease Commission, the first time a state had ever undertaken such a survey. Dr. Henderson had some influence in selecting the members and, as

he knew of my great interest in the subject, he included me in the group of five physicians who, together with himself, an employer, and two members of the State Labor Department, made up the commission. We had one year only for our work, the year 1910.[69]

The pioneering discovery of lead poisoning from paint resulted from this work.[70] Hamilton was able to document that the men breathed lead fumes into their lungs and were not responsible for their illnesses, as their American employers charged. Henderson also aided Hamilton in her travels to England and the continent, where she observed their methods of industrial protection and insurance.[71] Thus Henderson was directly instrumental in Hamilton's career in occupational diseases and, in particular, the discovery and documentation of lead poisoning among the working class.

Charles R. Henderson and Jane Addams

Like Small, Addams and Henderson had a long and close association that can be documented only in fragments. To briefly summarize their previously discussed interests, they both worked for changes in the garment industry, the establishment and continuance of the University of Chicago Settlement, and the Chicago School of Civics and Philanthropy (they even cotaught a course in the latter institution).

Both Addams and Henderson probably shared the platform on numerous occasions. Only one such instance was found, however. This occurred on 4 May 1897 at the University of Chicago when they spoke at a Conference on Day Nurseries. Addams chaired the session and Henderson presented the paper "The Social Function of the Day Nursery."[72] Similarly, Henderson probably spoke frequently at Hull-House, but only two lectures have been documented. In 1893 he spoke before the Working People's Social Science Club and in the fall of 1894 he addressed the same group on the topic of Sir Thomas More.[73]

Henderson and Addams also shared an interest in the social settlement affiliated with the Chicago Theological Seminary. This social settlement, the Chicago Commons, cosponsored an Economic Conference with Hull-House in 1896 and 1897. In 1896, Henderson addressed the group on "Society as an Evolution and Growth," and it can be safely inferred that Addams was involved in developing and planning these conferences. Not only was she the Head of Hull-House; she was also on the board of trustees of Chicago Commons.[74]

In 1896 Henderson sent her a detailed letter concerning travel in Germany. He included names of people and institutions she should visit during her European trip. Clearly, Addams sought his professional advice and entrée to his collegial network and he responded to this request in depth.[75]

He considered Hull-House and Addams' writings major resources for the study of social problems and reform. In 1912 he wrote Addams and thanked her for his autographed copy of *A New Conscience and an Ancient Evil*. He addressed her as "an honored friend" and judged the book courageous and rational. He added that he had read each chapter as they appeared in separate articles, indicating that he followed her work closely.[76]

The clearest information on their relationship can be found in Addams' funeral eulogy for Henderson. At that time she recalled that she had heard Henderson speak for the first time in 1884 at the National Conference of Charities and Churches. Addams noted the close and immediate ties between their work:

> When he came to the University of Chicago in 1892, he came to call at Hull-House rather early, I think, after his arrival in Chicago, and again I had the impression of a man who was anxious to know the poor people at first hand. He was not willing to take his sociology from the various pieces of paper which his students had brought him after they had gone through a street with a paper in one hand and a pencil in the other, but he wished to understand the social factors lying at the bottom of his subject from firsthand informations.[77]

Addams then recalled a conversation when she "met him down town one day and we stopped to comfort each other for a moment in the midst of this universal storm of disapproval."[78] Both had signed a public petition against capital punishment which had elicited an outraged response from the community. Thus it appears that Henderson and Addams were more controversial and withstood the pressure of public disapproval more tolerably than Small.[79]

Henderson's work in applied sociology overlapped considerably with Addams'. He studied the juvenile courts, social settlements, children's welfare, and workers' insurance—all topics of major concern to Addams.[80] Both were major figures in the National Conference of Charities and Corrections and served as presidents of the organization.

His work, however, was consistently more moralistic and statistical than hers. Addams was specifically concerned with the failure of traditional religion to address the needs of the disenfranchised and thus her approach was more secular than his. Similarly, she worked with a cadre of statisticians, especially Edith Abbott and Sophonisba Breckinridge, but Addams herself rarely incorporated data in the body of her writing. Despite these differences Henderson and Addams shared a series of common concerns and a thrust for reform that united their interests and sociological work.

Charles Zeublin and Social Reform

Charles Zeublin's career was similarly centered around applied sociology. Trained first as a minister, he combined sociological insight with

Christianity. Like Henderson, he thought that sociology was a medium for practicing the social gospel.

Supportive of Fabian socialism, he worked primarily out of the British tradition of sociology, despite his advanced training in Leipzig. An early resident of Hull-House, he worked closely with Addams and other Hull-House women in the cause of social settlements. He also specialized in the study of municipal playgrounds, becoming a national figure in the recreation movement. Furthermore, he was called a "municipal sociologist" because of his work in the city. It is vital to note that he, like Henderson, Bemis, Addams, McDowell, and other Chicago women sociologists, has been largely omitted from the sociological literature and neglected as an early founder of the Chicago School.

His Writings on Social Reform

Unlike many of the Chicago women, especially Addams, Zeublin was not an intellectual. Even sympathetic portraits of him stress his remarkable speaking abilities, and not his intellectual abilities.[81] For example, Taylor wrote:

> In the years succeeding [1892] in a hundred towns and cities of the Great Lakes region, Professor Zeublin's lectures were a leaven the value of which could scarcely be over-estimated. He made his audiences see social institutions, their communities, their economic life with fresh eyes. He combined a searching courage with an appreciation of the spiritual values of life and art and a robust faith in the processes of democracy.[82]

Similarly, Beatrice Webb succinctly summarized his strengths and weaknesses in the following passage from her diary:

> Professor Charles Zeublin is a Fabian who has been much in England: a sympathetic, pleasant person, well favored in body and mind, and with eclectic information of political questions. He is of the type of University Extension lecturer—neither a literateur nor a scientific man; just a cultivated right-minded individual who has a facile tongue and agreeable manner.[83]

Zeublin appears to have been more like McDowell, the Head of the University of Chicago Social Settlements, than Addams, Breckinridge, or Abbott. Nonetheless, he made some significant contributions to Chicago Sociology that have been largely unrecognized.

His courses at the University of Chicago "ranged over a wide area, including 'English Fiction and Social Reform,' 'The Industrial Revolution,' 'The Structure of Society,' 'British Municipal Reform,' 'Prophets of Social Morality,' 'Art and Life,' 'The Unity of Faith,' 'The Common Life,' and

'The Twentieth Century City.'"[84] Clearly this list of courses reflected an interest in the sociology of art and literature, a field largely neglected by contemporary sociologists.[85] His British, Christian, and urban concerns also loom large, but it was only his emphasis on the city that was continued in the work of later male Chicago Sociologists. For example, his course on "Municipal Sociology" focused on population movements and ecological studies. Students in this class prepared statistical and map materials about the city and some of this work was later adopted by Burgess.[86]

As noted in chapter 3, Zeublin contributed to the ground-breaking study, *HH Maps and Papers*. This early interest in regions of the city and the mapping technique was again used by Zeublin in 1899 with his analysis of municipal playgrounds and social class. Here Zeublin used a map to show the graphic relationship between poverty and the aesthetics of the urban environment.[87] Although he owed a considerable debt to Addams and other Hull-House women, his interests and ideas on urban environment were part of a large mosaic leading to the urban ecology school at Chicago that emerged in the 1920s.

In one of his few scholarly articles, Zeublin revealed the intellectual capacity he had but rarely displayed. In a concise article he traced the major figures in British sociology during the nineteenth century and their influence on socialist thought. Rejecting Marxism as dated and too deterministic, Zeublin believed that social reform was a variant of collective action embodied in the notion of socialism.[88]

Thus Zeublin believed that democratic cities would be governed by the people. As a group, they would act on their best interests through reforms in the economy, politics, and culture. His four books elaborated on these themes. The city, democracy, and the social gospel were all means for the working class to control its everyday life.[89]

Clearly adopting many of Addams' assumptions about society albeit with more religious and literary overtones, Zeublin became an expendable Chicago sociologist. Forced out of the academy in 1908 (see chapter 7), his "resignation" was an indictment not only of his worth to sociology, but also his practice of it. Nonetheless, his concern with urban problems and ecology were themes continued by Chicago sociologists who emphasized mapping, urban ecology, and social policy studies.

Zeublin's Social Reform Activities

An early resident of Hull-House, Zeublin later traveled to Toynbee Hall himself and subsequently founded the Northwestern University Settlement in 1893. No major work analyzing this institution has ever been completed and only a small file of clippings announcing the opening and ceremonial occasions in the settlement now exists.[90]

Active in the Chicago City Club, the Municipal Museum of Chicago, and the Pullman Strike, his social reform career, like his scholarly life, remains obscure. The scanty information available is linked directly to Addams.

Charles Zeublin and Jane Addams

There are several direct influences of Addams on Zeublin during the formative stages of the latter's career. As an early resident at Hull-House[91] he gave a number of lectures there, offered at least one course, and instigated the link between the social settlement and the University of Chicago Extension Division.[92] Clearly taking inspiration from Addams, he traveled to London and studied Toynbee Hall. Upon his return to Chicago, he appealed to Northwestern University for the establishment of its own social settlement. In 1892 this was completed.[93]

Zeublin and Addams kept in contact after his forced resignation from the University of Chicago in 1908. For example, in 1911 he wrote Addams that he did not need the complimentary copy of *Twenty Years* that she had intended to give him, because he already owned one.[94] Later that year, he wrote her that he was accepting the editorship of *Twentieth Century Magazine.* He asked if she had "anything in the barrel which is too 'strong' for the conventional magazines."[95] Again, their similar interests and "politics" were apparent. In 1913, they shared an active interest and leadership in the Progressive Party.[96]

Again, a pattern emerges based on common interests in writing and practice, but with a greater emphasis on the social gospel by the male. Zeublin, however, was more politically active and vocal than Small or Henderson. In this respect, Zeublin was closer to Addams. Predictably, this made him more problematic to the academy.

George Vincent and Social Reform

Little is known about Vincent: his social thought, biography, or reform ideas. Part of this lack of information can be traced to his extreme modesty. Moreover, like many of the other Chicago men who have been forgotten or neglected in sociological accounts, Vincent was a better orator than writer. One of his students, L.L. Bernard, recalled that "Vincent was a brilliant lecturer, perhaps somewhat less fundamental in his ideas than the other men in the department at Chicago, and altogether a bit of a heretic."[97]

Vincent's entire commitment to sociology and social reform revolved around education: first in the Chatauqua system, and later as an administrator in a series of institutions.

His Writings on Education

As the son of the founder of Chautauqua, Vincent spent his entire youth and most of his adult life in this setting. Throughout his years at the University of Chicago, a considerable amount of his time and energy was expended in this area. Bernard noted that "Almost invariably he left the University Friday afternoon or night and returned to it Monday night or Tuesday morning. He was said to be one of the most popular lecturers in America and to command top prices for his oratorical and educational performances in this connection."[98]

In 1896 his dissertation was completed and a year later it was published as *The Social Mind and Education*. Here "He interpreted education as the transmission to the child of the accumulated tradition formed from experience and reflection on the past."[99]

In many ways, this seminal book was compatible with the ideas of Mead and Addams on education. It is an early pragmatic account of the need for breadth and scholarship in a liberal education to help individuals reach a peak of human understanding and growth. Symbolic interactionism in its rudimentary form is an underlying theoretical approach in the text. Although Vincent has never been considered part of this school of thought, such an inclusion is warranted. Combining his Chautauqua background with his Chicago training (perhaps with John Dewey), Vincent's book is a significant statement on the development of the student through a generalized knowledge of the community and its symbolic meanings.[100]

Vincent's coauthorship with Small of *An Introduction to the Study of Sociology* created a landmark text in sociology, both pedagogically and professionally. The book preceded by a quarter of a century the now more famous introductory text of Park and Burgess. For these twenty-five years, however, the Small and Vincent text played a formative role in defining the profession.[101]

As a graduate student, Vincent was approached by Small to coauthor the book. According to Bernard, "Small wrote Part I, on the history of sociology, . . . Vincent contributed Part II, on an ecological analysis of the growth of a frontier community [Topeka, Kansas]. The other three parts were simply Vincent's rewriting of Small's abstract of Schaeffle's organismic theory of society."[102] Thus in this text, the authors were developing an ecological approach to studying society, combining it with ethical concerns about the process and direction of community development. Vincent's work in *The Social Mind and Education* was a more sophisticated analysis of the development of the person as a function of interaction than this introductory text. Together, the two books generated a basis for the subsequent work of Park and Burgess that has been largely unacknowledged.

In general, however, Vincent's strength was not in his publications, but in his administrative work for education. He was a major figure in the development of Chautauqua, the University of Minnesota, and the Rockefeller Foundation. It is his influence on American education that concerns us below.

Vincent and Reform Work in Education

Vincent was marginally active in local reform issues. He and Small were both members of the Chicago Civic Federation. He also worked with Mead to establish a committee to increase the efficiency and professionalism of the Chicago Public Library. Finally, he and Zeublin were members of the board of the Chicago Municipal Museum. Linkages between Vincent and the reform work of others in the department are, nonetheless, scant.[103]

Vincent choose, instead, to channel most of his time and energy into the educational process. Since this was a major issue for Mead and Addams, some overlap in their interests is apparent, although Vincent's work in education preceded and succeeded his work in Chicago. It was the underlying concern of his whole career while other reform issues and even being a sociologist were peripheral to his pragmatic development of American education.

This focus on education permeated his childhood which revolved around the Chautauqua movement. As an adult, Vincent moved up the ranks of this organization until he became its president.[104] From the late 1890s until 1915, he guided its programs. During his period of ascendancy Jane Addams, as well as many other sociologists, lectured there.

The Chautauqua movement ultimately became popularized and somewhat analogous to intellectual revival meetings. Originally, however, the ideal was less flamboyant and more challenging to the mind than the emotions.[105] These Chautauqua ideals advocated life-long education, correspondence courses (called "home study"), and oratory skills. In a similar vein, George Vincent emphasized adult education and public speaking. Bernard noted that by 1907 "Vincent's renown as a popular lecturer probably detracted somewhat from his standing as an educator on the campus."[106] This insight by Bernard points to the conflict between the "oratorical" versus written scholar that emerged even at that early stage at Chicago. It was to be written and not oral work that would distinguish "good academics." Moreover, the development of popular speaking, adult education, and administrative skills were seen as less important to an "abstract" versus "applied" discipline.

While working in the Chautauqua program, Vincent was also dean of the junior colleges and later the dean of the faculties at the University of

Chicago, working under Small. Clearly he helped shape the university there, but in a marginal role. It is not surprising, therefore, that he left the University of Chicago to become president of the University of Minnesota in 1911.

Stifled at the University of Chicago,[107] Vincent intended to take charge of the University of Minnesota. He wanted to make it an intellectual center that also reached out to the community. He succeeded a president who had managed a more traditional land grant institution, causing little sensation in or impact on the state. Vincent changed that and created both significant alterations in the nature of the university and a controversial administration. One of his major accomplishments there was the affiliation of the Mayo Clinic and Foundation with the university. This liaison, now recognized as an outstanding one, was soundly rejected at first by many members of the community. Vincent also tried to appoint young scholars and national leaders, trodding on the toes of local men and vested interests. This leadership was central in making the University of Minnesota a nationally recognized institution. This achievement, however, was bought at a high price and it was with relief that he left this post to become president of the Rockefeller Foundation in 1917.[108]

It is clear that in this latter position he achieved his peak of influence. An administrator with power and resources, Vincent wielded them successfully. He helped establish the programs and careers of a number of institutions and scholars although information on his specific contributions is scarce. Under his guidance the Rockefeller Foundation became one of the most significant private funding programs for scholarly research in the world.[109] Glowing eulogies and memorials to his leadership can be found, but little specific information and analysis.[110]

Vincent's achievements at the Rockefeller Foundation were a product of his painful experience at the University of Minnesota where he actively led reforms in education. For the first time, his commitment to liberal education based on high standards of scholarship and intimate ties with practical application of knowledge were institutionalized by him. No longer the son of a powerful leader or the assistant of still another strong administrator, Vincent had his first opportunity to shape a major institution. The result was in many ways analogous to the political repression experienced by his fellow sociologists at Chicago. Although he was not fired from the University of Minnesota, he left amid a storm of bitterness and hostility. He responded by becoming apolitical.

In 1924, Vincent along with three other Rockefeller board leaders prepared a memorandum to

> keep the Memorial safely away from any investigations that might cause trouble. Among the guidelines set forth were admonitions not to contribute

to organizations primarily seeking the passage of legislation or to involve the Memorial in any direct efforts toward securing social, economic, or political reform; to be careful about contributing to the current expenses of organizations engaged in direct activity for social welfare; and in all respects to confine the Memorial to assisting "responsible" groups and agencies.[111]

Although this policy was basically dropped in 1928, the year before Vincent resigned, it indicated a stance opposed to social welfare and reform that was radically different from Vincent's original work and roots. He had a major impact on a series of educational programs: Chautauqua, the universities of Chicago and Minnesota, and the Rockefeller Memorial Fund. His philosophy of education and sociology were originally based on the growth of the community and democratic education and finally resulted in increasing elitism, power concentration, and certification. Thus his early period of work was highly compatible with Addams while his later years were the epitome of an opposite approach.

George E. Vincent and Jane Addams

Vincent appears to have been a frequent visitor to Hull- House, a colleague of Addams, and interested in social reform issues related to both. Documentation of this tie, nonetheless, remains scanty. For example, Linn noted that both Small and Vincent firmly supported the work of the settlement.[112] Vincent is cited by Linn as writing of "her tolerant and even defensive attitude in behalf of people who opposed her."[113] As mentioned earlier, Vincent was involved in the Child Labor Campaign from 1894 to 1897, was a trustee at CSCP, and worked with the Municipal Museum. Nonetheless, extensive documentation of his social reform interest is otherwise lacking. His dedication to Chautauqua is slightly more established, and it is here that his relationship to Addams is clearer.

Addams, like Vincent, was an important figure in the Chautauqua movement. For example, her books were included in their home study courses. She wrote articles for *The Chautauquan*, on Count Tolstoy, and the humanizing tendency of industrial education.[114] She, in turn, was the subject of two other articles on Hull-House and her leadership there.[115]

Zeublin published an article discussing the new "civic spirit" in *The Chautauquan* where he cited Addams and Hull-House as the prime example of this buoyant energy and hope. He recommended reading *HH Maps and Papers* as a source for additional information, providing the only linkage, albeit tenuous, between Vincent and this central volume.[116] The acceptance of Addams and her work at Chautauqua is clearly indicated by this particular article, however.

Furthermore, in 1902 she gave a series of lectures for their summer program in Chautauqua, New York.[117] In 1905 she addressed this audience again when she begged the participants

> to break out still further into the world about you till it includes the man who seems quite unlike ourselves. Although his real experiences are so like our own this man is forlorn because he does not realize there is any fellowship in this land to which he comes; who thinks that all we want is money and muscle. As our land is growing cosmopolitan in its people, let us meet it with a cosmopolitan culture.[118]

Finally, the 1915 Chautauqua class was named for Jane Addams, with an accompanying ceremony recognizing her leadership in society and education.[119]

The close association between Addams and Vincent in relation to Chautauqua is documented in five letters they exchanged concerning her participation in various programs.[120] Such evidence merely documents what can be inferred from their leadership in this program of adult education. (It can also be inferred that Vincent was aware of Tolstoy's work although this is not indicated in the former's writings.)

More insightful correspondence occurred on two other occasions. In 1897 Vincent was asked by Addams to sign a petition on the Child Labor Bill associated with his earlier work on eliminating child wage-earners in the "sweat shops."[121] Furthermore, in 1920 he wrote Addams informing her that he had met Mrs. Barrett of Toynbee Hall during a visit to New York. This last letter indicated both a continuing interest in the work of Addams, some contact with social settlement leaders, and yet another link between Vincent and Addams even after he had left the University of Chicago.[122]

His acknowledgement of her leading role as a sociologist is found in his definitive article on sociology written for the *Encyclopedia Americana* in 1904. In this article, he divides sociology into three specialties: philosophical, scientific, and social technological. In the latter division, Vincent placed Addams in the forefront: "Men and women like Graham Taylor, Robert A. Woods, Jane Addams, John Graham Brooks are bringing to bear upon the pressing problems of the day scientific knowledge, tested and transformed into wise and effective action through their experiences of life. Sociology is not philanthropy, but as all scientific work must find its ultimate sanction in service to mankind, sociology seeks to increase the resources of "social technology."[123] Vincent saw the division of labor in sociology as compatible with the work of Addams and integral to the total task of sociological practice. A more complete analysis of this linkage, like the other early men, is clearly needed to more firmly establish the roots of their intellectual ties.

The Religious Men as a Group

Evaluated as a group, these early men were politically active in American life, particularly in education, religion, and urban reform. Each of them had unique relationships to these topics and subsequently to Addams. Small was a key figure in Addams' sociological career. Attracted to social reform yet tied to the academy and conservative values, Small was a paradoxical figure for the profession and more specifically for Addams' career in it. His writings on the economy reveal his vacillation and it is only in administrative skills that Small adopted a consistent stance: Sociology was to be established as a legitimate profession in the academy. Christian beliefs permeated his social reform writings making them appear unsystematic and unscientific. Only Becker's analysis has untangled the complexity of his ambiguity to reveal both his strengths and weaknesses. Addams and Hull-House were important influences on Small's work for years, but his close alignment shifted to a more distant one as he aged and the scars of social reform battles took their toll.

Both Henderson and Zeublin appeared to have maintained life-long interests in social reform, particularly urban reform. On the one hand, they formed a basis for later Chicago sociologists to study the city, used mapping techniques and statistics, and committed themselves to the analysis of urban problems. On the other hand, these men used religious values in their speech and writings, and their commitments to Fabian ideals were not carried on by later generations. Although they worked in social settlements, their professional networks were often distinct from those of Addams and other women sociologists. Henderson, through Chicago Commons, and Zeublin, through the Northwestern University Settlement, tied their social settlement work to the academy. These settlements, moreover, were part of a male sociological network with a religious emphasis that was not found at Hull-House.

Vincent was deeply committed to Chautauqua during his tenure at Chicago and this closely supported Addams' work outside of the academy and with adults. Starting from a religious background, Vincent increasingly distanced himself from this interpretation of social life. His work with Small on their introductory textbook illustrates his compatibility with the religious men, while his own dissertation dramatically signaled his own change and movement away from them. Like Small, Vincent's administrative skills in higher education were his strong point, stronger even than his social thought. Although Vincent was part of the beginnings of symbolic interactionism, it was Thomas, Mead, Park and Burgess who were major figures in the development and flowering of this form of social theory.

All the men, with the notable exceptions of Park and Burgess, were colleagues of Addams, frequent visitors to Hull-House, involved in social settlements, and specialized in areas of writing that overlapped with Addams'. The common core of work in the garment industry battles, in the Chicago City Club, and in the Chicago School of Civics and Philanthropy bound these men into a coherent group. Therefore, it is important to keep in mind that these two chapters, this one and the next, are part of a single group of early Chicago sociologists. If any dividing line between them is to be made, it would be one separating the work of Park and Burgess from the rest. But such a line is suggested too often, especially by Park and Burgess, and they, too, were a product of social reform, the training and social thought of these early Chicago men, and the work of Jane Addams and Hull-House.

Notes

1. Ernest Becker, *The Lost Science of Man* (New York: George Braziller, 1971), p. 5.
2. See *Chicago Tribune*, Hull-House Scrapbooks, Addams Papers, SCPC. Accounts of this battle can be found in Josephine Goldmark, *Impatient Crusader: Florence Kelley's Life* (Urbana, Ill.: University of Illinois Press, 1953), pp. 33-50. See also Jane Addams, *Twenty Years at Hull-House* (New York: Macmillan, 1910), pp. 198-230.
3. An account of the strike and Mead's work in it can be found in Mary Jo Deegan and John S. Burger, "George Mead and Social Reform," *Journal of the History of the Behavioral Sciences* 14 (October 1978):362-72.
4. A number of writings on the topic giving the general background are Howard Barton Myers, "The Policing of Labor Disputes in Chicago: A Case Study." Unpublished disseration, Department of History, University of Chicago, 1929. Leo Wolman et al., *The Clothing Workers of Chicago: 1910-1922* (Chicago: Chicago Joint Board of the Amalgamated Clothing Workers of America, 1922), pp. 17-71. Charles Zaretz, *The Amalgamated Clothing Workers of America* (New York: Ancon, 1934). These authors give the ACWA much of the credit for the strike and its development. For a more balanced picture of the role of socialist women see Mary Jo Buhle, "Socialist Women and the Girl Strikers, Chicago, 1910," *Signs* 1 (Summer 1976):1039-51.
5. One of the few documents supporting Mead's participation in the strike is found in the pamphlet he coauthored with Harold Ickes and Irwin Tucker. "Brief History of the Clothing Strike in Chicago," Starr Papers, Smith College.
6. Stephen Diner, *A City and Its Universities* (Chapel Hill: University of North Carolina Press, 1980).
7. Ibid., p. 5.
8. These lectures are listed in the weekly *City Club Bulletins*. Some of the important ones here are those where she shared the platform with Mead. See, for

example, their shared presentation "Labor Night," *City Club Bulletin* 5 (27 May 1912): pp. 214-15 and 222 for Mead and Addams, respectively.

9. Membership lists are given each year in the *City Club Bulletin*. Information is found in the respective year cited in the text.

10. A discussion of this transition can be found in Roy Lubove, *The Professional Altruist* (New York: Atheneum, 1965); Jessie Bernard, *Academic Women* (University Park: University of Pennsylvania Press, 1964), pp. 242-50.

11. Jane Addams, *My Friend, Julia Lathrop* (New York: Macmillan, 1931).

12. "Historical Sketch of the Development of the Course of Instruction in the CSCP, 1903-1913," Taylor Papers, Newberry Library.

13. See Course Catalogs, CSCP, 1903-19; Catalogs for SSA, 1920-24. Abbott Papers, University of Nebraska Archives.

14. See Abbott Papers, University of Nebraska Archives.

15. Faris, *Chicago Sociology* (Chicago: University of Chicago Press, 1967), pp. 11-12.

16. Harry Elmer Barnes, *History of Sociology* (Chicago: University of Chicago Press, 1948), pp. 788-90.

17. Ernest Becker, *The Lost Science of Man*, pp. 19-21.

18. Herman Schwendinger and Julia Schwendinger, *Sociologists of the Chair* (New York: Basic Books, 1974), pp. 493-96.

19. Vernon Dibble, *The Legacy of Albion Small* (Chicago: University of Chicago Press, 1975).

20. Edward C. Hayes "Albion Small," in *American Masters of Social Science*, ed. by Howard W. Odum (New York: Holt, 1927), pp. 149-50.

21. Dibble, *The Legacy of Albion Small p. 53*.

22. Reprint of Small, "Some Researches into Research: 1924 Address to Research Society," in Dibble, *The Legacy of Albion Small*, pp. 205-20.

23. See both Becker and the Schwendingers for consideration of these positions.

24. Albion W. Small, *Adam Smith and Modern Sociology* (Chicago: University of Chicago Press, 1907), pp. 23-24, 65, 235, 237.

25. Albion W. Small, *The Cameralists: The Pioneers of German Social Policy* (Chicago: University of Chicago Press, 1909).

26. Albion W. Small. *Between Eras from Capitalism to Democracy* (Chicago: University of Chicago Press, 1913). For a discussion of this central aim of sociology see Dibble, *The Legacy of Albion Small*.

27. Albion W. Small, *The Origins of Sociology* (Chicago: University of Chicago Press, 1924).

28. Barnes, *History of Sociology*, p. 791.

29. Albion W. Small, "Some Researches into Research," p. 219.

30. See references in Allen F. Davis, *American Heroine* (New York: Oxford University Press, 1973), p. 97; James Weber Linn, *Jane Addams* (New York: Appleton-Century Crofts, 1935), pp. 160, 163, 190-91; John C. Farrell, *Beloved Lady* (Baltimore: Johns Hopkins University Press, 1967), p. 67; Alice Hamilton, *Exploring the Dangerous Trades* (Boston: Little, Brown, 1943).

31. Albion W. Small, "The Civic Federation of Chicago," *American Journal of Sociology* 1 (July 1895):101. (P. 28 in Dibble, *The Legacy of Albion Small*.)

32. Diner, *A City and Its Universities*, pp. 81-85.

33. *Chicago Tribune* (10 January 1915), as cited in Dibble, *The Legacy of Albion Small*.

34. This first reference is noted by Davis, *American Heroine*, note 28, p. 308.

35. Ibid., p. 103.
36. Jane Addams, "A Belated Industry," *American Journal of Sociology* 1 (March 1896):536-50.
37. Small to Addams, 14 October 1899, DG1, Box 24, Swarthmore College Peace Collection (referred to hereafter as SCPC).
38. See "A Belated Industry," *American Journal of Sociology* 1 (March 1896):536-50; "Trade Unions and Public Duty," *American Journal of Sociology* 4 (January 1899):448-62; "Problems of Municipal Administration," *American Journal of Sociology* 10 (January 1905):425-44; "Recreation as a Public Function in Urban Communities," *American Journal of Sociology* 17 (March 1912): 615-19; "A Modern Devil Baby," *American Journal of Sociology* 20 (July 1914):117-18 (this was a considerably longer essay in *The Second Twenty Years at Hull-House* (New York: Macmillan, 1930), pp. 49-79); comment on John R. Commons, "Class Conflict in America," *American Journal of Sociology* 18 (May 1908):756-83 (Addams, pp. 772-73).
39. "Nationalism—A Dogma?" *The Survey* 43 (7 February 1920): 524-26. This was originally published in *Publications of the AAS* (1919):206-14, with the title "Americanization." A Comment by Walter S. Thompson was also included, pp. 214-15.
40. See *Publications of the Proceedings of the ASS*, 1906-20.
41. Small to Addams, 17 October 1904, Small Papers, box 1, #1, UCSC.
42. Small to Addams, 1913, Addams Papers, box 4, SCPC.
43. See course outline for a university extension course by Addams, "Survivals and Introduction to Social Ethics," 1900, Ely Papers, WSHS. Addams is listed as a lecturer frequently in the *Bulletins* of the Chicago School of Civics and Philanthropy, see Table 4.1 here. Her frequent lecture schedule is also mentioned in Davis, *American Heroine*, p. 125.
44. See accounts of this by Addams in "The Chicago Settlements and Social Unrest," *Charities and the Commons* 20 (2 May 1908): 155-66.
45. Small to Addams, 19 March 1908, University of Illinois Archives-Circle Campus (hereafter referred to as UICC).
46. *Hull-House Scrapbooks, I, 1889-91*, pp. 25 and 28, respectively, SCPC.
47. Linn, *Jane Addams*, pp. 16-18.
48. Barnhardt interview with James Carey, p. 2, "Sociology Interviews," UCSC.
49. Steven Diner, "Department and Discipline," *Minerva* 8 (Winter 1975), pp. 524-25.
50. C. R. Henderson, "Business Men and Social Theorists," *American Journal of Sociology* 1 (January 1896):395.
51. C. R. Henderson, "The Scope of Social Technology," *American Journal of Sociology* 6 (January 1901):480-81.
52. Steven Diner, *A City and Its Universities*, p. 32.
53. Ibid.
54. Ibid., p. 33.
55. Diner, "Department and Discipline," p. 524.
56. Charles R. Henderson, *Social Settlements* (New York: Lentilhorn, 1898).
57. Ibid., pp. 183 and 184, respectively. Henderson also recommended *HH Maps and Papers* in *The Social Spirit in America* (Chicago: Scott, Foresman, 1904), p. 332.
58. *The Social Spirit in America, Industrial Insurance in the United States* (Chicago: University of Chicago Press, 1909); *Citizens in Industry* (New York: D. Appleton, 1915).

59. *The Social Spirit*, p. 14. Henderson equated his concept of "social spirit" to Addams' "subjective necessity" wherein both ideas refer to the individual's need to help others, p. 234.
60. Ibid., p. 16.
61. Ibid., p. 56.
62. References to these offices are found in the memorials by Jane Addams and Graham Taylor in "Charles Richmond Henderson: 1848-1915," Henderson File, Taylor Papers, Newberry Library, pp. 22-37. See also *Publications of the University of Chicago Faculty, 1902-1916*, p. 464.
63. See Faris, *Chicago Sociology* (Chicago: University of Chicago Press, 1967), pp. 113-15; Patricia M. Lengermann, "The Founding of the American Sociological Review," *American Sociological Review* 44 (April 1979):185-98.
64. John Koren to C.R. Henderson, 3 December 1908, p. 4, box 62, Presidents' Papers 1889-25, UCSC. Henderson wrote a note to President Judson on this letter attesting to the support of Small and Vincent.
65. Judson to Koren, 23 February 1909, loc. cit.
66. *Publications of the University of Chicago Faculty, 1902-1916*, p. 79. Abbott held another recognized position in the Department of Sociology as a Lecturer in Political Economy in 1909-10.
67. Mary Jo Deegan, "The University of Chicago Settlement and Sociology," unpublished paper, 1981.
68. Steven J. Diner, *A City and Its Universities*, p. 44.
69. Alice Hamilton, *Exploring the Dangerous Trades*, p. 118.
70. Ibid., pp. 119-26.
71. Ibid., p. 127.
72. Program on Conference of Day Nurseries, Addams Papers, Smith College.
73. Both noted in *HH Maps and Papers*, p. 217.
74. *Hull-House Bulletin*, 1 (no. 7, 1 December 1896):n.p. Hull House Archives, UICC. Graham Taylor on Jane Addams, "The Great Neighbor," *Survey Graphic* 24 (July 1935):339ff.
75. Henderson to Addams, April 1896, Addams Papers, SCPC.
76. Jane Addams, address at Henderson Memorial Service, "Charles R. Henderson, 1848-1915," Taylor Papers, Newberry Library, p. 22.
77. Ibid., p. 25.
78. Ibid., p. 26.
79. Henderson to Addams, 22 July 1912, Addams Papers, SCPC.
80. Henderson's bibliography is listed in *Publications of the Faculty of the University of Chicago, 1902-1916*, pp. 464-67. See Addams' bibliography in Farrell, *Beloved Lady*, pp. 220-41.
81. See Diner, "Department and Discipline," pp. 525-26.
82. "Social Work Shoptalk," *The Survey* 53 (15 October 1924):108.
83. David A. Shannon, ed., *Beatrice Webb's American Diary*, 1898, (Madison: State Historical Society, 1963), p. 99.
84. Diner, "Department and Discipline,"[p. 525.
85. See Gaye Tuchman, "Women and the Creation of Culture," in Marcia Millman and Rosabeth Moss Kanter, eds., *Another Voice* (New York: Anchor, 1975), pp. 171-202.
86. Albert Hunter, with Nancy Goldman, "Introduction," in *Ernest W. Burgess on Community, Family, and Delinquency*, ed. Leonard S. Cottrell, Jr., Albert Hunter, and James F. Short, Jr. (Chicago: University of Chicago Press, 1973), p. 5.

87. Charles Zeublin, "Municipal Playgrounds in Chicago," *American Journal of Sociology* 4 (September 1898):145-58.

88. Charles Zeublin, "A Sketch of Socialistic Thought in England," *American Journal of Sociology* 2 (March 1897):643-61.

89. Charles Zeublin, *American Municipal Progress* (New York: Macmillan, 1902). (This was part of Richard Ely's Social Science Text-Books series. Ely's other series, Citizens' Library of Economics, Politics, and Sociology, published the writings of Addams, E.A. Ross, and Henderson.); *A Decade of Civic Development* (Chicago: University Press, 1905); *The Religion of a Democrat* (New York: B.W. Huebsch, 1908); *Democracy and the Overman* (New York: B.W. Huebsch, 1910).

90. See "Northwestern University Settlement," folder at the Northwestern University Library Archives.

91. Charles Zeublin, "The Chicago Ghetto," in *HH Maps and Papers*, pp. 91-114. See discussion in chapter 3 here.

92. "Report to University Extension," January 1893. See *HH Scrapbooks, II, 1889-94*, p. 28, SCPC.

93. Davis, *American Heroine*, p. 97. Ruth Austin, "Economic and Social Developments Which Led to the Philosophy of the Early Settlements." In *Readings in the Development of Settlement Work*, ed. Lorene M. Pacey (New York: Association Press, 1950), p. 290.

94. Zeublin to Addams, 6 January 1911, Addams Papers, SCPC.

95. Zeublin to Addams, 2 October 1911, Addams Papers, SCPC.

96. Zeublin to Addams, 18 July 1913, Addams Papers, SCPC.

97. L.L. Bernard, "George E. Vincent," box 2, folder 16, p. 1. Bernard Papers, UCSC.

98. Ibid., p. 3.

99. Diner, "Department and Discipline," p. 526.

100. George E. Vincent, *The Social Mind and Education* (New York: Macmillan, 1897).

101. Albion W. Small and George E. Vincent, *Introduction to the Study of Sociology* (Chicago: University of Chicago Press, 1896). Robert E. Park and Ernest W. Burgess, *Introduction to the Science of Sociology* (Chicago: University of Chicago Press, 1921).

102. Bernard, "George E. Vincent," pp. 10-11.

103. For a brief discussion of each of these issues, see Diner, *A City and Its Universities*, pp. 91, 162-63.

104. For a discussion of the sequence of roles he held see E. Bestor, "The Chautauqua Period," in *George E. Vincent, 1864-1944*, memorial addresses. (Stanford, Conn.: Overbrooks, 1941), p. 6.

105. Bernard, p. 2. Theodore Morrison, *Chautauqua* (Chicago: Universiy of Chicago Press, 1974).

106. Bernard, p. 3.

107. Guy Stanton Ford, "The Minnesota Period," in *George E. Vincent, 1864-1944*, p. 27.

108. Ford and Wallace Notester, in *George E. Vincent, 1864-1944*, pp. 25-29 and 47-49, respectively.

109. Martin Bulmer's recent article on the influence of the Laura Spelman Rockefeller Memorial on sociology failed to even note Vincent's presidency of the Rockefeller Foundation during these same years or the possible relation be-

tween this role and his sociological background. *American Sociologist* 17 (November 1982): 185-92.

110. See especially *George E. Vincent, 1864-1944* and the memorial address of Ernest W. Burgess, *American Journal of Sociology* 46 (May 1941):887. Bernard's comments are interesting but condescending in parts. Thus a partial view on Vincent is afforded there, but whether it is accurate is uncertain.

111. Robert Shaple, *Toward the Well-Being of Mankind* (Garden City, N.Y.: Doubleday, 1964), p. 130.

112. Linn, *Jane Addams*, p. 191.

113. Ibid., p. 439.

114. Jane Addams, "Count Tolstoy," *Chautauqua Assembly Herald* 26 (11 July 1902); id. "Humanizing Tendency of Industrial Education," *Chautauqua Assembly Herald* 30 (May 1904):266-72. This latter article was also on a course offered by Rhto Zeublin, the wife of Charles Zeublin. Farrell lists five short (1-2 pages) articles by Addams on pacifism and Tolstoy that were published in the *Chautauqua Assembly Herald* during July 1902. I have been unable to find copies of these articles and therefore only note their reference by Farrell, *Beloved Lady*, p. 223.

115. "Hull-House and Modern Charity," *Chautauquan* 50 (March 1908): 9-10; "Moral Power of Addams," *Chautauquan* 49 (January 1908): 259-65.

116. Charles Zeublin, "The New Civic Spirit," *The Chautauquan* 38 (September 1903):55-59. Zeublin includes three pictures of Hull House in the article to illustrate his points.

117. Davis, *American Heroine*, p. 143.

118. Cited by Theodore Morrison in *Chautauqua* (Chicago: University of Chicago Press, 1974), p. 60.

119. Ibid., p. 296.

120. Vincent to Addams, 11 November 1897, Vincent to Addams, 28 May 1900, Addams Papers, Smith Memorial Library; Addams to Vincent, 9 February 1898, University of Iowa, Redpath Chautauqua Collection; Vincent to Addams, 30 June 1900, Addams Papers, SCPC.

121. Addams to Vincent, 31 March 1897, Addams Papers, Smith Memorial Library.

122. Vincent to Addams, 29 October 1920, Addams Papers, SCPC.

123. George E. Vincent, "Sociology," *Encyclopedia Americana*, vol. 14 (New York and Chicago: Americana Company, 1904), no pagination (this was a seven page article and the citation is from the last page of this unit).

5

Jane Addams, Social Reform, and the Symbolic Interactionists

George H. Mead and W.I. Thomas are the recognized founders of the Chicago School of Symbolic Interactionism. This major stream of sociological thought has been consistently viewed as a theory of action without applied roots. This abstraction of their thought from its practice in social reform has obscured the profound impact of Addams and Hull-House on their sociological concepts. Although Mead had more direct connections between social reform and his epistemology, Thomas was also committed to the activities and ideas of Addams and her female associates. Thomas, moreover, was more financially and institutionally dependent upon the women's network than Mead was.[1] Therefore, both men were closely associated with social reform and its advocates.

The three sociologists, Mead, Thomas, and Addams, form a powerful network for critiquing the generation of social behavior and its capability for change in a community context. Addams' social thought is examined most fully in chapters 9, 10, and 11. In this chapter, the emphasis is placed on the thought of Mead and Thomas and its relation to Addams. Their interpersonal network is also documented, forming a basis for a long-term, face-to-face, and intricately connected professional and personal foundation for Chicago Sociology.

This chapter has many continuing themes with the previous one, because all of the Chicago men were concerned with urban problems and the systemic observation of social life. Social reform was also central to these men as a group. Mead and Thomas, however, signaled a new generation in reference to religion. More skeptical of religion, more optimistic about the potential for people to change and be reflective, and more "modern" in their appreciation of urban life, Mead and Thomas were intellectually closer to Addams than the other Chicago men. It is widely accepted that Mead and Thomas strongly influenced the work of Park and Burgess (whose work is discussed in the next chapter). It is largely unrecognized, however, that Mead and Thomas developed a sophisticated epistemology and practice of social science interlaced with the work of Addams and Hull-House.

George Herbert Mead and Social Reform

Social reform was central to Mead's pragmatism, ties to sociology, and relationship with Addams. Simultaneously, sociologists have consistently neglected to analyze Mead's reform and philosophical ideas, forcing their work into a narrowed focus on his posthumous book, *Mind, Self and Society*.[2] This profoundly inaccurate interpretation of Mead has even developed into an attempt to "remove" him from the Chicago School of Sociology.[3] This series of explanations of Mead's work and collegial influence reveals the deep ahistorical and antireform perspective of contemporary sociologists.

His Writings

Mead was a shy man with strong opinions. A prolific writer, over half of his work concerned reform issues directly related to Addams' interests; education, war, democracy, labor, immigrants, social settlements, and the relation between theory and practice. This wealth of knowledge, consisting of over eighty articles, has been swept away by users of his most influential book, noted above.[4] In fact, the paperback edition, with a statement on the back cover that has been reprinted by the tens of thousands, propagates the erroneous idea that Mead published little in his lifetime! A general summary of his theory followed by examples of its relation to practice is presented.

Society. Mead's seminal development of the concept of "self" was a revolution in social thought. Defining the "self" as a product of social interaction, Mead offered a unique theory of human behavior. Initially copying others' gestures, the infant progresses through play and game stages until a developed "mind" or rational ability to understand symbolic gestures appears. The mind, in turn, allows the individual to become an object to him/herself. In order to take the self as an object, a person has to have the capacity to "think," have a "mind," and be able to reflect on his and others' actions.[5]

These concepts were adopted and utilized by a wide variety of sociologists. What is often overlooked is that these concepts of "mind and self" are linked to the concept of "society." It is this latter idea that most clearly reveals the social reform roots of Mead. His concept of society was optimistic, rooted in progressive thought, liberalism, and pragmatism. These are precisely those aspects of Addams' work that have similarly been neglected in sociology.

For Mead, "society" emerged from collective "selves." There was a great deal of continuity between the individual and institutions, therefore. Individuals created and maintained institutions, using symbolic gestures to communicate with each other their intent and meaning. Society reached its peak performance in a democracy. The self reached its optimal development with "international-mindedness," or the ability to understand the "community" as embracing all people.[6]

Conflict in society occurred when people were unable to take each others "roles." The remedy to social problems became more open communication. "Scientific information" collected in an "objective" manner provided a mechanism to understand the issues involved in any given problem. All the participants in the dilemma could then listen to and understand the different perspectives and situations. Since people were rational beings and desired a peaceful and sociable existence, social reform girded with liberal values was the logical way to plan social change.[7] This approach to knowledge and its application is called "pragmatism."

Thus Mead's pragmatism is intimately linked with his theory of the self and its emergence from society. There are "better" selves which have a high degree of international-mindedness, compared to those selves built on parochial interests. The former types of selves generate stronger communicative skills needed to think rationally and make decisions based on scientific information.

"Scientific" rhetoric underscored Mead's ideals of social reform. Because he believed that humans were unique organisms, however, he strongly supported a "humanistic" approach to the collection of data. People needed to be respected and their ideas presented without distortion. Knowledge was intended to resolve social problems.[8]

It is obvious that Addams and Mead had considerable overlap in their thought. This fusion of ideas resulted from their common approach to a variety of issues, whether in the city or at Hull-House, and their mutual intellectual exchanges. Addams' significant contributions to Chicago pragmatism have been consistently omitted from any analyses of this school of thought, just as pragmatism's contributions to Chicago Sociology have been frequently neglected. Mead's social reform writings are discussed next, and chapters 10 and 11 more specifically examine his shared interests with Addams.[9]

Democracy. Mead's social theory was based on the American philosophy of liberal rights. Free speech had a special meaning in his theory, for communication was the basis of the self and society. The ability to speak openly and with intelligence became an integral part of the development of a reflective self.

Of all the rights guaranteed by the Constitution, to Mead, democracy was their basis and defense. The development of the concept of total equality among citizens was for Mead a major breakthrough in the progress of society.[10] As more and more individuals became part of the community, the self became more highly developed and sophisticated. This "international-mindedness" was the goal of all self and community development.[11]

It is important to understand the centrality of democracy in Mead's thought in order to see the close alliance between the self, the community, and society. Only when there was an equal opportunity for communication of meaning and symbols for all members of society could there be symbolic development and union between the individual and others. Although Mead did not state that such an ideal state of opportunity and equality existed, he believed it was possible through democratic society. Flaws in the ability of citizens and members of society to communicate their experiences and ideals could be remedied through education, as discussed below. It is important to remember that Mead's entire view of the relation between society, mind, and self was predicated on the belief and goals of total equality and access to ideas.[12]

Education. Education was a central social institution for Mead as it was for his close colleagues John Dewey and Jane Addams. Remarkably, this emphasis on the process of formal learning has not been analyzed in depth by sociologists who have emphasized, instead, the relevance of his work for the study of deviance.[13] Clayton, an educator, wrote an outstanding study of Mead's views on education which has long been overlooked in sociology. In his book, Clayton outlined the impact of education on Meadian theory:

> Mead's position indicates that the great moral undertaking of education should recognize its responsibility in the extension of the experimental method of emergent mind. . . . The educational task is so to encourage the scientific habit of inquiry that we will rely upon it in fields now dominated by pre-scientific ways of things. The educator who is thoroughly alive to the implications of the pragmatic view would be increasingly interested in seeing the breaking down of the barriers that keep our reflective method of intelligence from operating in the areas where existing thought patterns are unscientific.[14]

Education, for Mead, was part of the democratic process and the daily interactions that generate the self. Behavior emerged from learning the meanings of human symbols, and the process of teaching these social objects was intrinsic to the educational enterprise.

The marginal members of society, the worker and the immigrant, were particularly subject to ostracism because of their lack of integration into the powerful symbols and signs of the social group. Thus, education had a central role in bringing these individuals into the social group. Workers needed to have access not only to equal communication with owners of production, they also needed education that would allow them to work to their full potential. Thus, Mead strongly supported education tailored to the needs, interests, and social world of the students. Vocational education was the key to such a development. In an exhaustive national study of young males in school, Mead and other members of the City Club Education Committee documented that among working-class youth there were high rates of truancy and "dropouts." This was not due to lack of ability or interest but to the inappropriate goals and knowledge provided by the school system. The grammar schools catered to the needs of middle- and upper-class youths. The institutions failed to provide concrete means for working-class youth to learn how to maximize their skills for their future labor. School was "irrelevant" and "meaningless," and the opportunity to earn pay was too attractive for needy families. Teaching these young people salable skills as well as reflective thinking and democratic ideals would provide a new working class, proud of its labor and able to control its fate in the community.[15]

Immigrants, too, were particularly needy of sound education. Barred from full participation due to language and custom barriers, Mead anticipated that integration into the symbolic community was limited. He did not advocate the assimilation of immigrants in order to "improve" them but in order to aid them in translating their own needs, customs, and rights into a new social context.[16]

Similarly, in a series of editorials for the *Elementary School Teacher*, Mead advocated more democratic control in the classroom and for the Public School Board. This long battle concerned the rights of teachers to unionize, to professionalize, and to have democratic elections of the board. Mead's proposals were concrete and directed to the Chicago public school system, but reflected the larger issues of teachers' rights to control curriculum and certification.[17] These goals were also advocated by Ella Flagg Young, causing her controversial resignation from the Chicago superintendent position in 1914. At this time, he wrote an article supporting her administration and its need to be free of a "heckling school board." Education was a mechanism to develop reflective thinking, democracy, and egalitarian participation in the community.

Science and Creative Intelligence. Science was central to the development of a "progressive" society. By systematically studying problems, finding solutions that were then tested and revised in an ongoing process, "working hypotheses" for social betterment could be generated.[18] Because the self and others experienced a shared symbolic world, understanding between people was possible. "Objectivity" was always relative to social perspectives, but it still depended on the gathering of facts and the observations of others. Often adopting methods used by natural scientists (contrary to myriad assumptions made by followers of Mead), Mead broke with the ideas of natural scientists who studied nonreflective objects, positivists, and sympathetic introspectors. Because people had intelligence, changed their environment, and understood their world, social investigations were qualitatively different from physical ones. Nonetheless, the same procedures of data collection, hypothesis generation, reflection and interpretation of data, and reporting of the results were involved in both types of scientific enterprises. Positivists who used such techniques erred when they looked for unchanging, universal laws. Sympathetic introspection was too dependent on information that could not be verified by others. It was a useless technique when it came to the generation and testing of working hypotheses. Thus Mead combined scientific ideas with everyday ideas about the world to solve social problems. In the process, the interdependence of scientific technique, ideas, and social amelioration would be revealed.[19]

The usefulness of science arose precisely from the creative intelligence of individuals. The ability to communicate and reflect upon action enabled people to use the knowledge generated by scientists. Education became a systematic way to unite the average person with scientific data and learn the value of such procedures for the group. Thus, science and the mind were intimately linked with Mead's understanding of society, democracy, and education in a pragmatic approach to understanding behavior and its creation by humans.

War. Like all Americans, Mead was profoundly disturbed by World War I. Part of the reason for Mead's perturbation, however, was that his theory of the self and society was directly challenged. Addams' pacifism, however, was unacceptable to Mead. Although Mead and Addams shared a variety of pragmatic assumptions, they did not share her belief in cultural feminism (see chapters 9, 10, and 11).

To recapitulate, Mead believed that the individual and society were emergents of each other and that sociability and harmony were their mutual goal.[20] War was direct evidence to the contrary. Thus, Mead developed a complex theory to understand and justify war:

> There is but one justification for killing which nations or individuals are willing to accept, that of self defense. The function of social organization is to build up and enlarge the personality of nations as truly as that of individuals, and this cannot include the deliberate destruction of the very members of international society, the consciousness of whom is essential to national self-consciousness.[21]

Despite the power of nationalism to unite a people, Mead viewed patriotism as ultimately a destructive element of social consciousness. Bonds within the "international" community were the most desirable ones.[22]

Despite his criticisms, Mead viewed the outcome of World War I positively. He saw government organizations that were adopted during wartime as the basis for a more socialist, and just, society. Optimistically, he saw World War I as the generator of a series of international rights and organizations, pointing to a more sane and secure future.[23] Clearly, he was wrong.

His only stance that was compatible with Addams' pacifism was his defense of the conscientious objector, when such a status was considered a protection of the coward. Otherwise, Mead tried to protect the American vision of war and viewed it as a victory for democracy.[24]

His Social Reform Activities

Mead's reform activities were varied and well-known throughout Chicago. He was the leader of a number of local reforms and played a significant role in the Chicago City Club and its powerful educational committee. He worked actively in social settlements in the city, particularly Hull-House and the University of Chicago Settlement. Because of the range of his work, this sampling of his activities reveals only part of his role in shaping the city and progressive reform. Henderson and Zeublin were active in as wide a range of programs, but Mead and Addams were closer intellectually and interpersonally.

Education

The Chicago Laboratory School. Like Dewey and Addams, Mead worked closely with the Chicago Laboratory School. He was an editor of its house publication, *The Elementary School Teacher*, for two years as well as serving in an advisory capacity for many more years. This school was designed to test progressive ideas in education and established a new style of teaching where the child's interests were vital for generating a propitious learning environment (see chapter 10 below).

Mead's concern with education preceded his work with Dewey's experimental school. However, he was also deeply involved with another experimental program in education at the University of Chicago, the Chicago Physiological School.

The Chicago Physiological School.[25] In 1899 Mary R. Campbell, the founder and director of the Chicago Physiological School, approached officials at the University of Chicago about opening a school for children unable to function in public schools. The deaf and speech-impaired were the original target populations.[26] As early as October 1900, Harper contacted Mead concerning the school's association with the university. Because of Mead's later role as a school trustee, it is safe to assume that he strongly favored this affiliation.

The few remaining school records point to a shaky financial base and minimal institutional support by the university. The school's board, however, was fully committed to the enterprise, and it assumed full fiscal responsibility on 24 September 1902. One board member, Henry H. Donaldson, chief consulting neurologist at the university, even took out a personal note to pay the school's debts in 1903.[27] With a reorganization, increased tuition, and philanthropic help, the school survived this immediate crisis. Unfortunately, the improvement was only temporary. Two bills were outstanding in August 1903, and Mead and Donaldson negotiated their payment. A year and a half later, only three of the original seven board members remained, including Harper, Mead, and Donaldson. Shortly thereafter, the school folded for lack of funds.[28]

Despite the financial collapse of the school, Mead remained committed to it or a similar agency. In 1908 he wrote President H.P. Judson in an effort to reestablish such an institution because: "The work commanded the immediate interest of the psychological and neurological departments."[29] Nonetheless, he was unsuccessful in his efforts. Clearly, he did learn how to manage fiscal accounts, which was a useful skill in his work as treasurer of the University of Chicago Settlement Board from 1906 to 1916.

The University of Chicago Settlement Surveys. Under the auspices of Mead and Henderson, the settlement undertook a five-year study of the Stockyards District. But this massive community study was continually hamstrung by the politics of the meat packers, university interests, and the question of the appropriate relationship between sociology and its application.

Six volumes on the district were planned on the following topics: (1) wages in the packing houses, (2) family budgets, (3) housing, (4) sanitary and health conditions, (5) educational services and opportunities, and (6) the educational and vocational needs of youth between the ages of fourteen and sixteen.[30] The sanitary and health study was never completed, while Abbott and Breckinridge completed the housing survey. Wages and family budgets were collapsed into one volume, and volumes on education, sex roles, and vocational needs were published under the auspices of the settlement. All these studies were subjected to pressure from the packers, especially when it came to analyzing wages in the meat industry.

This series of studies is important to the development of Chicago Sociology, but a lengthy discussion of their contents and influence is beyond the scope or intent of this section. Instead, only Mead and Henderson's role in reference to the wages' volume is analyzed here. Their commitment to applied sociology is thereby illuminated as well as their failure to adequately defend their findings.

Wages and Family Budgets in the Chicago Stockyards was coauthored by J.C. Kennedy and Emily Durand.[31] The study was controversial from its initiation. The meat packers did not want to provide wage information nor be criticized. The meat packers, Armour and Swift, sent letters to the board inquiring about the study and access to their wage data. The board's reply to Armour represents their conciliatory stance:

> We are just as interested as you are in making all parts of this report abso-
> lutely accurate, and we shall be very glad, following your suggestion, to
> submit any of the statements and data prepared for publication relating to
> your business to you for inspection, and correction if necessary, before pub-
> lication. If you can point out to us any mis-statement of facts, or any state-
> ments of facts which while they are true would carry a false impression, we
> shall be glad to correct them.[32]

Clearly, the packers would not, and did not, want to hear that their wages were too low or lead to poverty. On 11 October 1911, the board acquiesced to complaints by the packers and moved "that any portions of the survey reports which are likely to contain debatable matter be duplicated before typing and be submitted to the board."[33] The board then planned to make the packers look better, by showing that they only followed the standard practices of other capitalists. Thus data were gathered for other low-wage industries. As a result, when Kennedy's volume on wages was released, almost half of it was written by Durand on wages in packing houses in other cities and in the men's ready to wear garment industry.[34] In a mere two months, Durand's report was completed, but in June, Kennedy's report was still problematic.

In July, Henderson and Mead conferred on how to approach the pack-ers. Although willing to meet with the packers, Mead did not want this to result in a weakened stance:

> I think that they should have the facts in regard to actual wages and their
> actual decline since the unions were destroyed clearly placed before them in
> such a way that we will not appear to be recognizing specifically the introduc-
> tion of unions among their employees but in a manner to emphasize further
> that in other industries within this period, such as the steel industry, wages
> have actually risen . . . and finally to emphasize the necessity of finding some
> other method of controlling the downward trend or stationary position of
> wages under our conditions of increasing cost of living. I think also it should
> be borne in upon the minds of the packers that the industry should provide
> means for amalgamating the foreign laborers whom they employ, and thus
> taking the place of the unions as Americanizing agencies.[35]

In this lengthy passage, Mead reveals his *naiveté* concerning the profit motive of businessmen. It also reveals an application of Mead's pragmatism that was being tested "in the field." Mead firmly believed that the packers were fair-minded people who would understand rational explanations of the harmful effects of their unjustifiably large industrial profits. He even supported paternalistic sponsorship of workers (which Addams strongly opposed), because he thought democratic citizens should be responsible for each other and nonexploitive.

By November of 1912, Mead felt "that it was unwise to publish Mr. Kennedy's report in its present form because of the unsympathetic tone toward the packers."[36] A special meeting was called (which Mead missed) and each controversial paragraph was discussed and modified.[37] This revised version of the report was then submitted to the packers, who wanted even further revisions. Mead and an investigator met with the packers in February of 1913 and the final changes were made.[38]

The volume was finally published in 1914 and was the last in the series to be completed. Although the book was not "sensational," the data were striking. The most telling and innovative criticism arose from an attempt to calculate a "poverty level." In their estimates of the cost of rent, food, clothing, and living expenses, the investigators noted that $800 per year for a family of five was a minimal income. The average family size in the district was larger than this (5.33), while the average yearly wages from the packing houses was only $634.80.[39] Families survived by having mothers employed in the marketplace, pulling children out of school at an early age, taking in boarders, having all family members working for income, and enduring considerable overcrowding, poverty, and ill health. The indictments of the packing industry were strong, but buried. These figures must be ferreted out from pages of other statistics and the implicit justification of the packing manufacturers by their extensive comparison to other low-wage capitalists.

For our purposes, this politically controversial study documents Mead's commitment to using social knowledge to benefit the community. It also reveals his failure to fully implement his goals and his attempt to rationally arbitrate the differences between the packers and the board. It is unclear whether Mead would have pursued this interest further and struggled more with the ramifications of community involvement if Henderson had not died shortly after the completion of this study. Together, they acted as staunch supporters of the settlement's sociological development. After Henderson's death, Mead's participation rapidly dwindled. Between November of 1915 until Mead's election as president of the board in 1919, he missed well over half of the meetings, appearing only two or three times per year and saying little. Perhaps Mead only wanted to focus his energies in another direction, an equally controversial one where he had more clout: the battles concerning Chicago's public education.

The Education Committee of the Chicago City Club. Mead worked from 1910 until 1916 on the Chicago City Club's Education Committee. This group was a significant force in Chicago's school system, and Mead was its chair.[40] Their vocational training report was based on voluminous statistical data collected from several cities. In it, the committee members documented the high rate of dropouts among youth between the ages of 14 and 16. This study was similar to the educational and housing surveys sponsored by the University of Chicago Settlement. The vocational training report of the City Club was one of a number of studies urging more progressive education, the raising of mandatory school age from 14 to 16, and the establishment of vocational programs in public schools.[41]

This committee also worked to revise the services of the Chicago Public Library. A series of changes were then instituted and managed under the auspices of the City Club's Library Committee with George Vincent as a supervisory member. One of the first steps was the hiring of a professional librarian as the head of the service, instead of making a political appointment. The wider circulation of books and the more efficient use and location of facilities throughout the city were other policies that were implemented and modeled after programs adopted elsewhere.[42] Mead's work in these areas was based on a scholarly model similar to that used by Henderson, Abbott, and Breckinridge, and involved statistical analysis and documentation.

Labor. Mead actively supported labor unions when such an act was radical. Chicago had been a hotbed of union organizing since the days of the Haymarket riot in 1889. Mead and Dewey were at least marginally interested in the Pullman Strike, central to the work of Addams and Bemis. In correspondence between Dewey and Mead, the former wrote of his support and interest in the union organizer Eugene Debs. The city was boiling over Debs' effect on the workers, and Dewey wanted Mead to hear these radical speeches.[43]

More concrete evidence of Mead's prolabor stance can be found in his work for industrial education,[44] noted above, and his open support of the bitter 1910 Garment Workers' Strike in Chicago. During October of 1910, two young women sparked a wildcat strike in the men's ready-made clothing industry.[45] The strike started due to wage cuts and poor working conditions. Workers at Hart, Schaffner, and Marx were the first to leave their benches, but within a few weeks, 40,000 garment workers were on the picket line, supported by the International Garment Workers' Union.

Hull-House residents were major leaders during the course of the strike, as was Mead. For example, on 10 October 1910 a citizens' committee held a meeting at the home of Louise deKoven Bowen, a member of the Hull-House board and its president after Addams' death. The citizens' group was organized to help bring an early end to the dispute, and many local civic leaders, including Mead and Henderson,[46] were present. The committee selected a subcommittee, consisting of Mead, Breckinridge, and Anna Nicholes, then head of Northwestern's Neighborhood House, to investigate conditions and worker's grievances.

Following its mandate, the subcommittee interviewed labor union leaders, strikers, and heads of manufacturing houses. As a result, the researchers found that the workers' long list of complaints were justifiable.[47] Meanwhile the manufacturers did not want to cooperate with the workers or the subcommittee members. The subcommittee, with Mead as its chair, issued a strong condemnation of the clothing manufacturers' association.[48] According to Mead, the businessmen "refuse to submit any grievances to arbitration. They state that they have received no statement of grievances from their employers. This is a subject which can deceive no one."[49]

Conditions worsened, with many workers returning to their jobs without a settlement due to lack of funds sorely needed in winter. Nonetheless, in December, Hart, Schaffner, and Marx began to negotiate with their workers, who remained on strike. For two months, the workers and manufacturers discussed a settlement although none of the unions were recognized as "official" bargaining agents.

Finally, in January of 1911, some of the smaller companies began to settle their differences. In many ways, the strike was unsuccessful. Workers did not have improved conditions, the unions were not yet organized, and some of the gains obtained were meager.

Despite this bleak picture, a major victory in labor negotiations was achieved. Hart, Schaffner, and Marx agreed to the establishment of an arbitration board, signaling a strategic shift in the power between workers and management. This had far-reaching effects on other labor uprisings and settlements of grievances.[50] The concept of an arbitration board, moreover, supported the ideas of both Mead and Addams. It utilized language to settle disputes instead of physical coercion and confrontations.

Women's Rights. Like Thomas, Mead supported women's suffrage. Unlike him, however, he rarely wrote on the topic. In 1912 Mead spoke at a suffrage meeting, and in either 1917 or 1918 he marched down Michigan Avenue in the company of John Dewey, Jane Addams, and other distinguished Chicago citizens, for the same cause.[51] English suffragists visiting Chicago also stayed at his home.[52] In 1919 he chaired a municipal committee that cooperated with city and federal officers to suppress vice in and around Chicago.[53] This provides a direct link between his interests in this topic and those of Henderson, Thomas, and Addams.

In 1913 he addressed the Women's Trade Union League about the need for vocational education, indicating his support of their work and interests, compatible with his views on labor and job-oriented training.[54]

Immigrants: The Rudowitz Case. Mead served for a number of years as vice-president of the Immigrants' Protective League, a voluntary progressive organization established by Hull-House residents. (It is discussed further in chapter 8 below, in conjunction with Mead's work with women colleagues and for women immigrants.) He was also actively involved in a Russian immigrant's fight against extradition to his motherland. Some background information on the local circumstances surrounding this case is needed.

In 1908, Chicago was in a turmoil over the threat of anarchy from its Russian Jews. One explosive incident involved the shooting of Averbuch, discussed in the previous chapter. Such outright violence against an immigrant divided the city into those who feared and hated Russians and those who defended them, including Jane Addams. Many Jewish immigrants, moreover, feared a pogrom could occur in Chicago.[55]

The Averbuch incident was only one of a number of incidents involving Russian Jews, and many of them were being extradited to Russia to stand trial for their revolutionary "crimes" against the Russian government. One such refugee, Rudowitz, lived in Chicago and became a *cause célèbre* in 1908. His extradition was demanded by Russia on the grounds that he was one of a group guilty of three homicides, arson, and robbery. These acts were said to have occurred in the village of Beren, Courland, in January 1906. A review of the case by John H. Wigmore, dean of the Northwestern University Law School, indicated that there was no evidence to support the contention that Rudowitz was a marauder or robber but only a member of a revolutionary committee.[56]

Mead, Addams, and Thomas were part of a larger group protesting the extradition proceedings, stating that Rudowitz had the legal right to execute spies as a representative of a revolutionary government. Graham Taylor, head of Chicago Commons and a Chicago sociologist,[57] stated that "the American spirit" was aligned against the Russian government who wanted to extradite "many political refugees on poorly substantiated charges of being common criminals."[58]

A citizens' group, which also included Thomas, was formed to provide public support for Rudowitz' asylum in America. This group specifically demanded that the local immigration commissioners, Mark Foote, and Secretary of State Elihu Root deny the Russian government's demands.[59] Mead and Thomas with other prominent academics and civic leaders organized the Rudowitz Conference which sought to uphold the doctrine of political asylum. In the words of an article in the *Nation*, this was a "demand that the accused be given the benefit of every doubt; and that the absence of all intention to punish him for political offenses be made a certainty."[60]

On 29 December 1908, a large public meeting was held.[61] After the outcry from leading Chicago figures, Rudowitz was allowed to remain in the United States and the citizens' group was disbanded. Later they considered extending their efforts to Mexican refugees but rejected the project.[62]

War. Mead became a noted spokesperson in defense of World War I. He worked for the National Security League, a group that was considered "superpatriotic" and engaged "in a far-flung and intensive propaganda drive."[63] Through this organization, he published the previously noted moderate pamphlet encouraging the expanded development and understanding of the conscientious objector.[64] He also organized a series of public lectures on the war, under the auspices of the University of Chicago Settlement, in 1918.[65] Finally, Mead wrote a series of newspaper articles on the meaning and cause of war that were published in the *Chicago Tribune.*[66]

George Herbert Mead and Jane Addams

Mead and Addams had a lengthy and deep personal and professional relationship. To briefly summarize topics already discussed, they worked together in the 1910 Garment Workers' Strike on a series of reforms concerning immigrants and on the Ella Flagg Young campaign. He advocated women's rights, spoke before the Women's Trade Union League, and worked for years at the University of Chicago Settlement which had close ties with Addams. These reform ties were augmented by Mead's friendship with Addams, review of her work, and shared ideas. These latter issues are emphasized here, filling out the wealth of data documenting their mutual influence and development.

Almost as soon as Mead arrived in Chicago he visited Hull-House and became involved in its activities. In addition to his interests in the settlement, shared with his close friend and colleague John Dewey, Mr. and Mrs. Mead became close friends with Addams. As Addams recalled at the time of Mrs. Mead's death:

> My friendship with Helen Mead was during those early years of her husband's connection with the University, when their lives were suddenly overshadowed by a great tragedy. The loss of her brother and his little daughter by sea, as they were returning from Europe to the Hawaiian Islands, seemed to set apart these young people so lately come to Chicago.[67]

This began a close friendship and collegial relation that spanned decades. Mead, like Thomas, often dined with Addams,[68] and a few references to their close and casual contact as friends are found in letters of Mead to his wife Helen. One brief excerpt can illustrate this: "we went to Hull-House for luncheon where we stayed till we returned to go to the Thomases for Sunday night supper."[69] As noted above, Thomas and Mead shared this close pattern of visiting, talking and exchange of professional interests, forming a close network that has been unanalyzed.

Addams visited the home of Helen Mead's parents in Hawaii,[70] and the Mead's niece "lived at Hull-House for some months before her untimely death."[71] In another letter, Mead wrote Helen that Addams had turned to them and sought their help when a close, female relative of Addams had wed secretly and was expecting a child: "What Miss Addams wished was that there should be no scandal and that if the matter came up there should be someone who would say that it had been accepted by both families."[72]

This intimate friendship was augmented by Mead's respect for Addams' writings and intellectual thought. His admiration for Addams' work is eloquently expressed in the following passage he wrote to her:

> I presume that you could not know how deep an impression you made last night by your very remarkable paper. My consciousness was, I presume, in the same condition as that of the rest of your audience—completely filled with the multitude of impressions which you succeeded in making, and the human responses which you called out from so many unexpected points of view.[73]

In light of Mead's philosophy, such a letter is remarkable. For he believed that social consciousness was directly tied to development of the self as well as the community. Addams' speech "called out" from him a response because of the variety of perspectives she was able to bring to her topic.[74] In another letter, Mead complimented her on a recent book (probably *Twenty Years*). He continued: "May I add my affectionate appreciation—the appreciation which I feel whenever I think of what you are to Chicago and to those who are fortunate enough to feel that they belong to the circle of your friends."[75] Mead also reviewed Addams' *Newer Ideals of Peace*. He called her the "preeminent" interpreter of immigrants and "of men and women who live in the congested districts of our cities, and of the conditions out of which they have arisen, and of the conditions of the whole social life which they determine."[76] Mead was not an "objective" reviewer here, but an advocate of Addams' ideas. Although he criticized the book's logical organization, Mead repeated her arguments that government must reflect the will of the people instead of being an arm of repression.

These collegial ties were shared on numerous other occasions. For example, in 1909, when Addams was president of the Conference of Charities and Corrections, she headed a committee on immigrants of which Mead was a member.[77] In 1917-18, this same group, renamed the National Conference of Social Workers, met and Mead chaired a committee on the

Social Problems of the War and Reconstruction. Mead presented a speech that strongly advocated the socialist policies of Britain and their institutionalization in the United States. Addams shared the platform, talking on world hunger and politics.[78] Addressing the issue of world poverty and hunger exacerbated by the aftermath of war, Addams was in the process of being vilified for her pacifism. For Mead to share the rostrum with her was a courageous sign of support as well as intellectual recognition. Finally Mead, as a member of the Chicago City Club, spoke with Addams on the topic of labor before that same group in 1912, during the course of another Garment Workers' Strike.[79]

Publicly, they were colleagues on a host of issues. They worked together as early as 1899 in order to find a location for the Parker School. Again, we find Addams resisting the influence of outside institutions on her domain. In that year, Mead wrote Dewey concerning an impending meeting with Addams on the topic.[80] Later he amplified on their discussion:

> I judge that matters are in such a condition that Miss Addams cannot avoid accepting the Parker Slum School if they decide to put it in the Hull-House block. She hopes they will find the ground too small in dimensions, however, it would be a good opportunity if the U.C.S. [University of Chicago Settlement] could get in a branch—but Miss Addams has committed herself both to Miss Blaine and to Miss Culver in getting her to put a price on the property $25,000 [sic]. This will leave $75,000 for the building. But the Colonel wants so much that there may be hardly room.[81]

The Parker School ultimately became a part of the University of Chicago and was subsumed later into its Laboratory School. There was a bitter battle about the two schools at the university, resulting in Dewey's resignation.[82] Again, however, Dewey, Addams, and Mead were joined in a project determining institutional control and domain.

Addams and Mead, among others, joined forces in opposing the segregation of the sexes at the University of Chicago in 1902. Mead signed his name to a petition opposing the action,[83] and he wrote to his wife that "Miss Addams has agreed confidentially to work up an agitation in the Woman's Club."[84] Thus, Mead's position was clearly antagonistic to Small and Vincent's, indicating his stronger support of women's rights and equality (see chapter 8).

Mead also lectured frequently at Hull-House. Only three of these have been documented, however: "The History of the Brain," "The Evolution of Intelligence," and "The Present Evolution of Man."[85] At this time, in 1897, Mead was still wrangling with the issues of Social Darwinism, as was Thomas, and their work at Hull-House helped them find an audience for these interests.

Mead's ideas on democracy and education were central to his emergent philosophy of the development of society, the mind, and the self. His pragmatic approach to knowledge, education, intelligence, and science was based on these central assumptions about the world and its generation through symbolic communication. This theory of human development was a product of his contacts with everyday life and problems in the city. By consistently trying to resolve pressing social crises, Mead refined his approach to studying people. This intellectual effort was based on his reform activities in Chicago, and dependent upon the leadership of social settlements in that city. Addams was a leading figure in these programs and her collegial influence on Mead was vital to his social amelioration and understanding of the process of human growth.

This is only a brief review, however, of life-long shared commitments and interests. Mead and Addams were both active in the Progressive Party, the fight for women's suffrage, higher education, and access to professional occupations, as well as the issues noted above.[86] Addams' philosophy, theory, and research affected that of Mead's, and vice versa. The evidence of their epistemological ties is overwhelming. Her influence on his pragmatism, and his on hers, can only be introduced here.

This section has emphasized the significance of Mead's social thought more than that of other Chicago sociologists, because Addams' ideas explicated many of Mead's, particularly in the topics examined here. Her stance on World War I, however, differed from his, and emanated from her different understanding of the role and values of women.

W.I. Thomas and Social Reform

W.I. Thomas was extremely involved with social reform, although he is usually portrayed as opposed to it and the founder of a more "objective" and "scientific" sociology than his male predecessors.[87] His work concerning women closely paralleled many of Addams' ideas on the same topic. Although not entirely adopting her ideas, he was nonetheless deeply affected by her work, particularly her ideas on the sociology of women. (Because of the centrality of the male sociologists' work and writings on women, this topic is discussed in greater depth in chapter 8. Addams' development of cultural feminism as a special field of study is analyzed in chapter 9.)

Thomas was vitally interested in the process of social change and the effect of the urban environment on everyday life. According to Thomas, Blacks and immigrants, in addition to women, were particularly subject to stress and rapid change. Although they often suffered as a consequence, they also obtained new opportunities for growth and liberation. Thomas not only studied these populations and their everyday life and attitudes, he also actively worked on a series of social reforms affecting them.

His Writings

The Individual and Society. Both Mead and Thomas were key figures in symbolic interactionism. Unlike Mead, however, Thomas saw the individual as more frequently in conflict with society. One consequence of this struggle was social disorganization, but another consequence was growth and challenge. As Mead defined the mind as an emergent process of language, Thomas defined

> the mind itself [as] the product of crisis. Crisis also produces the specialized occupations.[88]
>
> But it is quite certain that the degree of progress of a people has a certain relation to the nature of the disturbances encountered and that the most progressive had had a more vicissitudinous life.[89]

The individual was partially motivated through a flexible set of instincts, called "wishes." These elemental needs for new experience, love, security, and recognition were basic human factors underlying behavior. Human action was also motivated through the development of "attitudes"—subjective, learned predispositions to action, and "values" which were socially learned standards concerning social objects for judging action.[90] Of these concepts—wishes, attitudes, and values—the first has been consistently seen as a marginal and later denounced portion of Thomas' thought, although evidence of such a change in his thinking has not been found by this author.[91]

Thomas also developed his now-famous dictum: "If men define situations as *real* they are real in their consequences."[92] Thus, individuals enter any situation with the elements of a given environment, their attitudes, and socially generated values. People are able to reflect on the meanings for action and therefore chose their responses. These actions and decisions are repeated in a dynamic process, with each new situation involving new sets of activities and their concomitant definitions.

Mead and Thomas shared a consistent view of the individual as reflexive, capable of rational thought, dependent on social meanings and definitions for behavior, and a product of ongoing, dynamic factors. They differ, however, in their view of the individual, the relation of the individual to society, and the nature and function of social conflict. Recent scholarship has suggested that Mead and Thomas were from different schools of thought with Mead, a realist and Thomas an idealist.[93] Such dichotomization of their thought is rejected here, but there were differences in their approaches, as noted above.

Because of the emphasis on social conflict in Thomas' work, social disorganization and rapid social change were prominent factors. But the study of social organization was not a disinterested observation of what was occurring in social life, it was an integral part of social amelioration, discussed next.

Social Reform and Science. The "Methodological Note" in Thomas and Znaniecki's *The Polish Peasant* has generally been interpreted as opposed to social action. This is a distorted and inaccurate interpretation. Thomas and Znaniecki strongly stated their support of applied sociology:

> This demand of ultimate practical applicability is as important for science itself as for practice; it is a test, not only of the practical, but of the theoretical, value of the science, a science whose results can be applied proves thereby that it is really based upon experience, that it is able to grasp a great variety of problems, that its method is really exact—that it is valid.[94]

Thus in the famous "Methodological Note," which was strongly influenced by his coauthor Florian Znaniecki, Thomas continually stressed the necessity of applying social science to everyday life.[95] This concern with the practical aims of science continued throughout most of Thomas' writing career although his optimism about the discovery and implementation of social laws decreased through time.[96]

Parenti, in his preface to Thomas' book, *The Unadjusted Girl*,[97] commented on the lack of Thomas' condemnation of behavior that was considered "immoral" or "shocking" at the time.

> One of his goals in this book was to erase the line between "normal" and "abnormal" behavior, for he considered both forms to be varying manifestations of the same human and social phenomena. Behavior, as Thomas understood that term, was the manifold effort expended by human beings in attempting to come to terms with their environment. All behavior was adjustive striving, and "abnormal" behavior should be seen as "unsuccessful" adjustive striving which was symptomatic of stresses in the broader society.[98]

This sympathetic view of persons labeled "deviants" was also evident in his study of Polish crime.[99]

Thomas' interest in social problems was not limited to the adjustments of individuals. He also analyzed social groups and nations. Most notably, he focused on the peasant and his struggle to obtain a better life. In an innovative and overlooked article on Prussian-Polish relations from 1873-1914, Thomas presented the significance of primary group relations in reference to an imposed national policy. He depicted the peasant as part of a large primary group that included his community and kin (who generally coincided in rural areas). In addition, he had an innovative description of the relation between the peasant and the land: "If the primary group is distinguished by face-to-face and sentimental relations, I think it is correct to say that the land of the peasant was included in this group."[100]

The revolutionary potential of the peasant in Europe operated as a function of several major institutions—religion, the press, the commune, and the village.[101] By its very definition, revolution means an overthrow of the traditional institutional ties and definitions of the situation. "The only efficient method of dealing with the revolutionary attitude," reflected the authors, "is . . . the substitution of a new—and more satisfactory system for the old one—a substitution in which the revolutionary elements of society shall be made to cooperate."[102] The change in values, attitudes, and definitions of the situation were so rapid for Polish immigrants that they became disorganized in their behavior and had problems in meeting their personal needs or "wishes."[103]

Thomas' writings tended to analyze the lives of "marginal"[104] members of society: immigrants; women—especially prostitutes and delinquents—and blacks. In this section we have concentrated on Thomas' general statements on social reform and the role of science in it. Below, we concentrate on his more specific writings and activities that enacted these principles.

Immigrants. Thomas' and Znaniecki's *The Polish Peasant* was considered the most important sociological study of its time because of its innovative methodology using personal documents and its encompassing scope.[105] Comprising almost 2,300 pages, Thomas and Znaniecki examined the culture of Polish peasants in Europe, their traditional environment, and in the United States, as immigrants, a "modern" urban environment.

Originally written in five volumes, a major focus was the family's adaptation or maladaptation to stress and change. Approximately half of the volumes were devoted to a series of letters exchanged between extended families living in Poland and in the United States.[106] Changing "definitions of the situation" emerged in these letters, especially from the United States. New standards of behavior, changes in the home, problems with employment and unemployment, loneliness, and anxiety were often poignantly revealed. These "life histories" were the core data for the interpretations of social change found in the other volumes.

The numerous problems confronting the Polish peasant in urban America were analyzed as a function of rapidly altered definitions of the situations. The church, the work place, the home, the street, the family, and moral precepts were systematically altered in the new environment. The immigrant frequently became confused, despondent, and homesick. The community and family found it difficult to respond to such massive assaults on their collective meaning and role in the world.

The immigrants' behavior was a product of this confrontation between the socially trained individual who then enters a world that is fundamentally redefined. Such alterations were threatening, often painful and problematic, but they were also an opportunity for excitement, freedom, and growth. In the new context, changes were generally defined in individualistic rather than community terms. Thus immigrants were in a process of dramatic social change, but the result might be enhanced personal opportunity as well as broken or limited group ties.

Race Relations. Like immigrants and women, Blacks were often barred from full participation in mainstream institutions. Thomas' work in race relations underwent significant changes over time, as did his work with women. He was initially more Social Darwinist in his writings and often used the then acceptable word of "savage" to describe African societies, culture, and social structure. By at least 1909 he had radically changed his understanding of these people and their social world. His writings on race relations became increasingly sophisticated, so that by the time he met Robert E. Park and Booker T. Washington in 1912, he had developed a position on racial and ethnic differences that was a major advancement in social thought.[107]

Thomas first conceptualized prejudice as having a biological and instinctual origin that was easily eliminated through contact and association. In 1904 he wrote: "But for all its intensity, race prejudice, like the other instinctive movements, is easily dissipated or converted into its opposite by association, or a slight modification of stimulus."[108]

As Thomas saw it, the origins of prejudice, antipathy, and affection were found in groups which selectively noticed and remembered the positive characteristics of people close and familiar to them. Hostility, antagonism, and dislike were connected to those who were unfamiliar and dissimilar. There was affection for the one and antipathy for the other, and these characteristics became symbolically connected to physical appearance and social habits.

Thomas thought that the prejudice process could be reversed through communication, contact, similar systems of education, and equal access to knowledge. In his words, he wanted to remove the grounds of invidious distinction. Thus, in this area, Thomas supported the ideas and work of Mead and Addams concerning the role of education in social change and amelioration.

Thomas' attention then focused on the minds or conceptual styles of different races and their cultural development and socialization. He took a position similar to that of Franz Boas in 1909, claiming that there were no basic differences in the minds of "races," and that there was more variety *within* races than *between* them.[109] The differences between races, therefore, were based on cultural ideas. Afro-Americans had the ability to think abstractly and logically, but were educated through a foreign system developed by Whites. In 1912 Thomas took the advanced position that each individual understands the language of the "other" only imperfectly. This misunderstanding is compounded whenever a group is judged by criteria other than its own. A grave source of social injustice is generated and assumed to be logical.[110]

Thomas, like Mead and Addams, believed in industrial education for Black people and had high praise for Booker T. Washington's methods. Washington, in turn, admired the work of Thomas. In 1912 Thomas was invited to the first[111] International Conference on the "Negro," organized by Washington and his informal secretary, Robert E. Park.[112]

This was not to be a Pan African Conference like those organized by W.E.B. DuBois in 1900 and 1911, but the nationalists were there and their presence was felt. It appears Thomas held a middle ground position in the intellectual ferment of the conference. To the Left was Bishop Henry McNeal Turner, the leading advocate of the Back-to-Africa movement of the day, and Bishop Heard both of the AME church.

Thomas' paper focused on intellectual similarities and cultural differences of the races and echoed his more scholarly writing discussed above. The thesis of the paper was that he did not regard racial characteristics in the true sense as sufficiently fundamental to influence educational policy. The real problem is to adjust educational policy not to mental traits in the biological sense but to the types of culture existing among the different races.[113]

Although Thomas recognized that the prejudice of Whites was "very grave," he believed that Blacks could overcome these barriers through education. In particular, he supported Tuskegee as a "Negro cultural center" and favored industrial education. Moreover, he thought vocational education was closer to the everyday life of Blacks than the general educational system was to Whites.[114]

Thomas was clearly supportive of social reform for both Blacks and immigrants, but his platform was more articulated for Blacks whom he perceived as a distinct yet integral part of American culture who were limited in their opportunities and rights. He advocated education as a primary mechanism to bring Blacks into a more powerful community. Thus his ideas on the social construction of everyday life were directly linked to his specific reform activities.

His Social Reform Activities

Thomas' work in social reform was characterized by his frequent association in these projects with Mead and/or Addams and the Hull-House women. His significant work with women's rights is detailed in chapter 8, and this work was instrumental in generating some of his notoriety concerning women that resulted in his dismissal from the University of Chicago. Thus, he suffered political repression as a result of his open support of women's equality in all areas, including their sexuality. His work with Mead provides evidence of a strong shared commitment to each other as well as their joint reform interests.

Immigrants. Both Mead and Thomas were involved directly in the Rudowitz Case, discussed in detail in the section on Mead above. Thomas also wrote one of his books on immigrants for the Americanization series, a reform based group dedicated to using voluntary associations and education as mechanisms to integrate immigrants into American life.[115] Similarly, he wrote an article for the progressive journal on immigrants, *The Immigrants in America Review*, edited by Frances Kellor, a former Chicago sociology student and Hull-House associate.[116]

His work on *The Polish Peasant* reflects a direct concern with everyday problems of immigrants. His extensive travels in Poland also made him less available for local reform activities. The funding for this Polish research came from Helen Culver, who had donated the Hull-House land and building to Addams.[117]

War. Thomas' war activities were probably similar to Mead's. But since Thomas' dismissal occurred during World War I and he became very secretive about his activities after this event, information on his activities during this time are scant. We do know, however, that Thomas was in Washington, D.C. in 1917 and meeting with Colonel House of the War Department. The work that might have emerged from this alliance is unknown since it ceased after his dismissal from the University of Chicago.[118] He also gave a public lecture sponsored by the University of Chicago Settlement and organized by Mead on the topic of war. Unfortunately, no copy of his speech remains.[119] It is plausible, however, that Thomas supported America's role in World War I and his position was closer to Mead's than to Addams'.

Blacks. Thomas' only reform work concerning Blacks appeared to be his relationship to Booker T. Washington and his attendance at the Pan-African Conference in 1912. Because Thomas worked with Park, who was an assistant to Washington, and shared their intellectual concerns, he indirectly supported the vocational education emphasis of Tuskegee. In 1924, he did propose a race relation program, which was never completed.[120]

Education. Thomas was involved with a number of groups concerned with education outside of the university. For example, he wrote and presented a paper for the Chicago Educational Committee of the Society for Mental Hygiene on the role of the unconscious.[121] He also lectured at Hull-

House in their evening programs, as did most of his colleagues[122] and supported vocational education for blacks, as noted above.

Local Politics. Like Mead, there is some evidence that Thomas was a member of the Illinois Progressive Party.[123] Again like Mead, he was a member of the Chicago City Club, but for only two years.[124]

Social Settlements. His position on social settlements was favorable, as can be inferred from his above associations and activities. In addition to these, moreover, he frequently used the files of the Juvenile Court and Juvenile Protection Association (both founded by and associated with Hull-House) for his books, *The Polish Peasant, The Unadjusted Girl,* and *The Child in America.* The latter book, in fact, strongly endorsed the use of clinics and social agencies for social amelioration.

In 1922, five years after Thomas' dismissal from Chicago (see chapter 7) when he needed both friends and professional ties, Addams suggested to him that he work on a study of social settlements. His reply revealed his positive orientation toward social settlements and their work:

> I agree entirely as to the desirability of such studies and I will make out and send to you a little later a tentative program. I am very much interested in the race question and hope to prepare a volume which will be a contribution to your plan, even if not formally included.[125]

On August 18th we find that he wrote a short memorandum on the study of races, outlining his intended program. The intimate relationship between scholarship and social action emerges here:

> The general object of all studies of this character should be to establish the conditions in which all the members of a society can participate fully in the organized life of the group. It is desirable that work along these lines should be planned and distributed among the members of settlements who are interested in doing it, and that the results should be published preferably in the form of monographs. In this way it would be possible for the settlements to identify themselves with a valuable and unique series of behavior studies which would have a bearing in theory and practice in a number of fields.[126]

No known publications emerged from this proposal, but it does illustrate the continuing professional relationship between Thomas and Addams and his interest in and support of social settlements.

Thomas also attended a Housing Commission conference sometime in the 1920s, although his work for this group is unknown.[127] Thus, Thomas had a long-term commitment to voluntary social reform groups concerned with social amelioration, despite the many publications asserting the opposite.

W. I. Thomas and Jane Addams

Addams in particular and women sociologists in general were the life-force of Thomas' career. This was especially true after his dismissal from the University of Chicago. For a number of years, Addams dined with the Thomases on Tuesday evenings, for he was a friend and colleague of hers as was his wife, Harriet Thomas.[128]

Thomas was also involved in a series of local reforms: vice control, a *cause célèbre* concerning a Russian revolutionary, education for Blacks, social settlements, World War I, and women's rights. Each of these areas was a focus for Addams' work, too, although there are few records of their working on the same committees together. His writings, moreover, depended upon the resources of organizations first established by Addams and Hull-House associates. It is possible that Thomas, in fact, was persecuted in his work because of his wife's work with Addams for peace during World War I (chapter 8).

Addams and Hull-House residents were central to the political and social thought of Thomas. They were the primary means to challenge, develop, and implement his view of social change and science.[129] As early as 1897, Thomas presented a lecture at Hull-House entitled "Stories of the Soul Among Savages."[130]

Their close collegial relationship is evident in his letters to her:

> I have been intending to write you a little more fully on the question you raised at the suffrage meeting. I do not know Forel's statement, but I presume it refers to public prostitution. You are safe in saying this is connected with more advanced societies, where the girl is more easily lost sight of and is economically more dependent, but it is not true that it is never found among savages. . . . See for instance, Westermarck, "Origin and Development of the Moral Ideas," Vol. 11, page 440ff.[131]

There are no comparable letters between Addams and the other recognized men of the early department of sociology. Thomas' full collegial relationship is grounded in his attitudes towards women and political activities, as discussed in chapter 9. On another occasion, referring to his recently published *Sex and Society*, he wrote:

> I think I shall appreciate your noticing my book more than anything that could happen to it. At the same time, I want you to know that I hope you will not be sparing of your criticism and that anything of this sort will interest me almost more than anything good you may be able to say.[132]

In 1911 Thomas was angered by a statement made at a suffrage meeting that he and Addams had attended. Continuing his argument, Thomas noted "It is not true that public prostitution is not found among savages."[133] Thus Thomas and Addams exchanged ideas on prostitution and the sociology of women. This collegial discussion was lively enough to have Thomas write Addams even when they lived in the same city and frequently saw each other.[134]

Although Thomas never critiqued Addams' writings publicly, his wife Harriet and William James did review Addams' book, *The Spirit of Youth and the City Streets*.[135] Probably because of this association, Thomas received a letter from James lauding the book. Thomas, in turn, forwarded the letter to Addams. There, James wrote that Addams "simply *inhabits* reality, and everything she says necessarily expresses its nature. *She can't help writing truth*."(Italics in original).[136] Thus Addams, Thomas, and James shared a circle of influence unremarked in the literature of symbolic interactionism.

In 1922, five years after Thomas' dismissal from Chicago—when he needed both friends and professional ties after his abandonment by the "established" male sociologists—Addams suggested to him the study of social settlements, noted above. At this time, he had just completed Addams' *Peace and Bread* and he praised it as "one of the finest things you have done."[137] It is noteworthy that Addams was rejected by many male sociologists at this time whereas Thomas supported her pacifism when she was ostracized.

Thomas actively supported many social reform issues, particularly those associated with women's rights, discussed in chapter 8 here. He frequently worked with Mead and Addams on programs for social change thereby documenting their mutual influence and interaction.

Thomas supported a division of labor within the social sciences, with some social scientists, such as himself, concerned with developing particular theoretical and abstract interpretations of social life. Others, who were just as integral to sociology, emphasized action and application of knowledge. He did not, however, dichotomize social science into "good" and "bad" according to these distinctions. In effect, he worked with a division between "theoretical" and "applied" that reflected a division of labor and emphasis but without invidious comparisons accompanied by differential worth and value. He also frequently engaged in applied sociology, but his stong point was the area of theory rather than practice.

His perception of the role of science and knowledge in society was misinterpreted by his successors and later scholars. These sociologists depict Thomas as opposed to social reform and the application of knowledge by sociologists. A careful reading of Thomas and his reform activities provides a very different picture of his work and intellectual ties to Mead and other Chicago sociologists, including Addams.

TABLE 5.1
A Summary[1] of the Writings of Mead and Thomas
on Social Reform Topics

Topic	Mead's Writings	Thomas' Writings
Minority Rights		
1. Immigrants	1908	1921 *Old World Traits Transplanted; The Polish Peasant* (coauthor Florian Znaniecki), 5 vols. (c. 1918-1920; 1958[2])
2. Women	None	5 articles, 1908-09, *SEX and SOCIETY* (includes 9 articles printed prior to 1907-08.) Portions of *The Polish Peasant*, 1918-20; 1923
3. Blacks	None	1904 a,b 1912 a,b
4. Youth	1896	*The Unadjusted Girl*, 1923. *The Child in America* (coauthor Dorothy S. Thomas), 1928.
Education	7 editorials, *Elementary School Teacher*, 1907-09; 1912; 1903-04; 1906, a,b; 1907-07; 1908 a,b; 1913-14; 1015-16	1917 1912
Labor	1908, 1912 a,b 1909 1918 a,b; 1929; 1914-15	1907 ? None
Politics	1908 1913 1909	Portions of *The Polish Peasant*, 1918-20; 1914, 1915
Social Settlements	1899 1908	None

[1]A summary of the articles is presented because good bibliographic references exist for the writings of Mead and Thomas. For Mead, see Stevens (1967), or Reck (1964): lxii-lxix. For Thomas, see Volkhardt (1951: 319-322). Articles not listed in these resources are indicated by and listed in bibliography here.

[2]There were two "original" editions because the University of Chicago Press stopped publication due to the Thomas dismissal.

Clearly, Thomas and Addams were close associates whose work was mutually influencing. Because of Thomas' central role in forming the discipline, this intellectual tie would be enough to grant Addams a significant role in the discipline. Nonetheless, her influence on Mead was as great, if not greater, than on Thomas. The collaboration of Mead and Thomas is examined below to reveal an interlocking network between them and Addams that has never been examined before.

Mead, Thomas, and Addams as Colleagues

Mysteriously, Mead and Thomas are rarely portrayed by sociologists as colleagues or friends. Their ideas are often seen as independently developed, reaching a peak of differentiation in the analysis of Lewis and Smith.[138] There is considerable evidence of their close friendship and work, however. Both Mead's daughter-in-law and Thomas' granddaughter speak of the long and close ties between their families, spanning three generations.[139] References to their friendship usually noted by philosophers can be found scattered throughout several introductory writings on Mead, too.[140] Thomas somewhat grudgingly admitted in an autobiographical statement that Mead was an intellectual influence, but this brief statement was made over a decade after he left Chicago. Thomas, moreover, gave little recognition to any specific individuals as influences on his thought. He stressed, instead, his interdisciplinary background and training.[141] It is important, then, to document here the considerable overlap in their work and writings.

As significant cofounders of symbolic interactionism, they shared an approach to social life based on communication, using symbols to create meaning, and the emergent process of becoming human. In many ways their work is complementary although comparisons are almost completely lacking. Instead, the individualistic origin of Thomas' work, its lack of coherence, and piecemeal analysis have been stressed.[142] A thorough analysis of their commonality is beyond the scope of this book and deserves to be a separate monograph. Nonetheless, even initial comparisons of their shared social reform interests and activities illustrate the common substantive concerns that inform their work and writings (see Tables 5.1, 5.2, and 5.3). It is also important to note that Thomas received some of his earliest training at the University of Chicago as a student in Mead's class in 1896.[143]

The topics of common interest; vocational education, youth, immigrants, and war, complement the areas in which they differed. While Mead stressed co-operation, Thomas stressed social disorganization. While Mead studied the process of resolving differences, Thomas studied the process of creatively learning from differences.

A key to their common work is found in Addams and Hull-House, documented more fully in succeeding chapters; Thomas, Mead, and Addams formed a significant intellectual group that has been unnoticed. The separation of their thought can only be attributed to the succeeding generations of sociologists who disassociated the work of Mead and Thomas from

TABLE 5.2
The Separate Social Reform Activities of Mead and Thomas by Topic Area

Topic	Mead's Activities	Thomas' Activities
1. Immigrants	Immigrants' Protective League, 1st Vice President 1900-1917	Writings in Americanization Series (1921) and for immigrant rights groups (1916)
2. Women	Lectures, 1903- "Women and the New Education" at Univ. of Chicago; 1908- spoke before Women's Trade Union League; 1912- Suffrage address	1910- lecture of Suffrage to College Equal Suffrage League 1911- Member Chicago Vice Commission
3. Blacks	1920- ? Helped Harry Dean, a black pan-African sea captain, to get autobiography published	1912- Participant at the First International Conference on Blacks
4. Youth	1912, chair, social settlement committee, Child Welfare Committee	Use of records Juvenile Court and Juvenile Protective Assn. for publications from 1918-28.
5. Education	1919, President, 1917, Chair of Directors; 1908-20? Member, Chicago City Clubs Committee on Education 1914- Supportive of Ella Flagg Young battle for Chicago Superintendent of Schools 1907-08, editorials on education & politics in *Elementary Teacher* 1908- Chicago Vocational School 1908- Vocational Education study	1924- Proposed race relations program 1926- Educational Conference Chicago Educational Committee of the Society for Mental Hygiene
6. Labor	1912- Member of Chicago Federal Commission on Industrial Relations 1910-11- Member of Citizens Committee of Garment Workers' Strike, lectures on same 1902?- Supported Meatcutters' Strike	No comparable work

(Continued on next page)

TABLE 5.2 (Continued)
The Separate Social Reform Activities of Mead and Thomas by Topic Area

Topic	Mead's Activities	Thomas' Activities
7. War	1917- Chair, social work conference section on war and reconstruction 1917- Wrote newspaper articles on World War I	1917- lectures on war for U. of Chicago Settlement (Mead Board of Directors)
8. Politics	1912- Vice President, Illinois Progressive Party	Thomas perhaps a member
9. Social Settlements	1895- spoke at Chicago Commons 1890-1928?- Univ. of Chicago Social Settlement board of trustees; treasurer; president	
10. Housing	No comparable work	192?- Attended Housing Commission meeting

TABLE 5.3
The Joint Social Reform Activities of Mead and Thomas by Topic Area

Topic	Year	Activity
Immigrants	1908	The Rudowitz Case
Women	191?-20	Suffrage for Women
War	1917	Lecturers on World War I
Social Settlements	1897-?	Hull-House—lectures; participation in variety of associations initiated or sponsored by the settlement. The Juvenile Court; the Psychopathic Clinic, Immigrants' Protective League, the Juvenile Protective Assn.; close friendship with Jane Addams, working relationships with other residents such as Edith Abbott and Sophonisba Breckinridge
Local Politics	1913-14	Members of the Chicago City Club; Mead (1908-28)
Applied Sociology	1902-12	Special lecturers at the Chicago School of Civics and Philanthropy

their social reform roots and erased Addams' role in sociology from most accounts of the profession's development. Their intellectual, professional, and personal ties were deep, however, and reveal an exciting area for continued research and analysis. This peak of sociological liaison between Addams and the men of the Chicago School, however, contrasts dramatically with her relations to Park and Burgess.

Notes

1. Documentation of Thomas' dependence on the women's network can be found in Mary Jo Deegan and John S. Burger, "W.I. Thomas and Social Reform," *Journal of the History of the Behavioral Sciences* 17 (January 1981):114-25.
2. The extensive literature on Mead in sociology relates primarily to the Chicago School of Symbolic Interaction. See Herbert Blumer, *Symbolic Interactionism* (Englewood Cliffs, N.J.: Prentice-Hall, 1969) for the most abstracted and apolitical interpretation. Blumer trained many sociologists in his way of interpreting Mead, creating a consistent bias throughout the sociological literature. Historians are less vulnerable to this criticism. See Diner, *A City and Its Universities* (Chapel Hill: University of North Carolina Press, 1980). Philosophers, too, understand Meadian thought more accurately. See Darnell Rucker, *The Chicago Pragmatists* (Minneapolis, Minn.: University of Minneapolis Press, 1967). See also Mary Jo Deegan and John S. Burger, "George Herbert Mead and Social Reform," *Journal of the History of the Behavioral Sciences* 14 (October 1978):362-72. Educators, too, recognize the significance of his politics. See Alfred S. Clayton, *Emergent Mind and Education* (New York: Teachers College Bureau of Publications, Columbia University Press, 1943).
3. See David J. Lewis and Richard L. Smith, *American Sociology and Pragmatism* (Chicago: University of Chicago Press, 1980).
4. See Mead's bibliography in Andrew J. Reck, ed., *Selected Writings: Mead* (Indianapolis, Ind.: Bobbs-Merrill, 1964), pp. lxiii-lxix. In Reck's introduction, he also analyzes the relationship between Mead's ideas on reform and other aspects of his social thought. Reck is a philosopher. See also John Petras, *George Herbert Mead: Essays on His Social Philosophy* (New York: Columbia University, Teachers College Press, 1968).
5. George H. Mead, *Mind, Self and Society* (Chicago: University of Chicago Press, 1934).
6. Ibid., especially the section on "Society," pp. 227-36.
7. See Mead, *Selected Writings*.
8. Mary Jo Deegan, "Mead vs. His Interpreters," unpublished paper, 1981.
9. See C. Wright Mills, *Sociology and Pragmatism*, ed. by Irving L. Horowitz (New York: Paine-Whitman); John Petras, "John Dewey and the Rise of Interactionism in American Social Theory," *Journal of the History of the Behavioral Sciences* 4 (May 1968):18-27.
10. Mead, *Mind, Self and Society*, pp. 281-89.
11. George H. Mead, "National Mindedness and International-Mindedness," *International Journal of Ethics* 39 (July 1929):385-407.
12. For a discussion of Mead's adoption of democracy as a central concept, see John S. Burger and Mary Jo Deegan, "George Herbert Mead on Internationalism, Democracy, and War," *Wisconsin Sociologist* 18 (Spring-Summer 1981):72-83.
13. A number of these articles can be found in the reader by Jerome Manis and Bernard Meltzer, *Symbolic Interactionism*, 3rd ed. (Boston: Allyn & Bacon, 1979). Gregory Stone and Harvey Farberman, *Social Psychology through Symbolic Interaction* (Waltham, Mass.: Xerox, 1970).
14. Clayton, *Emergent Mind and Education*, p. 165.

15. Ibid.; George H. Mead, Ernest A. Weidt, and William J. Brogan, *A Report on Vocational Training in Chicago and in Other Cities* (Chicago: City Club of Chicago, 1912); George H. Mead, "Fitting the Educational System into the Fabric of Government," *City Club Bulletin* 10 (27 March 1917):104-8.

16. George Herbert Mead, "Educational Aspects of Trade Schools," *Union Labor Advocate* 8 (1909):19-20.

17. A list of the editorials can be found in Mead, *Selected Writings*, p. lxviii. See also George Herbert Mead, "A Heckling School Board and an Educational Stateswoman," *Survey* 31 (10 January 1914):443-44.

18. George Herbert Mead, "The Working Hypothesis and Social Reform," *American Journal of Sociology* 5 (November 1899):367-71.

19. See Deegan, "Mead vs. His Interpreters," for a summation of these arguments. See also George Herbert Mead, "Cooley's Contribution to American Social Thought," *American Journal of Sociology* (March 1930):693-706; id., "Scientific Method and the Individual Thinker," in *Creative Intelligence*, ed. John Dewey et al. (New York: Holt, 1917), pp. 176-227.

20. See Mead, *Selected Writings*, p.204; *Mind, Self and Society*, p. 271. Also John S. Burger and Mary Jo Deegan, "George Herbert Mead on Internationalism, Democracy, and War."

21. Mead, "The Psychological Bases of Internationalism," *Survey* 23 (6 March 1915):604-5.

22. Mead, "National-Mindedness and International-Mindedness," pp. 400-401. In this latter article, then, Mead was adopting Addams' long range goals for international peace. Also this is the specific critique raised by Addams in "Americanization," *Proceedings of the American Sociological Society*, 14 (1919): 206-14.

23. Mead, "Social Work, Standards of Living and the War," *Proceedings of the National Conference of Social Workers,* 15 (1918):637-44. Addams also spoke on war at this conference, "The World's Food and World Politics," pp. 650-56.

24. Mead, *The Conscientious Objector*, Pamphlet no. 33 (New York: National Security League, 1918).

25. The hospital had three different names during its brief existence: The Chicago Physiological School, The Chicago Hospital for Nervous and Delicate Children, and the Hospital School for Abnormal and Delicate Children.

26. Campbell to Harper, 24 September 1901, Presidents' Papers (hereafter referred to as PP), box 39, folder 16, UCSC.

27. Campbell to Harper, 24 September 1902, "Report of the Minutes of the Board of Trustees of the Chicago Hospital School," 19 April 1903, PP, Box 39, folder 16, UCSC.

28. For a more detailed account, see Mary Jo Deegan and John S. Burger, "George H. Mead and Social Reform," pp. 363-65.

29. Mead to Judson, 2 December 1908, PP, box 39, folder 16, UCSC.

30. Ernest Talbert, *A Study of Chicago's Stockyards Community*, vol. 1 (Chicago: University of Chicago Press, 1912). Louise Montgomery, *Opportunities in School and Industry for Children of the Stockyards District*, Vol. 2 (Chicago: University of Chicago Press, 1913). J.C. Kennedy et al. *Wages and Family Budget in the Chicago Stockyards District* (Chicago: University of Chicago Press, 1914). Edith Abbott and Sophonisba Breckinridge wrote a series of articles and a book. Five of these articles were published in the *American Journal of Sociology*. Their work was compiled and updated in *The Tenements of Chicago: 1908-1935* (Chicago: University of Chicago Press, 1935).

31. Emily Durand is not listed as the coauthor although she single-authored almost half of the book. Kennedy had been the director of all the studies and received little recognition of this status in the other volumes. Nonetheless, Durand's omission as second author is hard to explain.

32. *Settlement Minutes, 1896-1910*, vol. 1 (referred to hereafter as *Minutes 1*). Letter of 25 July 1910 was inserted between pp. 210 and 211. McDowell Papers, Chicago Historical Society.

33. *Settlement Minutes, 1910-1928*, vol. 2 (referred to hereafter as *Minutes 2*); 11 October 1911, p. 23, McDowell Papers, Chicago Historical Society (referred to hereafter as CHS).

34. Kennedy et al., pp. 24-57.

35. July 1912, Mead to Henderson, folder 15a, McDowell Papers, CHS.

36. 11 November 1912, *Minutes 2*, p. 44.

37. Ibid., 15 November 1912, pp. 44-45.

38. Ibid., 17 February 1913, p. 47.

39. Kennedy et al., p. 79, 62, and 10, respectively.

40. Diner, *A City and Its Universities*.

41. Mead, Weidt, and Brogan, *A Report on Vocational Training in Chicago and Other Cities*; Edith Abbott and Sophonisba Breckinridge, *Truancy and Non-Attendance in the Chicago Schools* (Chicago: University of Chicago Press, 1916).

42. See Diner, *A City and Its Universities*; also Mead's *City Club Bulletin* articles.

43. John Dewey to George Mead, Fall, 1893, Dewey Papers, University of Southern Illinois Archives.

44. For a more detailed account, see Deegan and Burger, "George H. Mead and Social Reform," pp. 365-68.

45. Mary Jo Buhle, "Socialist Women and the Girl Strikers, Chicago, 1910," *Signs* 1 (Summer 1976):1039-52.

46. *Chicago Examiner* (31 October 1910); *Chicago Record Herald* (31 October 1910).

47. There was a report filed by the subcommittee enumerating their procedures and findings. See Mead Papers, box 9, folder 22, UCSC. A summary statement of the report and the investigation can be found in Deegan and Burger, "George H. Mead and Social Reform," pp. 365-68.

48. Subcommittee report, Mead Papers, box 9, folder 22, UCSC.

49. *Chicago Record Herald* (30 November, 1910).

50. For a discussion of the importance of this strike on subsequent labor contracts see Charles Zaretz, *The Amalgamated Clothing Workers of America* (New York: Ancon, 1934).

51. Irene T. Mead to Mary Jo Deegan, 7 July 1975.

52. Ibid.

53. Darnell Rucker, *The Chicago Pragmatists* (Minneapolis, Minn.: University of Minnesota, 1969), p. 21.

54. George Herbert Mead, "Educational Aspects of Trade Schools."

55. *Chicago Record Herald* (28 November, 1910).

56. Ibid., 3 December 1910.

57. Mead Papers, box 9, folder 22, UCSC.

58. Graham Taylor, "The Rudowitz Case," *Charities and the Commons* 21 (6 February 1909):780.

59. Mead Papers, box 9, folder 22, UCSC.

60. Ibid., Sidney Hillman and Earl Dean Howard, "The Hart, Schaffner and Marx Labor Agreements," February 1914, p. 9.
61. Charles Zaretz, *The Amalgamated Clothing Workers of America*, pp. 110-11.
62. George Herbert Mead, "The Working Hypothesis in Social Reform."
63. Arthur A. Ekirch, Jr., *Progressivism in America* (New York: New Viewpoints, 1974), p. 244.
64. Mead, *The Conscientious Objector.*
65. Dummer Papers, Schlesinger Library, Radcliffe College.
66. The undated newspaper clippings are available in the Mead Papers, box 4, folder 34, UCSC.
67. Jane Addams, "Helen Castle Mead," memorial, 1929, p. 18, SCPC.
68. Irene Tufts Mead interview by author, 26 June 1979.
69. G.H. Mead to Helen Mead, 1 July 1906, Mead Papers, box 1, folder 5, UCSC.
70. Addams, "Helen Castle Mead," p. 19. Irene Tufts Mead believes there may have been more than one such visit. Interview, 26 June 1979.
71. Addams, "Helen Castle Mead," p. 19.
72. G.H. Mead to Helen Mead, 27 June 1901, Mead Papers, box 1, folder 5, UCSC.
73. Mead to Addams, 12 April 1907, p. 1, Addams Papers, box 2, SCPC.
74. See G.H. Mead, *Mind, Self and Society; The Philosophy of the Act* (Chicago: University of Chicago Press, 1938); "Social Consciousness and the Consciousness of Meaning," *Psychological Bulletin* 7 (1910): 397-405.
75. Mead to Addams, 1 December 1910, pp. 1-2, DG1, box 2.
76. G.H. Mead, "Review of *The Newer Ideals of Peace,*" *American Journal of Sociology* 13 (July 1907):121.
77. *Proceedings of the National Conference of Charities.* 1909.
78. Addams, "The World's Food and World Politics," pp. 65-56; Mead, "Social Work, Standards of Living and the War," pp. 637-44.
79. G.H. Mead, "Remarks on Labor Night," *City Club Bulletin* 5 (27 May 1912):214-15. Addams and McDowell also shared the platform with Mead. Their remarks are summarized on pp. 222 and 219, respectively, of the above bulletin.
80. Mead to Dewey, 2 June 1899, p. 3, Dewey Papers.
81. Mead to Dewey, 25 June, 1899, p. 2, Dewey Papers.
82. See Joan K. Smith, *Ella Flagg Young* (Ames, Iowa: Educational Studies Press and the Iowa State University Research Foundation, 1979). She extensively documents the politics, theory, and battle over the Parker School at Chicago, pp. 60-100.
83. See petition, "Coeducation at Chicago," PP, 1889-1925, box 60, folder 11, UCSC.
84. G. H. Mead to Helen Mead, 30 May, 1901, p. 3, Mead Papers, box 1, folder 5, UCSC.
85. February, 7 March, 21 March, 1897, reported in *The Hull-House Bulletin*, Hull House Archives, UICC.
86. More extensive documentation on Mead's role with the women's network of sociologists, including Addams of course, is found in Mary Jo Deegan, "G.H. Mead and the Sociology of Women," unpublished paper, 1981.
87. Kimball Young, "The Contributions of William Issac Thomas to Sociology," *Sociology and Social Research* 47 (October 1962):17. Addams and other female sociologists are never even mentioned as influences, although Small and Henderson are.

88. William I. Thomas, *Source Book for Social Origins: Ethnological Materials, Psychological Standpoint, Classified and Annotated Bibliographies for the Interpretation of Savage Society* (Boston: Richard G. Badger, The Gorham Press, 1909), p. 17.

89. Ibid., p. 18.

90. See "Methodological Note," in W.I. Thomas and Florian Znaniecki, *The Polish Peasant in Europe and America*, vols. 1 and 2 (hereafter referred to as *The Polish Peasant*) (New York: Dover, 1958, c. 1917-1918) for a discussion of each of their concepts, esp. vol. 1, pp. 72-73.

91. See Gisela Hinkle, "The Four Wishes in Thomas' Theory of Social Chicago," *Social Research* 19 (December 1952): 464-84; Edmund H. Volkhart, "Introduction," in *Social Behavior and Personality: Contributions of W. I. Thomas to Theory and Social Research*, ed. Edmund H. Volkhart, pp. 16-18.

92. William I. Thomas and Dorothy S. Thomas, *The Child in America* (New York: Knopf, 1928), p. 572.

93. See Lewis and Smith, *American Sociology and Pragmatism*.

94. Thomas and Znaniecki, *The Polish Peasant*, vol. 1, p. 16.

95. Ibid., pp. 16-18, 64, 66.

96. William I. Thomas and Dorothy Swaine Thomas, *The Child in America: Behavior Problems and Programs*; William I. Thomas, *Primitive Behavior: An Introduction to the Social Sciences* (New York: McGraw-Hill, 1937).

97. William I. Thomas, *The Unadjusted Girl: With Cases and Standpoint for Behavior Analysis*, ed. Benjamin Nielson, preface by Michael Parenti (New York: Harper Torchbooks, 1967).

98. Ibid., p. x.

99. William I. Thomas, *On Social Organization and Social Personality*, ed. Morris Janowitz (Chicago: University of Chicago Press, 1966), p. xxiv.

100. William I. Thomas, "The Prussian-Polish Situation: An Experiment in Assimilation," *American Journal of Sociology* 29 (1914):92.

101. Thomas and Znaniecki, *The Polish Peasant*, vol. 2, pp. 1265-1306.

102. Ibid., 1267.

103. Gisela J. Hinkle, "The Four Wishes in Thomas' Theory of Social Change," *Social Research* 19 (1952):464-484.

104. The concept of "marginality" was developed by Robert E. Park. It refers to individuals who are part of more than one culture, never fitting exactly into a single culture and becoming the epitome of the stranger or outsider. Their unique position creates the possibility for creative insight into the process of making social patterns. See Robert E. Park, "Human Migration and the Marginal Man," *American Journal of Sociology* 33 (1928):881-93.

105. Herbert Blumer, *An Appraisal of Thomas and Znaniecki's Polish Peasant* (New York: Social Science Research Council, 1939).

106. The volumes were accepted for publication by the University of Chicago Press. Two of the five volumes were published in 1917, but the remaining volumes were not. The University of Chicago Press sold its rights to Badger publishers, because of the scandal surrounding Thomas' firing from the university. See ch. 7 for a full discussion.

107. *Chicago Record Herald* (30 December, 1908):9.

108. Thomas, *Source Book of Social Origins: The Polish Peasant*; "The Psychology of Race Prejudice," *American Journal of Sociology* 9 (1904):593-611; "Race Psychology: Standpoint and Questionnaire, with Particular Reference to the Immigrant and the Negro," *American Journal of Sociology* 17 (1912):725-77.

109. Thomas, "The Psychology of Race Prejudice," p. 608.

110. Thomas, *Source Book of Social Origins*, pp. 143-55.

111. Thomas, "Race Psychology," p. 731.

112. This conference is significant in view of other International Conferences on Negroes, challenging Washington's claim of being first. Washington's involvement in international race politics was ambivalent. He did not attend the Black international conferences held in Atlanta in 1895, and in London in 1900 and 1911. At these conferences his political enemies were in control, supporting Black nationalism. Louis Harlan wrote that "Washington's call for the conference ignored the important but controversial issues of race nationalism, and stressed a more systematic development of constructive educational work on the part of missionaries and governments." Louis Harlan, "Booker T. Washington and the White Man's Burden," *American Historical Review* 71 (January 1966):441-67.

113. Fred H. Matthews, *Quest for an American Sociology: Robert E. Park and the Chicago School* (Montreal: McGill-Queen's University of Press, 1977), pp. 61-68.

114. Thomas, "Education and Racial Traits," *The Southern Workman* 41 (June 1912):378.

115. This book was falsely attributed to Park instead of Thomas due to the "scandal" surrounding Thomas' name. This is discussed in chapter 7 in this volume in detail. The book referred to is *Old World Traits in the New World* (New York: Harper.& Brothers, 1921). Because of the confusion surrounding authorship, I list the authors as W.I. Thomas with the possible help of Robert E. Park and Herbert A. Miller.

116. W.I. Thomas, "Five Polish Peasant Letters," *The Immigrants in America Review* 2 (April 1916):58-64.

117. Morris Janowitz, "Introduction" in *W.I. Thomas On Social Organization and Social Personality*, ed. by Morris Janowitz (Chicago: University of Chicago Press, 1966), p. xiii.

118. Information concerning Colonel House and Thomas was supplied by John S. Burger.

119. The University of Chicago Settlement Discussions on War, "The Present European War," pamphlet; W.I. Thomas, "Racial Traits Underlying War," box 231, Dummer Papers, Schlesinger Library, Radcliffe College.

120. "Memorandum on the Study of the Races," Addams Papers, DG1, box 26, SCPC.

121. "The Configuration of Personality" in C. M. Child, et al., *The Unconscious*, intro. Ethel S. Dummer (New York: Knopf, 1927), pp. 143-77.

122. "Stories of the Soul among Savages," *Hull-House Bulletin* 2 (1 March 1897). Hull-House Archives, UICC.

123. Both Mead and Thomas are listed as members of the Illinois Progressive Party on their respective biographical cards at Hull-House Archives, UICC. No other documentation of their work in this area has been found. Work in the Progressive Party would be consistent with their ideas, social reform activities, and association with Hull-House residents.

124. Chicago City Club membership lists, 1912, 1913.

125. Thomas to Addams, 9 August 1922, Addams Papers, DG1, box 97, SCPC.

126. "Memorandum on the Study of the Races," p. 2, Addams Papers, DG1, box 26, SCPC.

127. "Memorandum of Business to Come Before the Executive Committee," Addams Papers, SCPC, DG1, 13a, Box 96.
128. Interviews with Ruth Thomas Billingsley and Irene Tufts Mead, 29 June 1978, and 26 June 1979, respectively.
129. See Deegan and Burger, "W.I. Thomas and Social Reform."
130. *Hull-House Bulletin* (21 March 1897), Hull-House Archives, UICC.
131. Thomas to Addams, 20 March 1907, Addams Papers, SCPC.
132. Thomas to Addams, 27 December 1909, Addams Papers, SCPC.
133. Thomas to Addams, 12 December 1911, Addams Papers, SCPC.
134. Addams wrote a book and several articles on the subject, e.g., *A New Conscience and Ancient Evil* (New York: Macmillan, 1916). Thomas wrote about prostitution in *The Polish Peasant* and *The Unadjusted Girl.*
135. Harriet Park Thomas and William James, "Review of *The Spirit of Youth and City Streets,*" *American Journal of Sociology* 75 (June 1910):550-53.
136. Addams influenced James' thought and corresponded with him. Little substantive information about their relationship is found in the James Papers, however, at Harvard University Archives. Her influence on Cooley is also evident, and both men are discussed in chapter 10 here.
137. Thomas to Addams, 1 August 1922. Addams Papers, DG1, box 26, SCPC.
138. 1981. This is also seen in the work of Bernice Fischer and Anselm Strauss, "George Herbert Mead and the Chicago Tradition of Sociology," part 1, *Symbolic Interaction* 2 (Spring 1979):9-26.
139. Irene Tufts Mead, 26 June 1979 and Ruth Thomas Billingsley, 29 June, 1979, interviews with author.
140. David Miller, *George Herbert Mead: Self, Language and the World* (Austin: University of Texas Press, 1973), pp. xxvi-xxvii; Andrew Reck, "Introduction."
141. "The Life Histories of W.I. Thomas and Robert E. Park," *American Journal of Sociology* 79 (September 1973):243-60.
142. See esp. Manis and Meltzer, *Symbolic Interactionism;* Stone and Farberman, *Social Psychology through Symbolic Interaction;* and on Thomas alone, John W. Petras, "Changes of Emphasis in the Sociology of W.I. Thomas," *Journal of the History of the Behavioral Sciences* 6 (January 1970):70-9.
143. Lewis and Smith, *American Sociology and Pragmatism,* Appendix 2, p. 273.

List of Illustrations

Portrait of Jane Addams, circa 1890[1]
Portrait of Jane Addams, circa 1915[1]
Portrait of Jane Addams in Academic Robes, circa 1930[1]
Conference at Hull-House co-sponsored with the Chicago
    Commons, probably 1903 or 1904[1]
Jane Addams with Bishop John Vincent at
    Chautauqua Conference, n.d.[1]
Dining Hall at Hull-House[1]
Hull-House from Halsted Street, circa 1915[1]
Portrait of Albion W. Small, circa 1895[2]
Portrait of Charles R. Henderson, circa 1900[2]
Portrait of George E. Vincent, circa 1900[2]
Portrait of William Issac Thomas, circa 1945[2]
Portrait of George Herbert Mead, circa 1930[2]
Portrait of Ernest W. Burgess, 1923[2]
Portrait of Robert E. Park, 1944[2]

[1]Courtesy of the University of Illinois Library, Jane Addams Memorial Collection.
[2]Courtesy of the University of Chicago, Regenstein Library, Department of Special Collections

Portrait of Jane Addams, circa 1890

Portrait of Jane Addams, circa 1915

Portrait of Jane Addams in Academic Robes, circa 1930

Conference at Hull-House co-sponsored with the Chicago
Commons, probably 1903 or 1904

Jane Addams with Bishop John Vincent at
Chautauqua Conference, n.d.

Dining Hall at Hull-House

Hull-House from Halsted Street, circa 1915

Portrait of Albion W. Small, circa 1895

Portrait of Charles R. Henderson, circa 1900

Portrait of George E. Vincent, circa 1900

Portrait of William Issac Thomas, circa 1945

Portrait of George Herbert Mead, circa 1930

Portrait of Ernest W. Burgess, 1923

Portrait of Robert E. Park, 1944

6

Jane Addams, Social Reform, and the Urban Ecologists

The names of Park and Burgess have become synonymous with Chicago Sociology. They are the perceived leaders of a powerful school that signaled the beginning of "modern" sociology. This "new" approach was notable in one respect: It loudly and defiantly separated itself from social reform. In stark contrast to their predecessors, Park and Burgess developed a rhetoric of sociology based on a natural science model and in direct opposition to Addams' epistemology. Equating social reform with unsystematic analyses, religion, and "do-goodism," Park and Burgess were key figures in disassociating sociology from the appearance of doing social reform.

Identifying themselves as both symbolic interactionists and "urban ecologists," Park and Burgess saw society as socially created and maintained through conflict similar to that found in the natural world of plants and animals. They viewed the city as both a human product and a territorial settlement. They studied populations such as immigrants, minorities, and juveniles which their earlier colleagues had studied, but efforts to link sociological knowledge with application were truncated, at least in theory.

Nonetheless, Park and Burgess remained tied to social reform. Their statements and actions, especially those of Park, regarding its role in sociology are often contradictory. Their rhetoric against reform did succeed, however, in shifting sociology from work conducted in both the academy and the social settlement to that performed primarily in the academy. In the process, they emphasized the avoidance of political issues and their advocacy, and thereby evaluated their work as more "value-free" than their predecessors'. Although the major outlines of their substantive studies, their use of mapping techniques, and the subsequent "natural areas" of social settlements were all presaged in *HH Maps and Papers*, they claimed to be original and independent in their epistemology and practice.

Because Park and Burgess were intrinsically social reformers, they were similar in many ways to their earlier male colleagues. Park and Burgess, however, vacillated more in their applied commitments. They wanted re-

143

form but not the label of "reformers." They wanted to be interpreted as unemotional observers, separated from the hum-drum of political and vested interests. As a result, they derogated their predecessors and initiated a new form of "social policy" studies. This new approach was more acceptable to businessmen and the academic community, but much less powerful and effective in everyday life. They gained respectability but lost vitality and political effectiveness.

This chapter documents the change of social reform from a central pursuit of sociologists to a dubious and ambivalent activity. Concomitantly, Addams' status as a sociologist diminished drastically. For Burgess, she became a sentimental symbol of womanhood with a charismatic attraction for "doing good." For Park, she was important as a public leader who was personally admirable but not a colleague. The role of social reform, then, is a pivotal concept in understanding the work of Addams in relation to the Chicago School of the 1920s and 1930s. "Practical sociology" was no longer practiced in the academy.

Ernest W. Burgess and Social Reform

Burgess embodied the change between the early Chicago School and the later one. He helped establish the myths of the later Chicago School concerning its distinctiveness and separation from its roots. Not too surprisingly, Burgess had been a resident of Hull-House[1] and his ties with social reform were strong during his youthful career. This stage lasted from 1913, when he obtained the doctorate, until approximately 1921, when the *Introduction to the Sciences of Sociology* appeared. Caught between his acceptance of social reform and Park's vocal and strident antipathy toward it, Burgess eventually formally renounced his early values and stance. This struggle between his early training and his subsequent work is dramatically documented by his proposed autobiography.[2] The title and table of contents for the proposed work is as follows:

The title itself, "I Renounce Reform and the Reformer: The Story of a Conflict in Social Roles," reveals the depth of the struggle Burgess felt in making the transition from the early Chicago School to the later one. Unfortunately, Burgess never completed the manuscript, but since he did write on some of the topics to be covered in the proposed chapters, his views on these topics are partially known. For example, he viewed social workers, their agencies, and work as a kind of "auxiliary" to sociologists. Social workers' case records were a method for the sociologist to obtain data to be interpreted.[3] Moreover, he consistently stated in writings of the 1920s (described in more detail below) that sociology was more systematic, "scientific," and "objective" than social work or reform.[4] There is a con-

TABLE 6.1
The Table of Contents for Burgess' Proposed Autobiography

I RENOUNCE REFORM AND THE REFORMER:
THE STORY OF A CONFLICT OF SOCIAL ROLES
By E. W. Burgess
Table of Contents

Chapter 1	Introduction
Chapter 2	College and University. The Struggle Within Me: Individualism versus Socialization.
Chapter 3	Teaching and Research. The Conflict between the Reformer and the Social Scientist.
Chapter 4	The "Sob Story" and the Facts in Present Methods of Treatment Juvenile Delinquency.
Chapter 5	The Human Nature and the Ethics of Gambling.
Chapter 6	How Can the Crime Situation Be Brought Under Control?
Chapter 7	Can the Social Evil of Prostitution be Eliminated?
Chapter 8	Standards versus Friendliness in Social Work.
Chapter 9	What Kind of Records Should Social Agencies Keep?
Chapter 10	The Relation of Sociological Research to Human Welfare.
Chapter 11	The Emerging Profession. The Application of Sociology to the Solution of Social Problems.

tinuing theme in his interpretation of "social reform work" that it is not as powerful as sociology, especially in an intellectual sense. He critiqued the writings of the early women sociologists as if they were never members of the discipline and their writings themselves were "undisciplined."

This stance is very similar to the Doctrine of the Separate Spheres, discussed in depth in chapter 8. Briefly, Burgess was articulating the divisions between male and female sociology. Male sociology, to be further developed by Park and Burgess, was "superior," "more abstract," and "distinct" from the early Chicago sociologists' thought and work. These "value free" judgments were made despite the "facts" that he received his training from these early sociologists (see Table 1.1), did work similar to theirs, and continued to draw upon their ideas. He handled this conflict by denigrating the contributions of the early sociologists as a group, and then separating the women into a social work category and the men into a "founding," crude stage of sociological thought. Burgess' early support and later criticism of social reform is presented below.

Burgess' Positive View of Social Reform

Even in 1925, Burgess was writing positive evaluations of social settlements and reform; albeit as work distinct from sociology:

> Settlement work, especially, represents not only the most devoted and the most idealistic, but also the most intelligent, phases of social work of the past

generation. The settlement in its origin was an extension of the university. It carried over into a new environment the love of truth and, it may be added, the spirit of science.[5]

The characteristic contradictions of his and Park's writings are displayed in this paragraph. While partially praising the goals and work of the earlier social reform era, the statement attributes idealism to settlement work and the spirit of science to the university. "Truth" and "science" are seen to flow *from* the university *to* the settlement, not vice versa or reflexively.

Burgess, nonetheless, undertook a "social work" survey in 1916 while working at the University of Kansas. In this study he collected data on the regional characteristics of poverty, housing, and distribution of groups by occupations. Succinctly, he was familiar with the work of the early Chicago School and emulated them for a time.[6] As noted before, during this early era of Burgess' career, in 1916, he wrote highly of *Hull-House Maps and Papers*, but in 1924 he grouped this and other studies together as "local studies."

In 1927, he viewed such work favorably, too, when he wrote Graham Taylor, concerning the latter's biography:

> I also feel that you might quite properly stress the contribution of the settlement and settlement workers, not only in calling attention to social problems, but in providing concrete materials on family and neighborhood life from their own intimate experience. The recent trends in sociology seem to me to be following up the types of observations and studies which settlement residents instituted.[7]

Although Burgess asserted that his work was "scientific" and different from that of the "social reformer," Short has also noted Burgess' continuing interest in this area of research.[8] In his studies of marriage and the family, Burgess vacillated between attempts to be "value free" and to comment on "proper" behavior (see chapter 8). In many ways, Burgess adopted an untenable position. He attempted to bridge the gap between social work and sociology while simultaneously claiming that the groups and their work were distinct, and that sociology was superior.[9] It is important to understand that sociology and social work *did* take increasingly divergent paths after 1918. But Burgess went back in time and made this difference appear to have always existed, instead of noting that this was a complex phenomenon occurring over time. The history and origins of the distinctions were not elucidated by him. On the contrary, any confusion about this early work was only compounded.

Burgess' Negative View of Social Reform

Because most of his writings were done during or after the 1920s, the predominant message in Burgess' interpretation of social reform is negative. He had a central role in downplaying and denigrating the work of the early sociologists in Chicago, especially Addams. He frequently portrayed their work as without theory, order, and importance, while he held his own views to be theoretically coherent and objective. The following passage reveals this deep bias:

> The city has been the "happy hunting ground" of movements: the "better-government" movement, the social-work movement, the public-health movement, the playground movement, the social center movements, the settlement movement, the Americanization movement. All these movements, lacking a basic understanding or conception of the city, have relied upon administrative devices, for the most part, to correct the evils of city life. Even the community organization movement, theoretically grounded upon a conception of the city as a unit, had the misfortune to stake its programs upon an assumption of the supreme value of the revival of the neighborhood in the city instead of upon a pragmatic, experimental program guided by the actual conditions and trends in urban life.
>
> The tendency at present is to think of the city as living, growing; as an organism, in short. This notion of the city in terms of growth and behavior gives the character of order and unity to the many concrete phenomena of the city which otherwise, no matter how interesting, seem but meaningless flotsam and jetsam in the drift of urban life.[10]

This extensive passage summarizes many of Burgess' prejudices toward his predecessors. Beginning with his sarcastic and racist use of the religiously significant Indian term "happy hunting ground," Burgess proceeds to criticize precisely the reform interests and activities of the early sociologists. Small, Zeublin, Addams, and Mead were all involved in the "better-government" movement. Addams was a leader in what was later called the "social-work" movement, in which Henderson and Mead also participated. Henderson worked for the "public health" movement, and Zeublin and Addams specialized in the playground movement. All the early sociologists were involved in the social settlement movement. Finally, Thomas, Mead, and Addams were all concerned with immigrants, and Thomas published a book under the auspices of the Americanization Studies group. It is striking that Burgess omits the juvenile delinquency agencies and their organizational work during this period, the fights against "vice" or prostitution, or the movements affecting changing sexual mores and norms and related to marriage and the family. Each of these latter areas could be called part of a "movement," but they were areas of Burgess' interests. The "vocational education" movement, in which Park was active, was also omitted from attack.

Contrary to Burgess' assertions, there were a multitude of strategies used by the reformer sociologists to deal with urban problems: the collection of massive numbers of statistics, legal analyses, legislative hearings, public protests, large scale institutionalization of agencies and organizations, and considerable alteration of the shape of the city, governmentally, politically, physically, and socially. The major area left unchanged was the economic structure of the city, a topic which when analyzed led to considerable repression of free speech from the university (see chapter 7). Rather than being atheoretical, the early sociologists (not social workers) had a complex theory of social democracy based on liberal and progressive values. Several of the men overlaid this worldview with religious assumptions about behavior.

The early work was never static, or the sociologists would never have engaged in social reform. Stressing organizational and group consciousness, the early sociologists worked with the community as professionals. The city, to them, was an emergent form of behavior characterized by problems and great vitality.

Burgess was building a myth of early Chicago sociologists that disregarded the significant contributions of both men and women. Addams, in particular, was eliminated or downplayed as a significant sociologist in all accounts written by Park and Burgess after 1925.

Burgess and Social Reform Activities

The proposed autobiography of Burgess clearly reveals his dilemma, for Burgess was an active reformer throughout his life. Throughout his career, he acted as the liaison person to place the "scientific" students of the Chicago School in social agencies.[11] While Burgess placed such students, Park promoted the idea that such work was not associated with the settings in which the Chicago faculty and students labored.

Although the extensive reform activities of Burgess have never been documented, a few illustrations can be presented. In 1926, for example, Burgess was a member of the Committee of Fifteen, whose purpose was "To aid the public authorities in the enforcement of laws against pandering, and to take measures calculated to prevent traffic in women."[12] Four years later, Burgess was still a member of the board, and their nine-month report stated: "There were 162 commercial vice resorts closed by action of the Committee of Fifteen, in cooperation with the office of the State's Attorney during the first nine months of 1930."[13] Burgess was actively involved with the process of suppressing, not studying, houses of prostitution. This work, moreover, was unsuccessful. As impressive as 162 closings sound, 207 new resorts were opened during the same period.[14] Unlike the early reformers, Burgess was active in a group that changed little, was highly oriented towards control, and did not publish "scientific" analyses of urban problems. It is also revealing that Burgess continued the interests of Addams, Henderson, and Thomas concerning the topic of prostitution. Burgess did not acknowledge this heritage here or elsewhere. Burgess also advocated the adoption of parole procedures, following again a reform advocated by early Chicago sociologists, especially Addams and other Hull-House women.[15]

Finally, Burgess actively worked to establish the Section on Sociology and Social Work in the ASA. This subgroup, however, appointed primarily male sociologists to its committee structure, and the ASA presentations were generally given by men. The committee strove to have a structure permitting the exchange of information, but Burgess and other committee members wanted to "give" the social workers their concepts and knowledge while they would "take" the data collected by the social agencies and workers.[16] This colonization reflected the same "sociological laboratory" debate of the settlement workers and the sociologists of three to four decades earlier.

Thus, Burgess was actively involved in a number of social reform and work issues, but he tried to keep this aspect of his thought segregated from his "sociological" thought. Basing his interests in the same areas as his predecessors, he claimed distinctiveness and originality over the "biases" of the authors of "local studies." His ambivalence toward social reform, moreover, was amplified by Park.

Ernest W. Burgess and Jane Addams

Burgess' relationship to Addams reveals a strong shift in her collegial status with Chicago sociologists. Again, the conflict he felt between reform versus scientific sociology appears. For Burgess, the division between social work and sociology was at first blurred and only subsequently distinct. It was unlikely, for example, that he viewed his residency at Hull-House originally as at odds with his sociology.

He probably worked frequently with Addams on his many projects involving social agencies and community programs in Chicago.[17] Unfortunately, few records of this affiliation network are documented at this time.[18] One of the few references to their joint efforts is mentioned in a 1925 correspondence between Burgess and William Healy, then Director of the Judge Baker Foundation in Boston. Burgess noted that he had spoken with Addams about a "Mr. Bryon," probably William Bryon, a sociology graduate student who worked and lived at Hull-House in the 1920s. Burgess wanted Addams to help Bryon in "getting some relief from the obstacles which interfere with the completion of his work."[19]

Although there is little personal information available on Burgess, he did write a remarkable poem of admiration and inspiration concerning Jane Addams.[20] This poem was inspired by Burgess' reading of Graham Taylor's eulogy to her in the *Survey Graphic*.[21] Burgess hoped to have the poem

published in that same journal as well as in a book of verse he intended to
publish himself. The poem is reprinted here in its entirety.

To Jane Addams

Jane Addams, mother of the poor and helpless,
And of all humanity; loved and worshipped
By me, a youth in far-off Oklahoma,
Torn by conflicting impulses. You kindled
Into flame my dreams of service for mankind.
A graduate student, later, in Chicago,
On one not-to-be-forgotten afternoon,
I heard you tell of Tolstoi and world peace.
Years after, your dinner guest at Hull-House, I,
Tongue-tied and inarticulate, could not speak
Of my love and reverence. We talked of many things,
Great topics, but small to me in your presence.
Lady of Hull-House, hostess to the stranger;
As a tiny girl you drove through Freeport's slums.
You asked your father, Lincoln's friend, "Why do people
Live in shanties?" "Because they have no money."
"When I'm a grown-up lady I'm going to live
In a great big house, but it won't be near
Other nice ones. I'm going to live right next door
To the poor, and have children play in my yard"
The world was drawn there, to see and talk with you.
Prince Kropotkin, Altgeld, John Burns, Breshkovska,
The high and low knocked at your door and entered.
Jane Addams, supporter of every good cause;
But greater than any cause that you espoused;
You, like Lincoln, transcended institutions;
You rose beyond the confines of time and place.
Nothing human was alien to you; you proved
Our common humanity. Great neighbor
Of the poor, rarely gifted in sympathy,
You knew intuitively that one learns more
From others than one can ever teach them.
Beloved by the immigrant because you listened
To his tale, then proffered aid. Interpreter,
You told his story to the wise and powerful.
Jane Addams, inspirer to dreams and great tasks,
Graham Taylor went forth from your side to found
Chicago Commons, to enthuse theologians
With social purpose, to fight 'gainst civic wrongs.
Mary McDowell left to live Back of the Yards,
Champion of those who had no other champion.
Julia Lathrop, to head the Children's Bureau;
Florence Kelley, to defend the toiler;
Edith Abbott, to train youth for social work;
Sophonisba Breckinridge, to right old wrongs;
Grace Abbott, Robert Lovett, James Weber Linn,

And Hundreds more were fired to serve mankind.
Oft have I studied your face, striving to catch
The secret of your personality.
The look of brooding in your eyes, compassion
For man's inhumanity to man; patience
To wait for centuries till your dreams come true.
The spirit of friendship that illuminates
Your countenance and causes all to love you.
Friendship is, I think, the secret of your power.
You learned not to feel anger nor resentment;
For understanding all, you forgave all. You
Knew why King Lear's daughters were unfilial,
Why Pullman was outraged when his men struck:
"While he cultivated the noble impulses
Of the benefactor, the power of friendship
Went from him." "'Twas that word 'with' from Jane Addams,"
Explained a working-woman, "that took the sting
Out of my life. If I could work with her,
It gave my life new hope and meaning." "Is not,"
Queried Taylor, "the hope of democracy
In that word 'with'? Honored in death, you were attacked
In life. The Red Network, *roll of honor*
Of those who have kept faith (my name is there, though
Under served) named you our leader in the fight.
Jane Addams, you are now with the immortals!
Your spirit stays to bless our thought and work.
Magnanimous, returning good for evil,
With the dignity of humility. I
Recall that great dinner some eight years ago,
The memorable tributes: the President
Sent a glowing message, William Allen White
And others praised you far beyond the mead of
Mortal men. All wondered how you would respond.
"I cannot recognize the one described here;
I know it is not I." The spell was broken,
And you spoke simply to us, as friend to friend.

In this ode to Addams, he clearly acknowledges her preeminence and influence on his work and thought. This eulogy is, however, one that admires Addams' "womanly" strengths of compassion and goodness and her leadership of women "social workers." The words do not convey admiration of a great intellectual colleague; a person who could combine systematic analysis with personal greatness. Instead, this paean of praise is from a man who saw the ideal of traditional womanhood embodied in Addams, not the ideal of a scholar, sociologist, or the equal to men. Addams is on a pedestal, above the common thinking of "mere male sociologists." He ridiculously credits her with knowing she will found a social settlement as a child. He glosses over her struggles, conflicts, and victories to generate a coherent approach to study the social order and change it.

Burgess' ideas of women and social reform versus his own work as a sociologist created this image of "St. Jane" with its concomitant recognition of her significance as a "womanly" leader. Within this restricted vision, Addams influenced Burgess. The editor of *HH Maps and Papers*, empirical scientist, and critical pragmatist does not appear in his vision.

Park and Social Reform

Park was virulent in his dislike of social reform. This antipathy, however, is paradoxical given his own work in social reform. Because he is the only male sociologist studied here who was outspokenly opposed to social reform, his antireform stance is examined first and in depth. Then evidence documenting his reform interests and work is presented to reveal his contradictory behavior in light of his expressed opposition. Park was central in influencing later sociologists' views on the value of social reform. The consistent interpretation that after 1920 the Chicago School underwent a dramatic paradigm shift is deeply rooted in the distorted vision of Park. His derogatory attitude toward the applied roots of Chicago Sociology profoundly influenced Burgess and their students. Simultaneously, Park advocated reform interests and practices in his own life. This anomalous position must be explained to understand the decline of Addams and most of the work of the early men of the Chicago School in the eyes of contemporary sociologists.

Park and Anti-Reform

The first indications of Park's strong antireformism appeared in 1893 when he was a reporter in Detroit. In a condescending and bitter passage, Park wrote Clara Cahill, who later became his wife, that women reformers were ridiculous and misguided.[22]

Again and again this theme of antagonism toward "do-gooders" runs through his correspondence, teaching, and writings. "More than once he drove students to anger or tears by growling such reproofs as 'You're another one of those damn do-gooders.'"[23] In an undated leter, Rauschenbush (Park's biographer and assistant) quoted Park as writing:

> In developing the techniques of sociology we must escape both *HISTORY* and *PRACTICAL APPLICATIONS*. . . . The first thing you have to do with a student who enters sociology is to show him that he can make a contribution if he doesn't try to improve anybody. . . . The trouble with our sociology in America is that it has had so much to do with churches and preachers [italics in original].[24]

Furthermore, in an astonishing phrase, Park noted that "A moral man cannot be a sociologist."[25] Finally, one obituary of Park stated that if Park was intolerant of anybody, he was intolerant of reformers.[26]

He had a consistent, dramatic policy of great hostility toward the application of sociology. He had an established program of changing the views of his students, reinterpreting the contributions of early sociologists, and changing the direction of the discipline. Park employed the rhetoric of "objectivity" and "science," ambivalently used by Small in conjunction with his reform interests, to strip away the linkages between theory and application. The kernel for such distortion lay in the separate sexual division of labor, also associated with the divisions between "general" and "practical" sociology. But it was Park who made the complete severance and devaluation. The possible origins of this ideology are worth considering.

One explanation for this paradoxical antireform stance is Park's extreme ambivalence towards his own interests in reform. While he denigrated such commitments, his own career reflected a dramatic swing between opposition to reform and active engagement in it. This vacillation is examined more fully later in this chapter.

Another explanation of Park's hostility, compatible with the above, is that he felt extremely marginal to the early sociologists and was angered by their lack of acceptance of him. It is quite logical to assume that his six years within the Department of Sociology as an underpaid temporary instructor made him a "marginal man." This concept developed by him argues that those outside of a group gain special insights and strengths as sociologists.[27] He made extreme professional and financial sacrifices to remain in sociology during this period while others, including Edith Abbott and Sophonisba Breckinridge, held full-time positions.

This leads to a third possible reason for Park's ideology: his hostility to women in general and to Abbott and Breckinridge in particular. As noted in chapter 8, Park was strongly antifeminist. This stance, moreover, affected his acceptance of women as colleagues. For example, in 1921 Park was active in organizing panels of speakers for the ASS meetings. At that time, Ethel Sturgess Dummer wrote to him concerning past difficulties in getting men at these meetings to address issues of concern to her and other women. She asked him if a women's panel could be organized to discuss these topics of interest to women.[28] In his response, Park made an interesting correction in word choice. First, he wrote: "I want to assure you that the matter of sex is not considered in science." As an afterthought, Park penned in ink "except as a matter for investigation."[29] He concluded by saying, "We are eager to hear from anyone who has a contribution to make." Park obviously felt, upon reflection, that his original comment about sex not being considered in science was open to misinterpretation. Presumably, he meant to imply that science and truth are sex blind, that *even* women were welcome to speak if they had a "contribution to make". On the other hand, Park may have meant, perhaps subconsciously, that matters related to sex were not proper subjects for scientific investigation. The record demonstrates that Park did not study women, at least the study of women and women's issues are not found in his published writings in sociology. Park's students generally neglected the female half of the population in their massive volumes of sociological work. (The only book in the series that focused on women was written by Frances Donovan, a Chicago high-school teacher. She obtained a bachelor's degree from the University of Chicago in 1918 and was not a student of Park. He did, however, write the introduction to her book.) This lack of analysis of women's place in society represented a 180-degree turn from the tradition of studying women that was espoused by many of Park's predecessors, both male and female. So what can be made of Park's penned-in addition in his letter to Dummer? At best, he was magnanimously condescending to the contribution of women to science. At worst, and perhaps most revealing, he was momentarily confronted by the reality of his own deep neglect of women as a fit subject of study in sociology.

Park's relations with Abbott and Breckinridge were strained, although the nature of their deep fissure is difficult to trace and document. In interviews with the present author, three sociolgists who had graduated from the University of Chicago prior to 1935 remarked on Park's strong and active animosity to Abbott's and Breckinridge's research. All three requested that their names be witheld in conjunction with this information. All three vaguely alluded to fear of losing friendships and "face" if it were known that they had talked about this subject. Winifred Rauschenbush, Park's long-time assistant and biographer, was the only person who willingly stated publicly that such an estrangement existed. In correspondence with this author, she wrote that in an early draft of her biography on Park she had documented this conflict. She had removed this section, however, because she had been strongly advised to do so by unnamed persons.[30] The pressure to keep this information private was also evident when a noted sociologist and friend of Park's (whom this author decided should remain anonymous) wrote the author that "it was better to let sleeping dogs lie" rather than "stir up trouble." He subsequently told me I would be blackballed in sociology if I asked questions about the relations between Park, Abbott, and Breckinridge.

Fortunately, such control over relevant information is diminishing. Evidence of Park's conflicts with Abbott and Breckinridge can be found in the rich interviews conducted by James Carey with early University of Chicago sociology students. Laura Pederson noted that opportunities for women students were more limited than those available to men. She continued: "They [the other students] said that Park didn't like women at all."[31] Ruth Newcomb recalled that "They [the male sociologists in the 1920s] had some arguments with Sophonisba Breckinridge who was in social welfare. I don't remember just how those arguments went. But I was aware that they were having little disputes."[32] Harriet Mowers had a different interpretation of the conflict. In response to a question asking whether such divisiveness existed, she answered, "Absolutely." However, she attributed the problem to the women at SSA and not to the men in sociology: "The SSA at Chicago Social Service Administration did all they could to cause trouble as far as sociology is concerned."[33] Similarly, Robert Faris noted that an estrangement occurred between Park and Breckinridge, although the latter liked his father Ellsworth L. Faris.[34]

It is clear from all accounts that there was animosity between Breckinridge and Park, and to some extent between Abbott and Park. There is also evidence that the two women became hostile to sociology as a discipline.[35] Given their treatment in the department and Park's attitudes toward social reform, such an angry response is understandable and predictable. Thus, it is reasonable to conclude that part of Park's distance from reform and application can be attributed to the nature of his interactions with particular personnel, especially women personnel, at the University of Chicago.

The paradox of Park's reform position is also a function of Small's earlier search for respectability. This was amplified through Park's ideological rejection of any moral or community applications. Associating such practical applications of knowledge with "women's work," Park's antifemale and antifeminist stances augmented Small's institutionalization of academic sociology. Finally, Park's personal and historical situation in reference to Breckinridge, Abbott, and the SSA make his strong but contradictory stance more understandable. Nonetheless, for all his conflict and condescension, Park was strongly committed to social reform.

Park's Reform Activities

Everett Hughes, writing in 1950, interpreted Park's commitment to social reform as integral to Park's entire system of thought and action: "It is in a sense, the dialectic of his own life; reform and action as against detached observation; writing the news of the unique event as against the discovery of the eternal theme and process of history; sympathy for the individual man as against concern for the human race."[36]

Carrying out this theme of reform's significance, Park reflected in his autobiography "that with more accurate and adequate reporting of currents the historical process would be appreciably stepped up, and progress would go forward steadily, without the interruption and disorder of depression or violence, and at a rapid pace."[37] Such views are in strong contradiction to those cited in the section above.

In fact, Park felt that his sociological work began when he was a reporter. Such an interpretation reveals the kind of complexity of his relationship to "reform" and "science." For he freely admitted that when he worked as a reporter, both as an undergraduate and for ten years after that, he sought to "reform" the newspaper into something "more accurate and scientific."[38] Thus it appears that Park had a specific idea of what the word "reform" meant, and this unique meaning often referred to the work of others who were interpreted by Park to be moralists. Changes that institutionalized the use of "science" were seen as value-free, "factual" progress.

His initial journalistic career lasted for ten years after his completion of the bachelor's degree, i.e., from 1887 to 1897. He became dissatisfied with newspaper work, however, and returned to the scholarly life. But shortly after returning to college, he tired of the routine there and longed for more "action." When he was subsequently invited to become the secretary of the Congo Reform Association, he accepted. Later, he wrote:

> There were at the time reports of great scandals in the Congo, and the secretary of the Baptist Foreign Missions, Dr. Barbour, wanted someone to help advertise the atrocities in order to prepare for some sort of political action which would insure reform. I was not, at that time, strong for missions, but I undertook the job. Eventually, however, I became interested.[39]

In this position, Park wrote a series of muckraking articles exposing King Leopold of Belgium and his exploitation of the Congolese. He worked with Baptist missionaries and knowingly accepted a "reform" platform, as he did repeatedly throughout his life. Matthews notes that Park felt extreme ambivalence about muckrakers, yet the former cannot fully explain why he adopted this journalistic style.[40] Indeed, Park's stance is fundamentally ambiguous.

Rather than seeing this early newspaper work as something to be denied or segregated from his sociological endeavors, Park saw great continuity:

> According to my earliest conception of a sociologist he was to be a kind of super-reporter, like the men who write for *Fortune*. He was to report a little more accurately, and in a manner a little more detached than the average, what my friend Franklin Ford called the "Big News." The "Big News" was the long time trends which recorded what is actually going on rather than what, on the surface of things, merely seems to be going on.[41]

Park's selection of *Fortune* magazine as an example of "sociologically similar" work is very revealing. This magazine represented powerful business interests, not an "objective" position. The "superreporter" image is embedded in obligations to a particular community, the elites.

But even this depiction of Park's relation to reform is too simple, for Park was involved throughout his life in several major reform activities that aided Black people and the poor. In his capacity as Booker T. Washington's secretary, Park worked towards increased educational opportunities for Blacks. Although Park's students portray a rosy picture of his influence on Washington, Stanfield's recent scholarship has called these interpretations into question. Instead of Park being a "ghostwriter" who sustained Washington, Stanfield documents that "Booker T. Washington, through his sponsorship of Robert E. Park, was a founder of the Chicago school of race relations."[42] Stanfield documents Park's anxiety, insecurity, and financial dependence upon Washington, as well. Despite Stanfield's serious critique of Park's role at Tuskegee and the sociological myths surrounding it, Park was concerned with civil rights for Blacks. This commitment is visible in his role as president of the Chicago Urban League years after he left Tuskegee.

An excellent example of Park's complex—if not paradoxical—stance toward the poor, liberal social reform, and conservative politics can be found in his work on the Chicago Commission of Race Relations. The Commission, which was "established to study the race riot of 1919," was profoundly influenced by Park and his students. The riot itself was a bloody battle that started on the Chicago beaches when an ugly crowd of White bathers attacked two young Black men who had inadvertently crossed the "water line" into the White bathing area. One of the Black men was killed by the mob and the other was severely injured. Interracial fighting continued in the city streets for days. The liberal stance of the committee favored integration both racially and economically. But these ideals were not augmented by any concrete policy recommendations for their realization. Such a fatal flaw characterized Park's reform efforts. Carey evaluated the results of the commission's work as follows:

> The Chicago Commission of Race Relations, as an experiment in sociology-policy-making partnership, was a failure, if implementation of recommendations is the measure. Yet its report provided a model for the monographs written during the 1920s and early 1930s in presenting an integrated sociological perspective, in having a group of influential civic leaders commission the research, and in framing the recommendations a specific way.[43]

Carey is correct in saying that this report exemplified those that occurred after it,[44] but he is incorrect in attributing the juncture of sociological perspectives with influential civic commissions as a new experiment. All the early Chicago sociologists engaged in these activities. The distinctiveness lay in (1) the divorce of policy planning from social action and (2) the development of a more conservative stance initiated by Park's particular reform activities.

After Park retired from the University of Chicago, he joined the faculty at Fisk University, albeit on an intermittent basis, from 1936 to 1944.[45] Still committed to the Black movement, he did not identify his interests as "social reform."

Park was also president of the National Community Center Association from 1922 to 1924. This group tried to increase democratic involvement in urban life, a goal of the early sociologists.[46] He also helped to found Park House in 1924, although Rauschenbush noted: "His interest in the youth center mystified some of his friends. Had he, who detested do-goodism, himself become a do-gooder? They were also baffled by his attitude toward the religious tone of the enterprise."[47] As a board member, "Park spent a good deal of time there; it had for him the attraction that 'doing good' was combined with, or possibly masked by, an intellectual rationale and the opportunity to meet interesting people of a mildly bohemian character."[48] This Park House was a type of intellectual center for working-class people and was clearly built on the social settlement model.

Park House, however, never assumed an important role in the city, and it was ignored by the University of Chicago community. "The main attraction of the center seems to have been the opportunity to make friendships; the most successful activity was folk dancing, which seems to have served the same function as a T-group in lowering the inhibitions and defenses of middle-class males."[49]

Park's life and work were affected by social reform, but he despised this association. Contradicting himself at each step, he wanted people to be more fair and democratic, while at the same time wanting to disassociate himself with activities demanding such changes. Egocentric,[50] brusque, cantankerous, and charismatic, Park profoundly embodied the conflicts of the new sociology. He legitimized a conservative political role for sociologists and left a legacy to future sociologists who worked to maintain the staus quo while mildly condemning it. The "tragic paradox" plaguing Small was also characteristic of Park: an unacknowledged heritage of ambivalence in sociological thought and action.

Robert E. Park and Jane Addams

The distance between the early and later Chicago School is remarkable. Park epitomized the greatest distance. Although he did credit *HH Maps and Papers* as significant in his coursework and noted it briefly in one article, Park thought of himself as a professional distinctly different from Addams. Like Burgess, Park admired Addams within a restricted vision of female professionals. Rauschenbush, Park's late biographer and assistant, wrote the present author that "Park's daughter, Margaret Park Redfield, told me that Park admired Jane Addams very much. He admired anyone who accomplished anything real."[51] Thus, Addams was held in high regard, but this was not blended with a "professional" respect. This separation of reform and sociology also appears in Park's hostility toward Edith Abbott and Sophonisba Breckinridge.

When Ethel Sturgess Dummer, the first head of the family section in the ASS, wanted to have Addams as the major speaker for the 1922 meetings, Park responded: "It would be fine if Miss Addams could be induced to preside at the meeting when your program is presented. I [sic] would certainly add distinction to the program, and anything she had to say would be listened to by the whole country with interest and respect."[52] Again, this appears to be a situation where it is hard to interpret what Park meant. Did he really mean that he would add distinction to Addams' presentation? Or, more likely, is this yet another evidence of a typographical error when he intended to write that Addams' presence and not his would lend distinction to the session? It must be added that his correspondence does not appear to be replete with such Freudian slips. Park distinctly wrote in another passage of the letter that he and Mr. Eliot, a Northwestern University professor of sociology, should be associated with the program. This was needed to make the session "conform to the program of the other sections." Clearly, he wanted a more male and "sociological" influence to appear in conjunction with her work. He did not want to actively work with Addams, however, so he added that his connection would be purely formal and not an active one.[53]

No evidence of a close relationship between Park and Addams was found by this researcher. Those few indications of his contacts with her reveal only a peripheral involvement. Given their shared interest in Blacks and social settlements, they may have crossed paths on occasions which have yet to be documented. Given their even greater mutual concern with the study of urban life, it is hard to imagine them not having had a great deal in common. Nonetheless, Park's animosity to Addams' close friends and colleagues Abbott and Breckinridge would have been a barrier to their establishing a relationship. Park's strong rhetoric against social reform would have been yet another hurdle. Finally, Addams, the cultural feminist, stood for a number of ideas and ideals that Park vehemently denied. Whatever additional evidence may be garnered concerning their mutual influence and regard, it is safe to say that Park did not advance an understanding of Addams as a sociologist in his writings or professional life.

Park and Burgess as Colleagues

The close interaction between Park and Burgess is well documented. Coauthors of several influential books, coeducators of a series of students who subsequently assumed leadership roles in sociology, and the major acknowledged leaders of the Chicago School of Sociology, they were clearly major influences on each other. Park is usually described as the more dominant personality and leader while Burgess was the more careful and plodding partner.

Historical accounts of the development of the Chicago School after 1920 depend primarily upon Park's and Burgess' own writings and that of their later colleagues and students. In addition to Park and Burgess, the authors of books and articles who are frequently cited as reliable resources on and major interpreters of the Chicago School of Sociology include the following: Robert E.L. Faris, their student and the son of another faculty member, Ellsworth Faris; Morris Janowitz, a student of Burgess and a faculty member in his own right; Everett C. Hughes, a student of Park and Burgess who was related by marriage to Park and a subsequent member of the faculty; James F. Short, trained by Janowitz and yet another faculty member; Kimball Young, a student of the early Chicago men, including Thomas and Park; and Donald Bogue, a student of Burgess and again, another faculty member. Therefore, the influence of Park and Burgess on the interpretation of their work and era is particularly direct. These authors published works, moreover, were primarily published through the University of Chicago Press which provided an institutional support for elaborating and perpetuating a heroic view of their living faculty, successful students, and "scientific" Chicago School of Sociology. The foundation of these writings has been even further buttressed over the last twenty years through the Heritage of Sociology Series, edited by Morris Janowitz. Although over thirty titles on sociologists' lives and writings have been published in this series, women sociologists have yet to be included as subjects of the texts. Many Chicago faculty and students have been involved as subjects or editors in the series, so there are few accounts of the development of Chicago Sociology that have been written by sociologists that challenge the in-house view of the originality and vitality of the Chicago School headed by Park and Burgess.

Given this extensive and authoritative evidence of Park's and Burgess' collaboration, it is clear that they worked to establish a powerful and important vision of sociology. Their work has been shown here to be highly dependent on that of a number of other early sociologists. The role these latter men and women played in the development of the Chicago School of Sociology has been neither well delineated nor understood in the selective accounts of the historical development of sociology. The importance of women, especially Addams, in its establishment and maintenance, and the role of sexism in erasing or modifying the contributions of women to the development of sociology are all influences on the work of Park and Burgess that have been long overlooked.

Mead and Thomas on Social Reform Versus Park and Burgess

Mead and Thomas generated a strong theoretical basis for symbolic interaction, later selectively adopted by Park and Burgess. Park, in particular, claimed to have a close relationship to Thomas, although this friendship may have been more strained than Park admitted, as discussed in the next chapter. Burgess had taken coursework from Mead, so he claimed continuity between their work.

It was the "religious men" discussed in chapter 4 who were the most problematic to Park and Burgess. Rather than confront this conflict or shift in thought from Christian to secular, Park and Burgess attributed "religiosity" to "social workers" who were female and "unscientific."

Using rhetoric of ridicule and condemnation, Park and Burgess tried to segregate their thought from that of their male and female predecessors. Claiming to be influenced primarily by Mead and Thomas, they severed the latter men's work from that of the other early sociologists. Since Mead and Thomas were still writing and professionally active in the 1920s, this appears plausible. Much of their work, however, was developed in an earlier era and founded on social reform activities and the hopes of the progressive era.

In the process of disassociating Mead and Thomas from their work in social reform or "applied sociology," the commonality underlying their writings was erased and obscured. Similarly, Park and Burgess lived with an ambivalent commitment to social reform, trying to redefine the field as one of "social policy" characterized by "abstract, apolitical" analysis. The city as a focus for study derived from the heritage of the early sociologists, including the more "religious" ones and the basically "secular" work of Addams and the women of Hull-House. Abbott and Breckinridge, in particular, signified a way of working and thinking that aroused the ire of Park. A deep antagonism developed between them, and a subsequent division of labor occurred: sociology as a male discipline and social work as a female discipline. Park and Burgess, then, mark an important turning point for the early men of the Chicago School. The relations between them and the entire male group, can now be summarized.

Conclusion

The Chicago Men and Social Reform

This chapter and the previous two have documented the role of social reform in the early male Chicago School. Because of reform's centrality to the discipline, the ties between Addams and these men were fundamental to the development of sociology. Addams' role in sociology has been neglected partially because this vital topic has been consistently overlooked

TABLE 6.2
The Men of the Chicago School and Social Reform

Name	Significance of Social Reform	Areas of Specialization
Small	Central	the economy (Social Welfare State akin to a democratic" Germanic model)
Henderson	Central	the study of deviance, prison reform, social insurance, social hygience, alleviation of unemployment (akin to German and Fabian models)
Zeublin	Central	Fabianism, social settlements
Vincent	Central, prior to 1911	Adult education (Chautauqua)
Thomas	Integral	women, blacks, immigrants, impact of rapid social change, progressive
Mead	Central	education, war, immigrants, labor, science and working hypothesis, progressive
Burgess	Mixed, more positive than negative	delinquency, marriage and the family
Park	Mixed, more negative than positive	blacks, race relations

and even degraded in accounts of the development of sociology. Table 6.2 summarizes the Chicago men's relationships to social reform. The greater conservatism of Small, Vincent, and Henderson can be contrasted with that of Zeublin, Thomas and Mead. Despite their internal differences, these men generated a cohesive pattern of thought and action. Social reform was intrinsic to their conception of sociology. The struggle with "science" and "objective" standards was important to these men, but it was always conducted in the context of ethical concerns. The nature of social knowledge demanded a valid examination of the world, free from biases and corruption, but the purpose of such a study was to return this knowledge to the community. Sociology was part of a cycle of community life.

Park epitomized the problems of working within this model of social action and knowledge. Vacillating between an antireform stance and active commitment to a variety of causes, particularly Black rights, Park's stance wrecked havoc on sociology's relation to everyday life. His deep conflict over social reform, reflected also in the work of Burgess, was a product of numerous causes. In the next two chapters, two primary reasons for their behavior are examined: political repression by the monied elite and hostility toward women as intellectuals. All these factors, including the biographical situations of Park and Burgess, were products of a changing world. World War I devastated the hopes of social reformers and progressives. Park and Burgess worked in a modern society that rejected the optimism of liberals who worked before the Great War. These additional factors are discussed in the final chapter here, but for the present I will continue to study the pre–World War I era.

A common bond between these early men was their faculty status at the University of Chicago. This Department of Sociology was characterized by a particular relationship to social reform, augmenting and amplifying the social concerns of monied elite who financed it.

The Men and Addams as Colleagues

The pattern in collegial relationships between Addams and the Chicago School is marked (see Table 6.3). Small, Henderson, Vincent, and Zeublin (the "religious" men) were frequently close allies of Addams, treating her as a vital leader, although primarily within women's restricted sociological sphere. Since Small, Henderson, and Zeublin also practiced "applied sociology," the areas of specialization of these men and Addams were very similar. The men, however, tended more toward "armchair philosophy" and religious interpretation than did Addams, who worked closely with the empirical studies conducted through Hull-House. This "religious" Chicago School of men was profoundly influenced and closely associated with Addams. They accorded her recognition and respect as a colleague. Both Henderson and Zeublin were also recognized leaders in the social settlement movement.

Mead and Thomas had even more complex and significant relationships with Addams, primarily because of their greater openness toward women as colleagues and professionals. This liberated view, in turn, owed at least part of its development to Addams herself. She illustrated what intellectual women could accomplish. She provided access to empirical data, controversial audiences and speakers, and organizational skills to fight for social change. The work and writings of Mead and Thomas are intimately linked with Addams and she is a central figure in their careers and social thought.

With Burgess and Park, the transition to Addams as a figure of womanly and public leadership, especially of social workers, emerges. Burgess more openly recognized his debt to Addams, but she was once again the "ideal" symbol of a moral order separating men and women. Park afforded her respect as a person but not as a colleague. It is probable, however, that he visited with her on formal occasions and knew of her work.

Addams was integral to the early Chicago men's careers and social thought. Intellectually she was closest to the work of Mead and Thomas and the entire symbolic interaction tradition. Thus, Park and Burgess built

TABLE 6.3
The Chicago Men as Addams' Colleagues

Male Sociologists	Frequency of Contacts with Addams
Small	Frequent visitor, worked with her on at least three reform issues (Civic Federation, 1893 labor legislation) and on 1910 Garment Workers Strike
Henderson	Frequent visitor and worker with reform issues, (few documented other than Addams' acknowledgement at Henderson funeral), joint social settlement issues (Henderson at Chicago Commons and U of C Settlement)
Zeublin	Frequent visitor/associate, one-time Hull-House resident, joint social settlement issues (Zeublin at Northwestern University Social Settlement)
Vincent	Visitor at Hull-House, joint interests in Chautauqua
Thomas	Frequent visitor, life-time friendship, joint issues on women
Mead	Frequent visitor and life-long friendship, joint interest on immigrants, women, labor
Burgess	Some contact, did meet Addams, distant "admirer"
Park	Little if any personal contact, limited recognition of Addams' leadership or significance as sociologist

their work upon her concern with the city, the use of mapping, and her conception of the social development of the individual.

Notes

1. Winifred Rauschenbush, *Robert E. Park: Biography of a Sociologist* (Durham, N.C.: Duke University Press, 1979), p. 182.
2. Burgess File, Taylor Papers, Newberry Library.
3. "The Value of Sociological Community Studies to the Work of Social Agencies," *Social Forces* 8(June 1930):481-91.
4. "Can Neighborhood Work Have a Scientific Basis?" in *The City*, Robert Park, Ernest W. Burgess, and Robert D. McKenzie (Chicago: University of Chicago Press, 1967, c. 1924), pp. 142-55. See also "Research in Urban Society," in Ernest W. Burgess and Donald J. Bogue, eds., *Contributions to Urban Sociology* (Chicago: University of Chicago Press,1964).
5. Burgess, "Can Neighborhood Work Have a Scientific Basis?" p. 142.
6. F.W. Blackmar and Ernest W. Burgess, *Lawrence Social Survey* (Topeka: Kansas State Printing Press, 1917). Burgess also chaired the Central Philanthropic Council Survey Committee which produced *Columbus Pool Rooms: A Study of Pool Halls, Their Uses by High School Boys, and a Summary of Public Billiard and Pool Room Regulations of the Largest Cities in the United States* (Columbus: Central Philanthropic Committee, 1916).
7. Burgess to Taylor, 24 December 1927, Taylor Papers, Newberry Library.
8. James Short, Jr., ed., *The Social Fabric of the Metropolis* (Chicago: University of Chicago Press, 1971), p. xix.

9. See "The Value of Sociological Community Studies to the Work of Social Agencies," *Social Forces* 8 (June 1930):481-91; "Is Prediction Feasible in Social Work?" *Social Forces* 7 (June 1929):533-45. "Protecting the Public by Parole and Parole Predictions," *Journal of Criminal Law and Criminology* 27 (November-December 1926):491-502.

10. Ernest W. Burgess, ed., *The Urban Community*, Selected Papers from the Proceedings of the American Sociological Society, 1925 (Chicago: University of Chicago Press, 1926).

11. James T. Carey, *Sociology and Public Affairs* (Beverly Hills: Sage, 1975), pp. 142-43.

12. The purpose of the organization was stated on its letterhead. See the letter from Leslie Lewis, acting superintendent of the Committee of Fifteen to Ernest W. Burgess, 23 September 1926. Burgess Papers, box 6, folder 6, UCSC.

13. "Report to Directors," Committee of Fifteen, p. 1. Burgess Papers, Box 6, folder 5, UCSC.

14. Ibid., p. 2.

15. Burgess, "Protecting the Public by Parole and by Parole Prediction."

16. See the report of the committee's work in Maurice Karpf, "Sociology and Social Work: A Retrospect," *Social Forces* 6 (June 1928):511-24. For a report on the American Sociological Society meetings from an applied perspective, see Fay B. Karpf, "Sociology, Social Research, and the Interest in Applications: The Washington (1927) Meetings of the American Sociological Society," *Social Forces* 6 (June 1928):521-26. For a similar, but earlier report, see Maurice J. Karpf, "The Relation between Sociology and Social Work," *Social Forces* 3 (March 1925):419-27.

17. Burgess made numerous contacts for his students in local community agencies. This role is discussed in Burgess, "Research in Urban Society," and runs throughout the interviews conducted by Carey, "Sociology Interviews," UCSC.

18. Burgess has massive, unanalyzed papers at the University of Chicago library. Since these are not completely detailed or annotated, such a task would clearly be momentous. A book on Burgess' career is needed and is clearly beyond the scope of this project.

19. Robert E.L. Faris, *Chicago Sociology* (Chicago: University of Chicago Press, 1967), p. 32. Ernest W. Burgess to William Healy, 29 January 1925. Burgess Papers, box 8, folder 10, UCSC.

20. "To Jane Addams" in Burgess Correspondence, Graham Taylor Papers, Newberry Library.

21. Ibid. Graham Taylor's article that inspired the writing of this poem was "Jane Addams: The Great Neighbor," *Survey Graphic* 24 (July 1935):339-41ff.

22. See ch. 8 for a discussion of Park's attitudes toward women and citation of this letter, n. 107.

23. Faris, *Chicago Sociology*, p. 35.

24. Rauschenbush, *Robert E. Park*, p. 97.

25. Ibid.

26. Matthews' citation of a *Chicago Daily News* editorial, p. 17.

27. Robert E. Park, "Cultural Conflict and the Marginal Man," introduction to E.V. Stonequist, *The Marginal Man* (New York: Charles Scribner's Sons, 1937), pp. xiii-xviiii. Reprinted in *Race and Culture*, pp. 372-76.

28. Ethel S. Dummer to Robert E. Park, 5 November 1921. Dummer Papers, folder 699, Schlesinger Library (hereafter referred to as Dummer Papers).

29. Park to Dummer, 10 November 1921. Dummer Papers, folder 699.
30. Winifred Rauschenbush to author, 19 September 1979.
31. Carey Interviews, UCSC. Laura M. Pederson, p. 8, 18 March 1972.
32. Ibid., Ruth Newcomb, p. 16, 22 May 1972.
33. Ibid., Harriet Mowers, Section 2, p. 2, 17 April 1972.
34. Ibid., Robert E.L. Faris, p. 18, 24 May 1972.
35. See comments in Stuart A. Queen, "Seventy-Five Years of American Sociology in Relation to Social Work," *American Sociologist* 16 (February 1981):34-37.
36. Everett Cherington Hughes, "Preface" to Robert Ezra Park, *Race and Culture* (Glencoe, Ill.: Free Press, 1950), p. xiii.
37. Robert Ezra Park, "An Autobiographical Note," in *Race and Culture*, pp. v-vi.
38. Park to Howard Odum, 20 January 1936. Quoted in Rauschenbush, p. 158.
39. Park, "An Autobiographical Note," p. vii.
40. Fred H. Matthews, *Quest for an American Sociology: Robert E. Park and the Chicago school* (Montreal: McGill-Queen's University Press, 1977), p. 60.
41. Park, "An Autobiographical Note," pp. viii-ix.
42. John H. Stanfield, *Philanthropy and Jim Crow in American Social Science* (Westport, Conn.: Greenwood Press, 1985), p. 38.
43. Carey, *Sociology and Public Affairs*, p. 77.
44. Ibid., p. 80.
45. Rauschenbush, *Robert E. Park*, p. 149. Matthews lists Park's tenure as nine years, p. 178.
46. Matthews, *Quest for an American Sociology*, pp. 177-78.
47. Rauschenbush, *Robert E. Park*, p. 147.
48. Matthews, *Quest for an American Sociology*, p. 178.
49. Ibid.
50. Park's autobiographical statement is filled with self-aggrandizement and embarrassingly inaccurate statements, such as: "I expect that I have actually covered more ground, tramping about in cities in different parts of the world, than any other living man." P. viii.
51. Winifred Rauschenbush to author, 19 September 1979.
52. Robert E. Park to Ethel Sturgess Dummer, 28 October 1921, box 699, Dummer Papers.
53. Ibid.

7

Applied Sociology and the Politics of the Academy

Addams' sociology, which had a powerful impact on the community, was politically unacceptable to the academy. To understand the significance of her work and its suppression, the hostility of the university to this type of sociological practice must be documented.

It is evident that the men of the Chicago School used Addams' ideas to form their sociological thought, but they were institutionally bound to the university and not the social settlement. Although many American universities restricted free speech during this era (and today), the University of Chicago and its Department of Sociology have a particularly repressive record.[1] In this chapter, four specific instances of limitations on the Chicago sociologists' right to critique society and social mores are documented. (In addition, women's right to equal education was curtailed, but this is discussed in chapter 8, on the sociology of women.) Each case of restrictions on academic rights related directly to Addams' practice of sociology. Thus, a certain type of sociological work, applied sociology, was excluded from the academy. It was defined as outside the boundaries of the discipline, because sociology became increasingly defined as work done within the academy.

The general problem of academic freedom is briefly addressed below, followed by an analysis of the specific factors operating at the University of Chicago. Then, each of the instances of political suppression is documented with comments on their relation to Addams' ideas and practice of sociology.

Academic Freedom

The right to study a society unrestricted by its social and political mores is a necessary condition for the pursuit of knowledge in any social science. Sociology, in particular, is vulnerable to the problems of alienating vested interests of the community, since the community is the object of study in many sociological analyses. Sociology professors, therefore, have a particularly long record of social conflict. One of the major ways of avoiding this turmoil in the academy was the institutionalization of tenure and academic freedom. Another major way to forestall confrontations between the sociologist and the community was to become less controversial. Both these paths were selected by sociologists, with important consequences on the practice of academic sociology.

Tenure and the Issue of Academic Freedom

In the years studied here, 1892 to 1918, American universities fired a number of professors for their views. As a result, professors banded together and founded the American Association of University Professors (AAUP) to protect themselves. First meeting as a group in 1915, they were only a fledgling organization throughout the era studied here. World War I provided a crucial test for academic freedom, because in 1917 and 1918 a series of professors were fired for their alleged lack of patriotism.[2] The sociologists who were fired or forced to resign from the University of Chicago were part of a long line of professors similarly denied their constitutional rights.

Various reasons for the academy's repressiveness have been offered. Marxist critics interpret the academy as a tool of the monied interests of the community. Thus, the Schwendingers noted that American sociologists who worked in higher education were mainly articulating the hegemony of the ruling class. In a similar vein, Veblen wrote a scathing critique of university administrators as businessmen with little interest in the goals of education or the pursuit of knowledge.[3] But the most thorough analysis of the origins of academic oppression was done by Metzger. Acknowledging the power of the financial and vested interests, he added the factors of bureaucratization and increasing size as pressures on the academy to become more rule-oriented and anonymous. Furthermore, faculty status partially determined the rights to free speech, as well as the specific personalities of the contestants. The style of the conflict is also affected by the practice of the professor's views. The person avowing but not enacting a right is less likely to be punished than one who actually lives such a challenge. All of Metzger's factors are accepted here, including his view that the vested interests of the ruling class are the most powerful factor.[4]

In addition, in the particular case of the University of Chicago, all the people whose rights to free speech were constrained practiced a certain type of sociology. Thus, there was already a class structure within the discipline of "practical" versus "general" sociology, associated with acting on one's views versus merely espousing them. The vested interests of the ruling elite were more openly criticized by the "sociologists in the field" who visibly enacted their opposing views in their daily lives. Bureaucratically, three of the four Chicago sociologists subjected to repression were also outside of the main campus system. Only Thomas was a full faculty member, and his dismissal has never been analyzed as an academic freedom issue.

All these cases of political repression have been explained as outside the substantive concerns of sociologists or the issue of academic freedom in the following ways. (1) Three of the sociologists who are examined here—Bemis, Zeublin, and Addams—are omitted from traditional accounts of the discipline. They are not defined as sociologists. Following this logic, they could not be repressed as sociologists. (2) Chicago sociology and its influence refers only to full-status faculty men working in the Department of Sociology. (3) The only "recognized" sociologist, Thomas has been viewed as one whose rights were restricted because of the sexual mores of the time and his lack of discretion, not because of a political restriction on his right to sexual choice and freedom of speech.

Metzger's analysis of factors fostering academic restraints, then, omits several crucial influences: (1) the class structure of the discipline; (2) the sexual or racial status of the accused; (3) the extension of constraints on rights which occurs through biased accounts of the issues; and (4) the ability of the establishment to control data and interpretations of the cases. These additional constraints on freedom of speech limited faculty activism at the University of Chicago in the Department of Sociology.

Chicago Sociology and Academic Freedom. When it opened in 1892, the leaders of the University of Chicago were eager and determined to become a major intellectual force. They wanted to supersede the Eastern establishments then dominating higher education. In order to do this, they hired people with brains and ambition. Young scholars, in particular, were attracted to a school offering good positions, a beginning departmental base, money, and a chance to "make good" and pursue "new ideas." One way to legitimize this daring new venture in Chicago was to provide service to the community, to visibly aid in community progress. As Diner noted:

> This was not a time for introspection or self-criticism, but an era of growth and experimentation. Nothing in the experience of American universities thus far indicated that public service might harm the university; but the experience of the antebellum college suggested the shortcomings of a remote seminary learning for its own sake.[5]

This spirit of service was augmented at Chicago by its first president; William Rainey Harper, a former principal in the Chautauqua System of Education.[6] Harper was a strong advocate of useful education for the adult community. Simultaneously, he was an ambitious man who wanted to build a strong university. To meet this latter goal he needed money, a lot of money.

The University of Chicago quickly became noted for this dual base: an institution funded by vested elites, particularly Standard Oil money, as well as a daring venture in community education and scholarship. Harper mediated this conflict originally by wanting community activists and changes that were in the forefront of popular sentiment. He did not want radicals, he wanted liberals to articulate the modern thought of the day. This same strain underlies much of the work of Chicago sociologists, particularly Albion Small's. Clearly, the university was on a track leading to conflict. Chicago's business community poured vast sums into the university for the pursuit of knowledge; simultaneously they had strong opinions on what could and could not be written and said about the city. This business elite thought the city could be made more "efficient," more "modern," and in this sense more profitable. Veblen, writing a caustic book on the "conduct of Universities by business men,"[7] using the University of Chicago as its model, noted that

> it should be called to mind that the business men of this country, as a class, are of a notably·conservative habit of mind. In a degree scarcely equalled in any community that can lay claim to a modicum of intelligence and enterprise, the spirit of American business is a spirit of quietism, caution, compromise, collusion, and chicane.[8]

Therefore, the University of Chicago had many of the general problems associated with academic freedom: They were controlled by the monied elite, they were in the process of becoming a bureaucracy, they grew rapidly in size and influence, and they were in a city torn by rapid social change. The university avowed the right to pursue knowledge and to affect the political and social structure of the city at a time when Chicago was undergoing a massive influx of cheap immigrant labor and the rise of new elites.

Both Harper and Small were caught in this vortex of opportunity and power politics. They had a chance to create new institutional structures, but to do so they needed money and legitimation. Acceptance in the community hinged on community leadership and scholarship, and the city itself was in ferment.

Harper's successor, Charles Judson, was even more conservative and conciliatory toward the upper classes. He was more openly hostile to challenges to the status quo and more blatantly flaunted faculty rights. The era of his tenure, from 1906 to 1918, was increasingly conservative as well. Prior to World War I, he had begun the removal of faculty considered "threats" to the community. Even the established White, Protestant males were subject to rapid and unfair dismissals.

Thus, a convoluted pattern of free speech and criticism developed. Chicago sociologists during the first two decades of the university's existence developed a variety of powerful social critiques. These, in turn, came to be discredited as they increasingly threatened the upper classes. Ultimately, Chicago Sociology was severed from its early political stances and controversial studies. By 1918, almost all the early male sociologists had been dismissed, had resigned, or died. Park and Burgess emerged as major figures in the discipline, claiming to be "objective" and distinct from the early "social reformers" who were not true scientists.

Addams was a central figure in this disclaiming process of the roots of American sociology, for she was more radical than any of the men. Below, the specific details of increasing restraints on sociological practice are documented. Even during its most "outspoken" years, the university could not have retained Addams as a sociologist.

The Dismissal of Bemis, 1895

Chicago was the violent center of labor conflicts in the 1880s and 1890's. The site of the tragic Haymarket Riot in 1885, it again became the focus of warring factions with the 1894 Pullman Strike. The dispute arose because George Pullman, the railroad baron, had erected a "model" town for his employees while paying them low wages. The workers rebelled, wanting more humane working conditions and salaries, plus control over their homes and hours after work.

The strike rocked the city. Eugene V. Debs, the socialist union leader, became a recognized national figure as a result of the dispute, and Jane Addams entered the foray, siding with the rights of the workers. Although she had been an associate of Pullman prior to the issue, she wrote a scathing article calling him "A Modern Lear." This article was not published until 1912 because it was deemed too controversial, although Addams delivered it as a speech during the conflict.[9]

At this time, Bemis was a visitor to Hull-House and also sided with labor, albeit in a far more modified and conciliatory manner than Debs or Addams. This lead to his ultimate dismissal from the university, and one of the earliest cases concerning academic freedom in sociology. First, Bemis is introduced, and then the speeches leading to his dismissal are presented. Finally, documentation of the firing process itself and its aftermath is given.

Edward W. Bemis

Bemis had been trained as a political economist/sociologist by Richard Ely,[10] Addams' "sociological grandfather"[11] and Small's mentor. Thus,

Bemis studied the relations between the economic structure and society, sharing many of the assumptions made by Addams and Ely (see chapter 10 below). Each of these sociologists believed in the right of labor to organize, wanted changes in the distribution of ownership of certain industries and utilities, and adopted a generally conciliatory attitude toward the relations between capital and labor. Bemis and Small, however, were more religiously oriented than Ely and Addams.

In an 1892 course on the "Economic Questions of the Day," Bemis included writings by the socialists Beatrice and Sydney Webb, Richard Ely, and Ezra Seligman.[12] Bemis himself was a socialist. He wanted the gas and cognate commodities to be controlled by the government and not private owners. He clearly stated his position in an 1891 article, prior to his employment at the university in 1892.[13] Since Standard Oil money backed the University of Chicago, it is not surprising that conflict about Bemis would soon be generated.

By the summer of 1893 Bemis had so angered one gas magnate that the latter said: "If we can't convert you, we are going to down you. We can't stand your writing—it means millions to us."[14]

> The threat made to Bemis in the summer of 1893 was not an idle one. The first action taken to remove Bemis occurred that summer when the university's customary reduction in gas rates was disallowed by President Billings, then president of the so-called Chicago gas trust, which was then controlled by the Standard Oil Company. The second action consisted of direct persuasion to influence the University authorities to release Bemis.[15]

Although originally hired to teach in University Extension and Political Economy, in the summer of 1893 the head of the latter department asked that Bemis be removed from his staff. It was at this time that Bemis joined the Sociology Department. Unfortunately, his enrollments in the Extension Division declined in the Fall of 1893, and in January 1894, President Harper asked for his resignation. In his missive, Harper alluded to his hiring Bemis against the judgements of others. He bluntly stated that Bemis' extension work was a "failure" and with the "peculiar circumstances" at Chicago, Bemis could do better at another institution.[16] Harper wanted to "help" Bemis find alternative employment and to distinguish his personal response to Bemis from his professional one.

Bemis refused to resign, and he believed that his difficulties had been somewhat eased.[17] This was a short-lived peace. In July 1894, during the Pullman Strike, Bemis wrote Harper that he had heard "second-hand" that the trustees were displeased with his activities. He defended himself by noting that he urged Debs, as well as Gompers and several other union leaders, not to strike. When he was unsuccessful in preventing the strike, he felt his efforts were still not inflammatory:

> In every way have I tried to calm the troubled waters while making use of the opportunity to urge upon larger employers a conciliatory Christ-like attitude and the recognition of the trusteeship of wealth as suggested in the parable of the ten talents and endorsed by modern philosophy.[18]

This plea for understanding went unheard, for in August, 1895, Bemis was terminated at the university. This led to a series of vitriolic newspaper attacks. Bemis claimed that his rights of free speech had been violated and the university initially remained silent. Cries of outrage against such oppression arose in a variety of national periodicals.[19]

Finally, on 11 October Harper made his first public statements.[20] Subsequently more explicit statements were advanced by Albion W. Small and Nathaniel Butler, head of the Extension Division who publicly supported the firing and labeled Bemis an incompetent.[21]

Small's Role in the Dismissal

Repeatedly, Small appears as a liberal whose behavior was subverted by his conservative allegiance to the administration and his search for academic "legitimacy."[22] This character flaw is painfully evident in the Bemis case. For example, in an undated newspaper article, Bemis told the press that as of August 1895, the "head of the sociological department had, almost to the very end, pleaded for my retention."[23] Nonetheless, as the head of sociology, Small coauthored with the head of the Extension Division (Nathaniel Butler) a statement denying Bemis' right to protest his treatment by the university This statement was crucial to Bemis' academic career and its untimely end. A most telling indication of the nastiness of the fight is revealed by examining an early draft of this paper. Wherever Bemis was originally referred to by the title "Professor," this word was systematically crossed out in pencil and the title "Mr." substituted.[24] Therefore, this shred of collegiality was denied Bemis, and all published versions of the statement referred to him throughout as "Mr."

The public statement consists of twelve points refuting Bemis' position. The authors categorically denied that he was part of the larger faculty, and stated that he was not drawing enough students for his extension courses.[25] The two authors supported the president's decision that Bemis should go to another institution where he would not have to face the harsh judgements of the general public. Clearly, the initial points raised by Small and Butler all indicated a lack of competence, while the enrollment figures did not support their assertions. (After a low enrollment in the Fall of 1894, the figures began to meet and even exceed minimal standards.) Bemis had offered courses on the general campus, and Harper had admitted to Bemis in the letter of January 1894, that he had been considered originally for inclusion in the general faculty.[26]

Small, in particular, was involved in rejecting his full-time appointment to the Department of Sociology and clearly cites incompetence as the reason: "In attempting to be judicial he succeeded in being only indefinite. Instead of erring by teaching offensive views, the head and front of his offending was that he did not seem to present any distinct views whatever."[27] Citing their "friendly feelings," Small and Butler wrote that they regretted making their views public. They felt that the indiscretion of Bemis, i.e., fighting the dismissal publicly, led to this public denunciation.[28]

An appended note to the statement, dated 16 October 1895 and signed by Harper, attests to the validity of the views of Small and Butler. This was "necessary" because, according to Harper, "The proofs of the statement [intended only for Trustees] were stolen from the University printing office and given to the public. The employee who committed the theft has been discovered and discharged."[29] Thus, with the "leak," Harper, Small, and Butler united in a public stance averring that Bemis was incompetent. This was published in newspapers across the nation.

Although prior to the statement by Small, the sociologists/ economists E.A. Ross, Richard Ely, and John R. Commons had come to the defense of Bemis, the stature and power of Small dispelled many of their criticisms and doubts. Small's role was crucial in redefining the situation. Instead of being seen as political repression of free speech, it was reinterpreted as an "apolitical" issue of incompetence.[30]

There are at least two more indications that Small played a role in a conspiracy to get rid of Bemis. In one passage of his and Butler's statement, they defended Harper by saying that the president "only" wanted to limit Bemis in his speeches as a lecturer before a public, "promiscuous" audience. They were referring here to a prounion speech given in a Presbyterian Church during the Pullman Strike.[31] In a subsequent letter to Harper, Small wrote from Biddeford, Maine, that "At this distance it seems . . . clear that the Bemis case would have been bungled if you had given the papers more than you did. Denial that it had any connection with a principle of freedom was enough and it has been impertinence in the papers to ask for more."[32] Thus, it appeared from his interpretation of Harper's role and his congratulatory tone that they acted in collusion concerning Bemis. This is an unsavory reflection on them both.

The Consequences of the Dismissal

After being terminated at Chicago, Bemis was "politely" blackballed by Harper. In August 1895, Bemis wrote Ely:

> If I had evidence of Harper's directly attacking me the way would be plain, but he is likely to speak well of my character and work but shrug his shoulders and express the hope to other presidents "Try him." I hope you will like him (or get along with him) better than we did.[33]

But as noted above, Harper and others did become more "open" in their criticisms and Bemis was basically "finished" as an academic sociologist. Although he was able to procure a position at the Kansas State Agricultural College for a brief period, in 1899 he was dismissed under similar controversial charges. Bemis never held another academic position again.[34]

From 1901 until 1909, he was the superintendent of the water department in Cleveland. Appointed by a reform mayor, Tom L. Johnson, Bemis was able to work for a public utility, but in a less effective position to critique the oil and gas industries than he had earlier. From 1913 to 1923, Bemis was a member of the Advisory board of the Valuation Bureau of the Interstate Commerce Commission. He died in 1930.[35]

Addams' Relation to the Bemis Controversy

Clearly, Addams was a more vocal and radical leader of the workers during the Pullman Strike than Bemis. As author of "A Modern Lear" and a participant in the arbitration process itself, Addams had a key role in the conflict.[36]

Bemis, too, was a visitor to Hull-House during this period, so it is evident that Addams sided with his views, except that her own were more openly critical of the Pullman community and its goals.[37] Again, there is dramatic evidence that Addams and the university did not share basic assumptions about the nature of free speech and social change. This divergence in opinion and practice was even clearer in reference to her own ideas.

Denying Addams an Honorary Degree, 1906 (?), 1916

Addams was consistently too radical for the trustees of the University of Chicago, and this divergence in views increased from the founding of the university in 1892 until the end of World War I in 1918. Her unacceptability was evident in 1916 and perhaps also in 1906, when the faculty voted to bestow an honorary degree on Addams but their recommendation was turned aside by the trustees. Since these votes were "in-house," they were never made public. Only two references, supposedly documenting two different instances of the same type of trustee control, have been uncovered. Addams' biographer, nephew, and faculty member, James Weber Linn, gave one account of a faculty vote occurring in 1906 which was subsequently overturned by the Trustees:

In the early days of "Doctor Harper's Bazaar," as the University was often called, she was reproached by her "radical" friends for connecting herself however remotely with such a backward institution. But fifteen years later, when the professors of the University voted to confer on her an honorary degree, the conservative successor to Doctor Harper i.e., Judson, and his cautious board of trustees, declined to confirm the action. Professors Albion W. Small and George Herbert Mead, who in the fullness of their enthusiasm had neglected formalities and notified Jane Addams of the professorial vote, were forced to go to Hull House and with tears in their eyes explain the situation and apologize for the administration. It was to be more than twenty years from that time before the administration did confirm the early action of the faculty, and offer her a degree. She took it with one regret—that Professor Small could not know of it.[38]

This rather lengthy account is one of the rare references to this action.[39] Fortunately, however, it reveals the cast of characters relevant to the sociological drama at Chicago. It is evident that both Small and Mead wanted Addams to receive an honorary doctorate and they were probably active in obtaining the faculty vote for granting such a degree. Again, Small is revealed as a person who could be more "radical" than the university administration but acquiesced to the demands for legitimacy made by the business-minded president and trustees. Similarly, Addams' strong association with Small was uppermost in her mind when she did receive an honorary doctorate from the university in 1931.

In 1916, a similar incident occurred (or perhaps Linn was in error in his recording the fifteen-year interval). At this time, the university was celebrating its twenty-fifth anniversary and a gala convocation was planned. When the Trustees rejected the faculty's recommendation, James Tufts, chair of the Philosophy Department, wrote to Marion Talbot of his discouragement and ineffectual distress. This letter, too, is worthy of lengthy notice:

I have about concluded that I would not care personally to stir up the honorary degree situation. I do not expect now to recommend anybody and was disgusted with the whole method in which the Trustees treated the Senate's recommendations. . . . Personally I feel that for the University to confer honorary degrees after refusing the degree to Miss Addams is a stultifying performance, but the University has done a great many stultifying things and probably will continue. Still I consider that on the whole it is gradually contributing through its teaching to make this kind of thing less likely in the next generation.[40]

Chiding himself for his "moral cowardice or a half-hearted expediency," it appears that Talbot wanted to organize a protest against the trustees' actions. She did not do so and it is likely that frustration and not protestation was the usual response for faculty who remained at the university. Since these two references are the only evidence of the trustees' denial of faculty votes concerning Addams' honorary degree, it is possible that they refer to only one incident which was remarkably similar. Perhaps, too, this sorry event was repeated at two momentous occasions revealing the deep antipathy between the university's elite and Addams' sociological practice.

Whether one incident or two, this incident dramatically shows that Addams could not have been on the staff of the university and retained her ideas and leadership without considerable harassment and disapproval from the University of Chicago.

The nature of the relationship between Addams and the University of Chicago is crucial to understanding her role in sociology there. It cannot be stressed too strongly that Addams was effectively barred from recognition of her sociological leadership because of the limits on faculty activism embedded in the university structure. By the time that Addams was once again a "restored saint" she had travelled far from her early ties with sociologists at Chicago and her erasure as a sociologist of eminence was already firmly established.

"Resignation" of Zeublin, 1908

Addams and Zeublin shared a number of political positions and academic interests (see chapter 4). Like Addams, Zeublin favored more control for the workers and a more "democratic" government. These positions on social order and its control were the subject of many of his lectures and writings. Moreover, because his salary was so low at the Extension Department, he augmented his earnings by being a paid popular lecturer.[41] These latter speeches often drew public attention, much to the chagrin of the University of Chicago.

On 6 August 1906, the first mild reprimand to Zeublin is found in President Judson's correspondence. Judson had denied to the press that Zeublin had made a certain statement prior to contacting Zeublin. Judson was "gratified to see, however, that the reputable papers of Chicago responded to a correct attitude."[42] If this were the only reproof, such an incident could be interpreted as an error of the press.

A year later, however, Judson again wrote Zeublin that he was concerned about statements that Zeublin had made about "Mr. Field," a benefactor to the university.[43] Zeublin replied that he had been somewhat misquoted, but that the Fields and similar businessmen did not treat their workers fairly or pay them adequately. Zeublin also noted that criticism was a mild form of protest and that to allow free speech was to perhaps prevent even further forms of reprisals against the wealthy.[44] Needless to say, this was not the response that Judson wanted.

The president then began to ask whether there was a role for "the university to enter into present day polemics." Judson's rhetorical question was quickly answered by himself: "Personally I doubt it." Hastening to add that he was not criticizing Zeublin, he finished by writing: "I am merely raising the question whether it is worth while to allow one's self to get into that positions with reference to the press."[45] In other words, Judson wanted Zeublin to quietly conform to the university policy of not attacking people who donated money to the institution. Zeublin did not want to do this.

By March 1908, Judson was more strongly limiting Zeublin's right to free speech. He wrote:

> The embarrassments which have occasionally occurred in these last year [sic] seem to have arisen from the fact that you are at the same time a member of our faculty and an independent lecturer. Of course as an independent lecturer you have a right to discuss any matter you please in your own way. I have felt that as a member of our faculty it is not expedient for the lecturer on the public platform to attack individuals unless the University has been informed in advance and is willing to put itself in the position of supporting such policy. It is impossible to differentiate the lecturer on the public platform who bears the name of the University from the University itself.[46]

Judson tried to justify this action by calling it a "reasonable" limitation on the freedom of speech. By May, Zeublin had "resigned."

Newspapers picked up this "forced resignation," calling it instead a "firing." D.A. Robertson, Judson's secretary, for example, wrote the editor of *The Scimitar* in Memphis, Tennessee, asking for a correction on their editorial. In this paper, the university was called the "Standard Oil Institution of Learning," and Zeublin's loss of employment a termination and limitation of speech. Robertson denied this.[47]

Clearly, Zeublin was pressured to restrict his speech. When he resisted this control, Judson became increasingly oppressive. The resignation was a forced one, with Zeublin probably receiving a good recommendation as a price for his quiet dismissal. Once again, the university limited faculty activism and once again, in applied sociology.

Dismissal of Thomas, 1918

Addams and Thomas Influences

All the close ties between Thomas and Addams are notable, but their shared study of women, especially prostitutes, was a core commonality. Although Thomas is recognized as one of the most important sociologists of his day, his work on women is consistently ignored (see chapter 8) Part of this lack of academic appreciation is due to his "practical" interests and political views expressed in that body of work. He interpreted women's status in society as repressive and a barrier to social progress. These "radical" views were a component in the notoriety he received in 1918 and his vulnerability to attacks on his sexual life.

In addition, his association with Addams' pacifism through his wife's active work for this cause made the married couple a target of public opprobrium. The tale of his ostracism and brutal dismissal is rarely interpreted as a case of suppression of academic rights, or related to his writings on women, or his association with Addams' despised pacifism during World War I.[48]

The Event and Its Newspaper Reporting

In 1918, at the peak of his career and intellectual achievement, W.I. Thomas was fired from the University of Chicago.[49] This brutal termination of his career occurred rapidly, without due process, because of an unsubstantiated and dismissed charge of disorderly conduct.

The event leading to his firing began on 12 April 1918. Thomas and Mrs. R.M. Granger, a mother and the wife of an officer serving in World War I in France, were arrested by federal agents. They were charged with "violating the Mann act and the act forbidding false registration at hotels." In a short, buried announcement of the arrest in the *New York Times*, almost a third of the article was devoted to the "teachings" of Thomas on women. This article included the following statements attributed to Thomas:

> Women are better off for having had their fling as men do.
>
> Dissipated women often make excellent wives.
>
> Chivalry is the persistence of the old race habit of contempt for women.
>
> Any girl, mentally mature, has the right to have children and the right to limit their number.
>
> The morality of women is an expediency rather than an innate virtue.
>
> Marriage as it exists today is rapidly approaching a form of immorality.
>
> Matrimony is often an arrangement by which the woman trades her irreproachable conduct for irreproachable gowns.
>
> Children are not the result of a marriage, but marriage is the result of children.[50]

These statements were listed as examples of Thomas' "outrageous and immoral views."

This sensationalized account, however, paled in comparison to those in Chicago. The *Chicago Tribune* made it front page news with an "Extra" heading at the top of the column. According to this version: "The discrepancy in their ages caused the hotel people to suspect that they were not married and an investigation was started."[51] Clearly, this was a superficial reason for arresting anyone, as was later proved in court. Unfortunately, Thomas at first denied that he was arrested, but this strategy was bound to fail.

The Thomases were ridiculed by the press when the next day's *Tribune* ran another front-page account. A subheadline quoted Mrs. Thomas as calling her husband a "foolish boy." The opening paragraph referred to Thomas' "eccentric" writings on sex and Mrs. Thomas' national prominence as a pacifist. Again, their advanced views on sex and pacifism, largely shared by Addams, were an underlying factor in their treatment by the press. Simultaneously, the soldier husband and their "little child, only 3 years old, prattling fondly of the 'daddy' who is in far off France" were a dramatic contrast of patriotism, youth, and innocence to the Thomases' pacifism, mature age, and sophistication.[52]

The continuing story had Thomas behind an "iron door" uneasily pacing and trying to avoid "prying eyes"—all understandable events when arrested and hounded by the press, but transformed into high drama by the writing style. The Thomases were also depicted as hard-heartedly closing out reporters on the night of 13 April while "merry voices came floating down the speaking tube to the entry hall below."[53]

By the 15th, President Judson had "suspended" Thomas from the faculty via a long-distance telephone call to the head of the board of trustees, Martin A. Ryerson. Despite the fact that Judson was not even in the city, there was a supposedly "thorough investigation" done between the evening of the 12th and the morning of the 15th. It should be noted that Thomas was not charged with violating the Mann Act as originally reported, but instead went before a municipal court[54] on a morals charge.

By Wednesday, April 17, Thomas was officially dismissed while the "Trustees [were] Silent on Definite Charge Against Professor." Again, Judson only telegraphed his decision to the board. The account continued:

> Prof. Thomas was not present at the meeting which eliminated him as a factor at the university. The refusal of university officers to discuss the matter is in line with a desire on the part of all concerned, it is said, to dismiss from mind as soon as possible, a most unwelcome chapter in the school's history.[55]

Finally, on the 20th, all the government's charges were dropped against Thomas, because the formal allegation of "breaching the peace" clearly had not occurred.[56] Thus, there had been much ado about nothing, but it was sufficient to ruin the professional career and reputation of a sociologist who defended the rights of women and whose wife was a pacifist during wartime.

Clearly acting under the advice of his lawyer, the famous Clarence Darrow, Thomas issued a statement to the press on 22 April in his own behalf. Janowitz, the only sociologist who has commented on the defense noted:

> There has grown up a myth about the "brilliant" rebuttal and "profound criticism" Thomas presented in this essay. Unfortunately, the document is of little worth except as it represents a man tragically seeking to defend himself under circumstances of terrific personal pressure and therefore distorting his basic orientation both to social science and to contemporary social problems.[57]

Contrary to Janowitz' critique, Thomas' statement is interpreted here as a mixture of brilliance and tragedy. Indeed, it was a courageous statement written in a somewhat arrogant style, attempting to show the relationship between Thomas' views as a man and as a scientist. In an age when such views had cost him considerable humiliation and pain, his press release was a moving document, albeit too abstract and theoretical for its intended audience. In addition, Thomas had been effectively abandoned by his colleagues, who did not make this a *cause célèbre* and shunned him in professional interactions for many years. It is important to note, again, Small's role which was to privately work in Thomas' behalf but to publicly avoid such a stance.[58] In light of the significance of the event, a brief summary of Thomas' views is in order.

The Self-Defense

The introduction to the article was written by the newspaper staff, and was predictably sensational. In the Thomas statement, the major topics were the nature of free speech in the university; the difficulties of studying political and social questions, particularly sexual ones; the specific case leading to his dismissal, and his views on social reform.

The university. Although the University of Chicago was one of the "most liberal in America," it acted quickly and eagerly in response to public opinion, demanding a maximum in conformity and denying any freedom of sexuality in private life.[59] The university, in fact, was more interested in religious and moral conformity than in research.

Unlike businesses which show success through profit, university scholars show success through fulfilling social norms. For social scientists this became an impossible demand, because research had to be conducted within predetermined limits that structured the findings while the work was expected to be innovative. This was an unsustainable contradiction because creativity and innovation cannot be contained. Conformity, according to Thomas, was a higher value to the university than scholarship and truth. Moreover, "it does not wish any profound disturbance of the present economic organization."[60]

This repression had, for Thomas, a corollary in Russia which similarly repressed its universities and faculty by preventing the open study of social conditions. These problems were intrinsic to the nature of sociological analysis.

The study of controversial topics, especially sexuality. Thomas provided several examples of the limits on the study of sexuality and the arbitrary definition of "moral" and "immoral" behavior in different cultures at various stages in their development. Americans, in particular, found such studies offensive and "prurient." English suffragists found Thomas' early writings on women to be liberating and understandable, while many American women found them obscene.[61]

Commenting on his work for the Vice Commission, Thomas explicitly stated that the findings were consistently too tame and cautious.[62] Nonetheless, "The post office declared the report obscene literature, and the members of the commission were technically liable to a penitentiary sentence."[63]

By stating that sexuality was pervasive, Thomas adopted a stance similar to Freud's:

> The feeling of sex is not confined to the relation between man and woman. We have also the love of the mother for the child, and this is, in a wider sense, "sexual." Also, the more general "love of humanity" has in it an element derived from the fact that we are sexual and transfer some of the feeling for the baby to humanity.[64]

As Freud was ostracized by his medical colleagues, so too was Thomas shunned by his male, sociological ones.

The particular case. In this area Thomas was understandably less coherent. He brought up a series of examples where behavior could be misinterpreted. Finally, he noted that this particular case involved such an instance. He claimed that he and the named correspondent were waiting for another woman's arrival at the hotel where they were to work together on a project. Although this was highly plausible and never disproven, a strong case was not presented by Thomas who was in the awkward position of looking self-serving.

His views on social reform. Thomas clearly argued that social scientists involve their personal lives in their work, and the product of their labors was justified by their service to society. By raising issues that others thought solved, the social scientist endangered their reputations in the name of science. Such infractions of social norms, however, needed to be distinguished from individual, private actions.

For Thomas, the university tried to control the work of sociologists while simultaneously trying to dominate their "private lives." Both stances were insupportable. The scholar could not be creative, nor the individual free.

What was defensible, however, was calling intellectuals to task who were not doing their job: aiding society. In this regard, Thomas was a harsh and accurate critic. Society was not improving, despite the massive amount of resources expended for the goal.[65] This was because the "student of society" was caught in a double bind. In order to improve society, social customs and mores needed to be changed, while whoever attempted to change them was regarded as an enemy of society and one to be destroyed.[66]

In this public essay, Thomas defined both impersonal and personal freedom of speech and action. His closing paragraph summarized this tragic intersection of personal and public issues:

> I do not believe in social reform by the way of revolution, but by a knowledge of the laws of behavior and the development of a technique for the control of behavior. I do not believe in the reduction of the members of society to one class, but in a hierarchization of social classes based on efficiency. But perhaps my views on these and similar topics still contain vestiges of my academic fear-thought.[67]

Evaluating the Dismissal

Although Janowitz noted that Thomas had been involved in "previous personal complications" prior to this one,[68] the entire circumstances surrounding the arrest are questionable. For example, why did an agent of the Department of Justice go to the hotel room? Why not a hotel detective or the local police? How was Thomas immediately identified? Why were the initial charges dropped and a mere "charge" of disturbing the peace offered without any substantiating evidence? Why were the charges dropped so quickly but most of the articles hinted at "future charges"? Finally, why were the sensationalized accounts so biased against William Thomas, an author on the subject of women and sexuality, and Harriet Thomas, a nationally known pacifist? Why were the accounts so much more favorable to the "young wife and mother" with a soldier husband on the front? Clearly, the situation raises doubts about the "spontaneity" or fairness of the arrest.

Simultaneously, why did the university act so quickly? Less than forty-eight hours after the arrest, the university was making public statements about "allowing" Thomas to resign, a statement attributed to Albion W. Small.[69] Why did Thomas make a self-defense to the newspapers but not address the meeting leading to his firing, if, as reported, neither party wanted to make a bigger issue of the situation? Finally, why has this area of Thomas' writings, concerning women and sexuality, been largely overlooked while it was a major factor in his entire career and within his larger social thought?

All these questions cannot be directly answered, but as a group they suggest that Thomas was railroaded by the government, the university, and his academic colleagues. Furthermore, as Janowitz has noted, Mrs. Thomas' pacifism may have played a role in the matter.[70] This is highly plausible, given Addams' treatment by government agents and representatives.[71] Whatever the cause of the arrest, the study of women and sexuality was dangerous, and this hazard has rarely been raised as a professional issue of freedom of speech for men in America.

The Consequences

This unjust termination of Thomas' career had life-long consequences. Never holding a full-time faculty position again, Thomas was cut off from the mainstream work at Chicago. It is alleged that he frequently visited the University of Chicago in the 1920s and his work was continued by Park and others.[72] This picture of his ties with the department, especially with Park, is difficult to understand. Although close friends prior to his dismissal, in 1921 Park betrayed Thomas in a fundamental way.

After being terminated at Chicago, Thomas was employed to write a book on immigrants. This was published in 1921 under the title *Old World Traits Transplanted*. Despite the fact that Thomas was the primary, if not sole, author, his name did not appear on the title page. Instead, authorship was attributed to Park and Miller.

The circumstances surrounding the event are now difficult to determine. One account of it can be found in a note Thomas wrote to Ethel Dummer, who had commissioned Thomas to write *The Unadjusted Girl*. In this letter, Thomas explained the volume as follows:

> I am sending you a copy of the volume you read in manuscript a year ago, or less. It is called "Old World Traits Transplanted." This title was not chosen by me, but conforms to the general plan to get that sort of title. You will understand the fact that my name is not on the book. I really did the work in the place of Miller, who undertook it originally. Of course my name would have gone on except for my record. But it was a friendly arrangement, made on the basis of money.[73]

This picture of an amicable decision, however, is not the one portrayed by Rauschenbush, the life-long assistant and confidante of Park who wrote:

> When Thomas realized what was happening, he was enraged. A scholar of outstanding reputation, he had already suffered one body blow when he was asked to resign [sic] from his Chicago professorship, he was not prepared to take a second blow tamely. The situation created a short temporary strain in the Thomas-Park friendship, which both men were careful to conceal. Why could Park not have done more? Park was distressed, but powerless to alter the situation.[74]

Thomas is not mentioned in the 1921 text and in the 1951 version Park is excluded.[75] It is likely that Park is not a major author at all.

This humiliation penetrated deeply into Thomas' view of himself as a professional and a person worthy of respect. On 27 February 1921, Thomas wrote Dummer:

> I want to ask you what you think of the following plan—that I arrange an active cooperation with Miriam Van Waters in the further development of this study, that we together prepare a volume, and that she alone shall sign it. . . . I do not know how this idea will strike you. Possibly you have other plans for Dr. Van Waters, and possibly she would not wish to do it. At any rate I am just presenting it to you, not urging it.[76]

Dummer was outraged at his suggestion, in stark contrast to his male colleagues. Thomas reaffirmed his interest in the project, but repeated that the "shame" surrounding his name might influence the book's reception.[77] This plan was fortunately never adopted.

With the publication of *The Unadjusted Girl* in 1925 under his name and its wide public and scholarly acceptance, Thomas started to regain legitimacy. In 1927 he was nominated for president of the American Sociological Society (ASS). According to Janowitz, Thomas almost refused to be considered under the pretext of going to India, in order to avoid more scandal and disgrace. Burgess persuaded him to run and Louis Wirth, a later Chicago sociologist, organized the "Young Turks," Kimbell Young, George Lundberg, Stuart Chapin, and Stuart Rice.[78] This campaign was augmented by graduate students who, according to Everett Hughes, "jumped into their cars" and drove to New York City to cast their votes for Thomas. One result was that Thomas was elected president; another result was that students lost their rights to vote in future elections.[79] The latter policy still remains in effect.

Addams and the Thomas Dismissal

Addams was dismayed by the ostracism of Thomas by his former male colleagues. She and other women sociologists supported his career from his dismissal in 1918 until his triumphant restoration to the male sociology network a decade later.

Ethel S. Dummer, in particular, allowed Thomas to regain his scholarly reputation through her funding and moral encouragement of his work on *The Unadjusted Girl.* In 1922 Addams tried to involve Thomas in a survey of social settlements, which he considered doing.[80] Their female colleagues became resources for his documentation in both *The Polish Peasant* and *The Unadjusted Girl.*[81]

In general, Thomas was treated with fairness and esteem by women sociologists during his period of exclusion from the male network. He publicly recognized Dummer's significance to him and to sociology through her work with the ASS when he was president of that association.[82] The other women's support was not formally acknowledged, although his study of *The Child in America* carried on the women's work on childhood, therapy, and urban stress.[83]

Clearly, Addams would have suffered a termination of employment long before Thomas' work and lifestyle became an issue. Although punctilious in her personal life, Addams' public views were more radical than his. Her interest in women and pacifism was central to her entire corpus of thought. As a villain of the day, however, she was not the strongest sociological ally. Her separation from sociology during the 1920s created a gap between her work and the men's that was never bridged after Thomas was fired.

Conclusion

Jane Addams could not have functioned as a great American leader within the institutional structure of the University of Chicago. Although she was clearly concerned with her institutional independence per se, it is obvious that the academy was particularly repressive in America during her years of active sociological thought and practice.

Without a doubt, finances governed the university's policy on social reform issues. Governed by a monied elite, searching for more funds to expand their prestige and power, and led by presidents unsympathetic to the rights of the poor, the University of Chicago limited its faculty's political activism.

Within sociology, Addams was further restricted by her sex and area of study, "practical" sociology. Bemis, Zeublin, and Thomas were all removed from the university because of their espousal of ideas and study of topics shared with Addams.[84] Small was an unreliable ally for Addams because he played a conciliatory role toward the administration. At best, his stance in each of the above cases was one of feeble resistance to the repression of his faculty's rights to academic freedom.

The sociological history of the University of Chicago sheds considerable light on the ultimate practice of the discipline. Park and Burgess were major voices cutting themselves off from their roots in the writings of Addams and the other men. Rather than suffer the fate of their predecessors, Park and Burgess adopted a stance called "value-free." This allowed them to make a claim that they did not criticize or influence society, they only studied "facts" about it.

Although the inherently conservative political assumptions underlying the Chicago School perspective have frequently been critiqued, its linkage to political repression in the academy has rarely been analyzed. To understand the political conservatism of today's sociological analyses, this relationship must be considered. Contemporary American sociology is partially a product of repression at the University of Chicago, the most influential institution in the founding of American sociology.

Notes

1. This is discussed in Schwendingers, pp. 490-548. Thornstein Veblen's scathing attack on universities used the University of Chicago as its model. See *The Higher Learning in America* (New York: Hill & Wang, 1969, c. 1918). Veblen had this manuscript completed for over a decade before he could find a publisher for it. For a general discussion of the problems, see Walter P. Metzger, *Academic Freedom in the Age of the University* (New York: Columbia University Press, 1964, c. 1955).
2. Walter P. Metzger, "Academic Tenure in America: A Historical Essay," in *Faculty Tenure: A Report and Recommendations by the Commission on Academic Tenure in Higher Education*, William R. Keast, chair (San Francisco: Jossey-Bass, 1973), pp. 93-159. Metzger notes the pivotal role of E.A. Ross, sociologist and Addams' colleague, in bringing tenure issues to the fore.
3. Veblen's subtitle for *The Higher Learning in America* was "On the Conduct of Universities by Businessmen."
4. Metzger, "Academic Freedom and Big Business," in *Academic Freedom in the Age of the University*, pp. 139-94.
5. Steven J. Diner, *A City and Its Universities* (Chapel Hill: University of North Carolina Press, 1980), p. 48.
6. Theodore Morrison, *Chautauqua* (Chicago: University of Chicago Press, 1974), p. 78.
7. Veblen, *The Higher Learning in America*. Veblen did note that the pattern found at the University of Chicago was replicated in other academies.
8. Ibid., p. 51.
9. *Jane Addams: A Centennial Reader*, ed. Emily Cooper Johnson (New York: Macmillan, 1960), p. 31n; "A Modern Lear," *Survey* 29 (2 November 1912):131-37.
10. Herman and Julia Schwendinger, *The Sociologists of the Chair* (New York: Basic Books, 1974), p. 493.
11. Addams is cited as calling him this in Allen F. Davis, *American Heroine* (New York: Oxford University Press, 1973), p. 102. Ely had been considered for

Small's position at Chicago, but was not selected. Instead, Ely headed the Department of Economics and Sociology at the University of Wisconsin and is labeled by many contemporary sociologists as an "institutional economist" rather than a sociologist.

12. Syllabus of that title in Bemis File, Presidents' Papers, 1889-1925, UCSC (hereafter referred to as Bemis File).
13. Edward W. Bemis, "Municipal Ownership of Gas in the United States," *Publications of the American Economic Association*, 6 (1891):111-12.
14. Bemis Press Clippings, Bemis File.
15. Harold E. Berquist, Jr., "The Edward W. Bemis Controversy," unpublished history paper in Bemis File, p. 3. There are several footnoted references in Berquist alluding to correspondence on this topic which this researcher was unable to check. *Chicago Daily News*, 31 October 1895):4; the *Literary Digest* (31 August 1895):4, Bemis File.
16. Harper to Bemis, January 1894, Bemis File.
17. Bemis, press clippings, Bemis File.
18. Bemis to Harper, 23 July 1894, Bemis File.
19. See *Boston Herald* (2, 24 August 1895), "Prof. Bemis Secret Out," *The Voice* (17 August 1895); *The Literary Digest* (24 August 1895). Bemis File.
20. This was at the 11 October 1895 convocation at the university.
21. This was printed separately as a pamphlet and in the newspapers. See *Chicago Record* (21 October 1895), Bemis File.
22. Ernest Becker, *The Lost Science of Man* (New York: Braziller, 1971), pp. 3-70.
23. "Bemis Still Talking," *Chicago Times-Herald*, Bemis File.
24. See typescript in Bemis File.
25. Berquist documents that although there was low enrollment in the Fall of the 1894 term, subsequent enrollments were quite high and competitive with other lecturers. Bemis File.
26. See Harper to Bemis, January 1894, Bemis File.
27. "A Statement by Professors Small and Butler," pt. 8, no pagination. Bemis File.
28. Ibid., pt. 9.
29. Ibid., appended n.
30. For a discussion of the protests see the Schwendingers, *The Sociologists of the Chair*, pp. 493-94.
31. "A Statement by Professors Small and Butler," pt. 6.
32. Small to Harper, 27 August (no year), cited in Berquist, Bemis File.
33. Bemis to Ely, 24 September 1895, Ely Papers, Wisconsin State Historical Society, cited in Metzger, p. 157, n. 46.
34. The Kansas State Agricultural College controversy is briefly discussed in Metzger, pp. 150-51.
35. Edward W. Bemis, "Obituary," *New York Times* (27 September 1930).
36. Addams gave this speech, "A Modern Lear," in 1894 to the Chicago Women's Club and the Twentieth Century Club of Boston, but it was too controversial to publish. Addams waited eighteen years before it was accepted. See discussion in Christopher Lasch, *The Social Thought of Jane Addams* (Indianapolis: Bobbs-Merrill, 1965), p. 106.
37. Davis refers to Bemis as a visitor at Hull House, *American Heroine* (New York: Oxford University Press, 1973), p. 97. Kelley refers to Bemis and Zeublin as working with Hull-House residents during the Pullman Strike, although they were not as radical as Kelley. See Dorothy Rose Blumberg, *Florence Kelley* (New York: A.M. Kelley, 1966), p. 153.

38. James Weber Linn, *Jane Addams* (New York: D. Appleton-Century, 1935), p. 160.
39. No references to this action could be found in the archives searched, in particular the Presidents' Papers at UCSC.
40. James Tufts to Marion Talbot, Tufts Papers, box 1, folder 7, UCSC.
41. Zeublin's low salary was the topic of a series of letters. See "Zeublin," box 71, folder 13, Presidents' Papers, 1889-1925, UCSC (hereafter referred to as Zeublin File).
42. Judson to Zeublin, 6 August 1906, Zeublin File.
43. Judson to Zeublin, 18 November 1907. The "Mr. Field" is probably of the Marshall Field family in Chicago. Zeublin File.
44. Zeublin to Judson, 23 November 1907, Zeublin File.
45. Ibid.
46. Judson to Zeublin, 7 March 1908, p. 1, Zeublin File.
47. D.A. Robertson to the managing editor of the Memphis *Scimitar* 8 (May 1908), Zeublin File.
48. Janowitz alludes to the possible pacifist connection in his "Introduction" to *W.I. Thomas: On Social Organization and Social Personality* (Chicago: University of Chicago Press, 1966), p. xiv. Winifred Rauschenbush, *Robert E. Park: Biography of a Sociologist* (Durham: Duke University Press, 1979), pp. 88-89, however, analyzes the dismissal as a function of manners and morals of the times. The Schwendingers, *The Sociologists of the Chair*; and Robert E.L. Faris, *Chicago Sociology* (Chicago: University of Chicago Press, 1967), do not even discuss it as an issue of academic freedom.
49. Janowitz, "Introduction," p. xiv.
50. "Couple Arrested in Hotel," *New York Times* (13 April 1918):18, cols. 5-6.
51. "'Dr. Thomas' and Woman Taken in Loop Hotel," Chicago Tribune (12 April 1918):1.
52. "Takes Woman into Her Home," *Chicago Tribune* (13 April 1918):1, 8.
53. "Prof. Thomas Gives a Bond and Quits Cell," *Chicago Tribune* (14 April 1918):7.
54. "Prof. Thomas Suspended from U. of C. Faculty," *Chicago Tribune* (15 April 1918):13, col. 7.
55. "Dismiss Thomas from U. of C. on Judson's Order," *Chicago Tribune* (17 April 1918):17, col. 7.
56. "Raid Arrests at Stake in Thomas Case Decision," *Chicago Tribune* (20 April 1918):5, col. 1.
57. Janowitz, "Introduction," p. xv.
58. Ibid., p. xv.
59. "Thomas Defends Self as a Daring Social Explorer," *Chicago Tribune* (22 April 1918):16, col. 2.
60. Ibid., p. 16, col. 3.
61. Ibid., p. 16, cols. 2, 3.
62. Ibid., p. 16, col. 2.
63. Ibid.
64. Ibid., col. 7.
65. Ibid., p. 15, col. 7.
66. Ibid., p. 16, col. 1.
67. Ibid., col. 7.
68. Janowitz, "Introduction," p. xv.

69. "To Resign?" *Chicago Tribune* (14 April 1918):7, col. 2.

70. Janowitz, "Introduction," p. xiv.

71. See extensive documentation of this harassment in Davis, 1973, pp. 251-81.

72. Faris, *Chicago Sociology*, p. 19; Janowitz, "Introduction," p. liv; Rauschenbush, *Robert E. Park*, p. 255.

73. Thomas to Dummer, 4 February 1921, Dummer Papers, Schlesinger Library.

74. Rauschenbush, *Robert E. Park*, pp. 92-93.

75. Ibid., p. 93.

76. Thomas to Dummer, 27 February 1921, #1, Dummer Papers, Schlesinger Library, Radcliffe College (hereafter referred to as Dummer Papers).

77. Ibid., 3 March 1921.

78. Janowitz, "Introduction," p. xvii.

79. Informal group interview, Spring Institute, University of Chicago, Chicago, Illinois, May 1973.

80. A discussion of their ties and this issue are presented in greater depth in Mary Jo Deegan and John S. Burger, "W.I. Thomas and Social Reform," *Journal of the History of the Behavioral Sciences* 17 (February 1981):114-25.

81. See references to the Juvenile Court and to the work of Jessie Taft and Miriam Van Waters in W.I. Thomas, *The Unadjusted Girl*, ed. Benjamin Nielson, pref. Michael Parenti (New York: Torchbooks, 1967, c. 1923). The juvenile court was also central to the documents used by W.I. Thomas and Florian Znaniecki in *The Polish Peasant*, 2nd ed., vols. 1, 2 (New York Dover: 1958, c. 1917-18).

82. See Mary Jo Deegan, "Early Women Sociologists and the American Sociological Society," *American Sociologist* 16 (February 1981):14-24.

83. W.I. Thomas and Dorothy Swaine Thomas, *The Child in America* (New York: Knopf, 1928).

84. Mead resigned from the University of Chicago in 1931 due to a bitter political conflict over the governance of the faculty. Since he died in the spring of 1931, his resignation was a little-known fact. See background information in James H. Tufts to Frederic Woodward, 21 December 1929 and Frederic Woodward to James H. Tufts, 29 December 1929; John H. Moulds to James H. Tufts, 20 February 1930. Tufts Papers, Special Collections, Morris Library, Southern Illinois University. Mead's resignation is briefly mentioned by David E. Miller, *George Herbert Mead: Self, Language and the World* (Austin: University of Texas Press, 1973), p. xxxviii.

8

The Chicago Men and the Sociology of Women

Careers in sociology are created and maintained in three ways: through institutional practices of training and hiring, through the development and acceptance of sociological concepts, and through collegial networks. In a patriarchal society, these factors are structured differently for each sex, with men receiving better benefits and more power than women.

For Addams, her career in sociology was directly associated with the academy's barriers to hiring women as fully recognized professors. In fact, when she was a college student, women were rarely allowed even to matriculate in universities with advanced degrees. In this restrictive milieu, the University of Chicago was relatively open to the training of women and to their marginal employment in departments.

More specifically, the Department of Sociology admitted female students from the day it opened its doors in 1892, and even had a female faculty member, Marion Talbot. Soon, more women were hired in low-paid and low status positions. This "radical" policy was a result of sociology's zealous approach to "scientific" social change. The "woman question" was part of the social reform agenda. However, most of the Chicago men were more committed to urban reform than improving the status of women.

The Chicago men's views on the role of women in everyday life were central to Addams' career in sociology. The men's institutional support of women was dramatically reflected in 1902 by their support of or opposition to the introduction of sex-segregated classes during the first two years of training at the University of Chicago. Similarly, the men's sociological writings, particularly on women, provide a key to understanding their intellectual relationship to Addams' writings on cultural feminism. Another indicator of the sexual division of labor in the profession is found in the work relationships between male and female sociologists. These ties are exhibited through joint interests in teaching and research as well as overlapping ideas and patterns of social interaction. Before analyzing each man's writings and collegial network concerning women, the general milieu of women's higher education, particularly at the University of Chicago, is described.

The Higher Education of Women, 1892-1917

Since women had gained limited access to some universities and professional schools in the United States from the mid–nineteenth century, it is often assumed that the crucial battles in women's higher education had been "won" during these earlier confrontations. This was not the case.

Institutional discrimination against women in higher education flourished during the entire period analyzed here. As students or faculty members (especially the latter), women were systematically limited in their opportunities. Sometimes they were completely barred from entering a college or university. At other times more subtle forms of prejudice were exhibited, such as a lack of intellectual acceptance or financial support.

A leading advocate for women's rights to education during this era was Marion Talbot, an early Chicago sociologist who is rarely recognized as part of this school.[1] Her original interest in this program was a result of her personal struggle. In the 1870s, she discovered to her dismay that she could not obtain adequate training in Boston, a leading educational enclave, in order to enter college. Then, after a considerable battle to obtain a college degree, she could not find a job.

Working with women in a similar quandary, in November of 1881 she cofounded the Association of Collegiate Alumnae (ACA, later to become the American Association of University Women, AAUW). Most of the documentation on women's higher education during the 1890s was channeled through this group.[2] By 1884, they had 356 members. Of this number, only twenty-six held master's degrees and a mere four had earned doctorates.[3] As a group, they fought to gain access for women into universities and in 1892 they felt they had made considerable progress when four graduate schools opened their doors to women: Chicago, Yale, Pennsylvania, and Leland Stanford, Jr.[4]

Despite this relative progress in the United States, European universities remained more open to women students. These opportunities for higher education, however, were not supported by financial aid. Fellowships and faculty positions were available to men, not women.[5] But:

> there was no room in this masculine procession for young women, no fund available whereby they might, by virtue of their post-graduate training, become competitors for the college and university positions to which young men aspired. Very few graduate courses were open to young women, and no positions on college faculties outside of the women's colleges then developing.[6]

At the turn of the century, then, women with any college training, let alone graduate work, were pioneers. They fought for entry, financial assistance, and job prospects. This led to women taking degrees in any fields they could enter, and taking any jobs they were offered. Sociology was a relatively open field within this milieu of repression and restrictions.

At this time European theorists represented both the most conservative and most radical thought on the role of women in society. The conservative position can be found in the writings of Auguste Comte and Emile Durkheim.[7] Both "founding fathers" of sociology, they were also patriarchal in their analysis of society. The Schwendingers summarize Comte's views as follows:

> With regard to women, Comte maintained that women were constitutionally inferior to men because their maturation was arrested at childhood. He insisted that patriarchal authority (as well as a political dictatorship) was absolutely indispensable for "Order and Progress" in France. Accordingly, he proposed that women were justifiably subordinated to men when they married. Divorce should be unequivocally denied them: women should be pampered slaves of men.[8]

Durkheim noted in *Suicide* that "Women's sexual needs have less of a mental character because, generally speaking, her mental life is less developed."[9] He wrote that women must remain monogamous and that they participate less in the "collective conscience" or moral order of society.[10]

> As she lives outside of community existence more than man, she is less penetrated by it; society is less necessary to her because she is less impregnated [sic] with social ability. With a few devotional practices and some animals to care for, the old unmarried woman's life is full.[11]

Sexist attitudes such as these were targets attacked by radical sociologists. Engels, in particular, developed a complex theory of the relationship between women's status, the family, the accumulation of wealth, and the concentrated power of the state.[12] In the United States, Charlotte Perkins Gilman was writing on the political economy of women and their rights for full and equal participation in society.[13]

Thus the role of women in society was the subject of considerable debate. The major answer to the question of women's rights as professionals at the University of Chicago was to allow them entry, but expect them to "act" and have interests different from men's. During the era studied here, the predominant institutional response to women in sociology at the University of Chicago was the popular ideology of the "Doctrine of the Separate Spheres."

Women and Chicago Sociology, 1892-1902

When Chicago opened in 1892, women were included within its "pioneer" plans. As students and faculty, women were expected to be participants in a "radical" new approach to education. (It was this dream that partially attracted Addams during the early days, too.) There were more successful women within the university during its first three decades than during its succeeding five.[14]

This participation, however, was not the same as the men's. Women were expected to remain within their "special sphere," even though educated in an advanced manner. This "Doctrine of the Separate Spheres" was the dominant attitude towards women's place in society at this time. Each sex was expected to be distinct. Women "managed" the home, emotions, culture, morality, and children. Men "governed" the family, social and political institutions, especially the economy, and were more rational than women.[15] Thus Chicago made a forward step by including women within the university structure, but retained its belief in a "separate sphere" for women within this structure.

Sociology was particularly suited to this approach to the "new woman." It was a social science that was meant to "care for" social maladjustment. Albion Small adopted this separatist view, but he was not alone in this perspective. Addams, for example, thought women were different too, albeit superior; and in 1892 Samuel Dike articulated the male view as follows:

> Men and women are fundamentally different. Therefore, even if they received the same education, they would respond to it in unique ways. There must be subjects in which women will take deeper interest than men. The place of the family in the social order, and of women in the family, and their future as wives and mothers, will inevitably draw the attention of women to the family and the home as subjects of educational importance in proportion to their richness in educational material and value, and to their close connection with the life of women.[16]

Women were expected to study the "simpler forms of social life"[17] while men studied the "larger" ones. In this seminal article on the "sphere" of women in sociology, Dike noted that women sociologists would be best occupied in social settlements, where their philanthropic and benevolent spirits would respond to the needy. Dike also noted that the "major" concerns of women were often ignored in sociology coursework, and that this lack must be addressed.[18]

Fortunately, the women largely ignored this view of "their work." They, too, shared the vision of "special" aptitudes and interests, but they thought theirs were superior to the men's and wished to alter the shape of society *in toto*, according to their worldview. The women on the sociology faculty, five in number, were always "segregated" within the department: Mary McDowell as a "Special Lecturer," Annie Marion MacLean in Extension, Sophonisba Breckinridge and Marion Talbot in "Household Administration," and Edith Abbott as a "Special Lecturer in Statistics."[19] This separation was not entirely forced on the women, for they desired this status, too. In their "world," they were given considerable leeway to define sociology and the work they wanted to do. This segregation, moreover, created faculty jobs for women. For example, Talbot noted that in 1901 there were only twenty female faculty members. When the "women's sociology" group started the Chicago Institute (later to merge with the social work program), the number of employed women jumped to forty-one.[20] For the women, this desired separation was based on their strengths and not their inferiority. The women's view of their distinctiveness, however, did not govern the university. They were separate, but unequal, as scholars.

Writing in 1903, Talbot documented the superior performance of women in the university:

> Ninety-three men and 128 women received honors for scholarship based on class and examination grades. If the women had received honors in the same proportion to their numbers as the men the number of women would have been 81 instead of 128. In the same period of time 1,164 students have received the Bachelor's degree—614 men or 53 percent, and 550 women or 48 percent. One hundred and forty-five of the men and 199 of the women received honors for scholarship on graduation, and 44 men and 73 women received special honors. If the women had received honors and special honors in the same proportion to their numbers as the men, the number of women would have been 130 honors and 39 for special honors instead of 199 and 73, respectively.[21]

This overachievement was even more remarkable given the constraints within which women studied. Talbot also documented that despite women's academic excellence, they received a smaller proportion of the fellowship funds. Approximately 12 percent of the graduate men received aid; less than 5 percent of the graduate women did.[22]

The women clearly excelled the men in their scholastic performance. The men, in retaliation and in response to pressures and money supporting the segregation of the sexes, began to favor "separate training" for men and women. Thus, the "golden age" of the first decade came to an end. It was the pressure of women's outstanding performance that was the first impetus to decrease their student opportunities. As Talbot scathingly notes, on 3 July 1900, the University Congregation, (that grandiose organization which never lived up to President Harper's expectations and, after a period of coma, finally expired) the following topic was raised for discussion: Resolved that better educational results would be secured in the University by teaching the sexes in separate classes.[23]

Coeducation, supported during the first ten years, was then given a severe blow.

Women and Chicago Sociology, 1902-20

When coeducation was attenuated at the university, the women and some of the men strongly opposed it because it meant involuntary segregation. Thus, the early Chicago men's views on women can be partially traced through their response to this controversial coeducation issue. Small and Vincent supported sex segregation in the classroom, the former in public and the latter in private. In a more passive way, Thomas and Henderson also supported it by not visibly protesting it. Zeublin and Mead (as well as the Chicago women) protested it publicly. These stances are examined when each of the men is considered below.

Within the Sociology Department, sex segregation became increasingly apparent. Although each change between 1902 and 1920 cannot be documented here, the net result is that by 1920 the women faculty were administratively and professionally separated into the School of Social Services Administration.

Formally, the women were now social workers and the men were sociologists. The causes of these dramatic definitions resulting in two separate fields of specialization is the topic of chapter 12. Suffice it to be noted here, that women's place in sociology was first established through "special qualities" of mind and action and later removed from the field to another profession. The women's areas of specialization were only selectively continued by male sociologists during the 1920s and 1930s. Thus, sexism was institutionalized in sociological thought, but in a complex and changing pattern. Forces countering this prejudice were best articulated by Thomas and Mead, although their voices were unheeded. The "religious" men tended to be more conservative than Mead and Thomas, while Park and Burgess were the most repressive.

Small and the Sociology of Women

Small's attitude on women's place in society, especially in academia, was crucial for women sociologists' training and careers. He was central to job placement for the department's graduates. For in those days, people were "invited" to fill positions and these "calls" were first negotiated between the employer and Small. Students did not personally apply for them.[24] Such negotiations were extremely dependent on interpersonal relations, and Small was responsible for placing most male Chicago sociologists in academic positions from the 1890s until the early 1920s. He believed that women should be employed in "social settlements" and other types of "women's institutions." As sociology became increasingly academically defined and controlled, women were effectively barred from this vital job opportunity, particularly in sociology departments training graduate students.[25]

Small firmly believed in the separate domains of men and women. He repeatedly stated this in his writings on women. In 1902, he supported the still controversial belief that the intellectual capacity and "brain power" of men and women were equal[26] (thereby also reinforcing Thomas' conclusions in his dissertation).[27] Small believed that this equality was obvious and had been stressed. What needed to be addressed was the "separate but equal" nature of males and females:

> We are aware that the mental output of the two persons [sexes], with reference to a given subject, is not the same. There is a subtle difference of quality, perhaps like that between the same musical note produced, for example, by a cornet and a violin. Each has the same relation to other notes higher and lower in the scale, but neither could supply the place of the other in its own series.[28]

Acknowledging that some "modern" women were trained like men, he felt that this was a transitory and possibly destructive phase of social change. Although Small was a sexist, he wanted to venture on a non-controversial path toward more equality and rights for women. His contradictory ideas are evident in the following passage: "Equal pay for equal work is simple justice. But at best social ideals that train women to be competitors with men are like poisons administered as medicine."[29] Supporting the "complementary" roles of men and women exemplified in marriage, Small wrote that bachelorhood was a sign of maladjustment. In yet another contradictory statement, he noted the lack of high moral standards in society and given this "fact," remaining single could be a temporary "social sacrament."[30]

Small thought that women embodied humanness, emotional balance, harmony, and repose. (Since this was close to the image Addams projected, it is understandable that he admired her so much.) Simultaneously, he wrote that women were morally neither better nor worse than men. Women were cooperative and men competitive because of their social and sexual roles. Thus, when Park and Burgess developed their view of society as competitive, Small could have easily seen this as the "male sphere," but certainly not the female.[31]

Although Small was sexist in his views that women's place was in the home, he simultaneously believed that the "home" needed academic study. Women, by their "nature" would be the best scholars here, so his hiring of Marion Talbot and other women to study "women's subjects" allowed for a certain freedom and flexibility for women faculty. This ideology also allowed him to think of Addams as a colleague and sociologist, when many of his male successors did not.

Like all sexist visions, Small's reality always resulted in women's loss of social power and control. Agreeing in the abstract that males and females had equal *ability* to vote, he opposed the extension of suffrage on the ground of social expediency. Women should not vote because it would alter the complementary divisions of labor wherein men should have "the representative functions in our political system."[32]

Women were also not expected to be breadwinners. If they worked in the marketplace they would become competitive and devote less time to their homes and families. Work was like a new religion, fulfilling obligations to the community and to God. Thus, women who worked would be choosing a "holy" mission in competition with their other "holy" mission.

In 1903, after the instigation of segregation in education at the University of Chicago, Small wrote an article advocating this policy. Holding that women matured more quickly than men, he felt that the consequence was male discrimination in the classroom. He elaborated:

> The boy of seventeen or eighteen has grown up by the side of his younger, or even older, sisters and other boy's sisters, and has probably never wasted a minute on the purely academic question of their possible equality with himself. In the college environment the perspective changes. He is doggedly aware that the girls in his class are sophisticated beyond his years. He has always supposed himself at least as old as anyone of his age. Now, when he hears the girls of his class talk about "high school kids" he has a guilty feeling that it means him. While he is being guyed and hazed and, if lucky, "rushed," the chasm yawns wider between him and his girl classmate, who does not even shrink from the presence of the captain of the football team, and has already made a distinct impression upon some of the stars of the fraternities. Our freshman doesn't feel happy. These girls embarrass him.[33]

Sexually tempting, cold-hearted, competitive, and sophisticated, "college" women needed to be kept away from male freshmen. Keeping in mind Talbot's statistics on women's performance, it is clear that female students at Chicago did excel their male counterparts. This unexpected achievement lay beneath the subsequent attempt to "put women in their place."

Thus women sociologists were fairly welcome at the University of Chicago, if they knew, and kept, their place. Ironically, it was this extremely overt sexism which allowed a "place for women" to flourish. Subsequent policies toward women became increasingly restrictive and covert so that there were neither publicly sexist statements such as Small's, nor a place for women's control over a world where they were the "expert."

Henderson and the Sociology of Women

Henderson, like Small, was a "religious" sociologist. Unlike Small, Henderson was more involved with controversial reform. Henderson probably supported a more liberated variety of separate spheres ideology or even women's suffrage. Unlike many of his "liberated" colleagues, however, he did not protest the segregation policy at the university.

Regardless of his ideas about women, he did work closely with women professionals. For example, from 1894 until his death in 1915, Henderson was on the Board of Directors of the University of Chicago Settlement where he worked directly with Mary McDowell, the Head Resident. Henderson also worked with Edith Abbott and Sophonisba Breckinridge through the Chicago School of Civics and Philanthropy (CSCP), and with Alice Hamilton on the Illinois Commission on Occupations and Diseases. Although each of these relationships is discussed elsewhere, it is worth noting that these professional relationships were a group influence that helped to shape his thought. They also reveal the permeable boundaries of the sex segregated networks.

His attitudes toward sex education were also remarkably liberal for his day. Advocating sexual instruction in the school and home, Henderson adopted a stance still unacceptable to many "modern" communities. In a lengthy discussion of venereal disease, he argued for medical tests to be conducted before marriage to prevent infection of a new spouse. Similarly, he advocated public health clinics where treatment for venereal disease would be available to all without punishment or restrictions.[34]

Like Thomas, Addams, and Mead, Henderson advanced a more tolerant social acceptance of the prostitute, while arguing against state regulation or repression. Education, to this entire group, was a cornerstone for eliminating this "social evil and vice." Starting with "nature studies" and proceeding throughout the life cycle, Henderson mapped a program of sex education for students in public schools. Although opposed to masturbation and supportive of the home as the major source of explicit sex instruction, he nonetheless advocated that "some instruction" be included throughout the school curriculum.

Thus, Henderson was a mixture of "old-fashioned" sexual standards and more "progressive" ones. In addition to condemning masturbation, he defended chivalry and treating women "with modesty and respect."[35] In his favor, he did suggest that ignorant women were not modest and to be lauded, but the victims of a repressive ideal. Clearly, he was more advanced than Small and Vincent, the latter discussed next, but less open than the women sociologists or his male colleagues, Mead and Thomas.

Vincent and the Sociology of Women

Vincent did not specifically study women, so little evidence of his views on their place in society can be found in his formal studies. His position on the university's segregation policy, however, is known and reveals his support of Small's general approach.

In the fall of 1902, Vincent was asked by President Harper to publicly support the policy to segregate the sexes. Vincent refused to do so, although he supported the policy. In November 1902, Vincent explained his position:

> I regret to say that I am still of the opinion that the least said about the social and pedagogical aspects the better. Professor Small has done the thing as well as it could be done, but nevertheless the result is unconvincing. This material presents a marked contrast to the brief definite paragraphs of the earlier part of the paper. The reason is not far to seek. The later pages deal with opinion rather than with demonstrable facts. These assertions, however gently and qualifiedly made, are open to attack, and may provoke replies which will seem to make telling points. My attitude may be summed up in this aphorism: "When in doubt, don't do it."[36]

As dean of the Junior Colleges, Vincent actively enforced the policy. After he had worked with the sex-segregated policy for two years, Vincent was quoted by Marion Talbot as follows: "It meets most of the objections against throwing suddenly into constant association large numbers of young men and women just leaving home and entering on a new experience . . . it does not seem to have affected unfavorably the general social life of the institution."[37] Talbot went on to translate Vincent's opinions. First, the majority of the students came from coeducational high schools and it was only the elite private-school graduates who had sex-segregated education. Vincent was clearly more supportive of the elite's views than those of the general population of students. Second, Vincent supported social interaction but was more opposed to intellectual associations. Having fun with women was desirable but having them as equals was not.[38]

It is evident that Vincent can be placed in the "Doctrine of the Separate Spheres" category along with Small. Their lack of research on the subject of women reflects their biases as well.

Zeublin and the Sociology of Women

The generally more radical views of Zeublin again emerge. Contrary to the three "religious" men discussed above, Zeublin signed a petition protesting the university policy of segregation, as did Ira Woods Howerth, George H. Mead, and of course, Marion Talbot and Sophonisba Breckinridge.[39]

This "Memorial to President W.R. Harper and the Board of Trustees of the University of Chicago" begins by trying to placate the governing "gentlemen." The petitioners noted that the vote supporting sex segregation was the first taken by the united faculties of the junior and senior colleges. Many had not attended the meeting nor were they consulted. The dissidents wanted to know the long-term effects and plans and raised ten specific questions. Noting that all the women of the faculty opposed the plan, the petitioners wrote:

> That the measure will be coercive so far as concerns University women, that it will set back the cause of women's education wherever the University's influence is felt, that it will be a constant menace to the self-respect of women students, and will repel from the University some most admirable women, while attracting, with a probable increase of the total number of women, a less earnest class more interested in social diversions, and not assuring a corresponding increase in strong men, are consequences to be feared.[40]

This strongly worded protest was public, and Zeublin's endorsement of it was a sign of his openness toward women's rights.

His unusual mixture of radical thought, religiosity, and activism were combined in his article "The Effect of Woman on Economic Independence."[41] His opening passages contained Biblical quotations that presented "woman" as a vain and unproductive creature. He then proceeded to decry the lack of monetary independence of women and their enslavement in the household. Arguing that man controlled woman through the property instinct, Zeublin compared the wife and mother to a prostitute who must sell her body for survival. Finally, the conclusion was a poem that combined images of sweetness with equal partnership. Thus Zeublin tried to unite the social gospel, traditional roles, and radical thought into an American version of emancipation. Although the intellectual argument had numerous weak links, the overall themes were intriguing. These ideas were justifiably abandoned in future sociological analyses, but they do reveal Zeublin's commitment to a dramatically altered social status for women.

Similarly, he published a lengthy poem in *The Women Voter*, a publication of the National American Women's Suffrage Association (Addams' was its vice-president in 1912), concerning women's rights not only to vote but also to march in favor of their enfranchisement.[42]

Clearly, Zeublin's attitudes toward women favored greater equality than those of Small, Vincent, or Henderson. As we saw in chapter 4, however, it was Zeublin's politics that led to his subsequent dismissal.

Thomas and the Sociology of Women

W.I. Thomas was a major theorist in the sociology of women. He attained this status, however, by a labyrinthine path. At first he argued that biological traits limited women's ability to be creative and intellectual; then, that her weak social skills were a function of limited social contact; and finally, in one of the most sophisticated sociological analyses then available, he stated that women's behavior was a function of definitions of the situation that were socially and culturally derived. This latter view specifically countered Freudian interpretations of women's role in society, raised significant questions on the causes and social meaning of prostitution and delinquency; critiqued marriage and the nuclear family as frequently destructive to women; and actively supported women's suffrage.

To place such a strong emphasis on the study of women, however, made Thomas vulnerable to the same scholarly neglect in this area as his female colleagues suffered. For example, Janowitz, the editor of Thomas' selected papers, argued that the period from 1896 to 1908 (when Thomas wrote many articles on women) was a time that "can best be described as a self-education through which he freed himself from existing forms. Although it was a period of intense productivity, there is, in fact, no single essay from that time that warrants inclusion in this volume."[43] Similarly, Faris wrote that the Thomas collection of essays on women "was based on a soon-to-be discredited theory and was promptly forgotten."[44] Again, Volkhardt in his edited collection of Thomas' writings omitted all of Thomas' articles and books on women.[45] Finally, the Schwendingers wrote a reductionist analysis of this aspect of Thomas' career, stressing his early sexist biases and overlooking his struggle to break free from biological explanations of sex roles.[46] Thus there has been a consistent elimination of Thomas' sociology of women from the majority of the texts and articles written on his scholarly life.

The only serious consideration of Thomas' work in this area was done by Viola Klein, a British sociologist. Critiquing his collection *Sex and Society*, she evaluated it in this way:

From the point of view of the sociology of knowledge it is one part (but a very representative part) of the new perspective which functionalizes fixed traits of human character and explains them by the social context in which they have been acquired. It represents the most radical change in our outlook and in our approach to the problems of Man and Society.[47]

Thomas' large corpus on women can only be briefly summarized here, but even a cursory analysis can show its significance.

The Doctrine of the Separate Spheres and His Early Writings, 1897-98

In 1897 Thomas completed his dissertation on the origins of the sexual division of labor in society, basing his analysis on the two concepts of "katabolic" and "anabolic" energies. The former term refers to the patriarchal "fact" that men had the aggressiveness and impetus to go out and "conquer" the world. Men were able to manipulate objects (i.e., technologies, machinery, and other people) because of this instinctual strength. Women, on the other hand, were passive and had less "energy" to do these hard-working tasks. They preferred staying at home and caring for children and were less hostile and aggressive than men. The sexes, therefore, complemented each other. These "energies" were vaguely instinctual and augmented by social and cultural norms.[48] In other words, this dissertation was a "scientific" discussion and "documentation" of the Doctrine of the Separate Spheres.

A book review by Thomas in that same year also reveals his early sexism. Critiquing an antisuffrage text, Thomas lauds it as a remarkable and forceful dissent from the suffrage movement. Advancing the argument that women are best protected by strong men, it echoes the findings of his dissertation.[49]

But during these years, Thomas met Addams and visited Hull-House, and his ideas were to undergo a dramatic realignment. This shift is most evident in his collection of articles compiled in *Sex and Society* and published in 1907.

Sex and Society: The Problematic Book, 1897-1907

From 1897 to 1907, Thomas wrote steadily on the topic of women. In the latter year, these articles were collected and published in one text. The papers were unrevised and remain a record of his changes over the years. He started with a summary of his dissertation which articulated a Social Darwinist interpretation of the Doctrine of the Separate Spheres. He amplified these views a year later when he wrote that women had a weaker sexual appetite than men and needed males to protect them and their offspring.[50] It was "natural" for men to control their environment.[51]

Thomas was lecturing at Hull-House during these years, however, and had taken coursework with Mead. Gradually his ideas began to shift. Thus, in 1899, he still retained his belief in male's superior control over the world of politics (and crime), but he was attributing this more to social factors than biological ones. He even supported a matriarchal theory of society when he wrote: "In the earliest period of a society under the maternal system the woman had her own will more with her person; but with the formulation of a system of control, based on male activities, the person of women was made a point in the application of the male standpoint."[52] This loss of control included being used in exchanges negotiated by men, controlled by the tribe after divorce, killed as a human sacrifice, given in childhood as mates to unknown men, and sexual domination.[53]

This growing feminism is again mirrored in a book review. This time, however, in 1899, he agreed with the tenets of Mary Wollstonecraft: "For the gist of her quarrel with the world was that the activities of women did not have free play."[54] This same year, when the third major article in the collection was originally published, Thomas continued to explore his new views on women. Writing on clothing and modesty, he evaluated dress as a matter of social function and not "moral purity," a daring view in the Victorian age.[55]

By 1902, Thomas was examining the problems of monogamy and its resulting boredom, writing that "It is psychologically true that only the unfamiliar and not-completely controlled is interesting."[56]

Matriarchal societies continued to capture his interest, as they did Addams. His concern with social control, reflected in his studies of immigrants, was also connected to this aspect of his thought. As males increasingly dominated moral standards, freedom of action, economics, courtship, and marriage, women became increasingly dependent on men's approval. Because of this lack of control, women were charming, weak, and dependent. When community control lessened, as it did in the then-modern city, women more frequently engaged in behavior defined as "deviant" and "improper." These changes in behavior and expectations could be a source of new experiences and personal growth. Far from being "ruined," women could "pass" from a regular to an irregular way of life and back again, and this "change" could go unnoticed.[57] These sentiments were far from those advanced by Thomas in his earliest writings. All these explanations, moreover, were found in the same anthology!

The final paper in the collection, written in 1907, is the most radical critique of biological determinism. For example, he writes: "There is certainly great difference in the mental ability of individuals . . . but difference in natural ability is, in the main, a characteristic of the individual, not of race or of sex."[58]

Early men limited the range of women's activities restricting them to child-rearing and agricultural duties.

> Women were still further degraded by the development of property and its control by man, together with the habit of treating her as a piece of property whose value was enhanced if its purity were assured and demonstrable. As a result of this situation, man's chief concern in women became an interest in securing the finest specimens for his own use, in guarding them with jealous care from contact with other men, and in making them, together with the ornaments they wore, signs of his wealth and social standing.[59]

Continuing in his insightful analysis of control of women, he stated that

> we are apt to lose sight altogether of the fact that chivalry and chaperonage and modern conveniences are persistence of the old race habit of contempt for women, and of their intellectual sequestration.[60]

> [Women] are not readily admitted to the intellectual world of men; and there is not only a reluctance on the part of men to admit them, but a reluctance— or rather a real inability—on their part to enter.[61]

Commenting on the idea that women needed to be restricted from continuous hard work due to their relation to child-bearing, Thomas scoffingly wrote:

> The period of child-bearing is not only not continuous through life, but it is not serious from the standpoint of the time lost. No work is without interruption, and childbirth is an incident in the life of normal women or not more significant, when viewed in the aggregate and from the standpoint of time, than the interruptions of the work of men by their in-and-out-of-door games. The important point in all work is not to be uninterrupted but to begin again.[62]

Thus in this book Thomas developed from being a traditional sexist scientist to one with contradictory insights and finally to a strong advocate of women's fuller participation in society. By 1907 Thomas was obviously set in a direction of feminist thought that was to be clarified and expanded over the next twenty years.

Further Articles on Women by Thomas, 1908-09

Thomas published five articles on women in *American Magazine*, a popular periodical of the day, during 1908 and 1909. Still clinging to his views of instincts as a component of behavior, Thomas nonetheless made a series of strong statements on women's rights.

In "The Psychology of Women's Dress" he simplified his earlier scholarly article "The Psychology of Modesty and Clothing" discussed above. He also added more vivid language. For example, in the concluding paragraph, he made the following statement:

> The role of "half-angel and half bird" is a pretty one, if you can look at it in that way; but it denatures woman, makes her a thing instead of a person, a fact of the environment and an object of man's manipulation instead of an agent for transforming the world. It leaves society short-handed and the struggle for life harder and uglier than it would be if woman operated in it as the substantial and superior creature which nature made her.[63]

Speaking as an advocate of coeducation in "The Mind of Women," Thomas wrote that "few of the great schools are coed and in those which are so many of the instructors claim that they do not find it possible to treat the men and women on precisely the same basis, both because of their own mental attitude toward mixed classes and the inability of the women to receive such treatment."[64]

Since Thomas did not sign the petition in 1902 protesting the establishment of sex-segregated classrooms at the University of Chicago, but he was saying that such a practice was preposterous and destructive in 1909, either he was intimidated by the political milieu in the academy or underwent a change of mind. Given the evidence of his writings, the former reason is more logical, another sign of the political undercurrents of the day.

He continued his analyses of women's life in the "Older Newer Ideals of Marriage." There he asserted that monogamy could not settle all marital troubles, that working women did not destroy the family, and that divorce could be a reasonable approach to resolving marital conflicts. Condemning the religious idea of marriage as simultaneously holy and sinful, Thomas linked these attitudes with feelings of shame toward sexuality:

> This classing of marriage at once with the obscenities and the sacraments has much, though not everything, to do with the fact that marriage and sex remain among the questions which it is not safe or polite to handle. The whole question of sex is of profound interest to society but by its historical contiguity with the disreputable on the one hand and the sacred on the other it has been placed to a great extent outside the region of full examination and scientific control.[65]

In July of 1909, long before it was a socially acceptable position, Thomas defended women's suffrage. He lauded women's outrage with social problems, condemnation of the exploitation of working women, and efforts to remove incompetent politicians.[66] When he examined a series of reasons why women should not be granted the vote, he found them all wanting.

Only custom and emotions could explain the disenfranchisement of women.

His last paper in the series, "Woman and the Occupations," discussed women's need to share in the public work of a society. Matriarchies produced women who "were functional, strong, and normal, and they had a dignity and respect worthy of their work."[67] Arguing strongly for women to be integrated into the work of the whole society, Thomas saw political activities as an adjunct to full participation. This did not mean, however, that he advocated worker exploitation, for "our treatment of the working girl, particularly the factory girl, is scandalously out of harmony, not only to our romanticism but with our plain human sentiments."[68] Thomas, like Addams, saw women as less tainted than men by political corruption. Women, the argument continues, were more likely to engage in "civic housekeeping" if they were included more in powerful decision-making positions. He balanced these statements by writing: "No one is altogether male or female. The life of men and women corresponds more than it differs."[69] Acknowledging our androgeny in 1910 was, indeed, a significant insight.

Prostitution and Deviance

The topic of prostitution, a major one for Addams,[70] was also a central concern of Thomas. Both sociologists influenced each other's thought, although Addams was clearly more feminist than Thomas during the 1890s, suggesting that it was she who influenced him first.

In 1910-11 he worked on the Chicago Vice Commission which considered a range of reform issues on prostitution. After a year's investigation, the commission made ninety-six recommendations. Some of these included the establishment of a Federal Bureau of Immigration; medical certification of the lack of venereal disease for the issuance of marriage licences; increasing penalties for prostitution; establishment of municipal dance halls; prostitution rehabilitation centers; and a police morals squad.[71] Thomas was dissatisfied with the commission's conservatism and was amazed that the city later considered it a radical document.[72]

In his 1917-18 volumes of *The Polish Peasant*, Thomas again evaluated prostitution in the United States (see chapter 4). In 1923 he wrote *The Unadjusted Girl*, which examined the "social problems" of young women. Looking at the breakdown of traditional society and what he termed "social disorganization," he emphasized the social and not the moral origin of their behavior.

Prostitution and other forms of women's deviance were analyzed by Thomas as an indicator of social control over women and changing social structures. His interpretations were major, radical steps in transforming our understanding of women's behavior and place in society, rarely assessed or understood with sociological accounts.

Thomas and Women Sociologists

Thomas' career was directly tied to the women's network of sociologists. Funded by the philanthropists Helen Culver and Ethel S. Dummer who were closely associated with Hull-House, his research was directly dependent on their support.[73] Thomas also used numerous records collected by agencies associated with Hull-House, and he frequently cited the writings of women sociologists, such as Jessie Taft.[74] His close ties with Addams have already been documented.

It is clear that Thomas worked closely with women as colleagues and studied women's role in society as a significant component in his social thought. Moving from a restricted and biased perspective, he transcended these limitations to become a major interpreter of women's status. This ground-breaking work, like that of women sociologists, has been consistently neglected revealing the double bias: against women professionals and against the study of women.

George H. Mead and the Sociology of Women

Like his close friend and colleague W.I. Thomas, Mead was directly linked to the women's network and to Addams in particular. By analyzing Mead's professional network, his close affiliation with women professionals can be well documented. Unlike Thomas, however, he rarely wrote on this particular topic. Despite this fact, Mead developed a nonsexist theory of society written in egalitarian language.

Mead's Worldview

Mead's intrinsically positive approach to women is evident in his most influential book in sociology, *Mind, Self and Society*. This was published posthumously from student notes taken during his 1927 course in social psychology.[75] Throughout his lectures, Mead used sexually neutral words to describe human behavior and development. His major concepts—the self, the other, the generalized other, mind, society, institution, international-mindedness, universality, gesture, significant symbol, and the biologic individual—are all nonsexist. Mead's theory of the social genesis of the self is an excellent example of the ever-present (but rarely used) potential to write and speak without sexism. The structured absence of sexism is, therefore, part of Mead's conceptual process.

This equality in Meadian thought extends beyond the language used and is a pervasive theme in his explanation of people's behavior. His theory is a major challenge to biological determinism or theories of the "natural" differences between the sexes. With a perspective dependent upon the social creation of communication and thought, it is comprehensible, although unjustified, that men and women structure their worlds so that there are continual distinctions between the sexes. The sexes, moreover, separate their lives through the development of gestures signifying this socially created dichotomy; the nonsexist potential of Meadian theory has yet to be fully appreciated or applied. In fact, the major Meadian statement on the women's movement was written in 1913 by Jessie Taft, a doctoral student of Mead's.[76] Clearly, he was supportive of her interest and her product is a sociological classic unrecognized in the literature.

Mead's Ideas on Women

Mead actively advocated women's suffrage and signed the petition opposing the segregation of the sexes at Chicago.[77] As a suffragist, Mead marched in social protest against women's disenfranchisement and had many suffragists stay at his home.[78] In 1903, following the institution of segregation at the university, Mead addressed the Women's Fellows Club, which Marion Talbot sponsored. His talk was on "The Relation of Women to the New Education,"[79] and from all indications it was probably supportive of women's advanced education. Some of these signs are presented below.

In 1908 he spoke before the Women's Trade Union League on the topic of education, urging the development of industrial education.[80] In 1914 he wrote a strong letter to the mayor of Chicago, urging the appointment of a large number of women to the Board of Education.[81] Finally, he wrote an unpublished paper on the role of women and higher education. Referring to the proposed medical training of his daughter-in-law Dr. Irene Tufts Mead, he analyzed the need for the alteration of traditional sex roles. A passage excerpted below illustrates his general tone and advanced views. In this paper he averred that all women should have the right to careers, regardless of their economic resources. He continued:

> The pre-school training of children, the nursery schools, are coming to replace in some degree this type of natural development in early childhood. The nursery school is removing the child from the obsession of maternal devotion to the great advantage of the child, is approaching the objective training of infancy with an intelligence the mother does not possess. Institutional assistance of this sort should be at the disposal of the woman who is studying medicine and bearing children. . . . If such nursery schools exist a professional woman can find in them the means of providing for even prolonged absence from home without endangering the intelligent care of even very young children, nor do such occasional absences lessen the strength of the bond between the children and the mother.[82]

Mead was a strong, active, and outspoken advocate of women's rights. He is clearly the least sexist of the Chicago men, and he worked more closely with women sociologists than any other, as briefly outlined below.

Mead and Women Colleagues

It is difficult to separate any of the collegial relationships of Mead's from their association with Addams, Hull-House, and social reform. So these topics discussed elsewhere are not repeated here. Instead, his ties with Mary McDowell, Sophonisba Breckinridge, and Ella Flagg Young are analyzed.

Mary McDowell, the first head of the University of Chicago Settlement, was his close friend and colleague.[83] Mead was on the settlement's board from 1908 to 1921. He was treasurer of the board from 1908 to 1916 and its president from 1919 to 1921. During this period, he worked closely with Henderson, Abbott, and Breckinridge on a series of social surveys written under the auspices of the settlement.

Mead and McDowell shared a platform in 1907 when Mead spoke on the evolution of human relationships. He believed that the home and neighborhood were becoming increasingly important for human action while the significance of the church declined. McDowell continued his ideas, verifying and illustrating them with examples from her community.[84] Similarly, when McDowell gave the convocation address at the University of Chicago in 1923, it was Mead who introduced her.[85]

Probably many of his remarks on this occasion were similar to those he expressed in a paper on McDowell that was published in 1929. In it he stated that the University of Chicago "is after all another individual in the community, but an individual more like a business or corporation: an institution without a soul."[86] For Mead, McDowell provided the life and vision which the university lacked.

> It is a means of education that is not entered into the curriculum of our institutions of higher learning, this spiritual transportation, this opening of doors, this new orientation, this realization of one's own possibilities through other person's personalities, but it is without question a means of higher learning.[87]

Mead supported her contributions to the university two years earlier when he successfully lobbied for her retention as a special lecturer at the University of Chicago for the Social Services Administration, Department of Sociology, and Divinity School. There was an attempt to remove her from this position, but Mead counteracted it.[88]

Thus, from at least 1908, if not earlier, Mead and McDowell collaborated in working for the goals of the university settlement. It was this work which shaped Mead's writings and support of social surveys, industrial education, and community development that have long been overlooked as components of his social thought.

Another major female colleague of Mead's was Ella Flagg Young. He helped recruit her in 1893 for a position at the University of Chicago in the Department of Education.[89] She remained there until Dewey left in 1906. At that time she resigned due to her dismay at the political machinations and mistreatment of her at that institution.[90] (Yet another example of the limits of faculty activism and sexism.)

McDowell, Mead, Addams, and Breckinridge all joined forces in 1914 to support Young when she was forced to leave her position as superintendent of Chicago schools because of a "heckling schoolboard."[91] Their lobbying was successful in returning Young to her post and in gaining some teacher control over the classroom.[92]

During this same period, Mead worked frequently with Sophonisba Breckinridge. From 1908 until 1918, Mead served as the first vice-president of the Immigrant's Protective League, Addams as the second vice-president, and Breckinridge as secretary. This group worked for immigrants' rights, especially the female's.[93] Breckinridge also aided in the conduct of surveys at the University of Chicago Settlement,[94] and labored with Mead to establish a Chicago Bureau of Social Research. This latter organization was to be a municipal office to coordinate statistical data and "map" findings from a broad range of research topics. Ultimately such a bureau was established, although it was temporarily a victim of political appointments.[95] Mead, Breckinridge, and Abbott also worked to obtain vocational education and counseling for the working class, especially for immigrants and youths from fourteen to sixteen years of age.[96] Finally, Mead, Addams, Breckinridge, and McDowell were all involved in the 1910 Garment Worker's Strike, discussed in greater detail in chapter 4.

In summation, Mead was clearly the least sexist of all the Chicago men. Although at times conservative, Mead's work was usually highly supportive of women's equality and incorporated this goal within his sociological perspective. He advocated women's rights, labor unions for women, the extension of suffrage, and higher education for women professionals and college students. His record is by far more open and liberated than that of his later colleagues, Park and Burgess.

Ernest W. Burgess and the Sociology of Women

As can be expected, Burgess' view of women's status was a conflicting one. Sometimes he held egalitarian views and sometimes he did not. An egregious example of his sexism (and ethnocentrism) is found in his article on the preadolescent girl from an immigrant family. Written in 1923 (the same year as Thomas' *The Unadjusted Girl*), Burgess revealed a deep bias against immigrant women, their daily life, and family structure. In this article he drew on a series of settlement "anecdotes" to document his position, including several examples from Hull-House. His interpretation of these incidents, however, had little in common with Addams' views. For example, Burgess judged that "the relationship of mother and daughter is close in a formal rather than in a sympathetic sense." Finding immigrant mothers to be responding merely with "physical reflexes" rather than sympathetic ones, he perceived these mothers as isolated from their daughters. (The animosity toward the mothers is far exceeded, however, by his extreme insensitivity toward immigrant fathers[97].) Burgess summarizes each of his points in his conclusion:

> In our study of the personality of the little girl of the settlement we see human nature developing in the matrix of the human relations of the family under untoward influences, the blight of poverty, ignorance, and stupid kindness, the droughts of lack of sympathy and understanding; perceiving all this, we marvel and rejoice that the product has so little that is bad and so much that is good.[98]

Burgess' picture of the life of little girls is so sentimental toward the "little selfish drudges"[99] while being harsh in his judgement of her parents, it is hard to imagine him as a "sympathetic" figure toward these girls.

Burgess' attempt to move away from these extreme positions of emotional judgement can be seen in his later work. His explicitly repressive language is changed to more sophisticated wording that claims to be objective but is implicitly the same. For example, in 1943 he wrote a comment on Marvin K. Opler's analysis of the relationship between women's social status and various forms of marriage. Opler's thesis was that women's status was tied to views on marital and extramarital relations and her recognition in the economic structure of the community. Burgess missed Opler's point, however. Burgess presented an argument concerning the need to study "ideal types" of marriage, and Opler's central thesis concerning women's relative freedom and power was ignored. In this way, Burgess was trying to show his "value-free" position, but he missed the critical intent of Opler's argument.[100]

Further examples of his vacillating positions can be seen with the two passages cited below:

> One phase of this ambiguity in husband-wife relations—the nominally equal, but really inferior status of the wife—is often of decisive importance for success or failure in marriage. The husband may assume a position of domi-

nance in family relations. Or, conceiving the home to be the domain of the woman, as business is that of the man, he may withdraw as entirely as possible from responsibilities of the household and the rearing of children.[101]

The emancipation of youth, like the emancipation of women and the freeing of slaves, is a situation which must, I am forced to conclude, be recognized, whether or not we approve or it.[102]

These contrasting positions run through his extensive writings on marriage and the family, a topic in which he specialized. For example, working mothers were portrayed as leaving small children neglected and locked in the house.[103] He also portrayed these mothers as the victims of a romantic myth and ideology that restrained their freedom.[104] Numerous citations relevant to these two positions could be complied, but the more important issue is his general approach to the role of women in society, particularly in marriage and the family.

Within this broader perspective, Burgess is another "tragic paradox" wanting both more liberal mores and social acceptance of his ideas. Thus, he wrote that "companionate marriages" were desirable but never really analyzed the disparity in power inherent in marriages in the United States. His view of marriage and the family tends to be a mechanical analysis of this or that variable, such as length of engagement or degree of adjustment, or adaptability or assimilation. Consistently, Burgess neglected to ask questions about the meaning or goals of these factors.[105] In his efforts for "objectivity," his writings miss the essence of intimate relations or the nature of conflict within them. He continually stressed that Americans have individualistic rather than societal pressures, but he accepted the ideology of individualism instead of probing the real pressures of the economy or social structure upon marital unions.

In these writings, many able points are raised, for example that marriage would not disappear by 1977, as some of his colleagues predicted, and that divorce would be more accepted and frequent. Overall, however, Burgess had a dispassionate and hollow understanding of the forms of marriage and the family, reflecting his failure to understand sex roles or the status of women in society.

Robert E. Park and the Sociology of Women

Park was virulently opposed to feminism.

For Park, as for D.H. Lawrence, returning to nature meant opposition to feminism. Physical differences between the sexes seemed to imply barriers and separate spheres which were part of the order of nature and therefore proper. Among the press clippings from his Detroit days are little fillers, satirizing the reversal of sexual roles—women playing baseball, watched by daintily dressed men, the husband putting the children to bed while his wife rejoiced, there's none of the "new man" nonsense about him.[106]

As noted in the section on Park and social reform, Park was insecure as a scholar and person. His conflicts over social reform and "do-goodism" were closely associated with his ideas about masculinity and femininity. He associated applied sociology with women, as did the other supporters of the Doctrine of the Separate Spheres, but Park did not respect this "distinction" in the way the more "religious" men did. For Park, men were far superior to women. This derisive attitude is found in a letter to Clara Cahill, before they married. At this time, Park was a reporter and wrote to her:

> I will send you an article about the Women's Independent Voters' Association. I did not dare to tell all that I mean about them. I fear you would not like it because it is a trifle Mephistophelian and I cannot teach you to see the subtle delights of making people who are sincere but misguided appear ridiculous.[107]

This scorn, moreover, was expressed when Park himself was a muckraker!

This patriarchal worldview is intrinsic to his writings with Burgess, especially in their classic *Introduction to the Science of Society*. For this book portrayed society as a product of conflict, competition, and dominance. This societal theory directly opposed Addams' theory of cultural feminism. This ideological contrast helps explain their suppression of her ideas and influence. In order to understand the epistemological division between their work and Addams', their "patriarchal sociology" needs to be examined.

The Foundation of Patriarchal Sociology

The *Introduction to the Science of Society*, published in 1921, is sometimes claimed to be the most influential textbook in sociology,[108] if not one of its most influential books. According to Faris, it standardized views in sociology thereby making it a more unified discipline. This generalized acceptance of the text reveals the decline of opposing views, and the increasing power of the Chicago men to define sociology. The Chicago vision elaborated in this textbook was a patriarchal view of society and its control. Park, moreover, was the major force behind its writing.[109] Clearly believing in capitalism, Park and Burgess wrote that:

> Competition is a struggle for position in an economic order. The distribution of populations in the world-economy, the industrial organization in the na-

tional economy, and the vocation of the individual in the division of labor— all these are determined, in the long run by competition. The status of the individual, or a group of individuals, in the social order, on the other hand, is determined by rivalry, by war, or by subtler forms of conflict.[110]

This warring network of relationships and social order was deeply rooted in human interests.[111]

Using a Social Darwinist analogy, Park and Burgess reversed many of the laboriously won achievements of their predecessors at Chicago, both male and female. For example, Thomas slowly altered his Social Darwinist positions to ones favoring women's liberation, freedom from racism, and biological determinism. Mead, too, surpassed these ideas, as did Small.[112]

Calling this wedding of Social Darwinism with sociology "human ecology," the Chicago School engendered a view of social behavior in the city as basically a kind of adventuresome jungle, where the fittest survive and flourish (and are male). Thus we find that Park and Burgess viewed

> social organization, with the exception of the order based on competition and adaptation, [as] especially an accommodation of differences through conflicts. This fact explains why diverse-mindedness rather than like-mindedness is characteristic of human as distinguished from animal society.[113]

Instead of Addams' view of society as a group based on human cooperation Park and Burgess adopted the extreme counterview of society as a group based on competition. The incompatibility of their positions is evident at almost every point of comparison. For example, Addams theoretically opposed strikes because the working class used a means to obtain their short-term goals which was contradictory to their long-term goals. Strikes were "war-like" and generated further opposition and conflict. Park and Burgess, however, saw strikes as a mechanism for social change, social order, and "assimilation."[114] (Unlike Addams, however, they did not publicly defend strikers or aid in the labor struggle.)

Yet another example of the opposition of their theories was Park and Burgess' belief that war could be "a form of relaxation"! Citing Patrick on the "Psychology of War," they affirm such views as:

> It is by no means sure that what man wants is peace and quiet and tranquillity. That is too close to ennui, which is his greatest dread. What man wants is not peace but battle. He must pit his force against someone or something. Every language is most rich in synonyms for battle, war, contest, conflict, quarrel, combat, fight. German children play all day long with their toy soldiers. Our sports take the form of contests in football, baseball, and hundreds of others. Prize fights, dog fights, cock fights, have pleased in all ages.[115]

To Addams, the greatest pacifist leader of her day, such a worldview was anathema to everything she believed and wrote.

This intrinsic opposition between the ideas of Addams and Park is a fundamental reason for her almost complete erasure from the annals of Chicago Sociology and subsequently from sociology itself. Thus, attitudes toward women and their place in society are directly linked to the type of social thought produced, reaching an extreme of patriarchal analysis with the work of Park.

Conclusion: The Chicago Men and the Sociology of Women

As we have seen in this chapter, the Chicago men held a range of views in reference to women's status in society (summarized in Table 8.1). Contrary to the Schwendingers' claim, they were not all "sexists to a man."[116] The variations in the men's positions resulted in vastly different writings (see Table 8.2) and collegial relationships (see Table 8.3). These patriarchal or feminist positions directly affected the careers of women in sociology, as well as the receptivity of the profession to their ideas.

Small and Vincent clearly adopted the Doctrine of the Separate Spheres." Ironically, this form of sexism allowed women greater freedom than they had for decades after its eclipse. The reason for this flourishing of women sociologists is that the women themselves often believed themselves "different," too, although often superior to men. Thus, a kind of "accomodation" occurred. The women were given limited space and power to work, and they took it and created a space and world-view that flourished.

One response to the unanticipated success of the women who were "allowed" to enter the halls of higher learning in 1892 was the subsequent denial of their equal access to coeducation in 1902. Small's pivotal role in restricting women's rights in this case is clear. None of his "full-time" faculty opposed the policy, even Thomas who strongly supported women's rights. It was only the men less subject to his control, Zeublin in Extension and Mead in Philosophy, who signed the petition protesting this unfair

TABLE 8.1
The Male Chicago School and Their Attitudes
Towards Women on a Continuum

Anti-Feminist → Supporter of the Doctrine of → Liberal Supporter of
Women's Rights → Feminist the Separate Spheres

Park → Vincent → Small → Burgess → Henderson → Zeublin → Thomas
→ Mead

TABLE 8.2
The Chicago Men and the Scholarly Study of Woman

0 Articles	1-3 Articles	One Book	Two Books and Several Articles
Park	Small	Henderson	Thomas
Vincent	Burgess		
Mead	Zeublin		

TABLE 8.3
The Chicago Men and Contacts with
Female Sociology Colleagues (1892-1918)

Minimal Contacts	Primarily Addams	4 + Colleagues
Park	Small	Henderson
Burgess	Vincent	Mead
		Thomas
		Zeublin

policy. Small wanted women to have a place within the university but this was for him a restrictive "women's place" that was not as powerful as the men's. Nonetheless, this type of sexism created an opportunity for women to achieve that affected the work of many men as well as their female colleagues.

This "space" or "sphere" also directly affected the work of Zeublin, Henderson, Mead, and Thomas. All these men worked with women as colleagues and to varying degrees they were concerned with women's rights. Mead and Thomas have an intrinsically central position in the study of women as either scholars or colleagues. Almost all their work for and with women, however, has been overlooked.

Again, the pattern of Park's and Burgess' work revealed a central shift within the Chicago School. Burgess vacillated in his views, never strongly stating a position either way. Park was strongly antifeminist, generating a patriarchal style of social interpretation that shaped sociology until the present. The practitioners of sociology, predominantly male, found this world-view understandable and comprehensible. The "women's view" became increasingly restricted in sociology, and the sociology of women became a marginal subfield. The patriarchal perspective dominated sociology, paralleled by the removal of women from the profession and their segregation into "women's work" in social work.

Part of the reason why such a large-scale removal of a perspective and its proponents was possible can be found in the already existing dual division of labor within the profession. Since women were not acceptable as equal professionals in the academy, they found employment elsewhere. Social settlements, women's colleges and charity organizations employed women sociologists, and employees in this alternate institutional network looked to Hull-House for leadership. When Addams' ideas, institutional network, and sociological practice were labelled by male sociologists as "nonscientific" and "sentimental" social work, Addams continued in the same path with a new professional group. After all, she probably thought, "Why not?" She had developed a number of ties with social workers over the course of many years, and she had always felt independent of academic politics. This freedom from academic control was one of the reasons why she had not worked under the auspices of the University of Chicago on those occasions when she had been invited to join as a faculty member or as the head of an affiliated institution. Her failure to maintain a sociological base, however, marked a turning point for a whole segment of sociological epistemology and practice. Women sociologists as a group lost their professional recognition. Unlike Addams, some of them had developed a professional network that relied on academics and recognition within the sociological field. All the female sociologists had depended primarily on each other for their professional survival. Now they entered a new professional arena with psychological adherents, new professional networks, and different ideologies and practices. Addams, as a leader, changed little, but her contemporaneous women sociologists were often forced to change considerably. Addams' sociology, moreover, was buried in these professional realignments.

The loss of such a sociological vision was profound. To enable us to only speculate on the vastness of this vacuum, hypothetical questions can be raised concerning other great theorists. What would sociology be like if no one read Karl Marx, Max Weber, Emile Durkheim, or George Herbert Mead? More to the point, what would sociology be like if the famous faculty of the Chicago School of Sociology had discussed, debated, and understood Addams' ideas over the past sixty years?

Since these intervening years have yielded little sociological analyses of her work, such speculations can only lead to a partial understanding of what has been lost. Fortunately, Addams' theories of the social order were often anonymously incorporated into the Chicago School of Sociology and have thereby had a significant effect on the profession. But of even greater significance, her corpus has stood the test of time, and some of her books have become American classics. This national appreciation of her work has not been a scholarly one, however. Therefore, our next three chapters provide scholarly analyses of her written system of thought, its epistemology, and relevance to the practice of American sociology.

Notes

1. Talbot's place in the Chicago Department of Sociology is briefly discussed by Mary Jo Deegan, "Women and Sociology: 1890-1930," *Journal of the History of Sociology* 1 (Fall 1978): 11-34. Few references to her work can be found in any other writings on the Chicago School.
2. See the first chapter of Marion Talbot and Lois Kimball Mathews Rosenberry, *The History of the American Association of University Women, 1881-1931* (Cambridge, Mass.: Houghton Mifflin, 1931), pp. 3-11.
3. Ibid., pp. 144-45.
4. Ibid., p. 146.
5. Ibid., p. 143.
6. Ibid.
7. Writings by early male sociologists on the subject of women are considered by Herman and Julia Schwendinger, *The Sociologists of the Chair* (New York: Basic Books, 1974).
8. Ibid., p. 310.
9. Emile Durkheim, *Suicide*, tr. J.T. Spaulding and George Simpson (New York: Free Press, 1951, c. 1897), p. 272.
10. Ibid.
11. Ibid., p. 215.
12. Frederick Engels, *The Origin of the Family, Private Property and the State* (Moscow: Progressive Press, 1968, c. 1884).
13. Charlotte Perkins Gilman, *Women and Economics* (New York: Harper Torchbooks, 1966, c. 1898).
14. See the excellent documentation of women in social science at Chicago by Jo Freeman, "Women on the Social Science Faculties since 1892." Mimeograph of a speech given to a minority groups workshop of the Political Science Association, Winter 1969
15. See Eileen Kraditor, ed., *Up from the Pedestal* (Chicago: Quadrangle, 1970); Jessie Bernard, *The Female World* (New York: Free Press, 1981).
16. Samuel W. Dike, "Sociology of the Higher Education of Women," *Atlantic Monthly* 421 (November 1892):671.
17. Ibid.
18. Ibid., pp. 673-76.
19. Mary Jo Deegan, "Women and Sociology: 1890-1930," *Journal of the History of Sociology* 1 (Fall 1978):14-24.
20. Marion Talbot, "The Women of the University," *Decennial Publications of the University of Chicago* (Chicago: University of Chicago Press, 1903), p. 122.
21. Ibid., pp. 138-39.
22. Ibid., p. 139.
23. Marion Talbot, *More Than Lore* (Chicago: University of Chicago Press, 1936), p. 172.
24. Interview of Ruth Shonle Cavan by the author, October 1978.
25. They were similarly limited in participation in the "men's" organization, the American Sociological Society. See Mary Jo Deegan, "Early Women Sociologists and the American Sociological Society," *American Sociologist* 16 (February 1981):114-24.
26. Albion W. Small, "The Social Mission of College Women," *The Independent* 54 (30 January 1902):261-63.

27. W.I. Thomas, "On a Difference in the Metabolism of the Sexes," Ph.D. diss. Department of Sociology, University of Chicago, 1897. The equal capacity of the "female brain" and the "male brain" was a common theme in Thomas' early writings. See extended discussion below.
28. Small, "The Social Mission of College Women," pp. 261-62.
29. Ibid., p. 262.
30. Ibid.
31. See discussion of Park below.
32. Small, "The Social Mission of College Women," p. 263.
33. Albion W. Small, "Coeducation at the University of Chicago," *Proceedings of the National Education Association*, 1903, pp. 295-96.
34. Charles R. Henderson, *Education with Reference to Sex*, Eighth Yearbook of the National Society for the Scientific Study of Education (Chicago: University of Chicago Press, 1909).
35. Ibid., pt. 2, p. 33.
36. George E. Vincent to W.R. Harper, 11 November 1902, "Coeducation at Chicago," box 60, folder 11, Presidents' Papers, 1889-1925, UCSC.
37. Talbot, *More Than Lore*, pp. 178-79.
38. Ibid., p. 179.
39. The women were more overtly involved in the protest than the men. In addition to signing a general faculty protest, they wrote a pamphlet discussing the pros and cons of the issue and a strong dissenting editorial denied by the President as to its accuracy. See box 60, folder 11, Presidents' Papers, 1889-1925, UCSC.
40. "Memorial" in above file. Quotation taken from pt. "six," n.p.
41. Charles Zeublin, *American Journal of Sociology* 14 (March, 1909):606-14. For further discussion of these ideas see I.M. Rubinow, pp. 614-19, and Marion Talbot, pp. 619-21.
42. Charles Zeublin, "The Suffrage Parade," *The Woman Voter* 4 (June 1913):15-16.
43. Morris Janowitz, "Introduction" to *W.I. Thomas: On Social Organization and Social Personality* (Chicago: University of Chicago Press, 1966), p. xx.
44. Ellsworth Faris, "W.I. Thomas (1863-1947)," *Sociology and Social Research* 32 (1947-48):756.
45. Edmund Volkhardt, ed., *Social Behavior and Personality: Contributions of W.I. Thomas to Theory and Social Research* (New York: Social Science Research Council, 1951).
46. Schwendingers, *The Sociologists of the Chair*, p. 783.
47. Viola Klein, *The Feminine Character* (New York: International Universities Press), p. 162. Rosalind Rosenberg, a historian, has also favorably represented Thomas on the sociology of women. See *Beyond Separate Spheres* (New Haven: Yale University Press, 1982), pp. 114-31.
48. W.I. Thomas, Ph.D. diss., Department of Sociology, University of Chicago, 1897. Published as "On a Difference in the Metabolism of the Sexes," *American Journal of Sociology* 3 (July 1897):31-63.
49. W.I. Thomas, "Review of *Women and the Republic*," *American Journal of Sociology* 3 (November 1897):406-07.
50. W.I. Thomas, *Sex and Society* (Chicago: University of Chicago Press, 1907), p. 55.
51. Ibid., p. 73.

52. Ibid., p. 168.

53. Ibid., pp. 168-70.

54. W.I. Thomas, "Review of *A Study of Mary Wollstonecraft and the Rights of Woman*," *American Journal of Sociology* 4 (May 1899): 894-95.

55. Thomas, *Sex and Society*, pp. 201-20.

56. Ibid., p. 196.

57. Ibid., p. 242.

58. Ibid., p. 257.

59. Ibid., pp. 297-98.

60. Ibid., p. 301.

61. Ibid., p. 302.

62. Ibid., p. 314.

63. "The Psychology of Woman's Dress," *American Magazine* 67 (November 1908):72.

64. "The Mind of Woman," *American Magazine* 67 (December):150.

65. "The Older and the Newer Ideals of Marriage," *American Magazine* 67 (April 1909):548.

66. "Votes for Women," *American Magazine* 68 (July 1909): 292-301, p. 292. This article was so supportive of women's suffrage that it was reprinted as a pamphlet by the National American *Woman Suffrage* Association and distributed by their Massachusetts branch under the title of "Shall Women Vote?". Although there is no date on the pamphlet I found it bound with a series of similar pamphlets from 1912 compiled into one volume under the title *Woman Suffrage* at Notre Dame University. This was the same year that Addams was President of the National association, and Thomas included a picture of Addams in the article as well as a brief discussion of her special concern with working women voters.

67. "Women and the Occupations," *American Magazine* 68 (September 1909):464.

68. Ibid., p. 466

69. Ibid., p. 469.

70. See ch. 9 in this volume.

71. The Vice Commission of Chicago, *The Social Evil in Chicago* (New York: Arno Press and the New York Times, 1970, c. 1911).

72. W.I. Thomas and Florian Znaniecki, *The Polish Peasant in Europe and America*, 2nd ed., vols. 1 and 2 (New York: Dover, 1958, c. 1917-1918); W.I. Thomas and Dorothy S. Thomas, *The Child in America* (New York: Knopf, 1928).

73. Mary Jo Deegan and John S. Burger, "W.I. Thomas and Social Reform," *Journal of the History of the Behavioral Sciences*, (February 1981):114-25.

74. See references throughout *The Unadjusted Girl*, ed. Benjamin Nelson, pref. Michael Parenti (New York: Harper Torchbooks, 1967, c. 1923).

75. George Herbert Mead, *Mind, Self and Society*, ed. Charles Morris (Chicago: University of Chicago Press, 1934).

76. Jessie Taft, *The Woman Movement from the Point of View of Social Consciousness* (Chicago: University of Chicago Press, 1915). A dissertation of the same title was submitted to the Department of Philosophy of the University of Chicago in 1913.

77. See "Memorial" signed with Mead's name; "Coeducation at the University of Chicago," Presidents' Papers, 1889-1925, box 60, folder 11, UCSC.

78. Irene Tufts Mead to author, 7 July 1975. George Mead was also a major speaker at a suffrage meeting reported in "Society Women Talk Suffrage," *Chicago Tribune* (9 January 1912).
79. Talbot, "The Women of the University," p. 123.
80. George Herbert Mead, "Educational Aspects of Trade Union Schools," *Union Labor Advocate* 8 (1909):19-20. Audience noted on p. 19.
81. George Herbert Mead, "Report on the Chicago City Club Committee on Education," *City Club Bulletin* 7 (3 May 1914):14.
82. George Herbert Mead, "Women and Medicine," 1917, Mead Addendum, box 2, folder 31, UCSC.
83. Interview, Irene Tufts Mead with author, 2 June 1978.
84. Ethel S. Dummer Notes, "19th Century," Dummer Papers, folder 650, Schlesinger Library.
85. Caroline M. Hill, ed. *Mary McDowell and Municipal Housekeeping* (Chicago: Miller Publishing Co, 1937), p. 129.
86. George Herbert Mead, "Mary McDowell," *Neighborhood* 2 (April 1919), p. 77.
87. Ibid., p. 78.
88. University of Chicago administrator (unsigned) to G.H. Mead, 18 (May 1927), 2 pp.
89. Mead to Dewey, 23 June 1895, Dewey Papers, Southern Illinois University. McDowell Papers, Chicago Historical Society (hereafter referred to as McDowell Papers).
90. Joan K. Smith, *Ella Flagg Young* (Ames: Educational Studies Press and the Iowa State University Research Foundation, 1979), pp. 88-100.
91. Mead also gave a speech, later published. See "A Heckling School Board and an Educational Stateswoman," Survey 31 (10 January 1914):443-44.
92. Smith, *Ella Flagg Young*, pp. 200-219; Diner, *A City and Its Universities* (Chapel Hill: University of North Carolina Press, 1980), pp. 87-99.
93. This is discussed in more depth in ch. 6. See also Diner, *A City and Its Universities*, pp. 130-31.
94. Abbott and Breckinridge helped complete this project, particularly Montgomery's volume. Their work is acknowledged in the *University of Chicago Settlement Minutes I*, McDowell Papers.
95. For a discussion of this bureau see Diner, *A City and Its Universities*, pp. 127-29; and "A Bureau of Social Research in Chicago," Rosenwald Papers, box 4, folder 20, UCSC.
96. The intricate network between Mead, Abbott, and Breckinridge is discussed in Mary Jo Deegan, "Mead and the Sociology of Women," unpublished paper, 1981. As a group, these three authors—Mead, Abbott, and Breckinridge—published several books and articles and conducted overlapping social surveys in vocational education and guidance for immigrants and laborers.
97. Burgess' "analysis" of immigrant fathers is worthy of an extensive note. His spiteful tone is lodged in the words and no further comment is needed. "The attitude of the father toward the little girl varies decidedly with nationality. The Polish father apparently has little interest in his daughter or influence over her. . . . The control of the Italian father in the home is absolute, and his interest real, though crudely and unsympathetically expressed. . . . The father in the Jewish family seems to be on somewhat more friendly terms with his daughter than in the Polish or Italian homes. He usually makes pets of the

small children, although he pays considerably less attention to the little girl than to her brother. The average Irish father, if not a drunkard, takes a great interest in his daughter." Ernest W. Burgess, "The Pre-Adolescent Girl of the Immigrant Type and Her Home." *Religious Education* 18 (December 1923):353-54.

98. Ibid., p. 361.
99. Ibid., esp. pp. 352-53.
100. Marvin K. Opler, "Woman's Social Status and the Forms of Marriage," *American Journal of Sociology* 49 (September 1943): 125-46; Ernest W. Burgess, "Comment on Opler's 'Woman's Social Status and the Forms of Marriage,'" *American Journal of Sociology* 49 (September 1943):147-48.
101. Ernest W. Burgess, "The Effect of War on the American Family" (c. 1942), in *The Basic Writings of Ernest W. Burgess*, ed. Donald Bogue (Chicago: Community and Family Study Center, University of Chicago, 1974), pp. 200-201.
102. Burgess, "The Romantic Impulse and Family Disorganization" (c. 1926), in *The Basic Writings of Ernest W. Burgess*, ed. Donald Bogue (Chicago: Community and Family Study Center, University of Chicago, 1974), p. 163.
103. Ibid., "The Effect of the War on the American Family," pp. 195-96.
104. Ibid., pp. 200-201.
105. In Bogue's edition of Burgess' collected works, two of the seven sections are on marriage and the family, and these two sections contain fourteen articles. Other portions of the book also discuss the family, e.g. the family and the aging process (a third section of the book).
106. Fred H. Matthews, *Quest for an American Sociology* (Montreal: McGill-Queen's University, 1977), p. 16.
107. Cited by Winifred Rauschenbush, *Robert C. Park* (Durham, N.C.: Duke University Press, 1979), p. 23.
108. Robert E.L. Faris, *Chicago Sociology* (Chicago: University of Chicago Press, 1967), p. 37.
109. Ibid., p. 38.
110. Robert E. Park and Ernest W. Burgess, *Introduction to the Science of Sociology* (Chicago: University of Chicago Press, 1921), p. 574.
111. Ibid., p. 575.
112. The decline of Social Darwinism at Chicago occurred during the careers of all the early men. Its reemergence in subsequent writings by later Chicago sociologists is virtually unclaimed.
113. Park and Burgess, *Introduction to the Science of Society*, pp. 664-65.
114. Ibid., pp. 50, 544-50, 592-94.
115. Ibid., p. 598. This same article finds Vincent's Chautauqua unacceptably "peaceful," pp. 598-99.
116. Schwendingers, *The Sociologists of the Chair*, p. 290.

9

Jane Addams and Cultural Feminism

Jane Addams was an articulate cultural feminist who embodied her beliefs. She wrote extensively on the superiority of women's values, worldview, and behavior. She lived her life surrounded by women, and she trusted them more than she did men. Her cultural feminism was actualized in her lifestyle, self-presentation, and epistemology. That is, she was employing this perspective whenever she focused a very gentle and compassionate eye on the harsh world of the poor and the disenfranchised. She did not, however, sentimentalize their pain nor gently chide those who caused these conditions. Addams was a staunch fighter and persistent advocate. Her development of cultural feminism occurred throughout her lifetime, but it became increasingly apparent that this was her major intellectual stance and theoretical position.[1] For many years, she believed that the advantages of cultural feminism would become so evident that patriarchal society would give way in a rational recognition of its inferior power to order the world. She was grossly inaccurate in this judgment, and it was patriarchy and not cultural feminism that organized everyday life in the future.

Although cultural feminism is very distinct from the Doctrine of the Separate Spheres,[2] it is vulnerable to being absorbed by advocates of the latter approach. This problematic element in cultural feminism, especially in reference to the men of the Chicago School, is analyzed in this chapter. Before doing this, it is necessary to present some background on the theory and then analyze Addams' advocacy, development, and application of it.

Cultural Feminism

Many cultural feminists support their arguments by examining the behavior of women in both the distant past and the present. Bachoffen's groundbreaking work on early matriarchal societies is often used as evidence that women were the earliest and most important members of society.[3] In soceties led by women, or "matriarchies," there are vastly different rules governing sexuality and marriage, property inheritance, and the distribution of power than those rules operative in societies led by men, or "patriarchies." When women have greater social control than men, less stringent social sanctions are imposed on female sexual activities and choice of partners. Illegitimacy is absent, and inheritance and descent are organized through female ancestors. Matriarchal societies are generally nonmilitaristic, with the dramatic exception of Amazons. Religion, arts, and crafts are organized around female symbols of fertility and anatomy. Engels took the archaeological evidence developed by Bachoffen and Morgan and extended their analyses to include changing economic conditions as a cause for the transition from matriarchal societies to patriarchal ones.[4] Succinctly, Engels' argument is that as men accumulated capital, because of technological and social inventions, they altered the norms controlling sexuality, the family, and government. Women became a commodity of exchange who supplied men with both status and heirs. Recent anthropological evidence largely supports the existence of early societies where women had significantly greater power than they do today.[5]

A third major theorist of cultural feminism, Otis Tufton Mason, strongly influenced Addams' social thought and is discussed in the next section. All these theorists were part of a school of thought that was never viable in male American sociology. For female American sociologists, however, cultural feminism became the cornerstone of their thought.

Almost all women sociologists trained before 1915 were cultural feminists.[6] This branch of feminist thought suffered a severe blow immediately prior to, during, and after World War I. Most of these women theorists opposed the war on the basis that military values were destructive, masculine, and inferior to the more socially advanced feminine values of cooperation and pacifism. Addams, as the leading spokesperson for this view, was also the leading target. Pacifism was only one component in a complex set of assumptions made by cultural feminists, but its threat to patriarchal violence caused a savage response, and repression of this theory soon followed.

Jane Addams on Cultural Feminism

Addams was, and remains, one of the most articulate and sophisticated theorists of cultural feminism. Her major intellectual resource, especially during the 1890s, was Otis Tufton Mason's *Woman's Share in Primitive Culture*.[7] Addams used Mason's book in a course she taught through the University of Chicago Extension Division.[8] Therefore, a brief summary of his ideas is in order.

This feminist text is a radical statement on the role of women in the formation of culture and civilization. Mason attributed the development of many, if not all, the major innovations in art, language, religion, and industry to women. He documented that, in general, it was women who housed, fed, and clothed the species in early societies. Mason stressed the uniqueness of women's abilities and nature, even in the areas of public governance and speech: "Nothing is more natural than that the author of parental government, the founder of tribal kinship, the organizer of industrialism, should have much to say about that form of housekeeping called public economy."[9] Clearly, many of Addams' ideas are traceable to this influential book which not only stressed the significance of women, but even their superiority to men. Mason's concluding paragraph amply conveyed his view:

> It is not here avowed that women may not pursue any path in life they choose, that they have no right to turn aside from old highways to wander in unbeaten tracks. But before it is decided to do that there in no harm in looking backward over the honorable achievements of the sex. All this is stored capital, accumulated experience and energy. If all mankind to come should be better born and nurtured, better instructed in morals and conduct at the start, better clothed and fed and housed all their lives, better married and encompassed and refined, the old ratios of progress would be doubled. All this beneficent labour is the birthright of women, and much of it of women alone. Past glory therein is secure, and it only remains to be seen how far the future will add to its lustre in the preservation of holy ideals.[10]

This interpretation of women's place in early society contrasts markedly with most interpretations of "primitive" societies. Instead, such cultures and social worlds are often seen as "barbaric," "naturally" dominated by men, and strongly lacking in the benefits of "contemporary civilization." Such a patriarchal view was supported originally by W.I. Thomas, who examined the sexual division of labor in early societies as a function of "katabolic and anabolic energies" for males and females respectively. His interpretation of the male dominance of public life and activities based on this quasi-Darwinist position soon ended, however, and his later formulations of women's role in society were much more egalitarian.[11]

As scholars studying early societies, it is assumed here that Thomas was more influenced by Addams' cultural feminism than she was influenced by his ideas about sexual energies. Although Addams did believe in the existence of a "maternal instinct," this biological state was a sex-linked strength of women that was denied its full expression in patriarchal society. In his early writing Thomas justified the restriction of women's participation in society and their limitation to the "women's sphere." At this time, Addams valued the female world and wanted it to be extended throughout society. This does not imply, however, that his influence on her work was negligible. On the contrary, when the corpora of Addams and Thomas are compared, striking similarities emerge.

The study of women was central to both, and the specific concerns of the young delinquent, the immigrant, and the prostitute were common threads. Emphasis on the social origin of behavior and the significance of social meaning and interaction permeate both sets of writings. Both authors were more conservative in their earlier writings than in their later ones. Addams was more religious and elitist in her early years than in subsequent ones, and Thomas was originally more sexist. Both studied "primitive" societies and ultimately came to believe than women were increasingly oppressed as "civilization" spread. "The city" was viewed as the locale for changing social expectations, and the cost of such social dislocation was considered in depth by both.

With the frequent visits of Thomas to Hull-House, their long friendship, his activities in support of women's suffrage and rights of expression, it is clear that a deep intellectual and collegial bond existed that was reflected in both of their work on women.[12] It is possible that Addams was partially responsible for Thomas' broadening view of the role of women in society and his movement away from the then popular Doctrine of the Separate Spheres. Similarly, it is probable that Thomas aided in Addams' broadening perspective on social meaning and interaction as a basis for society rather than her earlier, more moralistic stance.

Despite these significant areas of overlapping interests and thought, there were important distinctions in their work. Addams was more politically active, more concerned with the plight of the poor and working class, and more involved in applied sociology than Thomas was.[13] On his part, he was clearly more scholarly, more influential in the academic world of sociology, and more supportive of a single standard for the sexes based primarily on the male model of society and social action. Thomas was also more supportive of women's testing of moral limits and standards than Addams. His view of the city and social disorganization held a key to interpreting city life as potentially exciting precisely because it was an adventure, albeit often an illegal or harrowing one. Addams, in turn, saw the underside of this glamour more poignantly and with more opprobrium. City life was far from an adventure for impoverished families in poor housing, with limited money, bad health, and underpaid employment. Addams emphasized the problems of the city and the dislocation of minorities: the poor, the aged, the immigrant, the young, and women.

Addams was a public leader because she acted on her vision of a new world, while Thomas was an intellectual leader because he systematically described his vision of the present. Together, they formed an important intellectual vision with a common base and a slightly different focus.

Another intellectual stream feeding her cultural feminism was radical feminism. In particular, she was strongly influenced by her life-long friendship with Charlotte Perkins Gilman, another early feminist theoretician and sociologist.[14] Gilman's writings were more materialist and militant than Addams', but they shared a deep interest in women's culture and emancipation.

One of the first indications of this friendship was Gilman's move to Hull-House in July of 1895. She left San Francisco amid much fanfare, for even at this time she was a noted figure. One newspaper claimed that she was to be Addams' "guest and first assistant."[15] She stayed less than a year, perhaps because of her failure to be an important leader within the group, but during that time she was an active participant at the settlement.

In October, Gilman offered a series of six weekly lectures. She discussed the labor movement, the advancement of women, childhood, social organization, the "body of humanity," and social ethics.[16] The following March she joined Addams, Kelley, McDowell, Vincent, and Small in a public protest against Chicago sweat shops.[17] Shortly after this, however, Gilman moved out of Hull-House and on to other projects. Her ties with Addams and the other Hull-House figures were never severed, however.

Gilman and Addams joined forces on at least two other occasions. They both worked on *The Women's Journal,* a feminist magazine advocating women's emancipation. This journal was notable in being one of the few women's publications that addressed working women's issues.[18] In 1915[19] Gilman and Addams also participated in the beginning of the women's peace movement.

In addition to these feminist activities, they were also intellectual colleagues. In 1898, Gilman's book *Women and Economics* was published and enthusiastically read by Addams and her female colleagues. Florence Kelley wrote Gillman that "'Ms. A.' has carried off one copy to Rockford [Addams' hometown], and given her other one to Mary Smith, so with our wonted frugality, the residents are waiting in rows for her to come back with it."[20] Kelley was able to "have a shot at it on our trip to Washington . . . and read it through on the way down and again, critically, on the way back."[21] Both Kelley and Gilman were socialists, and this materialistic interpretation of women's perspective was clearly known by Addams. Thus, the residents of Hull-House, including Addams, were not demurely reading "proper" or "saintly" literature, but were interested in radical changes in the structure of society, including feminist alterations in women's power and status.

Repeatedly, Addams advanced the argument that women were more humanitarian, caring, and "down to earth" than men. By restricting women's freedom to the home, the larger society was corrupt and unjust.

Everyday life functioned poorly because it was based on male values and ethics. This cultural feminism permeated the settlement movement, and provided a system of values for organizing life in these communal homes.

Cultural feminism was an underlying theme in all of Addams' writings. In addition she frequently used women as the source of her ideas and topics of analysis. She wanted to broaden the scope of women's activities, therefore altering the basic structure of values and relations throughout society. In addition to this generalized approach, Addams specifically studied prostitutes, women in the marketplace, especially working-class women, and pacifism. Each of these areas of study is examined below.

Addams on Women and the Larger Society

The most direct way to broaden women's sphere was the extension of their existing, home-oriented worldview into the realms of business, government, and formal institutions, such as education and the courts. Thus, Addams saw women as able to change and improve society by acting on their traditional values in the everyday masculine world. Society would be radically altered through the inclusion of values other than the display of power and force characteristic of men. Nowhere is Addams as scathing of this patriarchal world than in the article "If Men Were Seeking the Franchise."[22]

Taking the role of women in an imaginary matriarchal society, Addams noted that these rational and conscientious women could not see the value of having men empowered as citizens. In such a matriarhy, the state would develop along the lines of the family so that a primary goal would be the nurturance and education of children and the protection of the sick, the weak, and the aged.[23]

In a series of arguments against enfranchising men, Addams adopted the role of the mystified women:

> Can we, the responsible voters, take the risk of wasting our taxes by extending the vote to those who have always been so ready to lose their heads over mere military display?[24] . . . we know that you men have always been careless about the house, perfectly indifferent to the necessity for sweeping and cleaning; if you were made responsible for factory legislation it is quite probable that you would let the workers in the textile mills contract tuberculosis through needlessly breathing in the fluff, or the workers in machine shops through inhaling metal filings, both of which are now carried off by an excellent suction system which we women have insisted upon, but which it is almost impossible to have installed in a man-made state because the men think so little of dust and its evil effects.[25]

> Would not these responsible women voters gravely shake their heads and say that as long as men exalt business profits above human life, it would be sheer

folly to give them the franchise.[26] The trouble is that men have no imagination, or rather what they have is so prone to run in the historic direction of
the glory of the battlefield, that you cannot trust them with industrial affairs.[27]

Continuing in her defense of prostitutes, Addams is revolted by the
callous hypocrisy of men:

> Worse than anything which we have mentioned is the fact that in every man-
> ruled city the world over a great army of women are so set aside as outcasts
> that it is considered a shame to speak the mere name which designated
> them.[28] The men whose money sustains their houses, supplies their tawdry
> clothing and provides them with intoxicating drinks and drugs, are never
> arrested, nor indeed are they even considered lawbreakers.[29]

This satirical essay, one of Addams' most forceful attacks on male injustice,
was a cutting critique of the male world which fears the humanitarian
world of women.

This female realm is based in the home and family relationships. But
both men and women "do not perceive that as society grows more compli-
cated it is necessary that woman shall extend her sense of responsibility to
many things outside of her own home if she would continue to preserve the
home in its entirely."[30] A woman who remained at home and did not
participate in the life of the community was stunted. When such a woman
met a more active one, "she recognized that her hostess after all represents
social values and industrial use, as over against her own parasitic clean-
liness and a social standing attained only through status."[31] Nonetheless,
women were constantly urged to put the family and their needs before
other considerations. Addams called this demand "the family claim." Most
men were adverse to changing this standard, but so were women.

> This instinct to conserve the old standards, combined with a distrust of the
> new standard, is a constant difficulty in the way of those experiments and
> advances depending upon the initiative of women, both because women are
> the most sensitive to the individual and family claims, and because their
> training has tended to make them content with response to these claims
> alone.[32]

Modern women struggled to balance two "claims, the social and the
family." A prime resource for changing the relationship between these competing prescriptions for action was education. Predictably such a change
was problematic, for "the family has responded to the extent of granting
the education, but they are jealous of the new claim and assert the family
claim as over against it."[33]

After completing her education, the woman was expected to once again be loyal to the narrowly defined family boundaries. "The failure to recognize the social claim as legitimate causes the trouble, the suspicion constantly remains that woman's public efforts are merely selfish and captious, and are not directed to the general good."[34]

With critical insight, Addams noted that such education was not automatically liberating: "during this so-called preparation, her faculties have been trained solely for accumulation, and she learned to utterly distrust the finer impulses of her nature, which would naturally have connected her with human interests outside of her family and her own immediate social circle."[35] Formal education, in other words, often trained women for a male world.

Addams saw much of her work as a translation of the family claim into the world and work of the social claim. She did this by pointing to women's ability to care for "civic housekeeping."

> The men of the city have been carelessly indifferent to much of this civic housekeeping, as they have always been indifferent to the details of the household. They have totally disregarded a candidate's capacity to keep the streets clean, preferring to consider him in relation to the national tariff or to the necessity for increasing the national navy, in a pure spirit of reversion to the traditional type of government which had to do only with enemies and outsiders.[36]

Women were also "bread givers": nurturant people who fed others emotionally, spiritually, and physically.

> So we have planned to be "Bread Givers" throughout our lives; believing that in labor alone is happiness, and that the only true and honorable life is one filled with good works and honest toil, we have planned to idealize our labor, and thus happily fulfill Women's Noblest Mission.[37]

The development of this concept in 1880 at twenty years of age illustrates the profound continuity in Addams' thought. For in 1918 during World War I, she continued this theme in her passionate pleas for peace (see discussion below). Addams wanted society to be more nurturant; to value people more than profits; and to have the mores that governed the home and family as part of the rules of interaction for the entire community. The "nation" created boundaries between people, preventing cooperation and unity. Therefore, a new international-mindedness was needed to learn that all people were part of one community.[38]

This cross-national and cultural approach was the antithesis of the "competitive" perspective of Park and Burgess and their "Chicago" view of the basis of society. For the men described the patriarchal world in which they lived and participated, being both observers and advocates of this perspective.

Cultural feminism not only articulated the superiority of feminine values for Addams, it also provided a perspective to critique the oppression of women in everyday life. A group of women who epitomized the misuse of women in a capitalistic and exploitative society were prostitutes, discussed next.

Prostitution

Addams defined the commercial use of sex as a "social evil," a term "used to designate the sexual commerce permitted to exist in every large city, usually in a segregated district, wherein the chastity of women is bought and sold."[39] Prostitution was a continuing theme in her writings, and she even devoted an entire book to the subject. She firmly believed that prostitution would be eliminated as society advanced to superior levels of "consciousness."[40] For Addams, the position of the prostitute was analogous to that of a slave. The outlawing of commercial ownership of another's body was a step toward the outlawing of commercial use of another's sexuality. Addams, moreover, saw the Chicago Vice Commission, of which Thomas was a member, as an aid in dispersing information about this problem.[41]

Writing in 1911 on a socially unacceptable topic, Addams stated that "sympathetic knowledge is the only way of approach to any human problem."[42] Thus she predated by six years Thomas and Znaniecki's concern with the "human coefficient" in the study of society.[43]

Part of her work was devoted to a discussion of the White slave traffic, and the recruitment process for that and other forms of prostitution remains the same today as it was in the past: the betrayal of male lovers, loneliness, economic necessity, neighborhood and family influences, weariness, and discouragement. Writing on social isolation in the city she notes the dichotomy between our public and private lives.[44] "It is as if we had to build little islands of affection in the vast sea of impersonal forces lest we be overwhelmed by them."[45] Moreover, the lives of many working women were incredibly dreary. Often, young women would be required to turn over all their wages to meet the "family claim," and they were expected to live lives of constant drudgery. "Hundreds of working girls go directly to bed as soon as they have eaten their suppers. They are too tired to go from home for recreation, too tired to read and often too tired to sleep."[46] When they have the rare opportunity to be away from these constraints, they go too far, too fast. Again, predating Thomas' work on the "unadjusted girl" published in 1923, and *The Polish Peasant*, published from 1918 to 1920, Addams wrote about rapid social change that undermines the old order: "The social relationships in a modern city are so hastily made and often so superficial, that the old human restraints of public opinion, long sustained in smaller communities, have also broken down."[47]

The strain of domestic work, where women—not men—are the major employers, caused many women to seek a more profitable and less isolating existence. Women employed in this occupation accounted for half of the prostitutes at that time.

In an account of the social organization supporting prostitution, Addams portrayed the various members of the male recruitment and political process. The "spieler" tells the woman a false story, either that he loves her or that he is so wealthy that he can take her away from financial worry.[48] "Such a boy is often incited by the professional procurer to ruin a young girl, because the latter's position is much safer if the character of the girl is blackened before he sells her and if he himself cannot be implicated in her downfall."[49] After the initial sexual contact, the man would turn the "ruined" woman over to commercialized sex. This was possible because if a woman engaged in one "erring" sexual act, she became literally an outcast of society. Not only could one occasion cause a total change in her status, even the appearance of such an event could have serious, damaging consequences.

> A homeless young girl looking for a lodging may be arrested for soliciting on the street, and sent to prison for six months, although there is no proof against her save the impression of the policeman. A young girl under such suspicion may be obliged to answer the most harassing questions put to her by the city attorney, with no woman near to protect her from insult; she may be subjected to the most trying examination conducted by a physician in the presence of a policeman, and no matron to whom to appeal.[50]

As a group, men benefited from the exploitation of the prostitute with few social sanctions.

Addams pointed to the need to understand the "historic connection between commercialized vice and alcoholism, [and the] close relation between politics and the liquor interests, behind which the social evil so often entrenches itself."[51] Thus, prostitution is only able to continue as a result of police corruption and collusion.

> When the legal control of commercialized vice is thus tied up with city politics, the functions of the police become legislative, executive, judicial in regard to street solicitation: in a sense they also have power of license, for it lies with them to determine the number of women who are allowed to ply their trade upon the street.[52]

Addams assured women that it was logical to fear the prostitute when the circle of consideration was only one's immediate family. But again, this "narrow" family claim blinded women to their common sisterhood. "Nice girls" (a concept only recently revived) should learn to see the profit that men make from selling women.[53] Women needed to understand the harshness of sexual standards, and their false criteria when applied to only one of the sexes. Addams (contrary to the modern version of the rejection of the "double standard") believed that

> As woman, however, fulfills her civic obligations while still guarding her chastity, she will be in position as never before to uphold the "single standard" demanding that men shall add the personal virtues to their performance of public duties. Women may at last force men to do away with the traditional use of a public record as a cloak for a wretched private character, because society will never permit a woman to make such excuses for herself.[54]

Acknowledging that some women had, nonetheless, engaged in sexual intercourse outside marriage, she believed that "insofar as such women have been treated as independent human beings and prized for their mental and social charm, even although they are on a commercial basis, it makes for a humanization of this sordid business."[55] Optimistically, she ended her book with the assertion that social rejection of prostitution was inevitable:

> Certainly we are safe in predicting that when the solidarity of human interest is actually realized, it will become unthinkable that one class of human beings should be sacrificed to the supposed needs of another; when the rights of human life have successfully asserted themselves in contrast to the rights of property.[56]

Addams and Working Women

Women who worked in the marketplace suffered from a number of injustices including socialization detrimental to their development in the public arena. Trained to respond first to their "family claims," women had to respond instead to "social claims" in order to survive in the male-dominated business world. Women were taught to identify with their families to such an extent that they did not organize to defend their rights. Women undercut their fellow laborers when they limited their female vision to the immediate needs of their families. Addams strongly criticized this:

> The maternal instinct and family affection is [sic] woman's most holy attribute; but if she enters industrial life, that is not enough. She must supplement her family conscience by a social and an industrial conscience. She must widen her family affection to embrace the children of the community. She is wrecking havoc in the sewing-trades, because with the meagre equipment sufficient for family life she has entered industrial life.[57]

Because Addams supported the labor movement and many unions were organized by men and barred women as equal participants,[58] the women's labor unions in Chicago were organized primarily through Hull-House. In 1892 the cloakmakers were organized there, and in 1891 the shirtmakers. The Chicago Women's Trade Union League was also organized there, and yet another two women's unions met at the settlement.[59]

Union organizing required more than merely providing a setting. The women workers needed to define themselves in relation to the conflicting family and social claims. The residents, according to Addams, could facilitate this change in consciousness. They could also help working-class men and women to communicate with one another.

> The residents felt that between these men and girls was a deeper gulf than the much-talked of "chasm" between the favored and unfavored classes. . . . There was much less difference of any sort between the residents and working-class than between the men and girls of the same trade.[60]

Addams' approach to the methods of settling labor disputes was a dramatic illustration of her belief in feminine values. For she felt that strikes and violence associated with the labor movement were ill-fated and destructive.

> Men thus animated may organize for resistance, they may struggle bravely together, and may destroy that which is injurious, but they cannot build up, associate or unite. They have no common, collective faith. The labor movement in America bears this trace of its youth and immaturity.[61]

In the same vein, she believed that the working class and capitalists were not warring classes, but part of the same democratic society. The apolitical and largely economic character of American unions was foreseen by Addams as a limited and unsatisfactory direction. She advocated the workers' goals of a shorter workday, increased wages, better industrial and general education, and worker protection in the marketplace, but qualified her support when she wrote that the movement "does not want to lose sight of the end in securing the means, nor assume success, nor even necessarily the beginnings of success, when these first aim are attained."[62] Workers needed to struggle for self-definition and independence. Protection was only a stopgap measure and concern.[63] Addams saw the definition of society as warring classes as one that doomed society as a whole. The "literal notion of brotherhood" demanded a conception of universal kinship: "before this larger vision of life there can be no perception of "sides" and "battle array."[64] Labor unions became, in fact, the tools of capitalists by reducing their negotiations to single industry issues.

Addams clearly did not support the Marxist vision of labor, although she frequently read writers adopting this perspective (discussed in the next chapter). As a pragmatist, Addams advocated a number of laws to "protect" the worker, especially women workers, which led to her advocacy of positions far less radical than her long-term goals. For example, she was against the militant suffragists and their later proposal of the Equal Rights Amendment because of her defense of protective legislation. Her efforts to avoid class distinctions within the movement have also been criticized.[65]

Addams was intrinsically committed to a trade union movement oriented toward large-scale social change, and not the limited economic benefits of a short-term contract. She failed to have this vision adopted by the unions, and she became increasingly critical of their use of strikes. She saw the latter actions as generating severe hardships for the workers who wanted relief from such misery.[66]

Because Addams wanted to understand the strengths of the community as well as its problems, she described poor, aged, and working women as vital members of the community. They had a strength of spirit and power of mind to create a vision of happiness in the midst of degradation. She was fascinated by this "aesthetic sensibility":[67] "Years of living had taught them that recrimination with grown-up children is worse than useless, that punishments are impossible, and that domestic instruction is best given through tales and metaphors."[68] Older women, in particular, gained strength from their process of teaching, so that "the old people seemed, in some unaccountable way, to lose all bitterness and resentment against life."[69] The ability to do this was based on their verbal power and imagery. Women, according to Addams, developed mythical stories and fairy tales to establish some control and order in a world that was chaotic and oppressive.

Women who lived with bitter poverty and family abuse were able to transcend such squalor. Women thus developed "the strength of stout habits acquired by those who early become accustomed to fight off black despair."[70] This analysis of women's courage did not condone the conditions that generated the need for it. On the contrary, Addams felt that such conditions were useless and could be changed through community struggles. Moving women out of the home enabled them to widen their visions of life: Working women "possess the enormous advantage over women of

the domestic type of having experienced the discipline arising from impersonal obligations and of having tasted the freedom from economic dependence, so valuable that too heavy a price can scarcely be paid for it."[71] Thus,
working women were exploited in the marketplace in exchange for a degree
of freedom from the restrictions of domesticity. However, the feminine
values allowed these same women to bear their costs with dignity. Working
women were able to translate their unique experiences into an appreciation
for the community and loved ones whereas men's militaristic and warring
theories allowed them to only see their suffering and failures.

Thus working women were urged to accept their new roles in the community. This labor, however, was often misused and antithetical to their
training as women with "family claims." Despite these contradictory demands and the high costs of living in poverty, women were able to lead
courageous lives, generating social bonds and happiness. This triumph
could not be explained if the poor were seen only as oppressed and without
indigenous culture and values. Addams saw these paradoxical forces and
explained them as a function of cultural feminism.

Jane Addams and Pacifism

Addams did not believe that social change should be imposed on any
group. Education and good leadership could aid in forming the group
mind, but the democratic process held the highest priority. Although she
had a personal agenda for social change, she wanted to be part of the
people. Personally and politically, she was a good conciliator. Reflectively,
she noted: "My temperament and habit had always kept me rather in the
middle of the road; in politics as well as in social reform I had been for 'the
best possible.'"[72] Her belief in the masses and acceptance of their path
failed when nationalism was at a feverish pitch, even prior to the United
States' entry into World War I. The above quotation continued:

> But now I was pushed far toward the left on the subject of the war and I
> became gradually convinced that in order to make the position of the pacifist
> clear it was perhaps necessary that at least a small number of us should be
> forced into an unequivocal position.[73]

Repeatedly she presented her radical stance in her three books and numerous articles on pacifism. In 1907, she published a strong theoretical
analysis of the "newer ideals of peace."[74] These ideals were a progressive
basis for improved social relations that had been unarticulated, because
most pacifist terminology did not express the power behind the reality.

> The word "non-resistance" is misleading, because it is much too feeble and inadequate. It suggests passivity, the goody-goody attitude of ineffectiveness. The words "overcoming", "substituting", "re-creating", "readjusting moral values", "forming new centres of spiritual energy" carry much more of the meaning implied.[75]

In this passage Addams is explaining not only this new concept, but also her vision of cultural feminism. She wanted to regenerate the meaning for these values which had been linguistically limited by patriarchal thought.

These ideals of human relations were found throughout the populace. Urban life, however, was often organized to exploit these values and use them through competition.

> In the midst of the modern city which, at moments, seems to stand only for the triumph of the strongest, the successful exploitation of the weak, the ruthlessness and hidden crime which follow in the wake of the struggle for existence on its lowest terms, there come daily—at least in American cities— accretions of simple people, who carry in their hearts a desire for mere goodness.[76]

In 1907 Addams thought the exploited, the poor, and the immigrant were the most likely to exhibit compassion and the values supporting dynamic peace.[77]

Farrell has interpreted pacifism as the underlying theme of all of Addams' work after 1914.[78] Although there is no doubt of its significance within her social thought, cultural feminism embraced and explained pacifism. It was increasingly clear that Addams believed pacifism was most supported by women and the product of their culture.

Initially impressed by Count Tolstoy's pacifism,[79] she soon questioned his approach to nonresistance and began to formulate her own vision of the pacifist cause. An excellent example of how she adapted Tolstoy's thought can be seen in their discussion of the making of bread. For Tolstoy, every person needed to do "bread labor." This meant that each person worked the land and was personally involved in the production of food. As noted above, Addams thought that women were "bread givers" as early as 1880, long before she met Tolstoy. Therefore, she combined her own ideas with Tolstoy's. The latter's theory of the connection between working for one's literal bread and becoming a total community-oriented person was reinterpreted by Addams in relation to women who labored to make bread and therefore nurtured and sustained daily life. This union of labor with thought was carried even further for women than men because of women's values and "maternal instinct" which endorsed peace and social harmony.[80]

This interpretation of pacifism as a product of cultural feminism reached a clear exposition in her 1922 publication *Peace and Bread in Time of War*. The thesis of this book was that women knew it was better to nurture than to kill; to feed than to starve; to make laws for peace than for war; and to see people as part of one group rather than as individualized members of separate and antagonistic groups. To make the world more "woman-like" would require the removal of the economic causes of war, arms limitation, women's suffrage, and organized opposition to militarism.[81] Addams cited one soldier's demand for this role for women: "Ever since I have been in the trenches," he wrote, "I have been wondering what is the matter with the women. They would not be called cowards, and they need not be afraid. Why are they holding back?"[82] Addams' answer to this question would include an appreciation of women's conflicting social and family claims. These demands were partially based on instincts, but women had been trained for a narrowed family view. This perspective caused them to withdraw their wisdom and advice from the international arena of armed conflict.

Part of Addams' pacifism was also her continual portrayal of the war as it appeared to women. Writing on women in Egypt who were starving, like women in war zones, she and a friend

> came to realize with a sudden pang that the mothers feeding their children under these smoking roofs were clutched by the old fear that there was not enough for each to have his portion, and that simple scene before us with all its implication was but part of that unceasing struggle carried on by hard pressed women all over the world.[83]

Thus Addams linked women's values to a wide range of social problems: starvation, war, prostitution, unemployment, labor exploitation, and disenfranchisement. She also extended "women's work" into the special areas of child welfare, industrial pollution, and neighborhood recreation. Many of these "women's concerns" are discussed in the next chapters. Before proceeding to these discussions, "cultural feminism" is briefly critiqued in relation to the Chicago School of Sociology and evaluated as a school of thought.

Cultural Feminism and the Chicago Men

As noted in chapter 8, many of the Chicago men supported the Doctrine of the Separate Spheres. Small, in particular, believed that men and women were distinct beings. But this belief system was radically different from Addams', for the latter advocated not only women's world and values, but found them superior to men's. The former believed that the men's world and values were superior to women's while working within the rhetoric of equality between the spheres. Advocates of the separatist "sphere" doctrine, however, could work superficially with the separatist cultural feminists. Both had the appearance of supporting women's values, while there were sharp distinctions on the value, range, and proper arenas for enacting these differences.

When Addams was "vilified" for her pacifism, her separatist stance (and that of other women sociologists) enabled the male-dominated, academic world of sociology to "eliminate" women professionals as a group. Although there was a wide range of factors leading to the distinctions between female "social workers" and male "sociologists" (examined in chapter 12), the separatist values of Addams and her cohort facilitated their professional elimination.

This cultural feminism was also antithetical to the social thought developed by Park and Burgess. As early as 1911, Addams expressed her dissatisfaction with their view of society as based on conflict and competition. She waw, instead, the growth of a new, cooperative humanitarian emerging

> from the 19th century darkness which considered the nation as an agglomeration of selfish men each moved by self-interest, forgetful of the women and children, to a conception of a state maintained to develop and nurture the highest type of human life, and testing its success by the care afforded to the most defenseless women and children within its borders.[84]

Prophetically, she was denouncing the perspective that would ultimately characterize the thought of the men of the Chicago School: their stress on self-interest, competition, and the exclusion of women and children from topics of study and interest.[85] Addams believed the patriarchal view of the world was false and bound to fail.

She also opposed narrow definitions of society as a form of "social control." Literally, she thought that social scientists who emphasized this aspect of human behavior violated human freedom of action and dignity. When the social scientist "ventures to suggest that these forces should be controlled, he at once assumes the permanent dignity and value of human life, one of the tenets of all the great ethnic religions."[86] In a similar vein, she argued against the collection of statistics by detached observers. She felt that all researchers needed to deliberately put themselves in a "vital relationship, a living relationship, with the distressing aspects of industrial life."[87]

Although Addams' views were accepted in varying degrees by all of the early Chicago men, her cultural feminism was basically neither understood nor accepted by them. And it was this aspect of her thought that made her particularly critical of the sociological school that emerged in Chicago during the 1920s. Thus "cultural feminism" was, and continues to be, diametrically opposed to the theory of human competition and conflict developed by Park and Burgess.

Despite the lack of acceptance of cultural feminism by male sociologists, the strengths of this perspective are evident and significant. It is a clear-cut approach to a radical vision of society based on cooperation, equality of all people, the elimination of prostitution, the right of free speech, governance by the people, pacifism, and the priority of humanitarian goals over economic ones. These are vital visions of the social order, and their themes are found throughout Addams' work. Nonetheless, her work was not adopted by other sociologists. Where, then, did this vision falter?

Addams' Cultural Feminism as Problematic

Addams thought that women were biologically superior to men because of their maternal instincts. She practiced, then, a female chauvinism based partially on a biological explanation. She did not see parenting as equally valued and instinctual for both sexes. If she had remained consistent in her cultural feminism, she would have seen good parenting as a human potential and goal for everyone and an achievement that was particularly difficult to fulfill in a patriarchal society. In fact, it was even more difficult for men to attain than for women. Repeatedly Addams stressed the need for tolerance and compromise between groups. For men and women, however, she assumed not only the superiority of the women's vision, but also a biological advantage. To the extent that she relied upon such biological determinism, her arguments were weakened.

The second major difficulty with her theory was its lack of institutional, intellectual, and popular continuity. Although this may be a short-term criticism, a sign only of the fact that she was a leader of her time, it also indicated that her ideas were not institutionalized or incorporated within American society. Her dramatic establishment of many major social institutions cannot be denied. For example, she helped to found the Women's Bureau, the Children's Bureau, Social Security, and Workmen's Compensation.[88] Simultaneously, many other organizations she supported have been extinguished or languish: e.g. the social settlements and the National Consumers League. Her vision of the labor union movement was also not adopted.

A major reason for this lack of institutionalization and legitimation is that Addams did not entirely understand patriarchal power. Succinctly, she overestimated the power and organization of women's values and underestimated men's. For example Addams was correct in her assessment of the futility and destructiveness of war. She did not assess how pacifism would be attacked and ridiculed by her "competitors," however, until she had undergone their vilification. In the next chapter, her attempt to unify idealism and realism is examined in more depth. Her "pacifism" and her approach to "settling the great war" were too idealistic, too simplistic, and therefore defeated.

Thus, cultural feminism is strongest in portraying a *way* to order society. It does not adequately confront the problem of *how* to institutionalize this worldview in a patriarchal world dominated by violence and competition. Addams' partial answer to this problem was "critical pragmatism," the topic of the next two chapters.

Notes

1. There are a number of books published in this area, documented below. An excellent statement of the basic assumptions, however, can be found in Helen Diner, *Mothers and Amazons*, ed. and tr. Joseph Campbell (New York: Julian Press, 1965, c. 1922).
2. Discussed in ch. 4 and 8 in this volume, esp. in sections on Small.
3. Jacob Bachofen, *Das Mutterecht*. English translation and condensation, *Myth Religion, and Mother-Right*, tr. Ralph Manheim (Princeton: Princeton University Press, 1967).
4. Friedrich Engels, *The Origins of the Family, Private Property, and the State* (Chicago: Charles H. Kerr, 1902, c. 1884).
5. Kathleen Gough has updated the archaeological findings used by Engels. She has found his information to be basically sound even with the addition of new knowledge about early societies. See "An Anthropologist Looks at Engels," in *Women in a Man-Made World*, ed. Nona Glazer and Helen Youngelson Waehrer (Chicago: Rand McNally, 1977), pp. 156-68.
6. This is true of Emily Greene Balch and Anna Garlin Spencer, in particular. See Jane Addams, Emily Greene Balch, and Alice Hamilton, *The Women at the Hague* (New York: Macmillan, 1915). See Spencer's *Women's Share in Social Culture* (New York: Mitchell Kennerley, 1913).
7. Otis Tufton Mason, *Women's Share in Primitive Culture* (New York: D. Appleton, 1918, c. 1894).
8. "A Syllabus of a Course of Twelve Lectures, *Democracy and Social Ethics* by Jane Addams, A.B." (n.p., n.d.), SCPC. Cited by John C. Farrell, *Beloved Lady* (Baltimore: Johns Hopkins Press, 1967), p. 83, n. 5. Since Addams wrote a text by the same name (New York: Macmillan, 1902), Mason's ideas probably influenced her in writing this book.
9. Mason, *Women's Share in Primitive Culture*, p. 240.
10. Ibid., p. 286.
11. See W.I. Thomas, *Sex and Society* (Chicago: University of Chicago Press, 1907). Ch. 1 is based on Thomas' thesis, "Organic Difference in the Sexes," pp. 3-55. See also the discussions in this volume in chs. 5 and 8.

12. Thomas and his relationship to Addams is documented in chs. 5 and 8. His work in social reform and specific causes in Chicago also provided for a complementary division of labor between the applied and theoretical sociologist.
13. It is important to remember that Thomas' work on the topic of women was too political, as were his ideas on sexuality, for the academic community. The limits of faculty activism, documented in ch. 7, were so constraining that even the more modified politics of Thomas were too much for the business elite that dominated the university.
14. Gilman was closely associated with the sociologist Lester Ward, published in *The American Journal of Sociology*, and spoke at the American Sociological Society. A thorough analysis of her sociological thought has yet to be done. See a brief analysis of Gilmans's sociology by Carolyn Sachs, Sally Ward Maggard, and S. Randi Randolph, "Sexuality, the Home and Class," in *Midwest Feminist Papers* 2 (1981):31-44.
15. "Gone to Live at Hull-House," *San Francisco Chronicle* 25 (July 1895):15, Scrapbook 3, 1895-97, SCPC.
16. Ibid., schedule of lectures, p. 18 (the pages are not chronologically compiled).
17. Ibid., "Attack the Sweat Shop," 18 March 1896, p. 68; "To Abolish Sweat Shops," n.d., p. 69.
18. The affiliation of the *Woman's Journal* is noted in each issue.
19. Davis, *American Heroine*, p. 216.
20. Florence Kelley to Charlotte Gilman, 28 July 1898, Gilman Papers, 177; 138, one of 2 microfilms, Schlesinger Library.
21. Ibid.
22. Jane Addams, "If Men Were Seeking the Franchise," *Ladies Home Journal* (June 1913):104-7. In *Jane Addams: A Centennial Reader* (hereafter referred to as *Centennial Reader*), ed. Emily Cooper Johnson (New York: Macmillan, 1960), pp. 107-13.
23. Ibid., p. 108.
24. Ibid.
25. Ibid., pp. 110-19.
26. Ibid., p. 110.
27. Ibid.
28. Ibid., p. 111.
29. Ibid., p. 112.
30. Jane Addams, *Democracy and Social Ethics*, p. 104.
31. Ibid., p. 6. v
32. Ibid., p. 72.
33. Ibid., p. 84.
34. Ibid., pp. 89-90.
35. Ibid., p. 77.
36. Jane Addams, "Utilization of Women in Government," in *Newer Ideals of Peace* (New York: Macmillan, 1907).
37. Jane Addams, "Bread Givers," *Rockford (Illinois) Daily Register* (21 April 1880). Reprinted in *Centennial Reader*, p. 104.
38. George Herbert Mead, "National-Mindedness and International-Mindedness," *International Journal of Ethics* 39 (November 1929):392-407. Mead's concept of democracy and international-mindedness closely paralleled Addams' thought. See John S. Burger and Mary Jo Deegan, "George Herbert Mead on Internationalism, Democracy and War," *Wisconsin Sociologist* 18 (Spring-Summer 1981):72-83.

39. Jane Addams, *A New Conscience and an Ancient Evil* (hereafter referred to as *A New Conscience*), (New York: Macmillan, 1914), p. 9.
40. See also George Herbert Mead, "Social Consciousness and the Consciousness of Meaning," *Psychological Bulletin* 7 (December 1910):397-405; "Psychology of Consciousness Implied in Instruction," *Science* 31 (May 1910):688-93.
41. *The Vice Commission of Chicago: The Social Evil in Chicago* (New York: Arno, 1970, c. 1911).
42. Addams, *A New Conscience*, p. 11.
43. W.I. Thomas and Florian Znaniecki, *The Polish Peasant In Europe and America*, 2nd Ed., vols. 1 and 2 (New York: Dover, 1958, c. 1917-1918), vol. 1, pp. 1-89. Addams is clearly advocating the use of "sympathetic introspection," a methodological technique later formalized by Charles H. Cooley in "The Roots of Social Knowledge", *American Journal of Sociology* 32 (July 1926):59-79. Since Cooley was also influenced by Addams, her writings can be seen as a resource for him. See ch. 1, n. 36 for a discussion of this.
44. See Peter Berger, Brigitte Berger, and Hansfried Kellner, *The Homeless Mind* (New York: Random House, 1973).
45. Addams, *A New Conscience*, p. 33.
46. Ibid., p. 73.
47. Ibid., p. 34.
48. Ibid., p. 50.
49. Ibid.
50. Ibid., p. 191.
51. Ibid., p. 46.
52. Addams, "If Men Were Seeking the Franchise," p. 111.
53. G.L. Fox, "Nice Girl: Social Control of Women through Value Construct," *Signs* 2 (Summer 1977):805-17.
54. Addams, *A New Conscience*, pp.211-12.
55. Ibid., pp.216-17.
56. Ibid., p. 217.
57. Jane Addams, "The Settlement as a Factor in the Labor Movement," in *HH Maps and Papers* (New York: Crowell, 1895), p. 190.
58. See Heidi Hartmann, " Capitalism, Patriarchy, and Job Segregation by Sex," *Signs* 1 (Spring 1976):137-69.
59. Addams, "The Settlement as a Factor in the Labor Movement," p. 188.
60. Ibid.
61. Ibid, p. 194.
62. Ibid., p. 195.
63. Ibid., p. 197.
64. Ibid., p. 200.
65. Virginia Fish, "The Hull-House Circle," mimeo, n.d.
66. See the collection of articles on labor in the *Centennial Reader*, pp. 192-217.
67. Jane Addams, *The Long Road of Women's Memory* (New York: Macmillan, 1916), p. 6.
68. Ibid., p. 9.
69. Ibid., p. 10.
70. Ibid., p. 68.
71. Ibid., p. 100.
72. Jane Addams, *Peace and Bread in Time of War*, intro. John Dewey (Boston: G.K. Hall, 1960, c. 1922), p. 133.

73. Ibid.
74. Jane Addams, *Newer Ideals of Peace* (New York: Macmillan, 1907).
75. Ibid., pp. 7-8.
76. Ibid., p. 12.
77. Ibid., pp. 13-14.
78. Farrell, *Beloved Lady*, p. 140.
79. See Jane Addams, *Twenty Years at Hull-House* (New York: Macmillan, 1910); "Tolstoyism," pp. 259-80.
80. Jane Addams, "War Times Challenging Woman's Traditions," *Survey* 36 (August 1916), p. 478.
81. Addams, *Peace and Bread in Time of War*, pp. 7-8.
82. Jane Addams, "Aspects of the Woman's Movement," *Survey* 8 (August 1930):113-23. Reprinted in *Centennial Reader*, pp. 124-30, p. 129.
83. Ibid., p. 128.
84. Jane Addams, "The Social Situation," *Religious Education* 6 (June 1911):147-48.
85. See esp. Robert E. Park and Ernest W. Burgess, *The Introduction to Sociology* (Chicago: University of Chicago Press, 1923).
86. Addams, "The Social Situation," p. 148.
87. Ibid., p. 149.
88. For a discussion of some of these issues and accomplishments see Daniel Levine, *Jane Addams and the Liberal Tradition* (Madison: Wisconsin State Historical Society, 1971); Allen F. Davis, *American Heroine* (New York: Oxford University Press, 1973); Farrell, *Beloved Lady*; Addams, *Twenty Years* and *The Second Twenty Years at Hull-House* (New York: Macmillan, 1930).

10

Jane Addams and Critical Pragmatism: Her Intellectual Roots in Addition to Chicago Sociology

Addams' relationships with the male Chicago sociologists have been examined in depth throughout this book. In this chapter, additional intellectual influences on her sociological thought are examined. These varied roots help to account for her unique sociology and her varied resources for studying social behavior. These further epistemological influences do not negate the influence of the male Chicago sociologists, but instead reveal the intellectual journey that characterized Addams' quest for knowledge.

In addition to her role in Chicago Sociology, Addams was part of another school of thought, called pragmatism, a uniquely American philosophy. Its central concern is the human capacity for intelligent, purposive behavior.[1] A more succinct and narrow definition of the concept has yet to be developed and widely accepted.[2] "But if we look to their products as a whole we find that they have written on logic, on the nature of knowledge, on the interpretation of science, on art, on morality, on religion, on the nature of the cosmos."[3] Pragmatism attempted to avoid the idealism-realism dualism[4] by a combination of thought and action.

Morris characterizes American pragmatism as a product of the historical context and intellectual milieu of the United States from 1850 to 1930.

> The four major facets of the occasion for the development of pragmatic philosophy were the following: 1) the prestige which science and the scientific method enjoyed in the mid–nineteenth century; 2) the corresponding strength of empiricism in the then current philosophy; 3) the acceptance of biological evolution; 4) the acceptance of the ideals of American democracy.[5]

Although pragmatism originated at Harvard with Charles Pierce, James Royce, and later William James, philosophers at the University of Chicago rapidly generated a distinct approach, called "the Chicago School of Pragmatism." This new school was first noted by James in his correspondence with Dewey in 1904 when referring to the recently published *Studies in Logical Theory*.[6] This text was soon recognized as the herald of a new approach with John Dewey and George Herbert Mead as major figures.[7] Addams profoundly influenced both of these men, yet her role in their social thought has been consistently neglected by scholars assessing the roots of this Chicago School.

As noted in the discussions of Hull-House and *HH Maps and Papers*, Addams actively supported empiricism and the use of the scientific method. Similarly, she believed that social progress could be achieved through education, and she advocated a democratic basis for the social order.

For Addams, the social settlement was an institution that allowed for the union of theory and action; the translation of ideas across social groups and classes; and the analysis of society as it functioned in everyday life. Social progress was based on the goals of cultural feminism; embodied by women who were closest to enacting and defending feminine values.

Although pragmatism informed and influenced sociology, few analyses of its impact have been done.[8] This area of sociology which Addams influenced has been neglected in male sociological writings as well as in her own. But for Addams, this neglect is particularly associated with her politics, for Addams was a *critical* pragmatist. With this term, an emphasis is placed on her radical extension of the tenets of pragmatism developed by the Chicago School of Pragmatism. Education was a central concern to the male Chicago pragmatists, but Addams was more opposed to formal institutions of learning than were the men. Democracy was an underlying theme of the pragmatic program, but for Addams democracy included economic and social equality as well as its political dimensions. These two major concerns, education and democracy, informed a range of other substantive concerns about minority groups: the aged and youth, immigrants, Blacks; and, of course, women.

Critical pragmatism is important to understand for an analysis of Chicago School philosophers, but this is not the primary task here. Instead, Addams' critical pragmatism is important because it outlined the major topics of study for Chicago sociologists for several decades. In the 1920s and 1930s the critical pragmatism of Addams was considerably modified to fit the patriarchal program of Park and Burgess. This latter approach developed an emphasis on social policy studies which were built upon the major substantive concerns of Addams. Again, the Addams' influence was deep but modified, and her authorship was erased.

The American Pragmatism Connection

Addams was dramatically influenced by the Chicago School pragmatists. Mead, in particular, worked closely with her as he formulated his ideas over the decades he worked at Chicago (1894-1931). The earlier sections of the book have repeatedly revealed these close ties, and to reproduce them here would be redundant. Therefore, this section will focus on the other pragmatists who worked with Addams; particularly John Dewey, James Tufts, Ella Flagg Young, and William James. All but James were members of the Chicago School of Pragmatism, and James was an influence on both Dewey and Mead.[9] Thus this group had profound mutual interaction, albeit Addams' connection has rarely been noted before.

John Dewey: His Ideas

Dewey is one of the foremost pedagogues in American thought. His philosophy of education revolutionized the process of learning and teaching. Like Addams, Dewey's major assumptions about the structure of society were based on democracy and education. His definition of these concepts, too, were similar. For both, democracy was broadly defined.

> The political and governmental phase of democracy is a means, the best means so far found, for realizing ends that lie in the wide domain of human relationships and the development of human personality. . . . The keynote of democracy as a way of life may be expressed, it seems to me, as the necessity for the participation of every mature human being in formation of the values that regulate the living of men together; which is necessary from the standpoint of both the general social welfare and the full development of human beings as individuals.[11]

Democracy was built on faith in humanity to act rationally and with good intentions. All members of society were considered equal before the law and in politics.[12] Although no fully democratic society existed, the process of obtaining that goal was at least partially known:

> An obvious requirement is freedom of social inquiry and of distribution of its conclusions. . . . There can be no public without full publicity in respect to all consequences which concern it. . . . Without freedom of expression, not even methods of social inquiry can be developed.[13]

Dewey's books, *School and Society* and *Democracy and Education*, were products of his contacts with Addams. In both publications he stressed the interdependence of a free society and education. Government for him was found everywhere, not just in elected and formal positions: "There is government in the family, in business, in the church, in every social group."[14]

Similarly, he believed that "all institutions are educational in the sense that they operate to form the attitudes, dispositions, abilities, and disabilities that constitute a concrete personality."[15] Schools, in particular, were the source of democratic development and intelligent thinking. In these settings good "habits," shared symbols, and the process of learning to govern were all developed.[16]

In order to teach democratically, teachers needed full participation in decisions affecting their work. This belief was at issue during Ella Flagg Young's battle with the Chicago School Board (see chapter 8). Democracy had to be lived and experienced in the classroom and outside of it, with teachers as a connecting link between the wider society and the student. Progressive education was opposed to the imposition of ideas, authority, and interests upon children. Education, according to Dewey, was based on "the idea that there is an intimate and necessary relation *between* the process of actual experience and education."[17]

The ability to be democratic and develop intelligence was dependent on access to knowledge. Such information could best be provided through the use of logic and systematic analysis of data based on human experience. Dewey, like Mead and Addams, believed that social facts were radically and qualitatively different from physical facts. Furthermore, he wrote that "the building up of social science, that is, of a body of knowledge in which facts are ascertained in their significant relations, is dependent upon putting social planning into effect."[18] Social science needed to bring "a desired state of society into existence."[19] This pragmatic approach to knowledge was at the root of Dewey's philosophy of knowledge. "Fruitful thinking" terminated in valid knowledge.[20]

Dewey, Addams, and Mead had a fundamentally similar approach to social science, democracy, and education that bound them together as colleagues and friends. This foundation of similar ideas was based on a vision of the human as pliable and formed through social interaction.

Because of the dependence of the person upon the community, the person's role in shaping that community was intrinsic to its functioning. Language and symbols were a uniting factor allowing people to develop and function together. Subjectively, the meanings associated with behaviors were known and accepted by the person. Objectively, they became modes of natural interaction.[21] They emerged from language which, in turn, was based on the "mind."[22] "This ability to communicate was formed out of modifications of the self that have occurred in the process of prior interactions with environment. Its animus is toward further interactions."[23] Dewey's philosophy was broad and encompassing, and institutionalized through the work of Chicago sociologists, both male and female.

Dewey's Relation to Chicago Sociology

Dewey is recognized as a central albeit rarely studied figure in Chicago Sociology. Mills, Faris, Park, Matthews, Petras, and Mead have all recognized Dewey's influence on the Chicago School.[24] Lewis and Smith have raised the opposite thesis, suggesting even that "Dewey's psychology was an intellectual impediment to the development of realistic sociology at Chicago."[25] The latters' thesis is clearly rejected here. Relying on a division between the thought of Mead and Dewey as well as between Mead and other Chicago sociologists, the argument advanced by Lewis and Smith depends on artificial criteria of formal documentation in the academy only. Such criteria does not reflect the constant interaction and influence developed by these early sociologists and scholars in other settings. Therefore, the reader is urged to look at the documentation of Dewey's role in sociology found in the other works noted above, especially in Petras and Mills.

John Dewey and Hull-House

The significance of Addams and her settlement for Dewey was evident from his first visit to Chicago. Already a noted philosopher, Dewey stopped at the settlement before accepting the offer at the University of Chicago. He wrote Addams: "I cannot tell you how much good I got from my stay at Hull-House. My indebtedness to you for giving me an insight into matters there is great. . . . Every day I stayed there only added to my conviction that you had taken the right way."[26]

Like Mead and Thomas, Dewey frequently visited the settlement and dined there. In 1897 he became a member of the board at the settlement and served in that position until he left Chicago. He also taught at the settlement, sometimes officially through the University of Chicago Extension classes and other times through settlement-based groups. One of the latter included the Plato Club, composed of local workingmen who met weekly on Sundays to discuss philosophical issues. There, the debates were hot and involved Dewey's confrontation with anarchism and socialism.[27]

Dewey was also a moving force behind the Labor Museum. This was a mechanism to reveal to immigrants the continuity of their culture and experience from the Old World to the new one. Addams used Dewey's concept of "a continuing reconstruction of experience" to articulate this process. The disjunction between the two societies often made the old homesick and the young uncomprehending. The Labor Museum filled the immigrants with pride for their heritage, especially art. This institutionalization of Addams and Dewey's ideas dramatically reveals their pragmatism and its successful adoption through their collaboration.[28]

Addams' influence on Dewey's *School and Society* is widely acknowledged. Similarly, several authors have noted that Addams' *The Spirit of
Youth and City Streets* was a product of Dewey's influence. But it is Farrell
who has done the most careful analysis of the Dewey-Addams connection,
and his scholarship is drawn on freely here.[29]

Their joint emphasis on democracy and education was founded on their
interaction. Dewey's daughter, named after Jane Addams, wrote that
Dewey's faith in democracy as a guiding force in educaton took on both a
sharper and deeper meaning because of Hull-House and Jane Addams.[30]
As Davis has written:

> Dewey himself repeatedly used Hull-House and a few other settlements as
> models for what he hoped schools would become, but it was a reciprocal
> relationship and Addams and the other residents learned a lot from him. He
> made them realize the implications of some of their programs and experi-
> ments.[31]

Again, this mutual influence was noted by Linn who wrote that Dewey's
ideas "informed her frequent talks on public school methods, curricula
and her book, *The Spirit of Youth*."[32]

Lasch characterized their mutual obligations as "generously acknowledged." He continued:

> Hull-House and Dewey's experimental school at the University of Chicago
> constantly exchanged ideas and personnel. One of the teachers in Dewey's
> school was a Hull-House resident. . . . When she showed him the manuscript
> of "A Modern Lear," he exclaimed, "It is one of the greatest things I ever read
> both as to its form and its ethical philosophy."[33]

But these intellectual debts were only part of their mutual influence, for
they were lifelong friends. She wrote a speech for his seventieth birthday, he
spoke at her award ceremony for the M. Carey Thomas Prize of Bryn Mawr
College.[34] He attended her fortieth anniversary celebration and wrote the
introduction to *Peace and Bread in Time of War* for a new 1960 edition.[35]
This latter act was particularly poignant since they had differed regrettably
and sharply over America's involvement in World War I. Addams delivered
an eulogy on the death of Dewey's son, Gordon, who died at the age of
eight. In this message she talked movingly of Gordon's vivaciousness and
character which had been a gift and bond to all. Finally, Dewey dedicated
his volume *Liberalism and Social Action* "To the Memory of Jane Addams."[36] The ties between these two great intellectuals were enduring and
strong.

Dewey has long been recognized as a leading social critic, while acknowledgement of Addams' influence on his social thought has appeared primarily in books written about her and not in books written about him. Both share an intellectual greatness, but it is Dewey who is the most recognized. Fortunately, he did not suffer from the myopia of his followers.

The Other Chicago Pragmatists: James Tufts and Ella Flagg Young

To analyze adequately the relations between Addams and the entire University of Chicago faculty would require several volumes. To analyze her relationship to the Chicago pragmatists alone would require another book. Suffice it to be noted here that both Tufts and Young were frequent visitors to Hull-House.

Their basic ideas have already been mapped out in the analyses of the writings of Mead and Dewey. Tufts, however, specialized in the study of social workers and sociopolitical thought.[37] Tufts, moreover, was Mead's father-in-law and chair of the Philosophy Department where both Mead and Dewey worked. These interpersonal and interfamilial ties in the department were close, partially accounting for the strong ties underlying this school of thought.

Young's outstanding contributions were institutionalized through the Chicago public school system which united the educational interests of Dewey, Mead, and Addams. Young is rarely recognized as a member of the Chicago School of Pragmatism although, like Addams, a careful analysis of the school would reveal her basic and significant role in its development.[38] The broad interdisciplinary and interpersonal ties of these scholars was a basis for Addams' thought, as well as for Chicago sociologists.

Influence of the Harvard Pragmatists: Royce and James

The Chicago pragmatists were major colleagues of Addams, but her contact with pragmatists did not stop there. At one point she taught a course at Hull-House using Josiah Royce's *Aspects of Modern Philosophy* as a text.[39] Her major contacts with Harvard pragmatism, however, came through William James. They had met as early as October 1898. At that time they shared the same platform to discuss Tolstoy's ideas, "but both rejected his doctrine of non-resistance, and instead took a milder path of protest by joining the anti-imperialists."[40]

Their ideas concerning war were similar, although Davis claims that their work on finding "a moral equivalent for war" was worked out separately.[41] In fact in 1903, predating James' classic statement by seven years, Addams talked on the topic of "A Moral Substitute for War."[42] But whatever the origins of their ideas, it is clear that there were areas of overlap and mutual influence. Again, in 1904 they spoke together at the Universal Peace Conference in Boston.[43]

Correspondence between James and Addams documents his collegial admiration. In 1902, he wrote her that *Democracy and Social Ethics* was one of the great books of their age. Calling it a sympathetic interpretation of the religion of democracy, he continued, "I have learned a lot from your pages," and shared her "faith in the institution."[44] Similarly, in 1907 he wrote "a thousand thanks" for his copy of *Newer Ideals of Peace*. He critiqued it with passion: "Yours is a deeply original mind and all so quiet and harmless. Yet revolutionary in the extreme: I am willing to bet on you. Send it to George E. Shaw. It will stimulate his genius in the most extraordinary way."[45] James also wrote W.I. Thomas after publication of *The Spirit of Youth*. In his lengthy analysis, he reflected that it was hard for him not to cry in places since he found it so eloquent a document.[46]

Since James read the works of the Chicago School pragmatists, and Mead had taken coursework from Royce at Harvard, and Dewey was profoundly indebted to James,[47] the similar currents of thought found in the Harvard and Chicago Schools of Pragmatism run deep. Addams was a member of this network, enhancing and challenging the academic work of her predominantly male colleagues.

Critical Emancipatory Science

Addams has been incorrectly portrayed as a reformer and "do-gooder" who was a paternalistic liberal.[47] She has been seen, therefore, as rather moralistic, exhortive, and supportive of the status quo. This is a dramatically inaccurate understanding of her work, although it is a more accurate picture of some of the work of the male Chicago School. Her sociology of knowledge was based on a "critical-emancipatory" model while the men's was based on a "social-technological" model. Mead and Thomas were the closest to Addams in their writings, but she was far more radical than they.

Fuhrman has summarized the differences in these approaches, discussing the critical-emancipatory model first:

> There is a tendency for the sociology of knowledge to assume a critical attitude. The intellectual in the critical tradition sees himself as a critic of the existing order. The goal of the sociology of knowledge is conceived as the unmasking of the hidden interests of various dominant groups within society who hold decisive power over others. This unmasking process should make possible the transformation of the existing order. The social-technological paradigm, on the other hand, aims at establishing regularities between types of thought and general societal conditions. The goal of the sociologist of knowledge is to discover those regularities and to act as a professional advisor

to groups interested in maintaining order within society. There is an element of professional elitism in this theoretical tradition.[48]

Although there are areas of considerable overlap in the work of Addams and the early Chicago men, a major point of this book, the underlying difference in their assumptions about knowledge, its role in society, and the role of the scientist in everyday life created a major division between them. Academics needed to generate a belief in elites and their specialized knowledge to defend their profession within the academy. Addams did not support this stance and worked to eliminate the necessity for social settlements.

When Addams is called a *critical* pragmatist, it is her interests in empowering the community, the laborer, the poor, the elderly and youth, women, and immigrants that define her as such. Social technocrats, on the other hand, tend to look at cultural or societal totalities rather than minority or interest groups within a society. When she studied the everyday world, as social technologists did, she connected this analysis to the political and economic conditions that generated that mundane and oppressive reality.[49]

As a person engaged in a series of reforms in government, business organizations, and community institutions, Addams worked, often successfully, to change the existing order. Her alliance with labor, the women's movement, and pacifism were all deeply committed stances aimed at dramatic alterations in the social order. The Chicago men were also engaged in such changes, but they did not speak as forcefully for the oppressed and the rights of free speech. Knowledge, for the Chicago men, was seen as an accumulated "capital" which could be used to maintain stability and order.

Social scientists' roles were continually a source of frustration to Addams. For her, the critic should deepen the public consciousness and analyze concrete repressive conditions in light of ideal ones.[50] Few social scientists have ever captured the American conscience and imagination as she did. She translated abstract knowledge about oppressive conditions to the "common" person. She brought the experience of the poor into the mainstream of national understanding and debate. Social technocrats, on the other hand, addressed other experts to discover regularities in social behavior.

Addams was committed to a harmonic social order without elites and hierarchical relations. Basing these ideas on her cultural feminism, she did not stress the role of conflict but rather the way to achieve the cooperative society she envisioned. Unlike other critical-emancipatory scientists, Addams believed that adopting a conflict model of society reinforced the conflict process. For Addams, cultural feminism was better understood and enacted by women, but capable of adoption by both sexes. There was an important flaw in her emancipatory model concerning her perception of the innate nature of humans, when she assumed that women were "naturally" superior to men in their values, training, and maternal instincts. In these particular assumptions she was not critical-emancipatory.

Unlike social technocrats, she saw individual rights as more basic than those of social "forces." Both Addams and the Chicago men believed in reform of the society through democratic decisionmaking. This belief is seen as consistent with the critical-emancipatory model of society, although Fuhrman would take exception to it.[51] Her belief in the radical alteration of society, particularly away from conflict and aggression and toward cooperation and peace, was a part of her model rejected by the male Chicago School. Here there was a greater alliance between Mead and Addams than with the other men; but of the two, Addams was the more radical.

Most of the analyses of critical-emancipatory science have been done using a Marxist or conflict model as the basis for understanding society and social interaction.[52] The term "critical pragmatism" is adopted here to capture Addams' cooperative-democratic model of criticism and analysis which differs radically from the Marxist one.

In our next section, Addams' association with continental and British thought is examined more fully. Then, the two aspects of her writings concerning critical-emancipatory science and its American translation into social action and thought, are united.

Addams' Relation to Other Intellectual Traditions

In addition to the influences of the male Chicago School, feminism, and pragmatism, Addams drew upon a number of other intellectual traditions. Three subtypes are notable in this regard: Marxist-socialist writings, Russian writings on cooperative thought represented by Peter Kropotkin and Leo Tolstoy; and British empiricism, represented by the work of Charles Booth and the Webbs.

Marxist-Socialist Writings

Addams strongly supported the goal of economic equality advanced by Marx and Engels. She was clearly influenced by Kelley's early Marxist and socialist training during their writing of *HH Maps and Papers*. But socialism was problematic to Addams in several ways: She did not accept the conflict model on which it was based, she supported liberal values of democracy and free speech, and she wanted to accept the Marxist emphasis on economic equality while rejecting other basic assumptions. She was also critical of the concept of false consciousness of the working classes because all classes shared deep ties to their communities. Differences and inequities abounded, but so did commonalities and strengths. Her deep struggle with Marxist thought is discussed in depth in her autobiographical account *Twenty Years*. There she describes the socialists as "gallant company" who were devoted to relieving crushing poverty. She "longed for the comfort of a definite social creed, which should afford at one and the same time an explanation of the social chaos and the logical steps towards its better understanding."[53] Addams believed firmly in economic equality, but within a different matrix of explanation than that accepted by Marxists.[54]

This commitment to Marxist thought and experiments was revealed in her support of the Russian Revolution. This stance aided her opponents in labeling her a communist and resulted in persecutions by the government and public. In her second major autobiographical statement, *The Second Twenty Years at Hull-House*, Addams described this jingoism as similar to the fear following the French Revolution. At that time, people supported social repression, such as slavery, rather than be associated with the advancement of civil and political liberties. This defense of a bad social order arose from fear rather than a commitment to that order. Thus Addams supported the Russians because they were fighting an oppressive social order, although she did not support all their actions. She basically defended the Russian experiment while remaining a critic, but this thoughtful stance was intolerable to an enraged and stampeding populace.

Addams discusses Marxism primarily in her autobiographical accounts and in her analyses of cooperation, instead of conflict, as the preferred social change. These passages reveal her continuing consideration of Marxism. However, her support of British Fabianism indicated her greater acceptance of this form of socialism rather than of the German and Russian revolutionaries.

The Russian Connection: Bread and Peace

Addams was fascinated with the Russian experience for several reasons other than her interest in Marxism. Her Chicago neighbors were frequently Russian refugees, and they brought their culture, conflicts, and worldview with them. Russian anarchists, moreover, created a series of *causes célèbres* involving Addams who supported their right to speak, although not their ideas. Finally, Addams was profoundly influenced by the writings of Tolstoy and to a lesser degree by those of Kropotkin.

Tolstoy's philosophy was based on a "back to the land" movement. Deeply moved by the terrible depression that occurred in Russia in 1881, he labored to alleviate the unspeakable agony he witnessed. He came to the conclusion, however, that such efforts were futile. The problems of the poor were irresolvable in the city, and elite members of society could do little to ameliorate their conditions. Instead, each person needed to return to the land, raise his or her own food, make his or her own clothing, and give up the idle life of the rich. Because he was a noted literary figure at that time, his adoption of the peasant's life was a newsworthy event, affecting the thought and politics of many.[56]

Although Addams was originally drawn to his ideas concerning work with one's hands and the "simple" life, it was his philosophy of art and nonresistance that ultimately affected her the most. For Tolstoy, art should express and reflect the life of the people. It should reveal their experiences, honor their labor, and move them to a sense of community. All these concepts were accepted, extended, and practiced by Addams. Similarly, his concept of "nonresistance" was ultimately adopted by Addams, but with considerable struggle and pain. The path that led to her adoption of this view of social conflict and its elimination was a labyrinthian one.

The first documented account of Addams' reading of Tolstoy started in the Fall of 1885 when she read *My Religion*. This book accorded with her own beliefs and she was profoundly moved by it. In 1910 she recalled:

> The reading of that book had made clear that men's poor little efforts to do right are put forth for the most part in the chill of self-distrust; I became convinced that if the new social order ever came, it would come by gathering to itself all the pathetic human endeavor which had indicated the forward direction.[57]

She continued, however, that it was the application of his ideas and not their context which most fascinated her at that time. It must be remembered that this initial contact with his ideas occurred when she was recuperating from an illness which had precipitated her withdrawal from medical school.[58]

Her long and agonizing period of indecision[59] between 1885 and 1889 was characterized by her as a "snare of preparation," a concept taken from Tolstoy. It refers to the difficulty of finding meaning for one's life and labor when years are spent in preparing for but not engaging in action.

She had read his books early in her life, at the age of twenty-one and in 1893, after the founding of Hull-House, she was still reading them. For example after 1891, Addams was increasingly pressured by Kelley to question how much was accomplished with "only" reform: "The suffering of the poor during the depression of 1893 increased her doubts and made her more fascinated by the example of Tolstoy."[60] Finally in 1895 Addams suffered an acute case of typhoid fever. During her convalescence she again questioned the viability of her chosen path. She wondered whether she should chose a more radical lifestyle and was plagued by ambivalent feelings concerning the nature and role of settlement work. In 1910 she reflected:

> Doubtless the heaviest burden of our contemporaries is a consciousness of a divergence between our democratic theory on the one hand, that working people have a right to the intellectual resources of society, and the actual fact on the other hand, that thousands of them are so overburdened with toil that there is no leisure nor energy left for the cultivation of the mind. We constantly suffer from the strain and indecision of believing this theory and acting as if we did not believe it, and this man who years before had tried "to get off the backs of the peasants", who had at least simplified his life and worked with his hands, had come to be a prototype to many of his generation.[61]

In 1886 she traveled once more to Europe, the site of her earlier resolutions and inspiration. She first visited England, then continued her journey to Russia. There she sought out Aylmer Maude, a follower of Tolstoy, to arrange a visit. When they arrived, Tolstoy was working in the fields, dressed as a peasant, and tired by his long physical labor. He had never heard of Addams, and she recalled that while she was being introduced, he

> was standing by clad in his peasant garb. He listened gravely but, glancing distrustfully at the sleeves of my traveling gown which unfortunately at that season were monstrous in size, he took hold of an edge and pulling out one sleeve to an interminable breadth, said quite simply that "there was enough stuff on one arm to make a frock for a little girl," and asked me directly if I did not find "such a dress" a "barrier to the people."[62]

Addams was disconcerted and replied that it would be more of a barrier to dress as a peasant in the city. Also, since there were thirty-six nationalities in her neighborhood, selecting a peasant style could itself create a barrier.

This inauspicious beginning characterized her entire visit. When Tolstoy learned that Addams owned a farm tilled by another, he was aghast that she was an "absentee landlord." Then, at the end of the day, she was served by Tolstoy's family, who were weary and eating more modestly than their guest. Repeatedly, her self-presentation, lifestyle, and ideas were challenged. Tolstoy was clearly unimpressed by Addams.

Addams, however, was inspired and agitated by the visit. During the next month, she "read everything of Tolstoy's that had been translated into English, German or French."[63] Upon her return to Hull-House, Addams intended to spend two hours a day "making bread." Doing "bread labor," as

Tolstoy suggested, and drawing upon her knowledge as the daughter of a miller, Addams resolved to adopt this new course:

> until I actually arrived in Chicago when suddenly the whole scheme seemed to me as utterly preposterous as it doubtless was. The half dozen people invariably wanting to see me after breakfast, the piles of letters to be opened and answered, the demand of actual and pressing human wants—were these all to be pushed aside and asked to wait while I saved my soul by two hours' work at baking bread?[64]

This skepticism of Tolstoy's path has been considered by at least one biographer as an indication that she was interested in Tolstoy's ideas but rejected them as too radical and utopian.[65] But Addams did not stop here with her study and application of Tolstoy's thought.

Her letters at this time reveal her enthusiasm for Tolstoy and his profound effect on her. She wrote Maude that "a radical stand such as Tolstoy has been able to make throws all such effort as that of settlements into the ugly light of compromise and inefficiency."[66] She worried about her investments and began to live on her lecturing alone. She lectured on his ideas, and gradually took his adamant stance on nonresistance as a central core to her life and thought.

When Addams first visited Tolstoy, she was not concerned with national nonresistance. She kept her ideas of cooperation rooted in the community and neighborhood. When in 1898 the Spanish-American War broke out, "although she was not a prominent antiimperialist, the debate over imperialism, and her own experiences, helped her bring together some of the ideas aroused by Tolstoy and made her a full-fledged advocate of peace.[67]

There were several compatibilities between their writings. Tolstoy was an influence on Addams, but this was partially due to her independent theoretical development of these shared world views. In 1880, presumably before her contact with Tolstoy's philosophy, Addams was writing of women as "breadgivers."[68] Tolstoy's concept of "bread labor" carried this same association of fruitfulness and positive contributions in conjunction with making and creating food. Similarly, Tolstoy asserted that the salvation from evil for men of the wealthy class rested with women, a view that Addams shared.[69] Addams, too, believed in nonresistance reflected in her articles on Hull-House, but originally she viewed this on a more intimate scale than Tolstoy did.

> Miss Addams found confirmation for an increased pragmatism in her thought in Tolstoy's life. He had formulated a new moral insight, and he had reduced it to action. Moral principles that were not put into action, she said,

were not really believed. No start on a solution to vexing social problems was possible until new moral insights were formulated and tested in action.[70]

The connections between her thought and Tolstoy's are most apparent in a series of lectures she gave at Chautauqua in 1902. At this time she delivered five lectures using Tolstoy's concepts. The titles of the lectures reveal the association between his ideas and hers: "The Newer Ideals of Peace," "Arts and Crafts and the Settlement," "Count Tolstoy," and "Tolstoy's Theory of Life."[71] Of course, in 1907, Addams' *Newer Ideals of Peace* was published in which she discussed the evolution of new social standards honoring peaceful relations. There she criticized Tolstoy and other Russian pacifists as being too moralistic and individualistic. She described Tolstoy as "reducing all life to personal experience."[72] As a sociologist and pragmatist,[73] Addams felt new ideals were at work for practical reasons. War was inefficient, a waste of energy, a barrier to social progress. As a neo-Tolstoyian, Addams admired the stance of her mentor. As a pragmatist, she viewed the city as a living and positive step in human experience, one that was part of a growing understanding of the interdependence of people, not their separateness.

Again, in 1904, Addams discussed Tolstoy's ideas on a significant occasion. At this time she shared a platform with William James, and they both addressed Tolstoy's influence on their thoughts concerning war. Addams proposed a "moral substitute for war" while James similarly argued that the aggressiveness of humans needed to be channeled in constructive paths.[74]

Despite this "rejection" of Tolstoy, Addams continued to struggle with his works. Thus in 1922 with the publication of *Peace and Bread in Time of War*, she was still uniting her ideas on women, nurturance, and peace.[75] Five years later, she was writing that Tolstoy's *What Then Must We Do?* was a "book that changed" her life.[76] It was her struggle with Tolstoy's ideas that forced her to make the ultimate decision that she must take moral stances even when contrary to popular ("democratic") opinion. Tolstoy was the source of Addams' resolution of the basic conflict between "amelioration and pragmatic solutions" and a commitment to what is called here "cultural feminism." In 1931, she continued her study of Tolstoy by comparing his ideas with Gandhi's. Both men, however, did not combine enough realism with their idealism to satisfy her.[77] She admired them both, considered their work, and ultimately modified their thought with her sociological realism.

Finally, Addams read Tolstoy throughout her life, using his writings even in study groups at Hull-House.[78] Because Addams has not been characterized as a scholar, and because Tolstoy's ideas were ones she struggled to understand, modified, and at times mocked, his underlying vision that informed her own has been greatly underestimated.

Kropotkin's ideas were also central to Addams' although his thought was less central than Tolstoy's. Kropotkin, moreover, differed from Tolstoy in his relation to Addams, for Kropotkin was a loved visitor to Hull-House and his portrait hung there.[79] His publication *Mutual Aid* was the subject of at least one lecture, and Addams' ideas on social progress and cooperation as connected phenomena can be traced to similar ideas in Kropotkin. For example in his conclusion he wrote:

> In the practice of mutual aid, which we can retrace to the earliest beginnings of evolution, we thus find the positive and undoubted origin of our ethical conceptions; and we can affirm that in the ethical progress of man, mutual support—not mutual struggle—has had the leading part. In its wide extension, even at the present time, we also see the best guarantee of a still loftier evolution of our race.[80]

Like Tolstoy and Addams, Kropotkin stressed the need for "bread." His 1903 book entitled *The Conquest of Bread* dealt with the everyday struggle for existence and the need to survive. He saw the peasant revolution at that time as one resulting in immediate benefit for the peasant and only subsequently for the urbanite, again reflecting the bias against the city shared with Tolstoy but not with Addams.[81]

Kropotkin also addressed women's issues, recognizing that patriarchy was of recent historical origin and oppressive to women.[82] His support of women is also partially revealed through his stay and welcome at Hull-House when Emma Goldman was there. This convergence of their visits and to some degree their ideas later caused a considerable furor in the press. At that time, the newspapers inflamed the public about the radical ideas fermented at the settlement to the detriment of the "community."[83]

"Useful labor" was a key concept for Kropotkin who emphasized the need to perform manual labor and teach people how to make their living. Addams adapted this concept to fit her interests in industrial labor and pragmatism in urban America. In the process, she altered Kropotkin's idea which he tied directly to the land and rural living.

This bond with the land generated a concept of the environment as directly affecting human behavior. As a student of the city (like later Chicago sociologists), Addams stressed this influence. Kropotkin, however, was opposed to the division of labor in the city and factory. He saw it as a source of atomistic life, competition, and human destruction. The unity of the home and marketplace cried for decentralization. It is here that Addams' great ability to integrate different bodies of knowledge is apparent. She accepted Kropotkin's stress on the environment while she responded to the progressive concept of the new industrial city as a source of human liberation.[84] Thus the city and industry were not only negative forces, as described by Kropotkin, but also a means to provide the life and labor desired by the poor and disenfranchised. Industry and urban life provided the very mechanism for liberation, bringing the more utopian and naturalistic vision of Kropotkin into the world of twentieth-century America. This innovation does not negate the work of Kropotkin, which provided Addams with a way to articulate cooperation as an organic and evolutionary product of society.

Kropotkin and Tolstoy brought similar themes to Addams' work which she combined with those of cultural feminism and pragmatism. The result was a more emancipatory pragmatism than that developed by the male Chicago Pragmatists. Her model reflected her commitment to more fundamental change, to the people rather than the elite, and to radical democracy.

The British Connection: Empiricism, Social Settlements, and Fabianism

Throughout the book, the influence of Toynbee Hall and Charles Booth has been emphasized. It was Toynbee Hall that inspired Addams to found Hull-House, although she dramatically modified its practice and goals. Similarly, it was Charles Booth's monumental study of the life of the poor in London's East End that became a model for *HH Maps and Papers* (see chapter 2).

Booth's social survey was a turning point in British sociology. In fact, his study has been interpreted as the initiation of the discipline in that country and the termination of a long statistical movement that preceded it.[85] Booth's work was based on a tradition of British empiricism where social facts had a "scientific" status. Statistical "knowledge" about social conditions was considered an important component of government practice. This union of statistics with public agencies and commissions provided a basis for the later work of the Fabians who profoundly altered the conduct of British government with their use of statistical studies, public lectures, political platforms, and action on government committees. Although Booth himself was considered a disinterested observer, if not a conservative, his work was directly influential in changing the public's awareness of pervasive poverty and the pressing need to alleviate it.[86]

One of his early investigators, Beatrice Potter (Webb), was a major figure in the development of the welfare state in England and the abolition of the Poor Law. She and other like-minded colleagues visited Addams at Hull-House providing a link between British sociology, Fabian thought, and socialist democratic practice. These Fabian connections are worth close analysis, particularly the association between Addams and Beatrice Webb (*née* Potter).

Beatrice Webb, experienced conflicts as a professional and articulate woman, similar to those of Addams'. For example, she was caught between competing family and social claims. Between 1883 and 1887, Beatrice (then) Potter struggled with a profound depression. She felt that she must decide whether to marry the man she loved who wanted her to be sub-missive or remain independent but lonely.[87] Two years older than Addams, it is striking to note the similar ages in which they strove to achieve a place for themselves in the larger social order. Webb, however, nursed a paralyzed father for years, thereby prolonging her battle between incompatible de-mands on her as a professional and a dutiful daughter. During this time she was able to continue her "social" interests by studying and working with Herbert Spencer, the Social Darwinist.

In 1887, after turning down her marriage proposal, she began to work under the auspices of Charles Booth, a cousin by marriage. She completed an analysis of dock life and sweating shops, thereby earning a reputation as a "social analyst" and female explorer.[88] But she was restless with the apolitical role she was playing. With her marriage in 1892 to the Fabian Sydney Webb, she more directly entered the stream of British politics, albeit in the role of social investigator and analyst and not as an elected politician.

In 1893 the couple traveled to Chicago, visited the Columbian Exposition and stayed at Hull-House.

> Clarence Darrow gave a luncheon for them, with Jane Addams, and Gover-nor Altgeld as the other guests. Beatrice Webb smoked cigarettes, and in her desire to make the visitor feel at home, Jane Addams also took and smoked one, with the most regrettable results.[89]

This anecdote reveals a great deal about the two women. For although their interests were similar, their self-presentation and symbolic leadership as women were radically different. Addams was the more radical feminist, but Webb was far more connected to the male political world. Addams kept herself removed from electoral politics with notable exceptions, such as her disastrous role in the Progressive Party when she helped support a platform that was anti-Black and antisuffrage.[89] Nevertheless, there was a strong bond of similar interests between the women that has been overlooked. As sociologists, moreover, they had a leading role in the development of the disciplines in their respective countries.[90]

In 1896, Addams visited the Webbs on her journey to meet Tolstoy, discussed above. Addams noted that the Webbs were writing *Industrial*

Democracy at this time. She also attended a reception for Karl Marx's daughter, Mrs. Aveling, attended by the Fabian Bernard Shaw among others.[91] The Webbs again traveled to the United States in 1898, visiting the University of Chicago sociologist and Fabian Charles Zeublin and staying at Hull-House. Beatrice Webb found Zeublin a pleasant and sympathetic person, but condescendingly wrote that "he is . . . just a cultivated right-minded individual who has a facile tongue and agreeable manner."[92] Noting that the Zeublins "lived on the 'outskirts' of the University in more ways than one" Beatrice Webb summed up her opinion of the University of Chicago as a place of learning without form. Evaluating Harper as a businessman first, she recorded visits with Henderson and Small on the sociology faculty. Although she was not impressed by the male sociologists, her opinion of Addams was extremely favorable:

> Miss Jane Addams, the Principal, is without doubt a remarkable women, an interesting combination of the organizer, the enthusiast, and the subtle observer of human characteristics. Her article in the *International Journal of Ethics*—"Ethical Survivals in Municipal Corruption"—is an exact analysis of the forces of Tammany organization and its root in human nature. . . . She has made Hull-House; and it is she who has created whatever spirit of reform exists in Chicago.[93]

Both Webbs lectured while visiting at the settlement, where in her feisty style Beatrice recalled that they were exhausted, fed, and heckled.

This association between Addams and the Webbs was long-lived and marked by considerable cross-fertilization. Addams, for example, sent a copy of the *Newer Ideals of Peace* to the Webbs.[94] Similarly, Beatrice Webb wanted to enlist Addams as a contributor to *The New Statesman*, a major sociological and Fabian voice in England. Beatrice Webb wrote Addams in 1913 that

> I am so very sorry that you cannot find time to write directly for *The New Statesman*. But are there any articles you are contributing to American magazines which we might have for the Women's Supplement, or the general body of the paper? It seems a pity that they should be monopolized by America.[95]

Whether Addams did publish in the paper is unknown, but certainly Webb supported many of her ideas. Addams traveled to England in 1900 and in 1915, but does not provide any evidence that she visited the Webbs at that time. Since Addams was invited by the Webbs to visit in 1915, it is probable that they did meet then.[96] In 1919, however, it is known that she visited them as well as the Fabian sociologist Graham Wallas.[97]

In addition to the relationship between Addams and the Webbs, there were myriad other ties between the Fabians and Hull-House. Edith Abbott, a Hull-House resident and sociologist, studied for a year at the London School of Economics, working directly with Fabians, especially the Webbs.[98] Hamilton, moreover, summarized the range of these contacts at Hull-House in the following passages: "There were Liberals and Socialists of the moderate English type—Patrick Geddes, John Morley, J.A. Hobson, Sidney and Beatrice Webb, H.G. Wells, John Burns."[99] Patrick Geddes' ideas on "sociology as civics" closely parallel those of Addams, again providing a British sociology connection with her work.

Clearly an extensive analysis of Addams' thought and that of the Fabians would be an exhaustive one, far beyond the scope of this book on the Chicago School influence. What is vital, however, is that British sociology influenced Addams, Zeublin, and to some degree Henderson. The remainder of the Chicago male sociologists stressed German ideas and institutions and thereby followed a different sociological tradition.

Conclusion

Addams was a critical pragmatist, a term that refers to her unique combination of American thought with radical emancipatory practice and goals. Firmly enmeshed in the pragmatic sociological tradition, especially Dewey's and Mead's, Addams structured her arguments around the issues of democracy and education. These terms had a broad definition, encompassing the whole range of human experience and the meanings contained within their boundaries.

Always drawn to the experience of daily life found in her neighborhood, Addams struggled with the problems of the city. To find more radical answers to her questions, she turned to leading scholars in other countries. Fascinated by Marxism, she struggled with the concept of conflict, ultimately rejecting it as an unsatisfactory and limiting perception of social interaction.

In Russia she found intellectuals who addressed her deepest beliefs about pacifism and the importance of daily maintenance and labor. Less abstract and more grounded in the daily round of making bread, Addams found that these scholars took her restless search for radical answers seriously.

In England she was able to draw on the work of early social settlements to provide a new way of life for educated women social scientists. She wanted to do something with herself and her life while remaining true to her ideals, background, and skills. The Fabian program of social change was one that pragmatically provided guidelines for social amelioration and action. In particular, the Webbs with their programs of analysis and action aided Addams in her understanding of governmental powers and uses.

Addams wanted more than safe answers and compromises that keep society basically unchanged. Although she was firmly committed to democracy and the democratic method, she knew that the people's lives in the United States were radically oppressed and thwarted. She was torn between her own values based on cultural feminism and the society's patriarchal values based on material competition and exploitation.

Addams was drawn to a number of intellectual approaches and solutions while she tried to balance an antielite stance with a vision of peaceful cooperation in a society based on a vitality of life and emotions. She was never fully satisfied, however. It was this continual quest for a set of ideas that could articulate and explain her community that kept her an open and critical scholar. Her study of urban life, based on the work of so many others, forged a new approach to social amelioration and a broadening of consciousness. Her social thought was based on her American experience and historical context in Chicago.

Notes

1. Charles Morris, *The Pragmatic Movement in American Philosophy* (New York: Braziller, 1990), p. 11. See also Darnell Rucker, *The Chicago Pragmatists* (Minneapolis: University of Minnesota Press, 1969).
2. A brief review of the texts cited here resulted in a number of vague and conflicting definitions. Some of these divergences in the school are discussed by J. David Lewis and Richard L. Smith, *American Sociology and Pragmatism* (Chicago: University of Chicago Press, 1980). See also Morris, pp. 16-18.
3. Morris, p. 13.
4. Lewis and Smith (*American Sociology and Pragmatism*) argue that there are idealistic and realistic schools within pragmatism itself. This division in the theory is a contradiction of its basic assumptions, and there is not a separation as distinct as that suggested by Lewis and Smith. Nonetheless, the philosophical problems of uniting thought and action plagued pragmatism, which aimed to eliminate this dualism. This flaw in pragmatic logic also affected the work of Addams.
5. Morris, *The Pragmatic Movement in American Philosophy*, p. 5.
6. Ibid., p. 175. In a patriarchal omission, Morris only presents the names of male authors of the articles in this collection. However, Ella Flagg Young also contributed to this volume, establishing the Chicago School as a separate entity, but her contribution is rarely noted.
7. See Rucker, *The Chicago Pragmatists*; Morris, *The Pragmatic Movement in American Philosophy*, pp. 174-91.
8. Notable exceptions are the books by Lewis and Smith and by C. Wright Mills, *Sociology and Pragmatism*, ed. and intro. Irving Louis Horowitz (New York: Paine-Whitman, 1964). Mills, however, concentrates on the work of Dewey, James, and Pierce. Lewis and Smith (*American Sociology and Pragmatism*)

study the Chicago sociologists but emphasize many of the later Chicago sociologists, such as Blumer, Faris, and students of the 1920s and 1930s. Lewis and Smith come to the erroneous conclusion that Mead was an insignificant influence on Chicago sociologists. Such a hypothesis can be seen as a result of their ignoring the work of the early men and women. Despite disagreement with their thesis, however, their book is an important step in documenting some of the social trends of the Chicago School in later writings and years than that studied here. John W. Petras' work on John Dewey is also significant, but would lead us astray here into another major issue of Chicago Sociology. See "John Dewey and the Rise of Interactionism in American Social Theory," *Journal of the History of the Behavioral Sciences* 4 (1968):18-27.

9. Lewis and Smith (*American Sociology and Pragmatism*) emphasize the similarities of James and Dewey and their difference from Mead. Nonetheless, they are one resource for understanding the influence of James. For a study of the influence of Dewey on Mead, see Neil Coughlan, *Young John Dewey: An Essay in American Intellectual History* (New York: Free Press, 1976), pp. 113-33.

10. See John H. Dewey, "George H. Mead," *Journal of Philosophy* 28 (4 June 1931):309-14; id., "The Work of George Mead," *New Republic* 87 (22 July 1936):329-30; id, "Prefatory Remarks" in George H. Mead, *The Philosophy of the Present*, ed. Arthur E. Murphy (Chicago: Open Court, 1932), pp. xxxvi-xl.

11. "The Democratic Form," in *Intelligence in the Modern World* (New York: Modern Library, 1939), p. 400. This is a compilation of Dewey's writings drawing from over forty of his speeches and publications.

12. Ibid., p. 403.

13. Ibid., "Communication and Communal Living," p. 391.

14. Ibid., "Democracy in the Schools," p. 716.

15. Ibid., pp. 717.

16. See John H. Dewey, *Human Nature and Conduct* (New York: Henry Holt, 1922) pp. 14-15.

17. "Traditional vs. Progressive Education," *Intelligence in the Modern World*, p. 657.

18. Ibid., "Social Science and Social Control," p. 951.

19. Ibid., p. 954.

20. Ibid., "Experimental Verification and Truth," p. 937.

21. Ibid., "The Development of Meanings," p. 864.

22. Ibid., "Language and Mind," p. 807.

23. Ibid., "Mind and Consciousness," p. 813.

24. Robert E.L. Faris, *Chicago Sociology* (Chicago: University of Chicago Press, 1967); passim; C. Wright Mills, *Sociology and Pragmatism*; Petras, "John Dewey and the Rise of Interactionism in American Social Theory"; Fred Matthews, *Quest for an American Sociology: Robert E. Park and the Chicago School* (Montreal: McGill-Queen's University Press, 1977). Mead's close friendship with Dewey is documented in numerous places. See David Miller, *George Herbert Mead: Self, Language and the World* (Austin, TX: University of Texas Press), pp. xvi-xxviii, passim.

25. Lewis and Smith, *American Sociology and Pragmatism*, p. 168.

26. Dewey to Addams, 27 January 1992. Cited in John C. Farrell, *Beloved Lady* (Baltimore: Johns Hopkins Press, 1967), p. 68.

27. Jane Addams, "John Dewey and Social Welfare," *John Dewey: The Man and His Philosophy* (Cambridge: Howard University Press, 1930), pp. 140-51.

28. Addams, *Twenty Years*, pp. 236-37.
29. James Weber Linn, *Jane Addams* (New York: Appleton-Century Crofts, 1935), pp. 178, 235; Allen F. Davis, *American Heroine* (New York: Oxford University Press, 1973); Farrell, *Beloved Lady*, pp. 80-103; Daniel Levine, *Jane Addams and the Liberal Tradition* (Madison: State Historical Society, 1971), pp. 145-47; Jane Dewey, "Biography of John Dewey," in *Philosophy of John Dewey*, ed. Paul Schillip, (Evanston, Ill: Northwestern University Press), pp. 29-34.
30. Jane Dewey, "Biography of John Dewey," pp. 29-30.
31. Davis, *American Heroine*, p. 97.
32. Linn, *Jane Addams*, p. 254.
33. Christopher Lasch, ed., *The Social Thought of Jane Addams* (Indianapolis: Bobbs-Merrill, 1965), p. 176. Citing Dewey to Addams, 19 January 1896, SCPC.
34. Linn, *Jane Addams*, p. 386; Addams, "John Dewey and Social Welfare."
35. This introduction is also found in the 1960 centennial edition (Boston: G.K. Hall), pp. ix-xx.
36. John H. Dewey, *Liberalism and Social Action* (New York: B.A. Putnam's Sons, 1935).
37. For a brief discussion of Tufts see Morris, *The Pragmatic Movement in American Philosophy*, pp. 183-5.
38. See Joan K. Smith, *Ella Flagg Young* (Ames: Educational Studies Press and the Iowa State University Research Foundation, 1979).
39. Addams, *Twenty Years*, p. 347.
40. Davis, *American Heroine*, p. 141.
41. Ibid, p. 142. William James, "The Moral Equivalent of War," in *Pragmatism and Other Essays* (New York: Washington Equal, 1963, c. 1910), pp. 289-301.
42. Davis, *American Heroine*, p. 143.
43. Ibid.
44. James to Addams, 17 September 1902. Addams Papers, DG1, SCPC.
45. James to Addams, 24 January, 12 February, 1907, Addams Papers, DG1, SCPC.
46. James to Thomas, 13 December 1909, Addams Papers, SCPC.
47. Petras, "John Dewey and the Rise of Interactionism in American Social Theory," pp. 18-19.
48. Ellsworth Fuhrman, *The Sociology of Knowledge in America, 1883-1915* (Charlottesville: University Press of Virginia, 1980), p. 19.
49. The following discussion is based on Fuhrman's analysis of critical emancipatory interests and roles, pp. 19-20. He characterized Small as a social-technologist, although a more critical one than some other early male sociologists. Cooley, who shared many of Addams' ideas on society and social science, is seen as the most critical social technologist.
50. Ibid, pp. 19-20.
51. Jurgen Habermas, *Towards A Rational Society*, tr. Jeremy Shapiro (Boston: Beacon, 1970, c. 1968), pp. 81-122.
52. Fuhrman (*The Sociology of Knowledge in America, 1883-1915*), claims that these assumptions are parts of paradigms. This term is rejected here because Kuhn excludes the social sciences from paradigmatic analysis. See Thomas Kuhn, *The Structure of Scientific Revolutions*, 2nd ed. (Chicago: University of Chicago Press, 1970).
53. Addams, *Twenty Years*, p. 187.
54. *Newspaper*.

55. Addams, *Twenty Years*, pp. 153-56.
56. Davis, *American Heroine*, pp. 135-37. See also *What Shall we Do Then?*" vol. 17 of Leo Tolstoy, Complete Works, tr., ed. Leo Wiener (Boston: D. Estes, 1905).
57. Addams, *Twenty Years*, p. 261.
58. Davis, *American Heroine*, p. 42.
59. Addams, *Twenty Years*, p. 88; "The Snare of Preparation," pp. 65-88.
60. Davis, *American Heroine*, p. 136.
61. Addams, *Twenty Years*, p. 271.
62. Ibid., pp. 267-68.
63. Ibid., p. 274.
64. Ibid, p. 276-77.
65. See Linn, *Jane Addams*, pp. 291-92.
66. Quoted by Davis, *American Heroine*, p. 138.
67. Ibid, p. 140.
68. Addams, "Women as Bread-Givers," 1880. Partially reprinted in *Jane Addams: A Centennial Reader*, ed. Emily Cooper Johnson (New York: Macmillan, 1960), pp. 103-4.
69. Cited by Farrell, *Beloved Lady*, p. 142, n. 4.
70. Farrell (*Beloved Lady*), p. 142, summarized Addams' lecture on Tolstoy in 1902.
71. All summarized in the *Chautauqua Assembly Herald*, vol. 27 (1902, July 8:5; July 10:6; July 11:5; July 14:2-3).
72. Jane Addams, *Newer Ideals of Peace* (New York: Macmillan, 1907).
73. Lasch, *Social Thought of Jane Addams*, p. 218.
74. Davis, *American Heroine*, p. 143. James' famous pamphlet "The Moral Equivalent for War" was published six years later. See Davis for a brief comparison on the subject. James clearly emphasized more innate and masculine aspects of aggression than Addams, pp. 143-44. William James' pamphlet is reprinted in *Pragmatism and Other Essays* (New York: Washington Equal, 1963, c. 1910), pp. 289-301.
75. Addams mentions the Russian peasants' love of peace and Tolstoy in *Twenty Years,* pp. 91-4.
76. Jane Addams, "A Book That Changed My Life," *Christian Century* 44 (13 October 1927):1196-98.
77. Jane Addams, "Tolstoy and Gandhi," *Christian Century* 48 (25 November 1931):1485-88.
78. Jane Addams, *The Second Twenty Years at Hull-House* (New York: Macmillan, 1930), pp. 62, 409.
79. *Chicago Chronicle*, 16 September 1903, cited in *Eighty Years at Hull-House*, ed. Allen F. Davis and Mary Lynn McCree (Chicago: Quadrangle, 1969), p. 110. At Hull-House, picture.
80. Petr Kropotkin, *Mutual Aid: A Factor of Evolution*, foreword by Ashley Montagu and Thomas Huxley, "The Struggle for Existence" (Boston: Extending Horizons, 1955, c. 1902), p. 300.
81. Petr Kropotkin, *The Conquest of Bread*, ed., intro. Paul Avich. New York: New York University Press, 1972, c., 1892. See Jane Addams, *Peace and Bread in Time of War*, intro. by John H. Dewey (Boston: G. K. Hall and Co., 1960, c., 1922), p. 94.
82. Kropotkin, *Mutual Aid*, p. 313-20.

83. See Addams, *Twenty Years*, pp. 402-05; Alice Hamilton, *Exploring the Dangerous Trades* (Boston: Little, Brown and Co., 1943), pp. 86-87, *Chicago Chronicle*, September 16, 1903. See also Goldman to Addams (15 April, 1915) Addams Papers, DC1, 1a, SCPC.

84. See, e.g., Charles Zeublin, *American Municipal Progress* (New York: Macmillan, 1902); also Petr Kropotkin, *Fields, Factories and Workshops Tomorrow*, ed., intro. and additional materials by Colin Ward (New York: Harper & Row, 1974, c. 1904).

86. Michael J. Cullen, *The Statistical Movement in Early Victorian England* (New York: Barnes & Noble, 1975). Karl de Schweinitz, *England's Road to Social Security* (New York: A.S. Barnes, 1961, c. 1943).

86. de Schweinitz, *England's Road to Social Security*, pp. 178-80.

87. Norman and Jeanne MacKinzie, *The Fabians* (New York: Simon & Schuster, 1977), p. 257.

88. Ibid, pp. 132-33. Note that her interest in sweat shops was similar to that of Kelley, Addams, and the Chicago men during this period.

89. This compromise by Addams was a bitter one, pushing her away from politics. See Breckinridge cited in Lasch, *The Social Thought of Jane Addams*, p. 162.

90. Linn makes this comparison, citing Beatrice Webb's views on her sociological role. *Jane Addams*, p. 200, see also pp. 193-194.

91. Addams, *Twenty Years*, p. 264-65.

92. Beatrice Webb, *American Diary*, 1898, ed. David A. Shannon (Madison: State Historical Society, 1963), p. 99.

93. Ibid, p. 108.

94. Addams to Nelson (publisher), 11 January 1907, Addams Papers, SCPC. DG1, box 2. SCPC.

95. Beatrice Webb to Jane Addams, 11 August 1913, Addams Papers DG1 4, SCPC.

96. Beatrice Webb to Jane Addams, 10 May 1915, Addams Papers, DG1, box 5, SCPC.

97. Davis, *American Heroine*, p. 259.

98. Hamilton, *Exploring the Dangerous Trades*, p. 83.

99. See reprint of this 1915 chapter in *The Origins of British Sociology, 1834-1914*, ed. Philip Abrams (Chicago: University of Chicago Press, 1968), pp. 265-73.

11

Jane Addams and Critical Pragmatism: Democracy and Education as the Cornerstones of Urban Society and Sociology

Addams' theory of critical pragmatism was based on democracy to ensure social equality, and education as the mechanism to protect that right. She drew freely on the central concepts of symbolic interactionism, especially as they were articulated by Mead, Dewey, and Thomas. Social interaction based on equal participation for all, however, was stunted and blocked in American cities. As a result of capitalism, immigration, and changes in the home affecting primarily women, children, and the aged, communication and interaction were failing to work for the whole community. To resolve these problems, democracy and education needed to be used as tools to improve social institutions, community control, and the vitality of everyday life. In this way, Addams connected the social psychology of symbolic interactionism with the structural problems of city life. The male American pragmatists also shared her view of the social order, but Addams was more radical in her interpretation.

For her, democracy encompassed three levels: political, social, and economic. Because political rights were restricted for women, she demanded their full inclusion in the franchise. (She did not address the disenfranchisement of Native Americans, however.) Social rights could be gained through education which would provide access to full acceptance in a community shaped by its members. Economic rights could be won through militant action such as strikes, but she favored the development of economic equality through nonviolence. She supported union organizing, lobbying, and the use of the ballot to obtain economic goals of full equality and participation in the marketplace.

Democracy was also a central concern for Small, Zeublin, and Henderson. The latter two were particularly close to Addams' programs for action because of their emphasis on British Fabianism. Small and Henderson were both influenced by the German social welfare programs, but Addams was more supportive of the British than the Germanic social policies.

Democracy's power to generate social equality could be improved, articulated, and enacted through education. To Addams, education was a continuous process occurring throughout life. It had the potential to be activated in all situations, and it was the key to responsible action and reflective thought. Human intelligence could be brought to its maximum flowering through systematic knowledge, reflection, and analysis. Education needed to provide concrete information about everyday life. It was to be a tool for people to articulate their goals and needs. It was to create access to cultural ideas and knowledge for all rather than an elite. The desire to know was an intrinsic part of being human and striving for participation in a full community life. Traditional education was usually irrelevant and designed to interest the middle and upper classes, ignoring the culture, beliefs, and interests of workers and immigrants.

Traditional and progressive education were both central concepts and concerns of the Chicago sociologists and pragmatists. Mead and Dewey, in particular, supported progressive education throughout their lives. Zeublin supported progressive, adult education through social settlements, the popular lecture, and University Extension. Vincent was originally concerned with progressive education for adults through the Chautauqua system and for college students receiving liberal arts training. After his work at the University of Minnesota, however, he transferred his allegiance to more elite groups and researchers.

Small's concepts of education were closely linked to his program for professionalizing sociology. His concern with the elite development of the profession and legitimating its claim to authority fundamentally divided his work in education from Addams.[1] His search for respectability was continued by his successors, Park and Burgess. Basic divisions between Addams and these three men can be seen in relation to their stance on educational equality and their respect for knowledge both inside and outside of the academy.

Addams' close collegial work with Chicago sociologists and pragmatists must be seen in light of her other intellectual influences. One major competing set of ideas concerned cultural feminism. The conflict between critical pragmatism and cultural feminism will be considered later in this chapter, after a presentation of the major premises and arguments in critical pragmatism. Addams' intellectual roots in British and Russian thought also led to a distinct development of her concepts. The British sociologists, especially the Fabians, were important intellectual resources in terms of their program for social science and action, and for their particular methodological technique—statistical documentation. During the period of interest here, Chicago Sociology was frequently based on the use of statistical information. This was particularly true of the work of Henderson, Mead, and the female Chicago sociologists.

Park, however, was vehemently opposed to the use of statistics, and his stance was instrumental in the decline of this technique at Chicago for approximately a decade. Ironically, today's sociologists use quantitative methods extensively, but they have not recognized Addams and other Chicago sociologists' leadership in this endeavor.

Despite the significance of British epistemology, Addams adopted their ideas with modifications. On the one hand, she rejected the class and religious biases of English social settlements, and evolved a model built on American ideals and new opportunities for professional and working women. On the other hand, the British programs for the inclusion of labor in the political process and the establishment of minimal government standards for social welfare were ideas congenial to Addams' interests.

Finally, the Russian influence of Tolstoy and Kropotkin were central in her struggle to understand labor and exploitation. Rejecting the class struggle of Marx as too violent a depiction of social life and relations, she found more guidance in the cooperative goals of Tolstoy and Kropotkin. Their ideas on the significance of bread and labor were ultimately more congruent with cultural feminism than her critical pragmatism. The concepts of nonresistance and pacifism were central to her process of defining and changing class exploitation. Thus, the Russian intellectuals brought to the fore her concern with the process as well as the end of social change. The Russians' extreme, logical application of their ideas to all aspects of daily life prevented her from adopting *in toto* the American pragmatists' approach. The latter group tended to adhere to American ideals, including capitalism, more than she did.

Addams' thorough and consistent adoption of the goals of equality also led her to break from the educational programs adopted by the academic pragmatists. Although she is often characterized as antiintellectual,[2] such an interpretation is clearly wrong. She was opposed to separate elite education designed to segregate people from their experiences, family, and labor. Thus her ideals of education came out of a love for the people, best expressed in the works of Kropotkin and Tolstoy, rather than the elitist and academic biases pervading the social thought of men working in prestigious institutions of higher learning.

This blending of intellectual heritages can be seen in her analysis of the dual foundations of society: democracy and education.

Democracy

Democracy was the foundation of Addams' critical pragmatism. Her 1902 publication on the subject made it a central principle of all human action:

We are thus brought to a conception of Democracy not merely as a sentiment which desires the well-being of all men, nor yet as a creed which believes in the essential dignity and equality of all men, but as that which affords a rule of living as well as a test of faith.[3]

Democracy was a product of "diversified human experience and [its] resultant sympathy."[4] It was the method for discovering truth through the combination of rational thought with equal participation of all citizens in community processes. Although democracy was flawed and often inoperative, "the cure for the ills of Democracy is more Democracy."[5]

Democracy was a way of living, of experiencing life, of finding out the meaning of action. Social interaction was the core of daily life, and science was a method for gathering informaton about it. Addams averred that "we have come to have an enormous interest in human life as such, accompanied by confidence in its essential soundness."[6]

Thus democracy emerged from the good judgment and spirit of the community. Humans were basically good but they lacked information needed for full community cooperation and participation. In their daily lives, they could learn to generate and accept barriers to cooperation and egalitarian ways of living. They had to learn how to destroy such barriers and build more creative and life-giving skills.

Traditionally, Americans have interpreted democracy to mean equality before the law (especially for literate White men). Most of the arguments concerning human rights in a democratic society have emphasized suffrage as the route to political participation and governance. This definition and practice of democracy was too restrictive for Addams. For her, democracy was a more holistic concept. It encompassed the right of total equality: politically, socially, and economically. This definition of democracy makes it a radical interpretation of the assumption that all people are equal. Each of these components to her understanding of democracy is considered below.

Political Democracy

Addams fought for women's suffrage for years. As an active member and vice-president of the National American Women's Suffrage Association (NAWSA), she was a suffragist long before many other women joined the cause. This support of women's right to vote was intrinsic to women's participation in society. Thus, in this area, there was a considerable overlap between her cultural feminism and her critical pragmatism.

Farrell claims that Addams regarded women's suffrage as an instrumentality rather than a "right."[7] Her support of suffrage was radical but not militant. Since some feminists believe that radical support of women's rights must be couched in the language of inalienable rights that should be demanded,[8] it is worth exploring Addams' approach further.

Addams supported the franchise as a means for women to instill their values into the political sphere. She did not support the achievement of this goal through the use of armed conflict and physical confrontation. She marched in parades, delivered voluminous addresses, wrote articles, and became a national leader who was extremely influential in legitimating the right for women to vote. Access to the vote was only a limited reform goal. Such a narrow view was condemned:

> Reform movements tend to become negative and to lose their educational value for the mass of the people. . . . In trying to better matters, however, they have in mind only political achievements which they detach in a curious way from the rest of life, and they speak and write of the purification of politics as of a thing set apart from daily life.[9]

Political equality gained through suffrage was a major component of control over daily life, but it was a part of a system of justice, not the entire system.

Social Democracy

It is difficult to abstract only one of Addams concepts because they were usually interconnected. This union of ideas is exemplified in this passage concerning immigrant workers, democracy, education, and the right to social equality:

> Doubtless the heaviest burden of our contemporaries is a consciousness of a divergence between our democratic theory on the one hand, that working people have a right to the intellectual resources of society, and the actual fact on the other hand, that thousands of them are so overburdened with toil that there is not leisure nor energy left for the cultivation of the mind.[10]

When discussing problems of social democracy, Addams often focused on immigrant laborers and their children. For this populace, generational differences were amplified with their change of culture and country. Older immigrants lost in two ways: the art and history of their people were absent and often denigrated; while the worst values of American culture were emphasized, namely the search for money. Thus Addams noted that "this tendency upon the part of the older immigrants to lose the amenities of European life without sharing those of American,"[11] was a consistent loss and strain to immigrants, their communities, and their families.

Children of immigrants often found the rules enforced in the home to be too harsh. Parents misunderstood the behavior of their children as being loose and evil instead of normal or acceptable in a more informal society. Further stress was caused by the poverty of the families and lack of fun at home. Frequently, the children's wages were needed and controlled by their parents. This parental dominance made their children angry and the new generation sometimes turned to crime to get extra money and social freedom. Addams compassionately described this situation as follows: "Most of these premature law breakers are in search of Americanized clothing and others are only looking for playthings. They are all distracted by the profusion and variety of the display, and their moral sense is confused by the general air of open-handedness."[12]

Thus, an effort to be part of this society while another society had been lost was a key to understanding the need for social democracy. The right to have one's lifestyle and ethnic culture understood and accepted was a major concern. Such social equality was necessary for the immigrants' participation in the community. Moreover, Addams chided Americans for not wanting to risk their American customs and values.

> I hope to be able to sustain the contention that such danger as exists arises from intellectual dearth and apathy; that we are testing our national life by a tradition too provincial and limited to meet its present motley and cosmopolitan character; that we lack mental energy, adequate knowledge, and a sense of the youth of the earth.[13]

The symbolic meanings of action, according to Addams, should be a product of all members' ideas and backgrounds. Her efforts to "assimilate" immigrants arose originally from this same American provincialism, but her narrow ideas quickly changed to a cosmopolitan admiration of her neighbors and their right to have their own culture, dress, and way of life accepted by their American neighbors.

Thus social democracy was a cornerstone of her concept of equality. Since social customs generated everyday life and its meaning, total acceptance of individuals and their local lifestyles led to an understanding of the community's shared system of thought and aesthetics. Class differences, furthermore, were important causes of human suffering. Economic exploitation was a major source of this oppression, but other forms of exploitation were also significant. Restrictions on political rights, education, and social custom needed to be eliminated as well. Thus the worker needed equality on three distinct fronts: political, social and economic.

Economic Democracy

Expanding on the arguments developed above, Addams noted that the exploitation of immigrants occurred throughout their passage to America.

Beginning with steamship representatives, the process continued with brokers in manufactured passports and phony medical and physical exams. Educated for minimal literacy and impoverished by high-interest loans needed to pass the pauper's tests, the immigrants reached the United States indebted and financially exploited. "The sinister aspect of this exploitation," she wrote, "lies in the fact that it is carried on by agents whose stock in trade are the counters and terms of citizenship."[14]

Addams' concern with economic democracy encompassed all workers. Living in the midst of poverty, awareness of economic oppression filled her life. Anarchy and socialism, in particular, were advanced by her neighbors as solutions to the economic despair and misery around her. A beginning discussion of her lengthy struggle with these ideas was presented in the previous chapter and it is now elaborated here.

Addams and Socialism

During her first years at Hull-House, Addams admired the serious confrontations of the socialists with the bitter poverty that surrounded her. Her rejection of certain tenets, however, made her an outsider.[15] At this stage, then, Addams was struggling with the conflict of socialism with democracy and other liberal rights. In a biting critique, she wrote that socialism had replaced religious fervor and commitment:

> It is as if the socialists had picked up the banner inscribed with the promises of a future life, which had slipped from the hands of the ecclesiastic, as if they had changed the promise of salvation from individual to social, had substituted the word earth for heaven and had then raised the banner aloft once more.[16]

This socialist orthodoxy was particularly problematic for Addams who questioned the theory's emphasis on class conflict and its truncated analysis of women's status and values. In *HH Maps and Papers* she set forth her early disenchantment with the conflict model. Addams saw society as based on both conflict and cooperation, but if peaceful relations were the goal of society, the means to reach that end should be congruent with the end itself.[17] This harmonious goal was based on a feminine worldview and values. The vision of the world as warring was militaristic, and she rejected it.

Marxists also saw the world as based on material values. It was precisely this narrow view of the world that she decried in Americans. Rather than reinforcing this concept of the power of capital, Addams wanted to adopt a model of society that recognized the power of other resources and capacities. Art, literature, affection, and emotions were separate bases for being and acting in the world that had their own value and force. The socialist vision became a partner in perpetuating the false idea that the economy dominates life.

In a critique of John Common's article on class conflict, Addams clearly stated her view on class consciousness. She agreed that an increasing number of workers were uniting to support strikers, but this class struggle occurred in a context that was generating new meanings for group allegiances. For example, immigrants did change their class consciousness in the New World, but they were altered in other ways, too. Their new democratic perspective on the nation and community included more people, ideas, and values. This educational process of seeing new bonds generated between previously "hostile" groups was irreversible. Befriending other immigrants from different nationalities and religious backgrounds taught workers that the divisions between people were not as great as they had once believed. Addams observed a growth of personal identity and a breaking down not only of class distinctions, but also racial and ethnic ones.

Similarly, she felt that workers identified with the problems of management when the "bosses" were people with whom they interacted. The conflict in modern industry, then, was shifting from the owner and worker to the workers versus large businesses run by abstract and anonymous others. Thus Addams argued:

> The newer organization of industry brings the employer himself into a position subordinate to the trust; the trust is composed of the constantly changing stockholders; the trust can be controlled only by the government which after all in a democracy is composed of all the citizens, a universal class.[18]

In Commons' response, he did not stress his disagreement with Addams but the problems of discourse in formal settings. His answer is worth citing in full:

> The trouble about sociology is that if you get into it you are called upon to prophesy, and it is a difficult thing to prophesy. I am trying to answer the question put to me whether class struggle is inevitable and I have to put so many "ifs" around it that even Miss Addams, who agrees with me, has fault to find with some of the things I say.[19]

Addams remained partial to the socialist vision because of its emphasis on the primacy of economic exploitation and a program for its resolution. Nonetheless, her differences with its methods and underlying principles of addressing economic exploitation caused her to take a separate path. In particular, her support of democracy and education were her major mechanisms for nonviolent social change to yield a society composed of political, social, and economic equals.

Education

Education was closely linked with Addams' ideas on culture, and both concepts greatly altered after her first years at Hull-House. Originally, Addams thought that the traditionally defined arts and learning were the highest development of civilization. The industrial environment appeared to be at odds with this view of culture. Fortunately, this elite bias rapidly diminished in her ideas. Repeatedly, she praised the values and ideas of workers, especially immigrants. In 1897, citing Tolstoy, Addams told a settlement group that "music cannot be real . . . , painting is only an affection, unless we do it in the name of and for the mass of men."[20]

Initially favorable to formal courses and structures, Addams taught and sponsored college-level education. But she became increasingly dissatisfied with the effects of such endeavors and the intrinsic barriers generated between people by such an elite activity. In 1910, she reflected on these earlier efforts critically:

> But while we prize these classes as we do the help we are able to give to the exceptional young man or woman who reaches the college and university and leaves the neighborhood of his childhood behind him, the residents of Hull-House feel increasingly that the educational efforts of a Settlement should not be directed primarily to reproduce the college type of culture, but to work out a method and an ideal adapted to the immediate situation. They feel that they should promote a culture which will not set its possessor aside in a class with others like himself, but which will, on the contrary connect him with all sorts of people by his ability to understand them as well as by his power to supplement their present surroundings with the historic background.[21]

Traditional education, however, put the needs of employers first. Businessmen controlled the schools, and they wanted workers who could "write legibly and figure accurately and be punctual, and obedient."[22] Educators participated in this process because they suffered from their own background and training. They repeated what they had been taught, had been rewarded for learning, and continued to value.

Addams' ideas on education started with youth in the kindergartens and public schools, but these concepts soon informed her whole approach to learning and thinking. Speaking of adult laborers, she wrote:

> There is a pitiful failure to recognize the situation in which the majority of working people are placed, a tendency to ignore their real experiences and

needs, and, most stupid of all, we leave quite untouched affections and memories which would afford a tremendous dynamic if they were utilized.[23]

The solution for urban neglect and repression was, nonetheless, education: "Education alone can repair these losses."[24] Her efforts in education and her philosophy supporting it can be seen in her work with specific groups—the child, the adult, and the worker.

The Child and The Public School

The kindergarten movement was active in Chicago prior to the establishment of Hull-House, and Addams soon became a part of it. (McDowell, in fact, specialized in this subject.) In 1894, a kindergarten was opened at Hull-House and was an early success. Like Dewey, she drew extensively on the ideas of Froebel and encouraged the children to play and explore their worlds.[25]

The next stage in education, the public school, became the chief cultural and social method for obtaining a workers' democracy.

> The educators should certainly conserve the learning and training necessary for the successful individual and family life, but should add to that a preparation for the enlarged social efforts which our increasing democracy requires. The democratic ideal demands of the school that it shall give the child's own experience a social value; that it shall teach him to direct his own activities and adjust them to those of other people.[26]

Cutting into family loyalties, depreciating manual labor, separating the classroom from the work life—the public school systematically undermined the community and the family. Thus one of the ways to create a community of equals was to teach a new way of understanding the nature of work and its relation to the whole. In this sense, Addams saw education as a tool to eliminate class distinctions.

Public schools were especially harmful to immigrant children due to their failure to bring the immigrant experience into the American context. If teachers would bring the

> handicrafts and occupations, [the immigrants'] traditions, their folk songs and folklore, the beautiful stories which every immigrant colony is ready to tell and translate . . . into schools the material from which culture is made and the material upon which culture is based, they would discover that by comparison that which they had given them now is a poor meretricious and vulgar thing. Give these children a chance to utilize the historic and industrial material which they see about them and they will begin to have sense of ease in America, a first consciousness of being at home.[27]

Thus, through language, the symbolic context of the community is learned. Education which systematically taught such meanings and perspectives would generate a social democracy as well as an economic one.

Addams worked frequently with the Chicago public school system as well as having a school system at Hull-House itself. She joined with Mead in his campaign for teachers' rights to control their classroom and, in particular, became engaged in the battle over this issue involving Ella Flagg Young. Her efforts in education continued throughout the individual's life cycle, because education was a way of looking and being in the world as well as a formal time spent in institutions devoted to such processes.

The Adult Learner

A series of educational programs for adults were ongoing projects at Hull-House. In addition, Addams was active in the Chautauqua movement.

> To Addams settlement education needed to be used. This meant an application to a given neighborhood of the solace of literature, of the uplift of the imagination, and the historic consciousness which gives its possessor a sense of connection with men of the past who have thought and acted, an application of the stern mandates of science, not only to the conditions of sewers and the care of alleys, but to the methods of life; and thought application of the metaphysic not only to the speculations of the philosopher, but to the events of the passing moment; the application of the moral code to the material life, the transforming of the economic relation into an ethical relation until the sense that religion itself embraces all relations, including the ungodly industrial relation, has become common property.[28]

She was skeptical of all formal education, ultimately including University Extension courses in her criticism. Often taking the search for knowledge and research as more significant than teaching their students, professors became unintelligible to their students.

Part of the process of transmitting knowledge to others was making it understandable, and this was part of Addams' work. To intelligently apply information, however, people needed to comprehend the process of using the information and its relation to their daily lives and resources. This was adult education and this was Addams' goal. This general goal of generating reflective adults was made more specific and important in reference to labor. Through labor, people could affect their housing, sanitation, health, and general life chances. Therefore, industrial education was a primary concern.

The Worker

Addams supported industrial education in order to break down the artificial snobbishness against "working with one's hands,"[29] in addition to supporting its more pragmatic aspects of increasing a worker's wages and skills.

One of the founders of the National Society for Promotion of Industrial Education, Addams was part of a group that struggled from 1906 until 1917 to get industrial education subsidized through public funds. In 1917, the Smith-Hughes Act was passed providing precisely these federal subsidies for vocational education in high schools.[30]

For Addams, vocational education was not the restricted content and classroom training it has now become. "By industrial education she meant general training in the history of industrial processes."[31] Her work with the Labor Museum was indicative of the type of encompassing approach she wanted.

She equated industrial education with "cultural" education. Although having different contents and approaches, both could reveal the nature of being human, historical development, and complex ideas. Industrial education was needed to allow workers to understand the work process and to direct their fate in it. Thus the removal of alienation from work depended not only on good wages but also on an appreciation of the labor and process involved in creating a product. To obtain economic democracy, workers needed to understand their work, its place in society, and their role in production. To obtain social democracy, ideas about the nature of work needed to include an appreciation of manual labor and knowledge and the complexities of technology. Thus industrial education was a key factor in democratic life and community development.

The Role of Intellectual Thought

Addams has been victimized by antiintellectualism in two ways: first by not being considered an intellectual herself, and second by being considered a person who opposed intellectuals. These two misinterpretations are considered briefly here.

Recent scholarship on Addams has consistently addressed the problem of Addams being treated as a person of either saintly or villainous capacities.[32] Farrell and Lasch, stand out among the few authors who have emphasized her scholarship and significance as a social theorist, and even their work underestimates her epistemological stature.[33] Intellectual sexism has prevented Addams from receiving her full recognition as a major theorist. In addition to teaching, writing, and speaking on important issues of her day, Addams was a magnet to scholars. She was able to inspire them, encourage them, and penetrate their insights. She was widely read herself and managed what became a unique intellectual institution, Hull-House. She was fluent in not only English, but also Italian, Greek, French and German.[34] She authored numerous books, attended even more numerous professional conferences, published in leading academic journals, and addressed professional audiences. Nonetheless, because of her commitment to the community and a way of speech intended to address the average citizen, she has been viewed as a popularizer, often a sentimental albeit important public figure.

Ironically, it is Lasch who has also characterized her as an antiintellectual.[35] Addams was, indeed, opposed to college education that separated people, that made learning boring and abstract. Nevertheless, she was profoundly committed to the activities of intellectuals and to the people who exemplified the great potential of this type of learning. Addams was not an antiintellectual, she was an anti–elitist intellectual.

Addams wanted learning to be connected with life and experience. She thought each situation should be connected with the process of learning, discovery, and growth. She vehemently opposed the segregation of knowledge into the academy and the valuing of such ideas over other forms of knowledge and labor.[36]

This movement away from the academy is central here for understanding Addams' role in sociology. For the academy increasingly came to be defined as *the* home for sociology. The applied component of sociology languished. This death of sociological practice and concomitant legitimacy of academic labor will be considered in the conclusion, but it is important to note that it is linked to Addams' conception of knowledge, learning, and education. It was these concepts and her action in reference to them which was crucial for her removal from the sociological discourse.

Community Action and Organizing

Addams' faith in democracy and education are idealistic assumptions about the nature of society and social change. These were connected, however, with a realistic assumption: community organizing for group goals. Democratically based, emerging after education about an issue and methods to change the status quo had been acquired, neighborhood groups provided a mechanism for changing governmental action, laws, and restrictions. Addams excelled in this area of expertise, and it is this work for which she is most remembered. The list of organizations which she supported and often led is momentous.

Voluntary associations followed her beliefs in democracy and education as well as the underlying values of cultural feminism. The major groups in which she officially worked for women's rights were the National American Women's Suffrage Association (NAWSA) and the Women's International League of Peace and Freedom (WILPF). Many of the other groups in which Addams labored were dominated by women, although their members included both sexes. Often the elite leadership in these latter organizations had male representatives, thereby obscuring the fact that the groups were predominantly composed of women. Regardless of the sex ratio, in these groups Addams most fully integrated her cultural feminism and belief in nonviolent, democratic change. This congruence is part of the strength she exhibited in her work studied here. A partial list of the organizations in which she was active is presented in Table 11.1.

All these groups operated with a hierarchical administrative structure, usually democratically elected, but sometimes salaried and hired. Most salaried officers, however, were active in a variety of organizations in which they "volunteered" their time and expertise. There was a complex system of overlapping directories in these organizations. Addams and the Hull-House women were often major leaders in these organizations, implementing their ideas over and over again in a series of reforms that built upon each others' goals and methods.

This group structure and power ultimately led to charges in 1919 of a conspiracy to unseat the government and capitalism. These charges continued for over a decade and were particularly aimed at women sociologists. For example, in one anticommunist chart printed in 1927 the two most dangerous Americans listed were female sociologists, Jane Addams and Emily Greene Balch.[37] (They are also the only two American women to be awarded Nobel Peace Prizes, Addams in 1931 and Balch in 1946.) It is similarly noteworthy that although fifteen professors were also listed on the chart, none of them were male, academic sociologists. (This important topic is examined more fully in the concluding chapter.)

In addition to these groups, Addams also worked for the establishment of government bureaus: notably The Children's Bureau, the Women's Bureau, and the Immigration Bureau. Her long-term goals and programs for action were incorporated in many New Deal policies, particularly Social Security. Earlier, she had worked for causes such as Workman's Compensation, Unemployment Insurance, and governmental regulations of health and safety standards.

The profound structural effect that Addams and her organizations had on public life have been the primary source of documentation of the value of her work. In this book, the significance of these voluntary organizations lies in their intellectual union with a program of action and ideas about changing society in response to inequality.

Community organizing for the "neighbor" of the social settlement takes on a new meaning in this context. For the social settlement was a major component in community organizing. As a democratically run institution involved in community education, the social settlement became a mechanism to help the group to organize for its own interests. There was a tension

TABLE 11.1
Partial List of Organizations in which Addams Participated. Most organizations went through several name changes. Only the latest name of the organization is presented below.

EDUCATIONAL

Elite/Professional
American Economic Association
American Academy of Political and Social Sciences
American Sociology Association
American Association of University Women
Chicago Board of Women Education
National Education Association

Community
National Society for the Promotion of Industrial Education
Labor Museum

DEMOCRACY

Political
Progressive Party
National American Women Suffrage Association
American Civil Liberties Union
Women's International League of Peace and Freedom

Social
Chicago Playground Association

Economic
National Women's Trade Union League
National Consumers League

DEMOCRACY AND EDUCATION

Immigrants
Immigrants Protective League

Workers
supported the following strikes and attendant committees organized to settle them — Pullman Strike-1894; Building Trade Strike-1900; National Anthracite Strike-1902; Chicago Stockyards Strike-1904; Chicago Garment Workers Strike-1901, 1915

Youth
Juvenile Court
Juvenile Psychopathic Institute
Juvenile Protective Association

Blacks
National Association for the Advancement of Colored People
Chicago Urban League

Women
Chicago Women's Club

Settlements
National Federation of Settlements
College Settlement Association

in the elitism inherent in the institution which brought in White, middle-class, and highly educated Anglo-American women into a community based on a different ethnic, class, and educational background. Addams' charismatic leadership, moreover, was strong-willed and often dominating. Symbolically, she stood for a more compliant and "good" woman who could more easily be integrated into the goals of cultural feminism in a democratic neighborhood than her actual *modus operandi* would predict.[38] Because Addams' contributions in this area of social action have been well-documented, this work is not emphasized here except in conjunction with her intellectual thought and relation to sociology.

Critical Pragmatism and City Life

In American social thought the city has often signified corruption, dirt, and a distancing of the self from others.[39] This antiurban image has dominated American thought. Nonetheless, Addams and other American intellectuals of the Progressive era, began a new analysis of the city. They emphasized cities as places of human action and growth. What was needed was not the death of cities, but the end of certain repressive styles of urban life and exploitation. Poor housing, sanitation, low wages. and other specific social problems were targeted for elimination. Most importantly the loss of a meaningful community was defined as a source for social anguish and limitations.

This approach to the city was later to be the basis for the Chicago School of Sociology. For Addams, this was first codified and articulated in *HH Maps and Papers*. This work was continued by Addams throughout her life, and the major problems of specific city populations she studied are presented below. But before these special groups are analyzed, it is important to note that in each minority—the working class, immigrants, the young, and the old—it was the women within these groups who were of special interest to Addams.

These four groups were a special concern to Addams. They signified strains in city life. These groups suffered the most from the industrial and everyday life of the city. In this way, Addams was a student of social change, for the city was literally growing on the prairie around her. The interconnections between these groups and Addams' ideas about them are exemplified in the following short passage on city life:

> The first effect of immigration upon the women is that of idleness . . . children catch on faster . . . the children act not only as interpreters of the language, but as buffers between them and Chicago, resulting in a certain almost pathetic dependence of the family upon the child.[40] If we admit that in educa-

tion it is necessary to begin with the experiences which the child already has and to use his spontaneous and social activity, then the city street begins this education for him in a more natural way than does the school.[41]

City life was structured to remove the playful spirit. People were therefore thwarted and unhappy. To be human was to be playful.[42] In a typically biting passage she spoke of the retribution of such a restrictive and serious attitude: "This stupid experiment of organizing work and failing to organize play has, of course, brought about a fine revenge."[43]

Women and the City: The Overlapping of Critical Pragmatism and Cultural Feminism

Although there is overlap in each of the categories covered by Addams' two major approaches, it is primarily in reference to the city that Addams is clearest about the integration of her ideas. The city dramatically changed the home and family, and women's role had been dependent on these institutions. When the home was more central to society, whether in the old country or on the American frontier, women had a central role.

The industrialization of the city disrupted the power of the home to define behavior, to control the relation of its members to the environment and community, and to be respected as a significant part of material and cultural life. Discriminated against in the marketplace, women were doubly ostracized, for their homes were no longer a central part of the community and their labor was devalued in capitalistic terms. Succinctly, "women lost her earlier place when man usurped the industrial pursuits and created wealth on a scale unknown before."[44] Feminine values, nonsignificant before the rise of industry and capital, were also degraded. For example, in politics:

> The men of the city have been carelessly indifferent to much of this civic housekeeping, as they have always been indifferent to the details of the household. They have totally disregarded a candidates' capacity to keep the streets clean, preferring to consider him in relation to the national tariff or to the necessity for increasing the national navy, in a pure spirit of reversion to the traditional type of government which had to do only with enemies and outsiders.[45]

Cities were also the location of prostitution:

> Worse than anything which we have mentioned is the fact that in every man-ruled city the world over a great army of women are so set aside as outcasts that it is considered a shame to speak the mere name which designates them.[46]

Despite the considerable overlap between women and the major categories of her critical pragmatism—labor, immigrants, the young, and the
old—women as a special group always had a slightly different meaning and
focus. For example, women as laborers had problems in domestic life, as
prostitutes, and as discriminated workers. Immigrants had trouble surviv-
ing in their new environmet, but the woman's disruption in the home had a
different meaning from the man's disruption in the marketplace. Young
girls were more likely to be sexually exploited than were young men, and
older women were more likely to be poor and seen as an economic burden.
After all, in modern life what do women produce that is valued?

All these minorities were intrinsic to the urban way of life. The city was a
focal concern for both streams of Addams thought, critical pragmatism
and cultural feminism, often masking the consistent differences in these
approaches. Only the crisis of World War I brought these divergences into
stark contrast.

The city of Chicago was an "urban frontier" when Addams and the men
of the early Chicago School were working. In 1893 at the Chicago's World
Fair, Frederick Jackson Turner had announced the closing of the physical
frontier. There was no more land for physical expansion.[47] Changes would
occur henceforth in the urban milieu. Intellectual thought was needed to
explore the ramifications of rapid industrialization and social change attendant upon carving human settlements out of the social and cultural
wilderness.

When Addams arrived in Chicago in 1889, the city had recovered from
its devastating fire of 1871. Between 1880 and 1890 it had doubled its size
from half a million to over a million.[48] Despite this rapid growth, "it was
Western and fully aware that Easterners saw it as the frontier—wild, un-
civilized and lacking in social grace."[49] They were not far wrong.

As Florence Kelley recalled in her harrowing ride to Hull-House in the
Christmas season of 1891 (see chapter 2), the city streets were often only
muddy lanes. The city soon earned a reputation for being "rough and
tough." For example, the Chicago River was so unclean that its banks were
visibly covered with waste products from slaughtered animals, plus human
excrement. When such conditions were described by the editors of the *New
Republic*, they wrote that "the entire Middle West revels in the effluvia of
Chicago. It scents it joyously from afar, and young visitors still dream and
and rapture of walking on the face of the Chicago River."[50] On this urban
frontier, jobs were plentiful. The stockyards, steel mills, railroads, garment
industry, and McCormick agricultural works provided massive opportunities for manufacturers to increase their wealth, while their employees
labored under primitive working conditions and earned low wages. Despite

these drawbacks, by 1900 over a million and a half people lived in Chicago and by 1910, two million.[51]

Thus the urban conditions surrounding Addams were visibly emerging. Because the birth was witnessed, the possibility of shaping these forces was plausible. They appeared susceptible to change. These early sociologists were part of the process of *creating* a city, not just studying one. The city's "natural areas" and "zones of emergence," later identified by Park and Burgess, were produced by an earlier stage.

Addams' understanding of the city, then, was based on a concept of process and intervention into ongoing events. Democracy and education were the foundation for shaping the new urban citizen. Because of her holistic vision, she did not see portions of the city in a detached manner. She saw people suffering under the onslaught of massive social change and exploitation,who were also part of a new experiment in a land of growth and freedom. Scientific knowledge was intrinsic to understanding the city, as were other forms of knowledge brought to all situations by the people themselves.

Addams had a particular role to play in the city, witnessing what was happening and speaking about it. She articulated her experiences and reflected a wide range of social theory brought to bear upon this vast welter of humanity. In addition to women, who crossed all categories, she singled out the experiences of the worker, the immigrant, the young, and the old as signs of stress within the total system of urban life.

The Worker

Addams' concept of the worker was enmeshed in a series of assumptions. Most notably, she was concerned about women workers, the destitute who often were unable to work, immigrants, and child laborers. These other worker concerns are discussed elsewhere, but it is important to see that they were specialized factors in Addams general approach to labor.

Workers had more worries than just their low salaries. In addition to this problem, she enumerated five more misfortunes characterizing workers' lives: industrial accidents, preventable illness, premature death, unemployment, and neglected old age.[52] This five-pronged attack was combined with a concern for control over the workplace as well as wages. She actively supported labor unions as a method for obtaining better worker conditions and equity, but she combined this work with an emphasis on education, scientific documentation of the problems (especially industrial safety and sanitation), and community action in support of the worker.

Addams radically applied the concept of democracy to the workplace.

> The first real lesson in self-government to many immigrants has come
> through the organization of labor unions, and it could come in no other way,
> for the union alone has appealed to their necessities. . . . Although the spir-
> itual struggle is associated with the solitary garret of the impassioned
> dreamer, it may be that the idealism fitted to our industrial democracy will be
> evolved in crowded sewer ditches and in noisy factories.[53]

Her intellectual argument in support of unions can be found in chapter
2 here, but this work was combined with a massive program of social
legislation, impassioned speeches, and arbitration of labor disputes.[54]
Along with Mead, Dewey, and Bemis, Addams was involved in the
Pullman Strike of 1894. Similarly, Mead and Addams worked for the settlement of the 1910 Garment Workers Strike.[55] She helped organize at least
four women's labor unions as well as working with Alice Hamilton to
establish the first major industrial standards concerning health and safety.[56]

Addams' interpretation of labor was strongly mixed with her analysis of
rapid social change. Not only the employers, but also industry and its
technology were a new form of control. Employers and employees could be
on different sides of issues, but both shared the common fate of the market,
machinery, international costs, and the system of distributing and produc-
ing goods. Cities were unable to respond to the rapid demands for services
and the disruption of social norms and customs. Communities needed to
be constructed by people who knew each other and acted in partnership.
Industry, then, needed to be seen as existing in a context of life and a
physical environment as well as a market exchange.

Addams' long struggle with socialism was significant. After the 1919 Red
Scare and her villainization as a "commie," her acceptance of socialism
remained but was couched in more cautious terms. Advocating a *détente*
between Russia and the United States of America in 1930, she still favored
some form of socialist state: "A mixed type of state with competitive and
cooperative elements may have the greatest survival value and prove to be
the most serviceable."[57] Describing Russia as "now conducting perhaps the
largest piece of conscious social laboratory experiment that history records,"[58] Addams compared the necessary social revolution to the Coper-
nican one. That, too, caused an uproar and lack of acceptance at first,
although such a response now appears primitive and unreflective.

Although Addams worked for unions, she also foresaw their problems:
militaristic goals and the potential to be another source of oppression for
the workers. If they were not democratically run, they generated "trade-
union tyranny."[59] Her goal was always directed to the right of the people to
live a good life. She wished to move beyond definitions that limited the
struggle to either conflict or wages. Truly, she did not belong to any one
"camp" or position. Her continual effort was to see the pressing problems

of unequal wages and miserable labor as a product of a set of assumptions about life and its meaning. Thus, her position on labor was similar to her position on women. Opposing militance, her stance was nonetheless radical and rarely understood.

She continued to struggle for her earlier goals. As a result, she and her female colleagues, whom Lemons called the "Social Feminists," were the major advocates for policies incorporated in the New Deal during the Great Depression. They worked tirelessly for these goals from the end of World War I until the early 1930s.[60] Many of these programs were modeled after the Fabian ones, and were also promulgated by Henderson and Mead prior to World War I.

Such government support was needed, according to Addams, to avoid the punishing attitudes of employers and the unemployed. Both groups shared an interpretation of the failed economy as due to personal or employer/employee failure rather than the general system's failure.[61] Although Addams' long-term goals were for total economic democracy, her method for obtaining it was through democratic and nonviolent changes enacted through the ballot and social legislation.

Critical Pragmatism and Immigrants

Many scholars, particularly sociologists, have frequently misrepresented Addams' motivation and work with immigrants. For example, Mills interpreted her as a "social pathologist" who wanted to study social evils and remove them by "doing good." He portrayed her as naive and condescending, "paternalistic" in her approach.[62] This error arises primarily from his poor scholarship, citing from a scattering of passages in one book over a range of less than forty pages. Since he is one of the few sociologists to even evaluate Addams at all, his work has gained the status of being a "classic statement." Other sociological scholars such as Short, Burgess, Faris, and Park have revealed similar short-sightedness noted throughout this text.

Addams' thinking went through numerous stages of development. During her first years at Hull-House, she reflected her background as a White, middle-class, highly educated Anglo-American woman. At this stage, she was her most unknowing and unreflective in relation to the community surrounding the settlement. But with the arrival of Kelley in 1891, the intellectual influence of other thinkers, and her growing understanding of her neighbors' lives, Addams radically altered her views. Farrell has captured this shift:

> She soon learned that many Italian and German immigrants knew and loved
> Dante, Schiller, and Goethe. The Hull-House neighborhood contained tal-

ented immigrant craftsmen whose abilities had been ignored. Miss Addams discovered how much her neighbors loved to sing and with what pleasure they danced. She found her immigrant neighbors equal to many and superior to some Americans in their love of and respect for learning, and in their enthusiasm for drama, art, literature, and music. Her initial assumption that young college women possessed cultural superiority gave way.[63]

There were several ways in which Addams tried to bring the immigrants' values into American life. The Labor Museum, worked out with John Dewey, was one mechanism for visibly reenacting and recreating the values, customs, and industries of the immigrants. Another consistent program was through her speeches, where she continually stressed the intrinsic worth of the immigrants' backgrounds and experiences. Her frequent writings on the immigrants were also ways to bring that foreign way of life into the mainstream. Addams studied the problem of immigration long before most sociologists: first in 1895 with *HH Maps and Papers*, then a decade later in her convocation address at the University of Chicago. In this classic statement on the need to study immigrants, she urged scholars to understand and interpret the immigrants' experience so that other Americans could learn to appreciate it.[64] This work preceded Thomas and Znaniecki's by twelve years. This convocation address, moreover, was not unique. In her two autobiographical books, there were entire chapters devoted to developing these ideas.[65] Other speeches, too, emphasized the need to bring immigrants not only into American ways of life, but also to bring Americans into a multicultural way of life. Addressing Anglo-Americans, she wrote that "in our assertive Americanism we fail to understand and respect the family life, the many customs, the inherited skill they bring with them."[66] In this way, she acted as a member and critic of the wider society.

Addams' openness to the immigrant experience was built on a respect for it. Her democratic analysis stressed that the immigrants should bring their values to the community and not to erase their ways of looking at the world. To become a vocal member of the community, however, required education. It is in this context that her emphasis on learning must be interpreted.

Among the hundreds of immigrants who have for years attended classes at Hull-House designed primarily to teach the English language, dozens of them have struggled to express in the newly acquired tongue some of those hopes and longings which had so much to do with their emigration.[67]

Language, for all symbolic interactionists, was central to being a part of the community and its symbolic life. "Even a meager knowledge of English may mean an opportunity to work in a factory *versus* nonemployment, or it may mean a question of life or death when a sharp command must be understood in order to avoid the danger of a descending crane."[68]

Immigrants were segregated from community life, they lacked a voice in their own destiny, control over their workplaces, and participation in the spirit of a good life. This occurred partially because they were unable to understand their fellow Americans. But Americans, too, had to engage in an educational process to understand the immigrants.

During the 1920s Addams opposed immigration quotas, thereby adopting another controversial stance. Again, she deplored the narrowness of Americans: "As Spain in the sixteenth century was obsessed by the necessity of achieving national unity, above the variety of religions, so Twentieth Century America is obsessed by the need of national unity above all else."[69]

The consistent misinterpretation of Addams' stance on immigrants is truly difficult to understand. Although condescending passages can be found (and some of these are in *Twenty Years* which was a compilation of earlier essays), her overwhelmingly more frequent and articulate stance against such attitudes far outweighs these other portions of her writings. One reason to assert this, beyond the change in her thought and the sheer volume of her statements, is her clear and unwavering stance against the nativism expressed in the war fever prior to, during, and immediately following World War I. Repeatedly, Addams decried the narrowness of Americans' values and their intolerance of dissent. "Patriotism" in particular, was used as a catchall word to mask all sorts of oppression.[70] Similarly, Addams also found the American stress on homogenous behavior and conformity to be stultifying.[71]

Addams had a profound understanding of the immigrant experience. Depicting the disruptive factor of rapid social change that combined with cultural and social dislocation, she was part of a Chicago tradition of studying the urban experience of foreigners. One method to alleviate some of these problems was education, because a democracy needed to have intelligent citizens in order to respond to the community's values and needs. These new standards needed to be built on the immigrants' experience, art, and culture from the Old World which could enrich that of the new.

The Life Cycle in the City: Youth and the Aged

Adolescents and the elderly were the major age groups that Addams analyzed. She saw these two populations as structurally related: both were undervalued in the market place; both tended toward idealism, with the young idealizing the future and the old idealizing the past; and both were close to the effects of aging, with the young experiencing the birth of sexual interest and a desire for entry into adulthood and the old experiencing their biological decline and impending end. Both groups also have little financial control over their everyday life, and Addams always tried to articulate the situation of those in a weak social position who had difficulty in speaking for themselves.[72]

Addams' emphasis on the life cycle has no specific analogy in the work of the male Chicago sociologists. Although the men were consistently interested in youth, as students or delinquents, the problems of the aged were not seriously considered. Addams was also vitally concerned with the problem of child labor and its exploitation. In the 1890s, a number of male sociologists shared this interest, but none of the men paralleled Addams' continuing concentration on eliminating child labor.

Youth was often seen by the men as a "problem" to be controlled rather than a stage of life with strengths as well as weaknesses. Addams and the Chicago men worked closely to help establish the Chicago juvenile courts system, in particular the Psychopathic Institute and Juvenile Institute of Social Research. This aspect of their work is not stressed here. Instead, Addams' intellectual analysis of youth is emphasized. In this area, Dewey came closest to Addams with his vision of youth as a stage with great potential for both idealism and growth as well as immaturity and destruction.

Youth

Addams saw delinquency as a product of social malfunction and its maladaptation to the spirit of youth, and not as a result of the evil nature or pathology of the young. "The spirit of youth," in fact, was a major concept in Addams' interpretation of young people. This period in the life cycle was characterized by idealism, enthusiasm, a sense of adventure, and a desire to understand one's sexuality and future adult roles as both working and loving members of society. Each generation needed to find its own sense of value and charm in life.[73] Modern life made this difficult to achieve: for "Only in the modern city have men concluded that it is no longer necessary for the municipality to provide for the insatiable desire for play."[74] Failure to understand the spirit of youth was a societal weakness, creating a situation of strain when young people met this need in socially disapproved ways.[75]

Addams was interested in art, especially music, because it was a key mechanism to address the spirit of youth. But just as we failed to allow for our play activities, music too, was widely seen as something that could take care of itself. "Our attitude towards music is typical of our carelessness towards all those things which make for common joy and for the restraint of higher civilization on the streets."[76]

One of the most important areas where the biological drives and civilization's norms came in opposition concerned sexuality.[77] Addams transformed Freud's intrinsic conflict and suppression of human versus social needs into a potentially cooperative process achieved through understanding and compassion rather than repression and sublimation.

> It is neither a short nor an easy undertaking to substitute the love of beauty for mere desire, to place the mind above the senses; but is not this the sum of the moral obligation which rests upon the adults of each generation if they would nurture and restrain the youth, and has not the whole history of civilization been but one long effort to substitute psychic impulsion for the driving force of bland appetite?[78]

Instead of seeing children as primarily shaped by adults, as Freud did, Addams also described the way that children shape the adult world. Their capacity to love and respond is a resource for others to do likewise: "That wonderful devotion of the child seems at times, in the midst of our stupid social and industrial arrangement, all that keeps society human, the touch of nature which unites it, as it was that same devotion which first lifted us out of the swamp of bestiality."[79]

The "spirit of youth" was a vital force. Its "repression" could lead to illicit satisfaction.[80] This suppression of sexual interaction and activity was rooted in the American experience—in Puritanism. For the early Americans, however, their restraint was mediated by other social forms and pleasures lacking in modern urban life: "When the Puritan repression of pleasure was in the ascendant in the people it dealt with lives on farms and villages where, although youthful pleasures might be frowned upon and crossed out, the young people still had a chance to find self-expression in their work."[81]

Addams avoided the word "instinct" and, like Mead, preferred the word "impulse."[82] Her concept of the pliability of human nature was also close to Dewey's understanding of human development. Addams, nonetheless, did define three primary drives: sex, work, and survival. These came to a crucial stage during adolescence. For it was during this period that the individual prepared for the future and carved out a lived social location in it. To find one's status as an adult was the primary task of youth.[83] This task became increasingly difficult in a modern society with changing definitions of morality, occupations, and desirable futures.

Addams' analysis of this stage emphasized the existence of a variety of social resources and potential that could either enhance or limit the adolescent's choices. The family was a pivotal social force, but so too were other, independent interpersonal and community opportunities. For example, social change was occurring rapidly and bewilderingly for immigrants. The immigrant family needed to draw upon its own traditions, but it existed in an environment that was often hostile to these traditions. The family, too, lacked control over occupations, the economy, or the technology that structured it. These latter social institutions were crucial to the adolescent's future and were factors in the struggle to attain a meaningful adult life.

Thus, Addams studied society as problematic. Social forces in the city infringed upon the home rather than supported its goals. The home, in turn, could become a source of oppression and control, mimicking the destructive forces found outside of it: "In fact, the lack of vitality in youth is paralleled in the workplace of the adult: As it is possible to establish a connection between the monotony and dullness of factory work and the petty immoralities which are often the youth's protest against them."[84]

Some youths rebelled because they saw their fates as similar to adults': dull, controlled, unheroic, and uneventful. Other young people learned to become apathetic, to separate pleasure from learning and labor because the few areas of pleasure were ruled out of the educational and work worlds.[85] In this way, Addams emphasized the continuity between labor conditions and life outside the workplace. She did not see this situation as intrinsic to city life.

Similarly, although Addams stressed the social origin of delinquency, she did not say that society *caused* crime. Rather, illegal acts were a symptom of social maladjustment; a sign of a lack of accounting for and response to the human impulses to idealize, to strive for greatness and challenge.

Addams believed, like Dewey and Mead, in "the extraordinary pliability of human nature."[86] In a far-seeing statement, she noted that institutionalized babies had a high death rate because no one persuaded them to live.[87] Nonetheless, she rarely theorized about young children and concentrated instead on adolescence. A major concept she used to describe the plight of modern teens was Tolstoy's term "the snare of preparation." This refers to the process of "hopelessly entangling them [youth] in a curious inactivity at the very period of life when they are longing to construct the world anew and to conform it to their own ideals."[88] So not only was there a biologically induced crisis of sexuality and questions about future adult roles, but there was a peculiarly induced social problem of restraint of enthusiasm and restriction on exuberance. Youths dreaded the forthcoming fate of being encapsulated in a world dominated by technology and machinery. For the poor, this situation was compounded by the fact that men often earned their highest wages between the ages of twenty and thirty and would be put "on the shelf by thirty-five."[89]

Rigid control over young people in the family could generate apathetic withdrawal, a flight to illegal acts, or unloving obedience. The tyrannical rule of the parents could also "establish habits of obedience so that the nerves and will may not depart from this control when the child is older."[90]

One of the reasons for instilling these behavior patterns was to bind children to their financially needy family by ties of guilt. After discussing a case of parental injustice, Addams poignantly asked: "If love and tenderness had been substituted for parent despotism, would the mother have had enough affection, enough power of expression to hold her daughter's sense of money obligation through all these years?"[91] Since women did overwhelmingly support their parents in their adult years, as documented by Addams and Donovan,[92] this process of forming habits while young draws upon both Dewey's conception of "habit formation" as well as Addams' notion of the "family claim."[93] She was developing a theory of socialization of youth dependent on a broad understanding of communication, politics, and economics as factors shaping adolescence.

Despite her sympathetic analysis, Addams did not always see youth as either victims of society or seekers of truth. Her criticisms of young women of the postwar generation were marked and based on characteristics of the young as a group or generation unto themselves:

> They not only think differently, so that their opinions are unlike our own, but they exhibit a tendency to surround these differences with secrecy, lest the old become horrified and try to destroy what they cannot understand. I will confess that what disturbed me during this period and what seemed most unlike my own youth, was the spirit of conformity in matters of opinion among young people especially among college students.[94]

This tendency to conformity became a theme in her later analysis of the young. This sameness was expressed "in a dread of change, in a desire to play safe and to let well enough alone."[95] Her more critical view of youth occurred with the decline of the feminist movement in the 1920s, her increasing age, and her later experiences with young people who were generally not as poor and socially limited as the pre-war generations near Hull-House.

Old Age

In discussing the elderly, Addams generalized about the aging process, but most of her examples were drawn from women's lives and experiences. She reversed, therefore, what most male sociologists have done—generalized about aging from men's lives.

In an eloquent passage, Addams pointed out the similar relationship to time exhibited by the young who idealized the future and the old who idealized the past:

> For many years at Hull-House I have at intervals detected in certain old people, when they spoke of their past experiences, a tendency to an idealization almost to a romanticism suggestive of the ardent dreams and groundless ambitions we have all observed in the young when they recklessly lay their plans for the future.

> I have, moreover, been frequently impressed by the fact that these romantic revelations were made by old people who had really suffered much hardship and sorrow, and that the transmutation of their experiences was not the result of ignoring actuality, but was apparently due to a process inherent in memory itself.[96]

Addams noted (as a sociologist)[97] that these memories served another function in society besides "perfecting the past." This function, surprisingly, was to make changed standards of behavior acceptable and part of the established ways of doing things. This selective process

> often necessitates an onset against the very traditions and conventions commonly believed to find their stronghold in the minds of elderly people. Such reminiscences suggested an analogy to the dreams of youth which, while covering the future with a shifting rose-colored mist, contain within themselves the inchoate substance from which the tough fibered forces of social struggles are composed.[98]

This phenomenon creates a sense of "like-mindedness," of community unity.

Again comparing these groups, Addams wrote that it was difficult for youth to realize that the future blends with the present and for the elderly to realize that the present merges with the past. For the old, this past was usually perceived with nostalgia. This "rose-colored" view, however, was not maudlin but a sign of strength.

> This may be possibly due to an instinct of self-preservation, which checks the devastating bitterness that would result did they recall over and over again the sordid detail of events long past; it is even possible that those people who were not able then to inhibit their bitterness had died earlier.[99]

While Erik Erikson talks of the elderly's choice between "ego integrity or despair"[100] (or a sense of accomplishment and acceptance of one's life versus a rejection of it in one's advancing years), Addams talks of "acceptance" as a peaceful stage that is built on grounds of endurance: "Perhaps those women, because they had come to expect nothing more from life and had perforce ceased from grasping and striving, had obtained, if not renunciation, at least that quiet endurance which allows the wounds of the spirit to heal."[101] This process of aging with grace is similar to Erikson's but is placed by Addams in a more cultural role "as human vicissitudes are, in the end, melted down into reminiscence, and a metaphorical statement of the basic experiences which are implicitly in human nature itself, however crude in form the story may be, has a singular power of influencing daily living."[102] Rather than seeing despair as a final stage of life, as Erikson does, Addams portrayed it as a continual struggle for the poor.[103]

For women the generation of "folk wisdom" was necessary to protect themselves against their menfolk. Tales of justice meted out to the unjust helped restrain marital conflict. This function of folk knowledge was revealed to Addams when a story of a "devil baby" flourished in the Hull-House area. The old women rabidly gossiped about this personification of evil because they longed to see "one good case of retribution before they died." Rather than being passive, peaceful old "ladies," these women wished to see something vital that they had given up hope of ever happening: a verification of their dark sayings that those who did evil would have to pay for it.

Women survived their bleak lives of exploitation, loneliness, and pain by seeking solace in their stories, their comradeship, their endurance. Unlike men, they did not display aggression and dramatic acts. "Memory" became a key concept for Addams' understanding of the aging process. Not only individually based, it served as a social resource for integrating the personal and impersonal aspects of life.

When Addams discussed "women's memory," she accounted for her own past, thereby becoming a reflexive sociologist long before the term was coined by Gouldner in 1970.[104] She, too, had interpreted her past, and this "past" included the ancient Egyptians and their search for life after death.

> Certain it is that through these our living brothers, or through the unexpected reactions of memory to racial records, the individual detects the growth within of an almost mystical sense of the life common to all centuries, and of the unceasing human endeavor to penetrate into the unseen world.[105]

(With the recent American phenomenon of crowding to see the King Tutankhamen exhibit in art galleries across the United States, Addams' remarks are particularly applicable to contemporary society.)

A major component of Addams' thought was our passage through time. For the adolescent and the elderly, age became the ground for a particularly problematic stage in the social matrix. Historical expectations and cultural resources shaped each person's "perspective." (This latter Meadian term was amplified by Addams who documented this changing worldview for a "biologic individual" who ages.) Thus Addams established a sociological framework highly compatible with symbolic interaction, and her work in this context has not been fully explored.

The Conflict Between Critical Pragmatism and Cultural Feminism

These two streams of thought, critical pragmatism and cultural feminism, merged in many of Addams' writings. This occurred because she was a democratic and feminist leader who was able to frequently articulate the views and needs of the people as well as change them. There was a successful cycle of critique, leadership, and resolution of problems throughout Addams' early years, especially from 1889-1915. This appearance of harmony, however, dramatically broke down over the issue of pacifism. Here, she chose to abandon her usual advocacy of pragmatism and role as the "voice of the people" and opted for an unequivocal position.[106] Her values and perspective, articulated through cultural feminism, could not support the actions of the general public. More importantly, she did not powerfully understand nor critique war as an economic issue. Her analysis of it as a form of nationalism was only partially accurate. Although she understood (correctly) that her position was grounded in feminine values, she failed to move the necessary step to radically define this as a feminist versus patriarchal confrontation. Each of these lacks relates in a fundamental way to conflicting assumptions in her two positions: critical pragmatism and cultural feminism.

fragmatism suffers from a structural, logical weakness of what to do when a solution to a problem is considered morally right by the social scientist but is rejected by the majority. A good example of this conflict can be seen in Addams' advocacy of the Progressive Party's platform after they had rejected Black delegates. In this instance, she went against her "values" and selected the "will of the people." Making this decision caused her great anguish, and immediately after it was enacted, she deeply regretted it. Not only did she let down the Black populace, but she accepted an expedient policy. She was fundamentally more committed to her own values than to the racist majority's. The sad evening of this compromise is described by Lasch: When she failed to demand from the platform committee a declaration of racial equality as the price of her support, her friends "stood outside her door at the Congress Hotel and wept in the night hours.'It seemed as though she could not do anything,' said Sophonisba Breckinridge, a former Hull-House resident 'that was in the nature of an exercise of compulsion or control.'"[107] Perhaps because of this painful choice of "democratic" values over her own, Addams was aided in her later decision to opt for the latter when she was tested on the pacifism issue.

Because Addams was so committed to critical pragmatism, she struggled fiercely before she abandoned this tradition when it conflicted with her cultural feminism. Her dedication to being a member of the community and antielitist led to her conciliatory style of leadership and controlling her opposition to the group will—except on the issue of pacifism.

One way that she could have integrated her work would have been through an exploration of the ideas of Henry David Thoreau on democracy and conscientious objection. Although she must have been aware of Thoreau's work, if only through her contacts with Gandhi, Addams never adopted this model. To have integrated her feminist thought with an understanding of patriarchal society would have also been a major intellectual advance, but after World War I Addams did not continue to expand on the intellectual greatness of her first three decades. Not only age, but also the historical changes in the sociological profession, the academy, and the country took its toll on her innovativeness and creativity. Her later work is characterized by more compromise and fewer confrontations than her earlier work. She did not significantly alter her ideas, instead she primarily repeated what she had developed during her earlier years. Her work for pacifism continued, her struggle for democracy did too. But efforts to link democracy with pacifism, community ideals with the rights of workers, and the importance of education for the common good were all muted or segregated aspects of her thought. Addams' award of a Nobel Peace Prize in 1931 and the social questions awakened by the Great Depression restored her to eminence. But this new stature was a reflected one, a vindication and not a new journey.

Critical Pragmatism and Male Chicago Sociology

Of the two major components of Addams' thought, critical pragmatism is by far the closest to the male Chicago School of Sociology (see Table 11.1). It is clear that the latter's ultimate study of the city and its problems in a competitive society was fundamentally opposed to cultural feminism. In fact, women were almost entirely removed from sociology as topics of interest. Half of society's members were eliminated as well as their worldview and experience. Male Chicago Sociology was a specific rejection of Addams' central work for women.

Critical pragmatism was also altered. Although the men's interests clearly overlapped with Addams in many areas, their more elite biases and acceptance of capitalism were consistent differences in their approach. Before examining these differences more carefully, their similarities can be briefly examined.

Addams' basis for explaining social action as a function of democracy and education was implemented through democratic mechanisms to change the government and the economy. The Chicago men accepted this in its broad outlines. However, democracy was more narrowly defined by the men in terms of *political* rights, and education was more narrowly defined in terms of formal institutions that certified stages of learning, such as universities. These more narrow definitions of democracy and education applied particularly to Small, Vincent, Park, and Burgess. Mead's concepts were closest to Addams', with Thomas' concepts a close second. Both Zeublin and Henderson were particularly compatible with the social action component of Addams' thought. However, their intellectual interpretations were couched in Christian terms, thereby altering the content of their support for democratic and educational goals.

Although Mead came closest to sharing Addams' concepts of critical pragmatism, it was Thomas who most viably supported her ideas of cultural feminism. This aspect of his work has been consistently overlooked revealing his and Addams' similar fate in the hands of sociological interpreters. Thomas, moreover, interpreted "modern" forces concerning women's drives, behavior, and interests differently from Addams. A thorough analysis of their work in this area, beyond the scope of this book, would show an interesting development and mutual influence of their ideas.

The early men must be consistently seen as changing over time, as did Addams. Therefore, critical pragmatism was most accepted and understood by the men preceding Burgess and Park. The latter two also changed interpretations of their male predecessors' work. The "later" Chicago School distanced itself rhetorically from social action. They defined social action and voluntary organizations as outside the domain of "science." "Science" as a tool for the community was redefined on a model based on the physical world. Sociological observations and information were items for abstract study, purified from contacts with political interests.

From their so-called position of distance, the community became a problem of management. The political repression that haunted the work of the early academic men was amplified, made more public, and bitter for Addams. These later men therefore condemned political action for sociologists, while the ideas of the elite, in fact, permeated their work. Society as based on competition and conflict over scarce goods was a patriarchal and capitalist model of social action. Rather than condemn the exploitation and oppression of daily life, the later Chicago men described it. They justified it through their acceptance of it. The later Chicago men were basically aligned with the controlling interests of American society. Part of the process of legitimating these social forces of dominance was to eschew the work and influence of Addams, which they did with a vengeance.

Notes

1. Ernest Becker, *The Lost Science of Man* (New York: Braziller, 1971), pp. 14-61.
2. Christopher Lasch, *The New Radicalism in America*, 1889-1963 (New York: Knopf, 1965), pp. 286-349. Although Lasch does not single out Addams, he does criticize the pragmatists and includes Addams as a central figure in "the new radical" movement.
3. Jane Addams, *Democracy and Social Ethics* (New York: Macmillan, 1902), p. 6.
4. Ibid., p. 12.
5. Ibid.
6. Ibid., p. 7.
7. John C. Farrell, *Beloved Lady* (Baltimore: Johns Hopkins Press, 1967), p. 123.
8. See Shulamith Firestone, *The Dialectic of Sex* (New York: Bantam, 1971), pp. 19-21.
9. Addams, *Democracy and Social Ethics*, p. 223.
10. Jane Addams, *Twenty Years at Hull-House* (New York: Macmillan, 1910), p. 270 (hereafter referred to as *Twenty Years*).
11. Ibid., p. 234.
12. Ibid., p. 251.
13. Jane Addams, "Recent Immigration: A Field Neglected by the Scholar," *University Record* 9 (January 1905):274.
14. Ibid., p. 277.
15. She also raised this same argument in *A New Conscience and An Ancient Evil* (New York: Macmillan, 1916), pp. 94, 186-87.
16. Jane Addams, "The Social Situation," p. 148.
17. Jane Addams, "The Settlement as a Factor in the Labor Movement," *HH Maps and Papers*, pp. 183-206.
18. John R. Commons, "Class Conflict in America," *American Journal of Sociology* 13 (May 1908):756-66. See Addams' comment, pp. 772-73.
19. Commons, "Class Conflict in America," p. 783.
20. Cited in Farrell, *Beloved Lady*, p. 82.
21. *Twenty Years*, pp. 435-36.
22. *Democracy and Social Ethics*, p. 191.
23. Ibid., pp. 297-8.
24. Jane Addams, *The Spirit of Youth and City Streets* (New York: Macmillan, 1909), p. 109 (hereafter referred to as *Spirit of Youth*).
25. See an excellent discussion of this in Farrell, *Beloved Lady*, pp. 85-87.
26. "Education," 1902, in *Jane Addams: A Centennial Reader*, ed. Emily Cooper Johnson (New York: Macmillan, 1960), p. 146 (hereafter referred to as *Centennial Reader*).
27. Farrell, *Beloved Lady*, citing Addams, p. 92.
28. Jane Addams, *The Social Thought of Jane Addams*, ed., intro. Christopher Lasch (Indianapolis: Bobbs-Merrill, 1965), p. 189 (from "A Function of the Social Settlement," 1899).
29. "The Humanizing Tendency of Industrial Education," *The Chautauquan* 39 (May 1904):266. Sophia Smith Collection, Addams Papers.
30. Farrell, *Beloved Lady*, p. 98.
31. Ibid., p. 99.

32. See esp. Allen F. Davis, *American Heroine* (New York: Oxford University Press, 1973) for a sophisticated discussion of the media and popular image of Addams.
33. See comment by Balch cited by Lasch, "Introduction," in *The Social Thought of Jane Addams*, p. xiii.
34. See references to these skills in *Twenty Years*. She was so skilled in French and German that she was offered a temporary teaching position in the field at Rockford College. Davis, *American Heroine*, p. 43.
35. Christopher Lasch, *The New Radicalism in America: 1889-1963* (New York: Knopf, 1965), pp. 286-48.
36. Morton White has discussed the importance of different types of knowledge for the antiintellectualist. Addams partially fulfills this definition, but she also valued rational thought, did not want it to be isolated in the academy, or controlled only by those "certified" to teach in such settings. See "Anti-Intellectualism in America," in *Pragmatism and the American Mind* (New York: Oxford University Press, 1973), pp. 78-92.
37. For a discussion of the political repression of Balch's career, see Mary Jo Deegan, "Sociology and Wellesley College, 1900-1919, " *Journal of the History of Sociology* 6 (December 1983):114-25.
38. Davis, *American Heroine*.
39. See David W. Noble, *The Progressive Mind, 1890-1917.* (Chicago: Rand McNally, 1970); Fred H. Matthews, *Quest for an American Sociology* (Montreal: McGill-Queen's University Press, 1977), pp. 121-56.
40. *Democracy and Social Ethics*, p. 182, 184.
41. Ibid., pp. 186-87.
42. *Spirit of Youth*, p. 4.
43. Ibid., p. 6.
44. "Utilization of Women in City Government," 1907, in *Centennial Reader*, p. 122.
45. Ibid., p. 114.
46. "If Men Were Seeking the Franchise," 1913, in *Centennial Reader*, p. 112.
47. Frederick Jackson Turner, "The Significance of the Frontier in American History," *Annual Report for the Year, 1893* (Washington, D.C.: American Historical Association); id., *The Frontier in American History* (New York: Holt, Rinehart & Winston, 1920); id., "Later Explanations and Developments" edited by Ray Billington, *The Frontier Thesis* (Huntington, N.Y.: Robert E. Kreiger, 1977), pp. 21-30.
48. Steven J. Diner, *A City and Its Universities* (Chapel Hill: University of North Carolina Press, 1980), p. 52.
49. Ibid., p. 72.
50. *New Republic* (18 December 1915):158. Cited in Diner, *A City and Its Universities*, p. 73.
51. Diner, *A City and Its Universities*, p. 52.
52. Addams, "The Social Situation," p. 148. Addams credited this idea to "an anonymous economist."
53. "Militarism and Industrial Legislation," 1907, in *Centennial Reader*, p. 212.
54. See *Centennial Reader*, pp. 190-217 for an edited collection of Addams' statements on labor.
55. Mary Jo Deegan and John S. Burger, "George Herbert Mead and Social Reform," *Journal of the History of the Behavioral Sciences* 14 (October 1978):362-72.

56. Alice Hamilton, *Exploring the Dangerous Trades: The Autobiography of Alice Hamilton* (Boston: Little, Brown, 1943).

57. Addams, *The Second Twenty Years at Hull-House* (New York: Macmillan, 1930), p. 391 (hereafter referred to as *The Second Twenty Years*).

58. Ibid.

59. Ibid., p. 389.

60. J. Stanley Lemons, *The Woman Citizen: Social Feminism in the 1920's* (Urbana: University of Illinois Press, 1973).

61. "Social Consequences of Business Depressions," an address in the economics series sponsored by the National Advisory Council on Radio in Education," 24 October 1931, NBC, copy in Addams Papers, Smith College.

62. C. Wright Mills, *Sociology and Pragmatism*, ed., intro. Irving Louis Horowitz (New York: Paine-Whitman, 1964). See section on "social pathologists," esp. p. 309. He particularly misunderstands her paper on "The Subjective Necessity of Social Settlements."

63. Farrell, *Beloved Lady*, p. 65.

64. "Recent Immigration: A Field Neglected by the Scholar."

65. *Twenty Years*, pp. 231-58; *The Second Twenty Years*, pp. 263-303. Immigrants' stories and lives, however, are continually discussed in both books and should not be considered as limited to only these papers.

66. "The Settlement as a Neighbor," in *The Child in the City: A Handbook*, from the Child Welfare Exhibit, 11-25 May, 1911, p. 16. University of Nebraska, Abbott Papers, box 18.

67. *Twenty Years*, p. 436.

68. Ibid., p. 438.

69. *The Second Twenty Years*, p. 296.

70. "Americanization," *Proceedings of the American Sociological Society* 14 (1919):206-14.

71. *The Second Twenty Years*, pp. 188-98.

72. Jane Addams' primary books on the life cycle are *The Spirit of Youth* and *The Long Road of Women's Memory* (New York: Macmillan, 1916). References to the life cycle, however, can be found throughout her writings.

73. *The Spirit of Youth*, p. 3.

74. Ibid., p. 4.

75. Ibid., p. 6.

76. Ibid., p. 19.

77. See Sigmund Freud, *Civilization and Its Discontents*, tr. James Strachey (New York: Norton, 1961, c. 1931).

78. *The Spirit of Youth*, p. 30.

79. Ibid., p. 33.

80. Ibid., pp. 44-45.

81. Ibid., p. 108.

82. See G.H. Mead, *The Philosophy of the Act* (Chicago: University of Chicago Press, 1938).

83. Erik H. Erikson, *Childhood and Society* (New York: Norton, 1951).

84. *The Spirit of Youth*, p. 107.

85. Ibid., p. 111.

86. *Twenty Years*, p. 452.

87. Ibid., p. 354.

88. Ibid., p. 88.

89. *Democracy and Social Ethics*, p. 39.
90. Ibid., pp. 44-45.
91. Ibid., p. 46.
92. Addams, *The Long Road of Women's Memory*; Frances Donovan, *The School Ma'am* (New York: Frederick A. Stokes, 1938).
93. See John Dewey, *Human Nature and Conduct* (New York: Henry Holt, 1922). A discussion of Addams' "family claim" is found in ch. 9 here.
94. Addams, *Second Twenty Years*, p. 189.
95. Ibid., p. 190.
96. *The Long Road of Women's Memory*, p. ix.
97. Ibid., p. xi.
98. Ibid., pp. xi-xii.
99. Ibid., p. 2.
100. Erikson, *Childhood and Society*, 1950, pp. 258-73.
101. *The Long Road of Women's Memory*, p. 11.
102. Ibid., p. 23.
103. Ibid., p. 68.
104. Alvin Gouldner, *The Coming Crisis of Western Sociology* (New York: Avon, 1970).
105. The Long Road of Women's Memory, p. 163.
106. Jane Addams, *Peace and Bread in Time of War*, intro. John H. Dewey (Boston: Hall, 1960, c. 1922), p. 133.
107. Christopher Lasch, *The Social Thought of Jane Addams*, p. 162. Citation of Breckinridge, *Unity* 115 (15 July 1935):191.

12

The End of Addams' Career as a Sociologist: From Sociologist to Social Worker

After World War I, Addams and the men of the Chicago School traveled different paths. From her central place as an early leader in sociology, she moved to an undistinguished niche. Not only was she no longer a leader; her early influence was almost entirely erased in historical accounts. This remarkable slip in stature was presaged by a number of changes in her sociological thought and in that of the Chicago men, discussed throughout this book. The dramatic finale of her sociological career culminated with the social changes and upheaval attending World War I and its aftermath.

In this final chapter, three major issues are examined. The first section emphasizes the historical context, although the era affected all the issues examined here. World War I inaugurated massive changes in social thought, social institutions, and everyday life.[1] The decline of sociological activism and its association with cultural feminism is directly related to its zeitgeist. The defeat of Addams' ideas concerning elite education and the need to have a viable practice of sociology outside of the academy also occurred then. At the University of Chicago, personnel and policy changes resulted in a different practice of sociology and social work. For example, in 1920 all the women sociologists in the Department of Sociology were moved en masse out of sociology and into social work.[2] Consequently, Addams became more identified with social work at the University of Chicago and less identified with the now all male Department of Sociology. These local changes reflected national movements that finalized a shift of women from sociology into social work. By 1918 Addams' ties to Chicago sociologists were attenuated. Her life after this period is very briefly examined in my second major section. This completes her life story and the saga of her sociological career. This is followed by a brief recapitulation of Addams' contributions to sociology. An evaluation of her work as a contemporary resource concludes the book.

The Historical Context: Addams and Sociology

World War I and the Eclipse of Sociological Activism: The Test of Cultural Feminism

World War I was a watershed in American thought, history, experience, and politics. The dramatic difference between the eras before and after this war is a continual theme in historical accounts of these years. Optimism about the potential and power of social reform that characterized the earlier age changed into pessimism about the unchanging and pervasive quality of human destructiveness and aggression. Democracy and rational thought, in particular, were increasingly viewed with skepticism. Although pragmatism continued to be a viable intellectual force for at least another decade, the wide-scale belief in the continuing improvement of the individual and society was eroded. As a pacifist, social reformer, and applied sociologist, Addams symbolized the discarded values and acts of an old-fashioned age. Her sociological analyses of cultural feminism and critical pragmatism articulated an unacceptable approach to sociologists and the general public. Of her two streams of thought, her cultural feminism was the most problematic because of its defense of pacifism during the war.

Addams' emphasis on women's cooperative culture appeared particularly outdated, perhaps even dangerous. First viewed as a misguided "good" woman who was innocently ignorant of war, she was increasingly seen as deliberately misleading the American public. Finally, she was decried as a "menace" to society with her strange ideas of cooperation and dangerous beliefs in equality (this transition is discussed in the second major section here).

Her cultural feminism had never been fully accepted by male Chicago sociologists, and her pacifism drove a further wedge between her and the men of the Chicago School. Thomas, who was closest to Addams in this area of study, and even Dewey and Mead, differed from her concerning the war. Her position, which had always been strongly identified with women, was increasingly defined as oppositional to the men's. Since most women sociologists believed in cultural feminism and applied sociology, the differences between the groups were sharply accentuated.[3]

Disillusionment with the bitter war, an emotional distance from the fear and hysteria associated with the Red Scare and postwar unemployment, and a society based on "new" values were all factors that generated an apolitical 1920s. This opposition to political action was a fertile ground for Freudian ideas that attributed social action to individual drives and conflicts.

Like Addams, most of the women who had developed vital political programs and authored sociological analyses in the prewar era were unmarried. In this "new" age, their political interests were seen as acts of frustrated spinsters who missed the real excitement of life: sex. Their study of women's culture was seen as a "compensation" for their lonely lives. This interpretation of cultural feminism made it appear "ridiculous" and associated with sublimated drives "to do good" arising out of the emptiness of thwarted neurotic drives.[4]

Addams' ideas were thus attacked on several fronts, and her decline as a public figure mirrored her decline as a sociologist. The entire field of "applied" sociology was under attack for reasons similar to those leveled against Addams. This way of doing sociology was intimately related to pragmatic and progressive assumptions that were increasingly "passé". Its association with political controversies, the discredited theory of cultural feminism, and the "dangerous and neurotic" women sociologists made it appear to be a destructive and unscientific remnant of a bygone age. Application of knowledge was not only politically dangerous, it was "bad" sociology.

Cultural feminism was also challenged by new ideologies generated by confrontation with massive worldwide violence. The "new" sociology defined conflict and not cooperation as the basis for behavior. War was obviously not an archaic relic of primitive societies. In the modern world, it flourished and became even more deadly and sophisticated. This new world, with its urban milieu, was a challenge to the strong. Those who did not understand these "facts" were the losers. The old values, epitomized in cultural feminism, were the ideas of the weak and old-fashioned. Beliefs in social and economic democracy were also outmoded. World War I was not a victory for democracy but for the competitors who survived the modern jungle.

As cultural feminism and the women who supported it were disassociated from mainstream sociology, another profession was emerging: social work. This new profession accepted the disenfranchised women sociologists and a major realignment of careers occurred. Before this national movement is discussed, it is important to realize that both aspects of Addams' thought, cultural feminism and critical pragmatism, were attacked by sociologists after World War I. The end of the Great War ushered in an age of conservatism. The radical interpretation of liberal rights, including the hope for liberation through education and economic democracy, was now interpreted as the naive dreams of a bygone era.

The Institutional Debate: A Test of Critical Pragmatism

By 1918, Addams was strongly opposed to elite education and sociology as a science for the elite. For her, sociology was intended to serve the people and be a part of their everyday life. It was accountable to them and its home was in the neighborhood. Sociology was also a component in an interconnected web of social sciences and humanities.

Originally, Addams' ideas were more elitist and this made them more compatible with those of academic men. The male and female networks, moreover, provided a division of labor accepted by both groups. They also shared a fundamental belief in interdisciplinary work and the interdependent nature of theory and practice.

As Addams shifted in her relation to elitism, so too did the men of the Chicago School. When the University of Chicago opened in 1892, sociology was an ambiguous discipline. It needed legitimation, and a powerful reason to justify its existence was its work in social reform. At that time, the men in the academy defined their work as a partnership in community life. This original vision was lost in subsequent battles to locate sociology within the academy. The utopian goal of improving society was replaced by the conservative search for "pure knowledge." Becker analyzed the change as a resolution of a central problem:

> The whole story of sociology is summed up as a tension between these two poles: the human urgency of the social problem on one end and the quiet respectability of objective science on the other. This was the "dialectic" of the development of sociology, the story of its "success" and, as we shall see, the tragedy of its "failure."[5]

Becker's thesis is accepted here, including his interpretation of Small as the fulcrum of academic vacillation. This conflict-ridden role was inherited by Burgess, and the balance was tipped toward "respectable science" by Park. Over time, the sociologists lost the battle for a community science and opted for one that served the interests of the elite under the guise of "objective" knowledge. Within the profession, both sexes lost. The men became increasingly ensconced within the campus and internecine conflicts. The women lost their intellectual recognition within the academy and, ultimately, their institutional home in social settlements and similar organizations.

In addition to this discipline debate over the nature of sociology, there was political pressure from the elite who helped to govern the academy. Academies run by businessmen, as Veblen charged, became the controlling marketplace for sociologists. A double political force was exerted on sociologists: to be less political in their community work and to disassociate themselves from their more controversial colleagues outside of the academy. Those sociologists who opposed the vested interests of the elite were removed from the academy, voluntarily or involuntarily. Those remaining separated themselves from radicals, minorities, women, the poor, and immigrants. Male sociologists, in particular, distanced themselves from Addams and critical pragmatism.

This distancing by the sociologist from the "object" of study did not mean that these groups were no longer studied. Instead, the way that they were studied was changed, and sociologists' obligations to them were redefined. Sociologists became aligned with the governing interests by failing to comment on elite control. While they were rarely overt "lackeys of the bourgeoise," they were coopted under the rubric of "science" and "value-free" assumptions.

Thus, Addams' politically embedded concepts of critical pragmatism were not incorporated in the academy. Her ideas were stripped of their connection to social justice and community control, and then used by the later men of the Chicago School. Despite this radical alteration in her legacy, she was a vital influence on the profession (see the discussion of *HH Maps and Papers*, for example, in chapter 2). But her authorship of this tradition of ideas was buried, and her work was increasingly characterized by male sociologists as "social work," "sentimental," or "atheoretical." While this process of redefining Addams was occurring, the institutional homes for sociology outside of the academy were languishing. Many applied sociologists, including Addams, and the institutions that employed them were merged with a new profession—social work.

Sociology, Male Discipline: Social Work, Female Discipline

In 1918 there were two major occupational changes that were vital to female sociologists. Sociology was moving away from its early model of the discipline, its role in the community, and its institutional relations to work outside of the academy. Social work was just beginning to be affiliated with the academy, and in many ways it was beginning the "legitimacy" scenario that sociology was in the process of resolving. This change in social work practice was based on the confluence of forces associated with both the academy and World War I. As the academic sociologists increasingly defined "applied sociology" as social work, social workers were gaining prestige from their work with shell-shocked soldiers.[6]

Many female sociologists were already identified with social work, and they were increasingly marginal to the male network of sociologists. The national shift of women sociologists to social work occurred very dramatically at the University of Chicago. This process was accelerated by the political repression at the university and dramatic changes in sociology's personnel. A sociological era ended and a social work era began.

Changes in Sociology at the University of Chicago

As emphasized repeatedly throughout the text, Addams was a close colleague of Small, Henderson, Vincent, Zeublin, Mead and Thomas. By

1918, all of these deep ties had radically changed. Only Mead and Small remained, and they both became wary of social reform issues.

Meanwhile, Burgess and Park were building a new vision of sociology, a powerful one that dominated the discipline over the next decade. Although they drew heavily upon the ideas of the early Chicago School, they rarely acknowledged this debt. Thomas and Mead were singled out as contributors, but even their ideas were abstracted from their context of application and social reform.

Burgess and Park were key figures in shaping a sociological era in which Addams' work overtly disappeared. This change can be partially attributed to the coincidence of several forces. First, Burgess and Park were not close colleagues to Addams. They rarely interacted with her as a professional sociologist. They defined her as a social worker and never legitimated her decades of work as a sociologist. In their writings, they often explicitly denied the significance of her sociological contributions while they implicitly built upon them. Second, they instituted a new direction in Chicago Sociology during a historical era that was opposed to political rhetoric. Communism or any economic suggestions associated with governmental intervention and cooperative ownership were taboo. Addams was a symbol of these "dangerous" and erroneous ways. Third, they adopted a conservative political stance as a result of their predecessors' losing struggles with the academic establishment. Fourth, they worked in an era highly favorable to the "natural science" model. Although they resisted such a social movement, the positivist roots of Auguste Comte and Emile Durkheim were becoming increasingly important factors in sociological thought. Weber's concepts of a "value-free" sociology were also an influence, and sociology entered an era of scientific rhetoric concerning "objectivity." The struggle between "science" and "application" was a recurrent theme in the paradoxical work of Albion Small. Park and Burgess resolved this dilemma by legitimating a less active model for sociology in everyday life. Fifth, the popularity of feminism was rapidly waning. The suffrage victory was assured and, therefore, it was assumed that women were equal citizens. The Doctrine of the Separate Spheres had fallen into disfavor, and cultural feminism was seen as its counterpart. "Modern" women belonged in the home and were not very intellectual, but they could have more sexual and social freedom. Presumably, they could have all the benefits of a male life with few of its responsibilities. So the rhetoric of sexism adopted by Park and Burgess was legitimated. "Women's work" in sociology was defined as unscientific and unnecessary. It was really "social work" and not very intellectual anyway. Finally, Burgess and Park denied their intellectual roots and influences. They created a distorted image of sociology in the community and built an empire within an academic battlefield of prestige and honor. Thus a multiplicity of factors combined to change the reform basis of sociology. These changes were enacted by Park and Burgess, but they worked within the tides of widespread social movements.

Changes in Social Work

While sociology and society responded to massive realignments in social thought, social work was emerging as a profession. In other cities and contexts, social workers were developing a professional rationale and legitimacy. Social agencies were growing in number and influence. The government was responding to newer expectations and responsibilities, partially as a direct result of the work of the early sociologists.

The ties between social workers and female sociologists were strong. As sociology became increasingly defined as labor in an academic setting, women were concomitantly excluded from full-faculty status there. Women sociologists found employment in other institutions, and now these were being redefined as part of the "social workers'" domain.

At the University of Chicago, "sociology as a male discipline" and "applied sociology as affiliated with social work as a female discipline" was a theme developed over a period of fourteen years. From the founding of the Chicago School of Civics and Philanthropy in 1906 until the founding of the School of Social Services Administration in 1920, the Hull-House women struggled for recognition in sociology. They did not want this acceptance, however, at the expense of their ideas; including cultural feminism, critical pragmatism, and an active program of institutional freedom of opportunity for women.

Although Addams considered herself a sociologist, she was uninterested in academic recognition and employment. Some of her female colleagues, particularly Abbott and Breckinridge, were more tied to the academy. To paraphrase Virginia Woolf, the latter two women wanted a discipline of their own. They thought they had found it in social work.

These Hull-House women conceived of social work as based on the assumptions of critical pragmatism and cultural feminism. Many social workers in other cities and universities were more psychologically oriented in theory and practice. The Chicago social workers saw their mandate as change agents and effective leaders in this new society's programs. They were critics of the social order, not its representatives. These women did not want to enforce laws, they wanted to create them.

By 1920, all the Chicago female sociologists had become affiliated with social work. Increasingly isolated within sociology, the authors of a distinct sociological theory and practice, and the recent victors of a long suffrage campaign, they welcomed their movement out of sociology. As full citizens at the head of their own school, they anticipated a new age for women and an even more successful format for attaining their goals.

Alas, they were in error. For they were now members of an emerging discipline with its own leaders and agenda. As noted, other social work schools were more aligned with psychology than sociology. Many, too, worked out of the charity and philanthropy background and emphasized their religious basis for action. The Chicago School of Social Work became a component in a new intellectual stream. Simultaneously, animosity between male and female Chicago sociologists was fueled by their separation into different professions.

The Estrangement between Chicago Sociologists and Social Workers

A professional debate ensued after the separation of sociology from its roots in the social settlement and "application" of knowledge in the community. When all the Chicago female sociologists were segregated into SSA, the trend separating Addams' work from the men's culminated. But not only were the disciplines distinct, they were often hostile. As Faris described it: "Academic training in social work, once generally allied with sociology in one department, has almost universally withdrawn into separate departments and schools, leaving behind the chill that is characteristic of the feelings between divorced couples."[7]

Abbott and Park both summarized their vast differences in epistemology. On the one hand, Abbott wrote that the "scientific" view, espoused by sociology, led to "rejecting the academic theory that social work could only be 'scientific' if it had no regard to the finding of socially useful results and no interest in the human beings whose lives were being studied."[8] On the other hand, when Park was asked what help he had given an oppressed group discussed in a sociological course, he replied: "Not a damned thing."[9]

These dramatically different views of sociology were also recollected by Stuart A. Queen. During his years (1910, 1913, and 1919) at the University of Chicago, he heard little about the social services. However, there were rumblings about "'the old maids downtown who were wet-nursing social reformers' (at the Chicago School of Civics and Philanthropy). Occasionally, from the other side, on field trips and doing volunteer boys' club work, I heard slighting remarks about 'those ivory towered professors hiding from real life.'"[10]

Similarly, Faris who was a Chicago student from 1925 to 1931 wrote that "a few sociology graduate students whom I knew did transfer to SSA when they couldn't make the grade in sociology, but I know of no transfers in the other direction."[11] After taking a course at SSA late in his training, Faris recalled that the treatment of the subject was "incredibly naive and simplistic" and "some scorn for sociological contributions to the subject were openly expressed by the lecturer."[12] Relations were bitter indeed.

This destructive state was partially based on an intellectual and occupational division of labor, but it was also based on a sexual division of labor reflecting changing attitudes toward women and their expertise.

Summarizing the Transition from Female Sociology to Social Work

From the beginning, sociologists worked within a sexist milieu. Nonetheless, there was a particular type of opportunity and respect available to early women sociologists who worked in a sex segregated network. Through the passage of time, these differences, both ideological and prejudicial, yielded two separate fields: two sets of knowledge, two sets of practices, two institutional networks, and two sets of colleagues. Finally, the female network within sociology was eliminated by the men. The women relocated in another field where they felt deep ties and alliances, both professionally and as women.

The original sexual division of labor was continued, but social work became the female profession and sociology the male one. This separation differed from the two original sociological practices. Aplied sociology as a viable alternative network for women in sociology disappeared. Female sociologists became a distinct and deprived minority with few major figures to emerge during the ensuing decades. The cultural feminism of the early women sociologists was abandoned, critiques of women's role in a patriarchal society dramatically diminished, and the dominant intellectual model for male Chicago sociologists portrayed society as a product of conflict and competition. This conflict was not a war between the rights of the exploited against the exploiters. It shifted to a conflict and drive for power itself, the good of the community was a resultant factor for which no individual was responsible.

The tension discussed by Becker between social problems and their resolution versus the struggle for respectability resulted in not only one "lost dialectic" but two. Sociology buried its concern for humans, and social work abandoned its quest to change society. Social workers became administrative bureaucrats. They worked for the government instead of becoming its leaders and voice of reason and dissent.

Finally, the Freudian revolution and changes occurring in the 1920s denigrated the achievements of unmarried professional women. Not surprisingly, during this time of transition, Addams' life was in turmoil, and it was only partially calmed after more than a decade of controversy.

Addams: From Saint to Villain, Sociologist to Social Worker

Addams was always a controversial figure, a frequently forgotten fact. She supported labor when it was radical to do so, provided a meeting space for anarchists when the populace wanted them "out of town," and led a series of local battles on politics, education, and even the sanitary department. Such stances led to her being labeled a radical and troublemaker throughout her life. Simultaneously, she was often lauded, respected, and victorious in her battles with the government, capitalists, and repressive vested interests. Her survival of these many confrontations aided in establishing her notoriety and respect. As Davis has noted: "Probably no other woman in any period of American history has been venerated and worshipped the way Jane Addams was in the period just before World War I."[13]

Both her major intellectual contributions, critical pragmatism and cultural feminism, were coopted and accepted by others because their radical implications were not understood. Although her economic democracy and antielite stance on education were not thoroughly adopted, her beliefs in rational thought, systematic analysis, and social reform were core concerns of the Chicago pragmatists and male sociologists. This work also touched a chord in the mind and sentiments of Americans in general. Similarly, her cultural feminism advanced the idea that women were superior to men in terms of female values and their moral enactment. This aspect of her thought was coopted in two specific ways. First, she was able to work with individuals supporting the more conservative Doctrine of the Separate Spheres, which was particularly important in her relations with Albion Small. Second, she was able to combine this image of woman with her own image of "feminine benevolence, saintly devotion and practical usefulness, as well as the best of American democracy."[14] This uneasy peace between her ideas and those of male sociologists and the general public generated a tenuous position for Addams. But her considerable work and deep ties with many of these men were possible as long as the real intent of her ideas remained largely misunderstood and the goals she desired were being achieved.

Addams became a leader in the pacifist movement when war broke out in Europe in 1914. Half a year later, in 1915, Addams headed the Women's Peace Party but the group received little notice at this time. In the spring, a group of women met at the Hague at an international congress to unite in opposition to the war. After this meeting, some of these delegates spoke with world leaders in an effort to urge the heads of state to neutrality or peaceful negotiations.[15] At this time, some people were hostile to these trips and their mission, but in general there was little opposition and even some amusement. But by mid-summer, there were angry press releases concerning her naiveté and failure to understand the war's significance. According to Davis, "the animosity of the attack can only be explained by the fact that she had been an important symbol for Americans."[16]

Another interpretation is clearly available: sexism. Addams became a victim of the very hatred of women that was the complement to her previously loved position: women's place was in the home where she could be protected. Thus, one newspaper reporter described her as "a silly, vain, impertinent old maid, who may have done good charity work at Hull-House, Chicago, but is now meddling with matters far beyond her capacity."[17] Another editorial mocked her intellectual thought: "In the true sense of the word, she is apparently without education."[18] Addams was not allowed to speak on men's activities or against men's values when people understood what she meant.

Her own lack of integration of cultural feminism and critical pragmatism partially explains her reaction to the public outcry. She was deeply confused and disturbed; she was only acting on values that she had avowed for years. She did not perceive that the American value system was fundamentally at odds with cultural feminism. In 1915 and 1916 she continued to be troubled by the controversy she had stirred, but remained firm in her stance. When America entered the war she was again tested, and again she chose pacifism.

For most of 1917 she was out of step with the country, but in 1918 she was able to use her concept of women as food conservers to do some work for the Food Administration. In this capacity she was briefly and partially restored to public honor and notice, but the war had changed the country as well as the world. Social conditions were volatile:

> Runaway prices, a brief but sharp stock market crash and business depression, revolutions through Europe, widespread fear of domestic revolt, bomb explosions, and an outpouring of radical literature were distressing enough. These sudden difficulties, moreover, served to exaggerate the disruptive effects already produced by the social and intellectual ravages of the World War and preceding reform era, and by the arrival before the war, of millions of new immigrants.[19]

Americans who were roused to anti-German feelings during the war shifted their focus of fear and hatred to radicals who had resisted the war.[20] Four million men who had been drafted had either died or returned badly shaken by the carnage witnessed in the trenches. The government, too, had assumed a great deal more control and initiated new programs for social welfare.[21] Women had worked in large numbers in war industries, and Blacks had migrated to the North. Thus, vast social change and unrest were occurring in the United States while the Bolshevik Revolution was being fought in Russia. Americans began to retrench against these changes and their threats to individualism and traditional controls over minorities and women. The Red Scare began.

Returning veterans were particularly angry and confused by the changes that had taken place. In the early part of 1919, the majority of the mobs who stormed meetings held by immigrants or radicals was comprised of these disillusioned men.[22] Speeches exalting American institutions and way of life were more frequently given, and the American flag became a sacred symbol of capitalism and nativism.[23]

In January 1919, Archibald Stevenson, a young New York lawyer working for the War Department, testified before a Senate subcommittee. He presented a list of the sixty-two most dangerous and destructive people in the country. At the top of the list was Jane Addams.[24] Stevenson was able to convince the New York State Legislature that they should organize a full-scale investigation of radical, un-American activities and their results. This investigation was headed by Senator R. Luck, whose committee produced four volumes on revolutionary radicalism. This Luck Report haunted Addams "all through the 1920's and she never found an effective way to answer the charges which mixed fact, half-truth and outright lies."[25]

Many radical immigrants were deported[26] and Americans who could not be treated so crassly were vilified and made outcasts. Addams, the national symbol of goodness in an earlier age, became the country's scapegoat.

The two most castigated persons in this program of nativism and oppression were Jane Addams and Emily Greene Balch. These women were also the most notable women sociologists of their day. Male sociologists wanted to separate their occupation from this turmoil and were able to do so by supporting American militarism in World War I and by disowning the female sociologists during the War crisis.

The Red Scare ended quickly for most people. By the first half of 1920 the European revolutions were put down; by 1920 communism seemed to have been isolated in Russia. Bombings in America stopped abruptly after June 1919, and fear of new outrages gradually abated. Prices of food and clothing started to recede during the spring. Labor strife almost vanished from our major industries after a brief railroad walkout in April. Prosperity returned.[27]

Despite the general abatement, the Red Scare was far from over for female sociologists. It lasted almost a decade for Addams. One of the mechanisms for prolonging this animosity was the publication of various charts of "subversive radicals" called "Spider-Webs." (The charts had a list of name of "dangerous citizens" on one side, and on the other side was a list of "un-American organizations." Lines connecting the two lists made a complex pattern of interlocking networks similar to the pattern of a spider web.) On one Spider-Web published as late as 1927, Addams was at the top of the list, followed by Emily Greene Balch, Florence Kelley, and Mary McDowell.[28] Thus, although the country returned in many ways to "business as usual" in 1920, these women continued to be symbols of the problem of American socialism and its threat to national security. Their new programs for change were neutralized and ridiculed. Programs for a more equalitarian society instituted in the years before and during World War I were frequently undermined. As its most lasting accomplishments, the movement for "one hundred percent Americanism" fostered a spirit of conformity in the country, a satisfaction with the status quo, and the equation of reform ideologies with foreign enemies.[29] Simultaneously, male sociologists were changing their *attitudes* toward social reform and disaffiliated themselves from the stigmatizing labels of reformers or radicals.

By 1919, when Addams' work in sociology and with sociologists had radically diminished, she had turned primarily to the National Conference of Social Workers for professional activities. Here, too, many of her female sociological colleagues could be found. President of the organization in 1910, Addams was active in the group for years. She particularly worked for programs related to the central topics covered by critical pragmatism. She presented eighteen papers at the National Conference of Social Workers on these topics from 1897 to 1933, and Table 12.1 lists her extensive committee work in the organization.[30] It is evident that her greatest participation

TABLE 12.1
Addams' Committee Work for the National Conference of Social Workers*

Year	Committee Topic	Committee Titles and Offices
1904	Neighborhood	Neighborhood Improvement, Chair
1905	Neighborhood	Neighborhood Improvement
1926	Neighborhood	Neighborhood and Community Life
1928	Neighborhood	Neighborhood and Community Life
1929	Neighborhood	Neighborhood and Community Life
1930	Neighborhood	Neighborhood and Community Life
1931	Neighborhood	Neighborhood and Community Life
1909	Immigrants	Immigrants, Chair
1912	Immigrants	Immigration
1919-21	Immigrants	Uniting Native and Foreign-Born in America
1922	Immigrants	Immigrant
1924	Immigrants	Immigrant
1930-31	Immigrants	Immigrant
1932-34	Immigrants	Immigrant
1913	Immigrants	Immigrant
1911	Labor	Standards of Living and Labor
1918-21	Labor	Industrial and Economic Problems

*Other Committees on which she served included Social Hygiene (1914), the Executive (1910, 1913-1916, 1926-31), International Conference of Social Work (1925, 1932) and the Special Committee on the Jubilee Conference (1922).

occurred after 1918, when she had decreased her work in other professional organizations, especially the ASS.

Although Addams' eminence as a social worker is well established, for our purposes it is important to note that she never claimed to be a social worker. She did, however, claim to be a sociologist.[31] Moreover, long after Chicago Sociologists failed to identify her as a member of their profession, she was still publicly acknowledged as a sociologist.[32] There is no reason to suggest that Addams must be a sociologist or a social worker. (Many great intellectuals are claimed by a number of professions, e.g., Karl Marx, Max Weber, Sigmund Freud, and Emile Durkheim.) The only case being made here is that she was a sociologist. In the years following World War I she was increasingly close to social workers. But for nearly three decades prior to that time, she was an active, practicing sociologist.

Addams and other female sociologists faced a long and bitter decade during the 1920s. Fighting for a series of reforms, anticipating a female renaissance that never occurred, portrayed as frustrated and aging spinsters, the women were swimming against the tide of a new age. Most of the progressive organizations they had supported were disbanded, and Addams' influence had plummeted. They also became part of an ongoing profession, social work, with a number of leaders, institutions, and ideologies that were concentrated in the East. Addams became a "social worker," an anomalous one. She was respected and vital, but she was outside of the modern profession and its emerging goals. Again, she became a symbolic leader rather than an intellectually recognized force.

With the Great Depression, Addams was restored to favor. The American people returned to their earlier questions about national goals and priorities: what could be done to alleviate human misery? In this situation, Addams reemerged as a public leader.

> The economic crisis at home, and the threat of a new war abroad made her seem more relevant and less controversial. In the early years of the 1930's, the last years of her life, she was showered once more with honors, praised beyond reason, and treated, again, as a saint. . . . There was, however, something nostalgic about the honors bestowed on her in the 1930's, as if everyone were trying to recapture a more simple and idealistic age when Jane Addams was solving the problems of poverty and the slums.[33]

Although she made public speeches and did some writing, she was less controversial, less vital, and less intellectual in these efforts. Awarded a Nobel Peace Prize, an honorary doctorate from the University of Chicago, selected as one of the greatest American women in a magazine poll, Addams was restored to her public role as an American heroine. When she died in 1935 after a number of long illnesses, the country mourned her. But it was her image they mourned and not the demise of her vision of America. Fortunately, her dream of a liberated society has not been buried.

A Final Evaluation of Addams' Contributions to Sociology

Addams helped shape American sociology in a fundamental way. Her early work in *HH Maps and Papers* set the intellectual precedent for decades of work now recognized as "Chicago Sociology." Her participation in Chicago Sociology was intrinsic to its agenda, its brilliance, and it role in American life and politics.

Her two major streams of thought, cultural feminism and critical pragmatism, provide a rich heritage for scholars and Americans. She articulated a view of society based on the American experience and the social thought of her age. Patriarchal worldviews prevented an institutionalization of her work in sociology and her epistemological leadership was hidden.

Despite this historical distortion of her role as a sociologist, her work with the early men of the Chicago School was significant. Her influence on them and their relationships to her are categorized and summarized in Table 12.2. Three different patterns of relationships can be discerned.

The first network concerns Small, Henderson, Zeublin, and Vincent. Called here the "religious men," this group worked very closely with Addams for almost a quarter of a century. Small, Henderson, and Zeublin were all trained in the ministry and their use of religious assumptions marks their work in a distinctive way. Small and Vincent shared similar interests in elite education and a more conservative view of women. Henderson and Zeublin were particularly close to the social settlement movements and actively turned to Addams for intellectual and moral leadership. Mapping, education, social settlements, the economy, and criminal reforms were all topics central to Addams' sociological contributions and the work done by these men. She was more radical, less sexist, and more intellectually challenging than these men. Nonetheless, they shared a basic core of common interests, work, and historical context. All four men were actively associated with Addams, Hull-House, and the study of the city and its reform.

Mead and Thomas formed with Addams a significant intellectual force and influence on American thought. The least sexist of the men, they more willingly accepted Addams as a colleague and brought their personal lives and professional careers together. The considerable overlap in their ideas and work needs to be examined in greater depth than is possible here. Mead was most influenced by Addams' critical pragmatism, particularly supporting her concepts of democratic change, the need for communica-

TABLE 12.2

Table 12.2   SUMMARY OF INFORMATION CONCERNING ADDAMS AND THE MEN OF THE CHICAGO SCHOOL

MEN	SOCIAL REFORM	HULL-HOUSE	HHMAPS AND PAPERS	WOMEN	ADDAMS
SMALL	central, esp. economic issues	frequent visitor	used in class, supported publication	supported Doctrine of separate spheres, sex segregation at Chicago	admiring colleague; AJS honorary Ph.D. worked on social reform issues
HENDERSON	central, esp. social settlements	frequent visitor and lecturer	used in writings, probably also in classes	mixture of traditional religious views and liberal rights	colleague, working on numerous projects with similar social reform goals, supported social settlements
ZEUBLIN	central, especially social settlements	resident and frequent visitor and lecturer	contributor, used mapping methodology	supported suffrage	colleague, supported Fabian sociology
VINCENT	central, esp. Chautauqua Education	frequent visitor		probably more liberal than Small but believed in Doctrine of Separate Spheres	colleague in Chautauqua Programs
THOMAS	vital, but theory and practice part of division of labor	frequent visitor and lecturer, actively supported affiliated causes	studied immigrants and urban problems (social disorganizational)	dramatic change in ideas from Social Darwinist to egalitarian	colleague on topics of women, espec. prostitution, immigrants, and juvenile delinquency
MEAD	integral to theory of self and society	frequent visitor, lecturer, active support of affiliated orgs. and causes	favored mapping methodology	basically egalitarian	colleague, esp. in reference to pragmatism and role of social reform in everydaylife
BURGESS	mixed, more favorable in early part of career	distant admirer	used mapping methodology, mixed evaluation	mixed ideas; appeared to be enacting Doctrine of Separate Spheres	admired image of woman on the pedestal
PARK	mixed, virtulantly anti-reform ideologies	little or no contact	used mapping methodology studied urban life	sexist	knew of Addams

tion, and the flexibility of human nature. Thomas, too, shared an interest in immigrants and juveniles who were undergoing rapid social change in the new American city. Of all the men, he was the most influenced by her work with women and thereby formed a unique relationship to her thought concerning the role of women in modernizing society.

Finally, Park and Burgess inherited the wealth of concepts and methodologies generated by these early sociologists (see Table 1.1 showing the in-bred male patterns of recruitment). Park and Burgess had the most minimal contacts with Addams, but their intellectual debt to her was great. The most sexist of the men, the most opposed to social reform, and part of a new generation of sociological thought, Park and Burgess signaled the end of Addams' direct influence on the men of the Chicago School.

The changes in the relationships that occurred with these three subgroups of men were integrally related to their historical contexts. Political limitations on the academy; changing social currents fanned by unionization, the women's movement, progressive thought, and World War I; and the processes of increasing industrialization, urbanization, and bureaucratization were large social forces in which these sociologists lived, wrote, and acted. These larger tides are reflected in Addams' relationships to the Chicago men. Out of this vortex of change, a clear pattern emerges. Addams was not only integral to the developement of the "Chicago School," she was one of its founders.

Despite her brilliance, a number of errors in her thought are glaringly obvious. She overestimated the stability of the women's network and her leadership of it. She thought progress was more imminent and rational than it was. Her worldview was too idealistic in its interpretation of the power of patriarchy. Physical power and coercion were more dominant and accepted parts of society than she thought. Although she decried rampant inequalities in society, her power resulted from her being accepted by the elite. She thought this acceptance arose from the intrinsically human bonds that crossed lines of differences, but her role as an intellectual and public leader was more tied to the historical context than she realized. Despite her massive programs for social action (and most of them were successfully adopted), Addams believed more in the power of ideas than in the material world.

She basically segregated her ideas about cultural feminism from her ideas about critical pragmatism. Although these two epistemologies appeared to overlap, she wrongly assumed that society was embedded in the cultural feminism enacted by women. She thought that women voters would overturn the power of male viewpoints thereby showing the greater resiliency, justice, and humanity of the feminine, cooperative worldview. In this, she erred. Women voters turned to men for guidance, and women politicians did not gain ascendancy. Physical coercion and bedlam in World War I, World War II, Korea, and Vietnam, to list only a few conflicts, have repeatedly shown that ours is a murderous and violent age, supported by women voters.

Despite these major weaknesses in her thought, Addams' ideas were powerful and innovative. Her writings, lifestyle, commitments, and implementation of knowledge in everyday life dramatically altered the course of American life. She is one of the most influential American sociologists, and a comprehensive examination of her impact on sociology has only been initiated here.

As Americans enter another dark economic time, questions concerning the work of sociology, the meaning of community and democracy, and the social construction of equality are once more pressing issues. Although Addams partially failed in her work, she also succeeded beyond most of our dreams. Her own words are the most apt for guiding us in the future:

> If we believe that the individual struggle for life may widen into a struggle for the lives of all, surely the demand of an individual for decency and comfort, for a chance to work and obtain the fullness of life may be widened until it gradually embraces all the members of the community and rises into a sense of the common weal.[34]

Notes

1. There is an extensive literature on World War I and the shift in values it initiated. For writings particularly relevant to questions raised here see Allen F. Davis, *American Heroine* (New York: Oxford University Press, 1973); David Noble, *The Progressive Mind, 1890-1917* (Chicago: Rand, McNally, 1970); John Chamberlain, *Farewell to Reform* (Chicago: Quadrangle, 1965, c. 1932); S. Cohen, "A Study in Nativism: The American Red Scare of 1919-1920," *Political Science Quarterly* 79 (March 1964):52-75; John Higham, *Strangers in the Land, Patterns of American Nativism, 1896-1925* (New Brunswick, N.J.: Rutgers University Press, 1955). Addams discusses the era as well in *The Second Twenty Years at Hull-House* (New York: Macmillan, 1930), pp. 153-87 (hereafter referred to as *The Second Twenty Years*).
2. For documentation of the series of administrative shifts that moved female Chicago sociologists from sociology into social work, see Mary Jo Deegan, "Women in Sociology: 1890-1930," *Journal of the History of Sociology* 1 (Fall 1978):19-23.
3. Addams was not alone in her ostracism by male sociologists. A good example of this type of reaction to women sociologists can be seen in the life of Emily Greene Balch, a close colleague and ally of Addams. When Balch spoke on the topic of war and militarism at the ASS meetings in 1915, over twenty male sociologists declined an invitation to comment on her address. One of the discussants who finally accepted the invitation was Carey Thomas, the noted feminist and president of Bryn Mawr. She was surely an eminent speaker and,

just as surely, she was not a sociologist. Balch was ultimately fired from her sociology position at Wellesley College for her controversial ideas and work on pacifism. See Mary Jo Deegan, "Sociology at Wellesley College: 1900-1919," *Journal of the History of Sociology* 6 (December 1983):91-115.

4. Addams discusses the new and denigrating interpretation of unmarried women in *The Second Twenty Years*, pp. 192-99. Emily Greene Balch, mentioned in n. 3 above, wrote a section here supporting Addams' view and reporting on her similar experience.

5. Ernest Becker, *The Lost Science* (New York: Braziller, 1971), p. 6.

6. The process of creating a new profession was the product of myriad factors, although the work with returning veterans became an important turning point. For a detailed analysis of this process see Roy Lubove, *The Professional Altruist: The Emergence of Social Work as a Career, 1880-1930* (Cambridge, Mass.: Harvard University Press, 1965).

7. Robert E.L. Faris, *Chicago Sociology* (Chicago: University of Chicago Press, 1967), p. 13.

8. Edith Abbott, "Julia Lathrop and Professional Education for Social Work," Abbott Papers, UCSC, box 57, #2, p. 4.

9. Park quoted by Everett C. Hughes in a letter to the author, 26 October 1979.

10. "Seventy-Five Years of American Sociology in Relation to Social Work," *The American Sociologist* 16 (February 1981):35.

11. Correspondence from Robert E.L. Faris to author, 1 November 1979, p. 2.

12. Ibid.

13. Davis, *American Heroine*, p. 2.

14. Ibid., p. 207.

15. Jane Addams, Emily Greene Balch and Alice Hamilton, *The Women at the Hague* (New York: Macmillan, 1915).

16. Davis, *American Heroine*, p. 229.

17. Cited in Davis, *American Heroine*, p. 229.

18. Ibid.

19. Cohen, "A Study in Nativism: The American Red Scare of 1919-1920," p. 59.

20. Higham, *Strangers in the Land: Patterns of American Nativism, 1896-1925*, p. 222.

21. See Mead, "Social Reconstruction in a Time of War," *Proceedings of the Social Work Conference*, 44 (1917):637-44.

22. Cohen, "A Study in Nativism: The American Red Scare of 1919-1920," p. 68.

23. Ibid., pp. 68-71.

24. Davis, *American Heroine*, p. 252.

25. Ibid., p. 254.

26. Cohen, "A Study in Nativism: The American Red Scare of 1919-1920," pp. 72-73.

27. Ibid., p. 74.

28. "Spider-Web" is reprinted in Davis, *American Heroine*, p. 265. Written by Charles Norman Fay to Editor, Boston Herald (17 May 1927).

29. Cohen, "A Study in Nativism: The American Red Scare of 1919-1920," p. 74.

30. This information can be found in the memorial program from Addams' funeral. *Jane Addams* (privately printed, 1935).

31. Lionel James documented that Addams never labeled herself a social worker. "Jane Addams and the Development of Professional Social Work," Unpublished paper, p. 2. DG1, box 10. ser. 4, SCPC. Addams did, however, call

herself a sociologist. Jane Addams to Alice Addams Halderman, 7 January 1908. Deloach Deposit, SCPC. Cited in John C. Farrell, *Beloved Lady* (Baltimore: Johns Hopkins Press, 1967), p. 68.

32. Addams was considered a sociologist by others for years. The 1930 issue of *The National Cyclopedia of American Biography* identifies her as a sociologist. *White's Conspectus of American Biography* listed her under sociology and not social work in 1937. As late as 1948 Harry Barnes said the largest group of sociologists were "social economists" or "practical sociologists." He listed Addams as part of this group. My thanks to Jan Fritz for pointing out these references.

33. Davis, *American Heroine*, p. 282.

34. Jane Addams, *Democracy and Social Ethics* (New York: Macmillan, 1902), p. 269.

Bibliography

A. Manuscript Collections

Cambridge

Radcliffe College, The Arthur and Elizabeth Schlesinger Library on the History of Women in America
- Ethel Sturgess Dummer Papers
- Charlotte Perkins Gilman Papers

Carbondale

University of Southern Illinois, Dewey Collection
- John Dewey Papers
- James Tufts Papers

Chicago

Chicago Historical Society
- Mary McDowell Papers
- University of Chicago Settlement Records
Newberry Library
- Graham Taylor Papers
Northwestern University, Northwestern University Library
- Northwestern University Settlement Papers
University of Chicago, Regenstein Library, Special Collections
- L.L. Bernard Papers
- Ernest W. Burgess Papers
- George H. Mead Papers and Addendum
- Presidents' Papers, 1889-1925
- Julius Rosenwald Papers
- Albion W. Small Papers
- Sociology Interviews
- James Tufts Papers
University of Illinois at Chicago, University Library, Jane Addams Memorial Collection
- Addams Papers
- Hull-House Bulletin

Iowa City

University of Iowa
- Redpath Chautauqua Collection

Lincoln

University of Nebraska, Love Library Archives
• Abbott Papers

Madison

Wisconisn Historical Society
• Richard T. Ely Papers
• Edward Ross Papers

Northhampton

Smith College, The Sophia Smith Collection
• Jane Addams Papers
• Ellen Gates Starr Papers

Swarthmore

Swarthmore College, Swarthmore Library, Swarthmore College Peace Collection
• Addams Papers
• Hull-House Scrapbooks

B. Correspondence

Irene Tufts Mead to author, 7 July, 1975.
Winifred Rauschenbush to author, 19 September 1979.
Robert E.L. Faris to author, 1 November 1979.
Everett C. Hughes to author, 26 October 1979.

C. Interviews

Nels Anderson by the author, 28 August 1979.
Jessie Bernard by the author, 29 June 1978.
Ruth Thomas Billingsley by the author, 29 June, 1978.
Ruth Shonle Cavan by the author, October 1978.
Everett C. Hughes, Informal Group Interview, Spring Research Institute, University of Chicago, Chicago, Illinois, May 1975.
Irene Tufts Mead by the author, 2 June 1978.
Irene Tufts Mead by the author, 26 June 1978.
Irene Tufts Mead by the author, 29 June 1978.

D. Periodicals Read

Chicago City Club Membership Lists, 1912, 1913
Chicago City Club Bulletin
Publications of the Proceedings of the American Sociological Society, 1906-31. Chicago: University of Chicago Press.

E. Works by Jane Addams

Addams, Jane. "Bread Givers." In *Jane Addams: A Centennial Reader*, ed. Emily Cooper Johnson. New York: Macmillan, 1960, c. 1880. Pp. 103-04.

———. "The Subjective Necessity of Social Settlements." In *Philanthropy and Social Progress: Seven Essays by Miss Jane Addams, Robert A. Woods, Father J. O. S. Huntington, Professor Franklin H. Giddings,and Bernard Bosanquet Delivered before the School of Applied Ethics at Plymouth, Mass., during the Session of 1892*. Intro. Henry C. Adams. New York: Crowell, 1893. Pp. 1-26.

———. "Prefatory Note" and "The Settlement as a Factor in the Labor Movement." In *Hull-House Maps and Papers, by Residents of Hull-House, a Social Settlement. A Presentation of Nationalities and Wages in a Congested District of Chicago, Together with Comments and Essays on Problems Growing Out of the Social Conditions*. Boston: Crowell, 1895. Pp. vii-viii and 183-204 respectively.

———. "A Belated Industry." *American Journal of Sociology* 1 (March 1896): 536-50.

———. "Trade Unions and Public Duty." *American Journal of Sociology* 4 (January 1899): 488-62.

———. *Democracy and Social Ethics*. New York: Macmillan Co., 1902.

———. "The Humanizing Tendency of Industrial Education." *The Chautauquan* 39 (May 1904): 266-72.

———. "Problems of Municipal Administration." *American Journal of Sociology* 10 (January 1905): 425-44.

———. "Recent Immigration: A Field Neglected by the Scholar." *University Record* 9 (January 1905): 274-84.

———. Discussant of John Commons, "Class Conflict in America." *Publications of the American Sociological Society*, 2 (1907): 152-55.

———. *Newer Ideals of Peace*. New York: Macmillan, 1907.

———. Comment on an article by John R. Commons, "Class Conflict in America." *American Journal of Sociology* 13 (May 1908): 772-73.

———. "The Chicago Settlements and Social Unrest." *Charities and the Commons* 20 (2 May 1908): 155-66.

———. *The Spirit of Youth and the City Streets*. New York: Macmillan, 1909.

———. *Twenty Years at Hull-House*. New York: Macmillan, 1910.

———. "The Social Situation." *Religious Education* 6 (June 1911): 145-52.

———. "Recreation as a Public Function in Urban Communities." *Publications of the American Sociological Society*, 6 (1911): 35-39.

———. *A New Conscience and an Ancient Evil*. New York: Macmillan, 1912.

———. "Recreation as a Public Function in Urban Communities." *American Journal of Sociology* 17 (March 1912): 615-19.

———. "A Modern Lear." *Survey* 29 (2 November 1912): 131-37.

———. "If Men Were Seeking the Franchise." In *Jane Addams: A Centennial Reader*. Ed. Emily Cooper Johnson. New York: Macmillan, 1960, c. 1913. Pp. 107-13.

———. "A Modern Devil Baby." *American Journal of Sociology* 20 (July 1914): 117-18.

———. "War Times Challenging Woman's Traditions." *Survey* 36 (August 1916): 475-78.

———. *The Long Road of Women's Memory*. New York: Macmillan, 1916.

———. "The World's Food and World Politics." *Proceedings of the National Conference of Social Workers* (Kansas City, Mo.) 45 (1918): 650-56.

———. "Americanization." *Publications of the American Sociological Society* 14 (1919): 206-14.

———. *Peace and Bread in Time of War.* New York: 1922.

———. "A Book That Changed My Life." *Christian Century* 44 (13 October 1927): 1196-98.

———. "Pioneers in Sociology: Graham Taylor." *Neighborhood* 1 (July 1928): 6-11.

———. "The Settlement as a Way of Life." *Neighborhood* 2 (July 1929): 139-46.

———. *The Second Twenty Years at Hull-House.* New York: Macmillan, 1930.

———. "John Dewey and Social Welfare." In *John Dewey: The Man and His Philosophy.* Ed. Henry W. Holmes. Cambridge: Harvard University Press, 1930. Pp. 140-51.

———. "Aspects of the Woman's Movement." *Survey* 8 (August 1930): 113-23.

———. "Tolstoy and Gandhi." *Christian Century* 48 (25 November 1931): 1485-88.

———. *The Excellent Becomes Permanent.* New York: Macmillan, 1932.

———. *My Friend, Julia Lathrop.* New York: Macmillan, 1932.

———. *Peace and Bread in Time of War.* Intro. John Dewey. Boston: Hall, 1960, c. 1922.

———. *Jane Addams: A Centennial Reader.* Ed. Emily Cooper Johnson. New York: Macmillan, 1960.

———. *The Social Thought of Jane Addams.* Ed., intro. Christopher Lasch. Indianapolis: Bobbs-Merrill, 1965.

Addams, Jane, Emily Greene Balch, and Alice Hamilton. *The Women at the Hague.* New York: Macmillan, 1915.

F. Other Works

Abbott, Edith. *Women in Industry.* New York: D. Appleton, 1910.

———. "Grace Abbott and Hull-House, 1908-21. Part 1." *Social Service Review* 24 (September 1950): 374-94.

Abbott, Edith, and Sophonisba P. Breckinridge. *Truancy and Non-Attendance in the Chicago Schools,* Chicago: University of Chicago Press, 1916.

———. *The Tenements of Chicago, 1908-1935.* Chicago: University of Chicago Press, 1936.

American Journal of Sociology Index, 1895-1935. Chicago: University of Chicago Press, 1936.

Austin, Ruth. "Economic and Social Developments Which Led to the Philosophy of the Early Settlements." In *Readings in the Development of Settlement Work,* ed. Lorene M. Pacey. New York: Association Press, 1950. Pp. 282-91.

Bachofen, Jacob. *Das Mutterecht.* English trans. condensation, *Myth, Religion, and Mother-Right.* Tr. Ralph Manheim. Princeton: Princeton University Press, 1967.

Baker, Paul J. "Introduction: The Life Histories of W.I. Thomas and Robert Park." *American Journal of Sociology* 79 (September 1973): 243-60.

Barnes, Harry Elmer. *History of Sociology.* Chicago: University of Chicago Press, 1948.

Becker, Ernest. *The Lost Science of Man.* New York: Braziller, 1971.

Bemis, Edward W. "Municipal Ownership of Gas in the United States." *Publications of the American Economic Association* 6 (1891): 111-12.

_____. "Obituary." *New York Times* (27 September, 1930).

Bestor, E. "The Chautauqua Period." In *George E. Vincent, 1864-1944*. Memorial Addresses. Stanford, Conn.: Overbrooks, 1941. P. 6.

Berger, Peter, Brigitte Berger, and Hansfried Kellner. *The Homeless Mind*. New York: Random House, 1973.

Bernard, Jessie. *Academic Women*. University Park, Penn.: University of Pennsylvania Press, 1964.

_____. *The Female World*. New York: Free Press, 1981.

Blackmar, F.W. and Ernest W. Burgess. *Lawrence Social Survey*, Topeka: Kansas State Printing Press, 1917.

Blumberg, Dorothy Rose. *Florence Kelley*. New York: A.M. Kelley, 1966.

Blumer, Herbert. *An Appraisal of Thomas and Znaniecki's The Polish Peasant*. New York: Social Science Research Council, 1939.

_____. *Symbolic Interactionism*. Englewood Cliffs: Prentice-Hall, 1969.

Bogardus, E.S. "Leading Sociology Books Published in 1916." *Journal of Applied Sociology* 4 (May 1917).

Blumberg, Dorothy Rose. *Florence Kelley*. New York: A.M. Kelley, 1966.

Booth, Charles. *Life and Labour of the People in London*. 9 vols. London and New York: Macmillan, 1892-97. 8 additional vols. London: Macmillan, 1902. (The first volumes were originally published under the title *Labour and Life of the People: London*. 2 vols. London and Edinborough: Williams & Norgate, 1891).

Breckinridge, Sophonisba, and Edith Abbott. *The Delinquent Child and the Home*. Intro. Julia Lathrop. New York: Charities Publication Committee, 1912.

Buhle, Mary Jo. "Socialist Women and the Girl Strikers, Chicago, 1910." *Signs* 1 (Summer 1976): 1039-52.

Bulmer, Martin. "Quantification and the Chicago Social Sciences in the 1920s: A Neglected Tradition." *Journal of the History of the Behavioral Sciences* 17 (July 1981): 312-31.

_____. "Support for Sociology in the 1920s: The Laura Spelman Rockefeller Memorial and the beginnings of Large-Scale, Sociological Research in the University." *American Sociologist* 17 (November 1982): 185-92.

The Bulletins of the Chicago School of Civics and Philanthropy, 1903-19. Chicago: University of Chicago Press.

Burger, John S., and Mary Jo Deegan, "George Herbert Mead on Internationalism, Democracy and War." *Wisconsin Sociologist* 18 (Spring-Summer 1981): 72-83.

Burgess, Ernest W. "The Social Survey." *American Journal of Sociology* 21 (January 1916): 492-500.

_____. "Can Neighborhood Work Have a Scientific Basis?" *Proceedings of the National Conference of Social Work* 51 (1924): 406-11.

_____. "The Pre-Adolescent Girl of the Immigrant Type and Her Home." *Religious Education* 18 (December 1923): 352-61.

_____. "Protecting the Public by Parole and Parole Predictions." *Journal of Criminal Law and Criminology* 27 (November-December 1926): 491-502.

_____. "The Romantic Impulse and Family Disorganization." In *The Basic Writings of Ernest W. Burgess*. Ed. Donald Bogue. Chicago: Community and Family Study Center, University of Chicago, 1974, c. 1926. Pp. 156-64.

_____. "Sociology and Social Work: A Retrospect." *Social Forces* 6 (June 1928): 511-24.

_____. "Is Prediction Feasible in Social Work?" *Social Forces* 7 (June 1929): 533-45.

_____. "The Value of Sociological Community Studies to the Work of Social Agencies," *Social Forces* 8(June 1930): 481-91.

_____. "George Edgar Vincent." *American Journal of Sociology* 46 (May 1941): 887.

_____. "The Effect of War on the American Family." In *The Basic Writings of Ernest W. Burgess*. Ed. Donald Bogue. Chicago: Community and Family Study Center, University of Chicago, 1974, c. 1942. Pp. 194-201.

_____. "Comment on Opler's 'Woman's Social Status and the Forms of Marriage.'" *American Journal of Sociology* 49 (September 1943): 147-48.

_____. *Ernest W. Burgess on Community, Family and Delinquency*. Ed. Leonard S. Cottrell, Jr., Albert Hunter, and James F. Short, Jr. Chicago: University of Chicago Press, 1973.

_____. *The Basic Writings of Ernest W. Burgess*. Ed. Donald J Bogue. Chicago: Community and Family Study Center, 1974.

Burgess, Ernest W., Chair, Central Philanthropic Council, Survey Committee. *Columbus Pool Rooms: A Study of Pool Halls, Their Uses by High School Boys, and a Summary of Public Billiard and Pool Room Regulations of the Largest Cities in the United States*. Columbus: Central Philanthropic Committee, 1916.

Burgess, Ernest W., ed. *The Urban Community*. Selected Papers from the Proceedings of the American Sociological Society, 1925. Chicago: University of Chicago Press, 1926.

Burgess, Ernest W., and Donald J. Bogue, eds. *Contributions to Urban Sociology*. Chicago: University of Chicago Press, 1964.

_____. "Research in Urban Society." In *Contributions to Urban Sociology*. Ed. Ernest Burgess and Donald Bogue. Chicago: University of Chicago Press, 1964. Pp. 1-14.

Carey, James T. *Sociology and Public Affairs*. Beverly Hills: Russell Sage, 1975. Sage Library of Social Research, #16.

Chamberlain, John. *Farewell to Reform*. Chicago: Quadrangle, 1965, c. 1932.

Clayton, Alfred S. *Emergent Mind and Education*. New York: Teachers' College Bureau of Publications, Columbia University Press, 1943.

Cohen, S. "A Study in Nativism: The American Red Scare of 1919-1920." *Political Science Quarterly* 79 (March 1964): 52-75.

Cooley, C.H. *Social Organization*. New York: Scribner's, 1909.

_____. "The Roots of Social Knowledge," *American Journal of Sociology* 32 (July 1926): 59-79.

Coughlan, Neil. *Young John Dewey: An Essay in American Intellectual History*. New York: Free Press, 1976.

Course Catalogs for Chicago School of Civics and Philanthropy, 1903-19. Chicago: University of Chicago Press.

Course Catalogs for School of Social Services Administration, 1920-24. Chicago: University of Chicago Press.

Cullen, Michael J. *The Statistical Movement in Early Victorian England*. New York: Barnes & Noble, 1975.

Curti, Merle. "Jane Addams on Human Nature." *Journal of the History of Ideas* 22 (April-June 1961): 240-53.

Davis, Allen F. *American Heroine*. New York: Oxford University Press, 1973.

Davis, Allen F., and Mary Lynne McCree, eds. *Eighty Years at Hull-House*. Chicago: Quadrangle, 1969.

de Schweinitz, Karl. *England's Road to Social Security*. New York: A.S. Barnes, 1961, c. 1943.

Deegan, Mary Jo. "Women in Sociology, 1890-1930." *Journal of the History of Sociology* 1 (Fall 1978): 11-34.

_____. "Edith Abbott," "Emily Greene Balch," and "Sophonisba Breckinridge." In *American Women Writers*, vol. I. New York: Ungar, 1979. Pp. 3-5, 96-98, and 219-23, respectively.

_____. "Feminist Sociology." Paper presented at the Midwest Sociological Society Meetings, April 1979.

_____. "G.H. Mead and the Sociology of Women." Unpublished paper, 1981.

_____. "Mead vs. His Interpreters." Unpublished paper, 1981.

_____. "The University of Chicago Settlement and the Department of Sociology." Unpublished paper, 1981.

_____. "Early Women Sociologists and the American Sociological Society," *The American Sociologist* 16 (February 1981): 14-24.

_____. "Helen Merrell Lynd." *American Women Writers*, Vol. 3. New York: Ungar, 1981. Pp. 59-60.

_____. "Marion Talbot," *American Women Writers*, vol. 4. New York: Ungar, 1982. Pp. 202-3.

_____. "Annie Marion MacLean: The Chicago Sociologist Who Taught by Correspondence." Unpublished paper, 1982.

_____. "Sociology at Wellesley College, 1900-1919." *Journal of the History of Sociology* 6 (December 1983): 91-115.

Deegan, Mary Jo, and John S. Burger. "George Herbert Mead and Social Reform." *Journal of the History of the Behavioral Sciences* 14 (October 1978): 362-72.

_____. "W. I. Thomas and Social Reform," *Journal of the History of the Behavioral Sciences* 17 (February 1981): 114-25.

Dewey, Jane. "Biography of John Dewey." In *The Philosophy of John Dewey*. Ed. Paul A. Schilpp. New York: Tudor, 1951, c. 1939. Pp. 1-45.

Dewey, John H. "George H. Mead." *Journal of Philosophy* 28 (4 June, 1931): 309-14.

_____. "The Work of George Mead." *New Republic* 87 (22 July, 1936): 329-30.

_____. "Prefatory Remarks." In George H. Mead, *The Philosophy of the Present*. Ed. Arthur E. Murphy. Chicago: Open Court, 1932. Pp. xxvi-xl.

_____. *Intelligence in the Modern World*. New York: the Modern Library, 1939.

_____. *Human Nature and Conduct*. New York: Holt, 1922.

_____. "Introduction" to Jane Addams' *Peace and Bread in Time of War*. Boston: Hall, 1960, c. 1918, 1922.

Dibble, Vernon. *The Legacy of Albion Small*. Chicago: University of Chicago Press, 1975.

Dike, Samuel W. "Sociology of the Higher Education of Women." *Atlantic Monthly* 421 (November 1892): 668-76.

Diner, Helen. *Mothers and Amazons*. Ed., tr. Joseph Campbell. New York: Julian, 1965, c. 1922.

Diner, Steven J. "Department and Discipline." *Minerva* 8 (Winter 1975): 514-53.

_____. *A City and Its Universities: Public Policy in Chicago, 1892-1919*. Chapel Hill: University of North Carolina Press, 1980.

Donovan, Frances. *The School Ma'am*. New York: Frederick A. Stokes, 1938.

Durkheim, Emile. *Suicide.* Tr. J. T. Spaulding and George Simpson. New York: Free Press, 1951, c. 1897.

Ekrich, Arthur A. *Progressivism in America.* New York: New Viewpoints, 1974.

Elson, Alex. "First Principles of Jane Addams." *Social Service Review* 28 (March 1954): 3-11.

Engels, Frederich. *The Origin of the Family, Private Property and the State.* Moscow: Progressive Press, 1968, c. 1884.

Erikson, Erik H. *Childhood and Society.* New York: Norton, 1951.

Faris, Ellsworth. "W.I. Thomas (1863-1947)." *Sociology and Social Research* 32 (March-April 1948): 755-59.

Faris, Robert E. L. *Chicago Sociology,* 1920-1932. Chicago: University of Chicago Press, 1967.

Farrell, John C. *Beloved Lady.* Baltimore: Johns Hopkins University Press, 1967.

Firestone, Shulamith. *The Dialectic of Sex.* New York: Bantam, 1971.

Fish, Virginia Fish. "The Hull-House Circle," Mimeo, n.d.

Fisher, Bernice, and Anselm Strauss, "George Herbert Mead and the Chicago Tradition of Sociology (Part 1)." *Symbolic Interaction* 2 (Spring 1979): 9-26.

_____. "George Herbert Mead and the Chicago Tradition of Sociology (Part 2)." *Symbolic Interaction* 2 (Fall 1979): 9-20.

Ford, Guy Stanton. "The Minnesota Period." In *George E. Vincent, 1864-1944.* Memorial Addresses. Stanford, Conn.: Overbrooks, 1941. P. 27.

Fox, G.L. "Nice Girl: Social Control of Women Through Value Construct." *Signs* 2 (Summer 1977): 805-17.

Freeman, Jo. "Women on the Social Science Faculties since 1892." Mimeograph of a speech given to minority groups workshop of the Political Science Association, Winter 1969.

Freud, Sigmund. *Civilization and Its Discontents.* Tr. James Strachey. New York: Norton, 1961, c. 1931.

Fuhrman, Ellsworth. *The Sociology of Knowledge in America, 1883-1915.* Charlottesville: University Press of Virginia, 1980.

Fulcomer, Daniel. "Instruction in Sociology in Institution of Higher Learning." *Proceedings of the Twenty First National Conference of Charities* 21 (1894): 67-85.

Gilman, Charlotte Perkins. *Woman and Economics.* New York: Harper Torchbooks, 1966, c. 1898.

Gough, Kathleen. "An Anthropologist Looks at Engels." In *Women in a Man-Made World.* Ed. Nona Glazer and Helen Youngelson Waehrer. Chicago: Rand McNally, 1977. Pp. 156-68.

Goldmark, Josephine. *Impatient Crusader: Florence Kelley's Life.* Urbana: University of Illinois Press, 1953.

Gosnnell, Harold F. *Machine Politics.* Foreword W.F. Ogburn. Chicago: University of Chicago Press. 1937.

Gouldner, Alvin W. *The Coming Crisis of Western Sociology.* New York: Avon, 1970.

Guterbock, Thomas. *Machine Politics in Transition.* Chicago: University of Chicago Press, 1980.

Habermas, Jurgen. *Towards A Rational Society.* Tr. Jeremy Shapiro. Boston: Beacon Press, 1970, c. 1968.

Hamilton, Alice. *Exploring the Dangerous Trades: The Autobiography of Alice Hamilton.* Boston: Little, Brown, 1943.

Harlan, Louis. "Booker T. Washington and the White Man's Burden." *American Historical Review* 71 (January 1966): 441-67.

Hartmann, Heidi. " Capitalism, Patriarchy, and Job Segregation by Sex," *Signs* 1 (Spring 1976): 137-69.

Hayden, Dolores. *The Grand Domestic Revolution*. Cambridge, Mass.: MIT Press, 1981.

Hayes, Edward C. "Albion Small." In *American Masters of Social Science*. Ed. Howard W. Odum. New York: Holt, 1927. Pp. 149-50.

Henderson, Charles R. "Business Men and Social Theorists." *American Journal of Sociology* 1 (January 1896): 385-97.

_____. *Social Settlements*. New York: Lentilhorn, 1898.

_____. "The Scope of Social Technology." *American Journal of Sociology* 6 (January 1901): 465-86.

_____. "Review of Jane Addams' *Democracy and Social Ethics*." *American Journal of Sociology* 8 (July 1902): 136-38.

_____. *The Social Spirit in America*. Chicago: Scott, Foresman, 1904.

_____. *Education with Reference to Sex*. Eighth Yearbook of the National Society for the Scientific Study of Education. Chicago: University of Chicago Press, 1909.

_____. *Industrial Insurance in the United States*. Chicago: University of Chicago Press, 1909.

_____. *Citizens in Industry*. New York: D. Appleton, 1915.

Higham, John. *Strangers in the Land: Patterns of American Nativism, 1896-1925*. New Brunswick, N.J.: , 1955.

Hill, Caroline M., ed. *Mary McDowell and Municipal Housekeeping*. Chicago: Miller, 1937.

Hinkle, Gisela. "The Four Wishes in Thomas' Theory of Social Chicago." *Social Research* 19 (December 1952): 464-84.

Hughes, Everett C. "Preface" to Robert E. Park, *Race and Culture*. Glencoe, Ill: Free Press, 1950. Pp. xi-xiv.

Hull-House Maps and Papers, by Residents of Hull-House, a Social Settlement. A Presentation of Nationalities and Wages in a Congested District of Chicago, Together with Comments and Essays on Problems Growing out of the Social Conditions. New York: Crowell, 1895.

Hunter, Albert, with the assistance of Nancy Goldman. "Introduction," to *Ernest W. Burgess on Community, Family, and Delinquency*. Ed. Leonard Cottrell, Jr., Albert Hunter, and James Short, Jr. Chicago: University of Chicago Press, 1973. Pp. 3-15.

James, William. "The Moral Equivalent of War." In *Pragmatism and Other Essays*. New York: Washington Equal, 1963, c. 1910. Pp. 289-301.

Janowitz, Morris. "Introduction" to *W.I. Thomas: On Social Organization and Social Personality*. Ed. Morris Janowitz. Chicago: University of Chicago Press, 1966. Pp. vii-lviii.

Karpf, Fay B. "Sociology, Social Research, and the Interest in Applications: The Washington (1927) Meetings of the American Sociological Society." *Social Forces* 6 (June 1928): 521-26.

Karpf, Maurice. "The Relation between Sociology and Social Work." *Social Forces* 3 (March 1925): 419-27.

_____. "Sociology and Social Work: A Retrospect." *Social Forces* 6 (June 1928): 511-24.

Käsler, Dirk. "Methodological Problems of a Sociological History of Early German Sociology." Paper presented at the Department of Education, University of Chicago, 5 November 1981.

Keating, Barbara. "Elsie Clews Parsons." *Journal of the History of Sociology,* 1 (Fall 1978): 1-11.

Kelley, Florence. "The Need of Theoretical Preparation for Philanthropic Work." Association of Collegiate Alumnae Pamphlet, 1887.

――――. "Review of Jane Addams' *A New Conscience and an Ancient Evil.*" *American Journal of Sociology* 18 (September 1912): 271-72.

――――. "I Go to Work." *Survey* 60 (1 June 1927): 271-74.

Kennedy, J.C., (Emily Durand), and Others. *Wages and Family Budget in the Chicago Stockyards District.* Vol. 3, *A Study of Chicago's Stockyards Community.* Chicago: University of Chicago Press, 1914.

Klein, Viola. *The Feminine Character: The History of an Ideology.* Foreword by Karl Mannheim. New York: International Universities Press, 1948, c. 1946.

Kraditor, Eileen, ed. *Up from the Pedestal.* Chicago: Quadrangle, 1970.

Kropotkin, Petr. *The Conquest of Bread.* Ed., intro. Paul Avrich. New York: New York University Press, 1972, c. 1892.

――――. *Mutual Aid: A Factor of Evolution.* Foreword Ashley Montagu. And Thomas H. Huxley, "The Struggle for Existence." Boston: Extending Horizons Books, 1955, c. 1902.

――――. *Fields, Factories and Workshops Tomorrow.* Ed., intro., additional material Colin Ward. New York: Harper & Row, 1974, c. 1904.

Kuhn, Thomas S. *The Structure of Scientific Revolutions.* 2nd ed. Chicago: University of Chicago Press, 1970.

Kurtz, Lester R. *Evaluating Chicago Sociology: A Guide to the Literature, with an Annotated Bibliography.* Chicago: University of Chicago Press, 1984.

Lasch, Christopher, ed. Introduction to *The Social Thought of Jane Addams.* Indianapolis: Bobbs-Merrill, 1965.

――――. *The New Radicalism in America, 1889-1963.* New York: Knopf, 1965.

Lathrop, Julia. "Hull-House as a Laboratory of Sociological Investigation." *Proceedings of the Twenty First National Conference of Charities* 21 (1984): 313-20.

Lemons, J. Stanley. *The Woman Citizen: Social Feminism in the 1920's.* Urbana: University of Illinois Press, 1973.

Lengermann, Patricia. "The Founding of the *American Sociological Review.*" *American Sociological Review* 44 (April 1979): 185-98.

Lerner, Gerda. "Placing Women in History." *Feminist Studies* 3 (Fall 1975): 5-15.

Levine, Daniel. *Jane Addams and the Liberal Tradition.* Madison: State Historical Society of Wisconsin, 1971.

Lewis, J. David, and Richard L. Smith. *American Sociology and Pragmatism.* Chicago: University of Chicago Press, 1980.

Lindsay, Samuel McCune. "Review of *Hull-House Maps and Papers.*" *Annals of the American Academy* 8 (September 1896): 177-81.

Linn, James Weber. *Jane Addams.* New York: Appleton-Century-Crofts, 1935.

Lubove, Roy. *The Professional Altruist.* New York: Atheneum, 1965.

Lundberg, George A., Read Bain, and Nels Anderson, eds. *Trends in American Sociology.* New York: Harper, 1929.

Lynd, Staughton. "Jane Addams and the Radical Impulse." *Commentary* 32 (July 1961): 54-59.

McDowell, Mary. "The Settlement as a Way of Life." *Neighborhood* 2 (July 1929): 146-58.

MacKinzie, Norman and Jeanne MacKinzie. *The Fabians*. New York: Simon & Schuster, 1977.

Manis, Jerome and Bernard Meltzer, eds. *Symbolic Interaction*. 3rd ed. Boston: Allyn & Bacon, 1979.

Marx, Karl. *Capital*. Ed. Frederick Engels. Tr. Samuel Moore and Edward Aveline. New York: Modern Library, 1906, c. 1859.

Mason, Otis Tufton. *Women's Share in Primitive Culture*. New York: D. Appleton, 1918, c. 1894.

Matthews, Fred H. *Quest for an American Sociology: Robert E. Park and the Chicago School*. Montreal: McGill-Queen's University Press, 1977.

Mead, George H. "The Working Hypothesis in Social Reform." *American Journal of Sociology* 5 (March 1899): 369-71.

_____. "Review of Jane Addams' *The Newer Ideals of Peace*." *American Journal of Sociology* 13 (July 1907): 121-8.

_____. "Educational Aspects of Trade Union Schools." *Union Labor Advocate* 8 (1909): 19-20.

_____. "Psychology of Consciousness Implied in Instruction." *Science* 31 (May 1910): 688-93.

_____. "Social Consciousness and the Consciousness of Meaning." *Psychological Bulletin* 7 (December 1910): 397-405.

_____. "Report on the Chicago City Club Committee on Education." *City Club Bulletin* 7 (13 May 1914): 141.

_____. "A Heckling School Board and an Educational Stateswoman." *Survey* 31 (10 January 1914): 443-44.

_____. "The Psychological Bases of Internationalism." *Survey* 23 (6 March 1915): 603-7.

_____. "Remarks on Labor Night." *City Club Bulletin* 5 (27 May 1912): 214-15.

_____. "Fitting the Educational System into the Fabric of Government." *City Club Bulletin* 10 (27 March 1917): 104-8.

_____. "Scientific Method and the Individual Thinker." In *Creative Intelligence*. Ed. John Dewey et al. New York: Holt, 1917. Pp. 176-227.

_____. "Social Reconstruction in a Time of War." *Proceedings of the Social Work Conference*. 44 (1917): 637-44.

_____. "Social Work, Standards of Living and the War." *Proceedings of the National Conference of Social Workers*. 45 (1918): 637-44.

_____. *The Conscientious Objector*. Pamphlet 33. New York: National Security League, 1918.

_____. "Mary McDowell." *Neighborhood* 2 (April 1929): 77-78.

_____. "National-Mindedness and International-Mindedness." *International Journal of Ethics* 39 (November 1929): 392-407.

_____. "Cooley's Contribution to American Social Thought." *American Journal of Sociology* 35 (March 1930): 693-706.

_____. *The Philosophy of the Present*. Chicago: Open Court, 1932.

_____. *Mind, Self and Society*. Ed. Charles Morris. Chicago: University of Chicago Press, 1934.

_____. *The Philosophy of the Act*. Ed., intro. Charles W. Morris et al. Chicago: University of Chicago Press, 1938.

_____. *Selected Writings*. Ed., intro. Andrew Reck. Chicago: University of Chicago Press, 1964.

Mead, George H., Ernest A. Weidt, and William J. Brogan. *A Report on Vocational Training in Chicago and in Other Cities*. Chicago: City Club of Chicago, 1912.

Metzger, Walter P. *Academic Freedom in the Age of the University*. New York: Columbia University Press, 1964, c. 1955.

———. "Academic Tenure in America: A Historical Essay." In *Faculty Tenure*. A Report and Recommendations by the Commission on Academic Tenure in Higher Education. William R. Keast, chair. San Francisco: Jossey-Bass, 1973.

Miller, David L. *George Herbert Mead: Self, Language and the World*. Austin: University of Texas Press, 1973.

Mills, C. Wright. *Sociology and Pragmatism*. Ed., intro. Irving Louis Horowitz. New York: Paine-Whitman, 1964.

Morris, Charles. *The Pragmatic Movement in American Philosophy* New York: Braziller, 1970.

Morrison, Theodore. *Chautauqua*. Chicago: University of Chicago Press, 1974.

Montgomery, Louise. *Opportunities in School and Industry for Children of the Stockyards District*. Vol. 2, *A Study of Chicago Stockyards Community*. Chicago: University of Chicago Press, 1913.

Myers, Howard Barton. "The Policing of Labor Disputes in Chicago: A Case Study." Ph.D diss., Department of History, University of Chicago, 1929.

Notester, Wallace. In *George E. Vincent, 1864-1944*. Memorial Addresses. Stanford, Conn.: Overbrooks, 1941. Pp. 47-49.

Noble, David. *The Progressive Mind, 1890:1917*. Chicago: Rand, McNally, 1970.

Opler, Marvin K. "Woman's Social Status and the Forms of Marriage." *American Journal of Sociology* 49 (September 1943): 125-46.

Palmer, Vivien M. *Field Studies in Sociology*. Chicago: University of Chicago Press, 1928.

Park, Robert E. "The City as a Social Laboratory." In *Chicago: An Experiment in Social Science Research*. Ed. T.V. Smith and L. White. Chicago: University of Chicago Press, 1921. Pp. 1-19.

———. "An Autobiographical Note." In *Race and Culture*. Ed. Everett C. Hughes. Glencoe, Ill.: Free Press, 1950. Pp. v-xiv.

———. "Human Migration and the Marginal Man." *American Journal of Sociology* 33 (May 1928): 881-93.

———. "Cultural Conflict and the Marginal Man." Intro. to E.V. Stonequist, *The Marginal Man*. New York: Scribner's, 1937. Pp. xiii-xviii.

———. *Robert E. Park: On Social Control and Collective Behavior*. Ed. Ralph H. Turner. Chicago: University of Chicago Press, 1967.

Park, Robert E., and Ernest W. Burgess. *Introduction to the Science of Sociology*. Chicago: University of Chicago Press, 1921.

Petras, John W. *George Herbert Mead: Essays on His Social Philosophy*. New York: Columbia University, Teachers College Press, 1968.

———. "John Dewey and the Rise of Interactionism in American Social Theory." *Journal of the History of the Behavioral Sciences* 4 (May 1968): 18-27.

———. "Changes of Emphasis in the Sociology of W.I. Thomas." *Journal of the History of the Behavioral Sciences* 6 (January 1970): 70-79.

Philanthropy and Social Progress: Seven Essays by Miss Jane Addams, Robert A. Woods, Father J. O. S. Huntington, Professor Franklin H. Giddings, and Bernard Rosanquet. Intro. Henry C. Adams. New York: Crowell, 1893.

Publications of the University of Chicago Faculty, 1902-1916. Chicago: University of Chicago Press, 1917.

Queen, Stuart A. "Seventy-Five Years of American Sociology in Relation to Social Work." *American Sociologist* 16 (February 1981): 34-37.

Rauschenbush, Winifred. *Robert E. Park: Biography of a Sociologist.* Durham, N.C.: Duke University Press, 1979.

Ravitch, Jessie S. "Review of Jane Addams' *The Child, the Clinic and the Court.*" *American Journal of Sociology* 31 (July 1925): 834-35.

Rosenberg, Rosalind. *Beyond Separate Spheres.* New Haven: Yale University Press, 1982.

Rossiter, Margaret. *Women Scientists in America.* Baltimore: Johns Hopkins University Press, 1982.

Rucker, Darnell. *The Chicago Pragmatists.* Minneapolis: University of Minnesota Press, 1969.

Sachs, Carolyn, Sally Ward Maggard, and S. Randi Randolph. "Sexuality, the Home and Class." In *Midwest Feminist Papers.* (no. 2, 1981): 31-44.

Schwendinger, Herman, and Julia R. Schwendinger. *The Sociologists of the Chair: A Radical Analysis of the Formative Years of North American Sociology, 1883-1922.* New York: Basic Books, 1974.

"Settlers in the City Wilderness." *Atlantic Monthly* 77 (January 1896): 119-23.

Shannon, David A., ed. *Beatrice Webb's American Diary.* Madison: State Historical Society, 1963.

Shaple, Robert. *Toward the Well-Being of Mankind.* Garden City, N.Y.: Doubleday, 1964.

Shils, Edward. "Tradition, Ecology and Institution in the History of Sociology." *Daedalus* 94 (Fall, 1970): 760-825.

Short, James F., Jr., ed. *The Social Fabric of the Metropolis.* Chicago: University of Chicago Press, 1971.

Simmel, Georg. "The Sociology of Secrecy and Secret Societies." Tr. Albion W. Small. *American Journal of Sociology* 11 (January 1906): 441-98.

Small, Albion W. "The Civic Federation of Chicago." *American Journal of Sociology* 1 (July 1895): 79-103.

_____. "Scholarship and Social Agitation." *American Journal of Sociology* 1 (March 1896): 564-82.

_____. "The Social Mission of College Women." *The Independent* 54 (30 January 1902): 261-63.

_____. "Coeducation at the University of Chicago." *Proceedings of the National Education Association* (1903): 265-96.

_____. *Adam Smith and Modern Sociology.* Chicago: University of Chicago Press, 1907.

_____. *The Cameralists: The Pioneers of German Social Policy.* Chicago: University of Chicago Press, 1909.

_____. *Between Eras from Capitalism to Democracy.* Chicago: University of Chicago Press, 1913.

_____. *The Origins of Sociology.* Chicago: University of Chicago Press, 1924.

_____. "Some Researches into Research; 1924 Address to Research Society." In Vernon Dibble, *The Legacy of Albion Small.* Chicago: University of Chicago Press, 1975. Pp. 205-20.

Small, Albion W., and George E. Vincent. *An Introduction to the Study of Society.* New York: American Book, 1894.

Smith, Joan K. *Ella Flagg Young.* Ames: Educational Studies Press and the Iowa State University Research Foundation, 1979.

"Social Work Shoptalk." *The Survey* 53 (15 October 1924): 108.

Spencer, Anna Garlin. *Women's Share in Social Culture.* New York: Mitchell Kennerley, 1913.

Stanfield, John H. *Philanthropy and Jim Crow in American Social Science.* Westport, Connecticut: Greenwood Press, 1985.

Stone, Gregory P., and Harvey Farberman, eds. *Social Psychology through Symbolic Interaction.* Waltham, Mass.: Xerox, 1970.

Suttles, Gerald. *The Social Order of the Slum.* Chicago: University of Chicago Press, 1968.

Taft, Jessie. *The Woman Movement from the Point of View of Social Consciousness.* (Ph.D. diss., Department of Philosophy, University of Chicago, 1913.) Menasha, Wis: Collegiate Press, George Banta, 1915. Repr., no. 6, Philosophic Studies, Department of Philosophy, University of Chicago. Chicago: University of Chicago Press, 1916.

Talbert, Ernest. *A Study of Chicago's Stockyards Community.* Vol. 1, *A Study of Chicago's Stockyards Community.* Chicago: University of Chicago Press, 1912.

Talbot, Marion. "The Women of the University." *Decennial Publications of the University of Chicago.* Chicago: University of Chicago Press, 1903. Pp. 122-45.

_____. *More Than Lore: Reminiscences of Marion Talbot, Dean of Women, The University of Chicago, 1892-1925.* Chicago: University of Chicago Press, 1936.

Talbot, Marion, and Lois Kimball Mathews Rosenberry. *The History of the American Association of University Women, 1881-1931.* Cambridge, Mass.: Houghton Mifflin, 1931.

Taylor, Graham. "The Rudowitz Case." *Charities and the Commons* 21 (6 February 1909):779-80.

_____. "1848—Charles Richmond Henderson—1915", *Survey* 34 (10 April 1915): 55-56.

_____. "Jane Addams: The Great Neighbor" *Survey Graphic* 24 (July 1935): 339ff.

_____. "The Rudowitz Case." *Charities and the Commons* 21 (6 February 1909): 779-80.

Taylor, Lea. "The Social Settlement and Civic Responsibility." *Social Service Review* 28 (March 1954): 33.

Thomas, Harriet, and William James. "Review of Jane Addams' *The Spirit of Youth and City Streets.*" *American Journal of Sociology* 15 (January 1910): 550-53.

Thomas, W.I. "On a Difference in the Metabolism of the Sexes." Ph.D. diss., Department of Sociology, University of Chicago, 1897.

_____. "Review of *Women and the Republic.*" *American Journal of Sociology* 3 (November 1897): 406-7.

_____. "On a Difference in the Metabolism of the Sexes." *American Journal of Sociology* 3 (July 1897): 31-63.

_____. "Review of *A Study of Mary Wollstonecraft and the Rights of Woman.*" *American Journal of Sociology* 4 (May 1899): 894-5.

_____. "The Psychology of Race Prejudice." *American Journal of Sociology* 9 (1904): 593-611.

_____. *Sex and Society: Studies in the Social Psychology of Sex.* Chicago: University of Chicago Press, 1907.

_____. "The Psychology of Woman's Dress." *American Magazine* 67 (November 1908): 66-72.

_____. "The Mind of Woman." *American Magazine* 67 (December 1908): 146-52.
_____. "The Older and the Newer Ideals of Marriage." *American Magazine* 67 (April 1909): 548-52.
_____. "Votes for Women." *American Magazine* 68 (July 1909): 292-301.
_____. "Women and the Occupations." *American Magazine* 68 (September 1909): 463-70.
_____. *Source Book for Social Origins: Ethnological Materials, Psychological Standpoint, Classified and Annoted Bibliographies for the Interpretation of Savage Society.* Chicago: University of Chicago Press; Boston: Richard G. Badger, 1909.
_____. "Race Psychology: Standpoint and Questionnaire, with Particular Reference to the Immigrant and the Negro." *American Journal of Sociology* 17 (May 1912): 725-77.
_____. "Education and Racial Traits." *The Southern Workman* 41 (June 1912): 378-86.
_____. "The Prussian-Polish Situation: An Experiment in Assimilation." *American Journal of Sociology* 29 (March 1914): 624-39.
_____. "Five Polish Peasant Letters." *The Immigrants' in America Review* 2 (April 1916): 58-64.
_____. *The Unadjusted Girl: With Cases and Standpoint for Behavior Analysis.* Boston: Little, Brown, 1923.
_____. *The Unadjusted Girl: With Cases and Standpoint for Behavior Analysis.* Ed., Benjamin Nelson, pref. Michael Parenti New York: Harper Torchbooks, 1967, c. 1923.
_____. "The Configuration of Personality." In C. M. Child, et al., *The Unconscious.* Intro. Ethel S. Dummer. New York: Knopf, 1927. Pp. 143-77.
_____. *Primitive Behavior: An Introduction to the Social Sciences.* New York: McGraw-Hill, 1937.
_____. *Social Behavior and Personality: Contributions of W. I. Thomas to Theory and Social Research.* Ed. Edmund Volkart. New York: Social Science Research Council, 1951.
_____. *W.I. Thomas: On Social Organization and Social Personality.* Ed., intro., Morris Janowitz. Chicago: University of Chicago Press, 1966.
Thomas, W.I., with Robert E. Park and Herbert A. Miller. *Old World Traits Transplanted.* A volume in the Americanization Studies, Allen T. Burns, dir. New York: Harper, 1921.
Thomas, W. I. and Dorothy S. Thomas. *The Child in America: Behavior Problems and Programs.* New York: Knopf, 1928.
Thomas, W.I. and Florian Znaniecki. *The Polish Peasant in Europe and America.* 5 vols. Boston: Richard G. Badger, 1918-20. (Vols. 1 and 2 orig. pub. University of Chicago Press, 1918.) 2nd ed., 2 vols., same content but different pagination. New York: Knopf, 1927. Boston: Little, Brown, 1923, c. 1917, 1918. Repr., 2 vols. New York: Dover, 1958.
Tolstoy, Leo. *What Shall We Do Then?* Vol. 17, *The Complete Works of Count Tolstoy.* Tr., ed. Leo Wiener. Boston: D. Estes, 1905.
Tuchman, Gaye. "Women and the Creation of Culture." In *Another Voice.* Ed. Marcia Millman and Rosabeth Moss Kanter. New York: Anchor, 1975. Pp. 171-202.
Turner, Frederick Jackson. "The Significance of the Frontier in American History." *Annual Report for the Year 1893.* Washington, D.C: American Historical Association, 1893.

————. *The Frontier in American History.* New York: Holt, Rinehart, & Winston, 1920.

————. "Later Explanations and Developments." In *The Frontier Thesis.* Ed. Ray Billington. Huntington, N.Y.: Robert E. Kreiger, 1977. Pp. 21-30.

Veblen, Thornstein. *The Higher Learning in America: On the Conduct of Universities by Businessmen.*" New York: Hill & Wang, 1969, c. 1918.

The Vice Commission of Chicago. *The Social Evil in Chicago.* New York: Arno Press and the New York Times, 1970, c. 1911.

Vincent, George E. *The Social Mind and Education.* New York: Macmillan, 1897.

————. "Sociology." *Encyclopedia Americana,* vol. 14. New York and Chicago: Americana, 1904. N.p.

Volkhardt, Edmund, ed. "Biographical Note." In *Social Behavior and Personality.* New York: Social Science Research Council, 1951. Pp. 323-24.

White, Morton. *Pragmatism and the American Mind.* New York: Oxford University Press, 1973.

Wilson, Howard Eugene. "Mary E. McDowell and Her Work as Head Resident of the University of Chicago Settlement, 1894-1906." M.A. Thesis, Department of History, University of Chicago, 1927.

Wirth, Louis. *The Ghetto.* Chicago: University of Chicago Press, 1928.

Wisner, Elizabeth. "Edith Abbott's Contributions to Social Work Education." *Social Service Review* 32 (March 1958): 1-10.

Wolman, Leo, et al. *The Clothing Workers of Chicago, 1910-1922.* Chicago: The Chicago Joint Board of the Amalgamated Clothing Workers of America, 1922.

Woods, Robert A. *The Neighborhood in Nation-Building.* Boston: Houghton Mifflin, The Riverside Press of Cambridge, 1923.

Young, Kimball. "The Contributions of William Issac Thomas to Sociology." *Sociology and Social Research* 47 (October 1962): 3-24.

Young, Pauline. *Scientific Social Surveys and Research.* New York: Prentice-Hall, 1942.

Zaretz, Charles. *The Amalgamated Clothing Workers of America.* New York: Ancon, 1934.

Zeublin, Charles. "The Chicago Ghetto." In *Hull House Maps and Papers.* Pp. 91-114.

————. "A Sketch of Socialistic Thought in England." *American Journal of Sociology* 2 (March 1897): 643-61.

————. "Municipal Playgrounds in Chicago." *American Journal of Sociology* 3 (September 1898): 145-58.

————. "The World's First Sociological Laboratory." *American Journal of Sociology* 4 (March 1899): 577-92.

————. *American Municipal Progress.* New York: Macmillan, 1902.

————. "The Civic Renascence: The New Civic Spirit." *Chautauquan* 38 (September 1903): 55-59.

————. *A Decade of Civic Development.* Chicago: University of Chicago Press, 1905.

————. *The Religion of a Democrat.* New York: B.W. Huebsch, 1908.

————. "The Effect on Woman of Economic Dependence." *American Journal of Sociology* 14 (March 1909): 606-14.

————. *Democracy and the Overman.* New York: B.W. Huebsch, 1910.

————. "The Suffrage Parade." *The Woman Voter* 4 (June 1913): 15-16.

Subject Index

Name Index

Abbott, Edith, 42, 43, 44, 45, 48, 51n.1, 68n.15, 87, 102n.66, 112, 153-55, 161, 195, 210, 316; *Women in Industry*, 44

Abbott, Grace, 45

Addams, Jane: biography, 4-15, 258; and E.W. Burgess, 149-52; and critical emancipatory science, 254-56; contribution to sociology (summary), 323-26; and critical pragmatism, 247-67, 273-304, 311-13; and cultural feminism, 6, 159, 191, 225-43, 263, 288, 302-3, 310-11; on democracy, 273-304; and J. Dewey, 249-53; on education, 274, 281-304; on the elderly, 299-302; and feminism, 5-7, 13, 230-33; and C. Henderson, 88-89; as ideal of womanhood, 80, 150-51; influence on Chicago School, 55, 248, 252, 253; intellectual roots of, 247-67; and Marxist writings, 256-57; and G.H. Mead, 118-21, 132-34; and the men of the Chicago School, 163-64, 240-42, 303-4; and pacifism, 6-7, 110, 238-40, 302, 310, 318; and R.E. Park, 158-59; professional demise of, 6, 144, 177, 216, 218; on prostitution, 233-35; as too radical, 175-77, 188n.36, 320; and academic repression, 169, 171; and the religious men, 71-99; and A.W. Small, 80-83; and social reform, 71-99, 105-34, 143-64; and socialism, 279-81, 292; from sociologist to social worker, 309, 317-23; as suffragist, 276-77; and the symbolic interactionists, 105-34; and W.I. Thomas, 129-34, 178-79, 185-86, 227-28; on Tolstoy, 96, 104n.114, 257-62; and the urban ecologists, 143-64; as woman leader, 7, 13-15, 186, 218, 228, 286, 288, 318; winner of Noble Peace Prize, 7, 286, 303, 322; on working women, 235-38; on youth, 296-99; and C. Zeublin, 92. Works: *Democracy and Social Ethics*, 11, 12; *A New Conscience and an Ancient Evil*, 12, 89; *Newer Ideals of Peace*, 11, 119, 254, 261; *Peace and Bread in Time of War*, 130, 240, 252, 254, 261; *The Second Twenty Years at Hull-House*, 257; *The Spirit of Youth and the City Streets*, 12, 130, 252, 254; *Twenty Years at Hull-House*, 12, 52n.32, 92, 257. *See also Hull-House Maps and Papers*, and passim

Bachofen, Jacob, 243

Balch, Emily Greene, 286, 320, 326n.3

Becker, Ernest, 76-77, 98, 312

Bemis, Edward W., 17, 73, 90, 115, 169, 188n.38; dismissal of, 171-75

Bernard, L.L., 92, 93, 94, 104n.110

Bogue, Donald, 160

Booth, Charles, 56, 65-66, 263, 264; *Life and Labour of the People in London*, 56

Breckinridge, Sophonisba, 42, 43-45, 68n.15, 112, 153-55, 161, 195, 201, 302; and G.H. Mead, 210-14

Brooks, John Graham, 97

Bulmer, Martin, 45, 103n.103; *Symbolic Interactionism*, 135n.2

Burgess Ernest W., 22, 25, 37, 52n.20, 59, 61, 62, 63-65, 66-67, 72, 75, 79, 91, 99, 105, 143, 159-61, 164n.6, 165nn.17,18, 171, 185, 187, 241-42, 248, 314-15; and social reform, 144-52, 161, 162-63; and the sociology of women, 196, 211-13, 217, 222n.97; *Introduction to the Sciences of Sociology*, 144. *See also* Park, Robert E.

Butler Nathaniel, 173, 174

Carey, James T., 154, 157

Clayton, Alfred S., 108

Commons, John R., 174, 280

Comte, Auguste, 193